EVANGELICALS ENGAGING EMERGENT

A DISCUSSION OF THE EMERGENT CHURCH MOVEMENT

EDITED BY

WILLIAM D. HENARD AND ADAM W. GREENWAY

FOREWORD BY THOM S. RAINER

ACADEMIC

Nashville, Tennessee

ISBN: 978-0-8054-4739-2

Published by B&H Publishing Group
Nashville, Tennessee

Dewey Decimal Classification: 262
Subject Heading: EMERGENT CHURCH MOVEMENT\
POSTMODERNISM\CHURCH

Printed in the United States of America

3 4 5 6 7 8 9 10 11 12 13 • 17 16 15 14 13 12 11 10
BP

CONTENTS

PART THREE: PRACTICAL SECTION

FOREWORD

THOM S. RAINER

I AM EXTREMELY pleased that my friends Bill Henard and Adam Greenway accepted the challenge of taking a rigorous look at the Emergent Church. Much has been written on Web logs and argued over coffee regarding the Emergent and Emerging Church, but there is always room for an objective and informed examination of ideas when the gospel is at stake.

There is a cold breeze howling across the landscape of American Evangelicalism, and I am concerned it is chilling the hearts and minds of people desperate to hear an unadulterated gospel. Instead of hearing the depth of God's righteousness, His offense at our sin, His demand for justice, and His great mercy, grace, and forgiveness extended to us through the blood of Jesus, people in churches are hearing lukewarm spiritual porridge offered as a way to help them feel better about themselves. In a day when people need big thoughts about an infinitely capable God, they seem to be gathering to themselves teachers who tell them what they want to hear instead of what they need to hear, which is that Jesus Christ came into this world to save sinners.

Unfortunately what is too often happening in churches across America is that the cross of Christ is being "emptied of its effect" (1 Cor 1:17) because too many preachers are trying too hard to be clever.

I'm flipping through my Bible as I write this. There are so many verses that seem so deeply relevant to the conversation that follows in this book—and actually to all of life. Here are two passages:

> If anyone teaches other doctrine and does not agree with
> the sound teaching of our Lord Jesus Christ and with the

teaching that promotes godliness, he is conceited, understanding nothing, but having a sick interest in disputes
and arguments over words. From these come envy, quarreling, slander, evil suspicions, and constant disagreement
among men whose minds are depraved and deprived of
the truth, who imagine that godliness is a way to material gain. But godliness with contentment is a great gain.
(1 Tim 6:3–6)

For to those who are perishing the message of the
cross is foolishness, but to us who are being saved it is
God's power. For it is written: I will destroy the wisdom
of the wise, and I will set aside the understanding of the
experts.

Where is the philosopher? Where is the scholar? Where
is the debater of this age? Hasn't God made the world's
wisdom foolish? For since, in God's wisdom, the world
did not know God through wisdom, God was pleased to
save those who believe through the foolishness of the message preached. For the Jews ask for signs and the Greeks
seek wisdom, but we preach Christ crucified, a stumbling
block to the Jews and foolishness to the Gentiles. Yet to
those who are called, both Jews and Greeks, Christ is
God's power and God's wisdom, because God's foolishness is wiser than human wisdom, and God's weakness is
stronger than human strength. (1 Cor 1:18–25)

These verses are so rich, but I will offer two observations. The
first: it is vitally important that we draw sound doctrine from a
comprehensive view of Scripture. We must see the Bible from
beginning to end as God's story to graciously redeem godless
people—through the cross of Christ—from a self-inflicted tragedy
that results in an eternal and deserved hell. Doctrine becomes the
stepping-stones that guide us from Genesis to Revelation.

The second truth is that we must not attempt to be wiser than
God. The message of the cross—the propitiation of wrath; the
imputation of righteousness—must be preached. It is the only

hope sinners have. Drift from this truth and we drift hopelessly away from the only anchor capable of saving us.

Thank you, Bill and Adam, for assembling this great group of scholars and churchmen to write about this critical issue. And thanks to all the writers for your contributions in this much-needed volume.

I pray that God will use this book as an encouragement to all who read it to commit themselves "to preach the gospel—not with clever words, so that the cross of Christ will not be emptied of its effect" (1 Cor 1:17).

Thom S. Rainer
President and CEO
LifeWay Christian Resources

INTRODUCTION

WILLIAM D. HENARD

IN ROB BELL'S *Velvet Elvis* he writes,

> Jesus at one point claimed to be "the way, the truth, and
> the life." Jesus was not making claims about one religion
> being better than all other religions. That completely
> misses the point, the depth, and the truth. Rather, he was
> telling those who were following him that his way is the
> way to the depth of reality. This kind of life Jesus was
> living, perfectly and completely in connection and coop-
> eration with God, is the *best possible way for a person to
> live*. It is how things are.[1]

Bell correctly asserts that Jesus' statement quoted in John
14:6 is not about pitting one religion as better than another, but he
misses the point completely in determining that Jesus was speaking solely with regard to "the best possible way for a person to
live."[2] Biblically, faith in Christ is the only way for a person to live
and not to perish (John 3:16).

Just a few pages later, he offers a provocative look at the virgin birth in asking, "What if tomorrow someone digs up definitive proof that Jesus had a real, earthly, biological father named
Larry . . . and prove(s) beyond a shadow of a doubt that the virgin birth was really just a bit of mythologizing the Gospel writers
threw in to appeal to the followers?"[3] Bell does affirm that he personally believes in the virgin birth, the Trinity, and the inspiration

---

[1] Rob Bell, *Velvet Elvis: Repainting the Christian Faith* (Grand Rapids: Zondervan, 2005), 21 (emphasis added).

[2] Ibid.

[3] Ibid., 26.

1

of the Bible. The difficulty arises in the fact that he seems to think that the Christian faith does not find its foundation in these biblical truths. He rightly leads his church to ask the tough questions. Yet he creates a distinct problem, in that he does not seem to believe that any definitive answers exist.

I was watching television some time back and heard this statement, "Christianity is not primarily propositional truth; it is not primarily an experience; Christianity is primarily a conversation." Unfortunately, I did not watch the rest of the program to see how these statements would play out. Those arguments represent, though, the crux of where many find themselves within Emergent. They demonstrate clearly why Bell insists that the Bible should be interpreted as a communal book,[4] and why Doug Pagitt importunes that the traditional concept of preaching is nothing more than speaching.[5] The Emergent Church says preaching must be a dialogue, a conversation, not an insistence on personal interpretation.

This book purposes to be a provocative look at the Emergent Church. The task is not a simple one. Just defining "Emergent" provides an incredible difficulty within itself. Few of us like to be pigeon-holed into particular titles or labels. This fact holds true in most areas of the Christian life and theology. The old joke is that if you get five Baptists together you will have seven different opinions. To help with this dilemma, Ed Stetzer has provided an excellent means of defining Emergent and which streams will be addressed in this book.

Evangelicals Engaging Emergent is not intended to be an attack on the Emergent Church. The movement (or conversation) asks good questions, ones that the bridger generation[6] is pres-

---

[4] Ibid., 53.

[5] Doug Pagitt, *Preaching Re-imagined: The Role of the Sermon in Communities of Faith* (Grand Rapids: Zondervan, 2005), 18.

[6] See. Thom S. Rainer, *The Bridger Generation* (Nashville: B&H, 1997). Rainer identifies bridgers as ones who were born between 1977 and 1994. They encompass more than seventy-two million people. He names them bridgers for three reasons. First, their age group spans two centuries and two millennia. Second, they are bridging between a time of uncertainty and a time of hope. Third, the bridger designation fits the alliteration with builders, boomers, and busters. Rainer, *The Bridger Generation*, 2–3.

ently asking. It is true that bridgers make up one of the largest unreached people groups in America.[7] More specifically, George Barna estimates that 74 percent of teenagers have not trusted in Christ as Savior. While those in their teens are somewhat spiritual in their perspectives, the fact remains that "only one out of four (26%) . . . claims to be absolutely committed to the Christian faith."[8] Even within our own churches, 70 percent of those who constitute the student ministries end up dropping out of church sometime between the ages of eighteen and twenty-two.[9] That fact alone demonstrates that something is vitally wrong and must be addressed. The Emergent Church provides a tension that forces all of us to take a very hard look at our churches, our ministries, and our priorities.

Problems, though, do exist among some who serve as Emergent proponents. When theology comes into question, or when morality is sidelined because of cultural relativism, then serious issues do abide. It is the hope of the editors that those within the Emergent Church and those on the outside would read and learn from this book. The chapter authors are some of the best minds in the Evangelical world. All of us can learn from them. Many of them are personally reaching out to the younger generation and the leaders to whom they gravitate. They cautiously agreed to write their chapters because they did not want this book to seem to be a witch hunt. Yet they also recognized that the penchant for moral and biblical relativism must be addressed. With these thoughts and cautions in mind, this book is written.

[7] Ibid., 6.

[8] George Barna, "Teenagers Embrace Religion But Are Not Excited About Christianity" [on-line]; accessed 12 March 2008; available from http://www.barna.org/FlexPage.aspx?Page=BarnaUpdate&BarnaUpdateID=45; internet.

[9] Thom S. Rainer and Sam Rainer, *Essential Church* (Nashville: B&H, 2008), 15.

THE EMERGING CHURCH: ONE MOVEMENT— TWO STREAMS

MARK DEVINE

THE EMERGING CHURCH PHENOMENON continues to grow, both in numbers and in influence, and particularly among young Evangelicals.[1] In this chapter I shall provide an overview of the movement, attempt to define the movement by identifying distinctive values and goals at work within it, and argue that the movement includes two major streams. I shall contend that these two streams must be carefully distinguished if Evangelicals hope to develop approaches to the emerging movement in keeping with their own deepest evangelical commitments.

PATERNITY OF PROTEST

Major leaders within the emerging church have resisted the designation of the phenomenon as a movement. "Conversation" more closely suited their self-perception. But the volume of books, blogs, and bona fide communities of faith involved compels the acknowledgment that the emerging conversation has morphed into a full-blown movement—a movement that seems, in significant measure, to have sprung from seeds of discontent. Seeds were sown producing fragile plants (often within Evangelical churches), which were then nurtured but eventually found

[1] See for example, Robert E. Webber, *The Younger Evangelicals: Facing the Challenges of the New World* (Grand Rapids: Baker Books, 2002).

themselves deprived of the spiritual water, sunshine, and nutri-
ents needed for continued growth. This fated spiritual husbandry
occurred largely within conservative congregations of various
configurations from traditional PCA to Vineyard to the Assemblies of God to Southern Baptist churches of both mega and mini
varieties and everything in between.

Many of these dissatisfied believers struck out on their own,
at first in search of a new place to call home, but eventually on
a quest to plant communities of faith themselves, communities
responsive to the yearnings and hankerings left unsatiated within
the congregations from which they emerged and those they sub-
sequently sampled. These disgruntled seekers were largely white,
twenty-something, and internet-savvy; and so they soon found
each other in the blogosphere from Seattle, Washington, to Kansas City, Missouri, to Manchester, UK. And they found some older
folks with whom to commiserate as well—preachers, pastors, and
writers who could scratch some of their itches—people such as
Brian McLaren[2] and Leonard Sweet,[3] Tim Keller[4] and Robert
Webber.[5] Eventually some even caught John Piper[6] slipping up

[2] Brian McLaren was the founding pastor of the nondenominational Cedar Ridge Community Church in the Baltimore-Washington, D.C., region. He served in that capacity from
1986 to 2006. McLaren is a major influencer within the emerging church community and
the author of many best-selling books, including *A New Kind of Christian: A Tale of Two
Friends on a Spiritual Journey* (San Francisco: Jossey-Bass, 2001); *A Generous Orthodoxy*
(Grand Rapids: Zondervan, 2004); and *Everything Must Change: Jesus, Global Crises, and
a Revolution of Hope* (Nashville: Thomas Nelson, 2007).

[3] Leonard Sweet is E. Stanley Jones Professor of Evangelism at Drew University in
Madison, N. J., and the author of many books, including *The Gospel According to Star-
bucks: Living with a Grande Passion* (Colorado Springs: WaterBrook, 2007), and editor of
The Church in Emerging Culture: Five Perspectives (Grand Rapids: Zondervan, 2003).

[4] Tim Keller, pastor of Redeemer Church on Manhattan Island in New York City,
once responded to the question "Are you part of the emerging church?" thusly: "I don't
think so. I didn't mean to be." Nevertheless, in this chapter I treat Keller as a major figure
within the emerging church movement because, wittingly or not, his church, sermons, and
writings provide models, encouragement, and guidance to an expanding audience of self-
consciously emerging ministers.

[5] The recently deceased Robert E. Webber served as Myers Professor of Ministry and
director of M.A. in worship and spirituality at Northern Baptist Theological Seminary in
Lombard, Ill. Webber authored more than forty books on worship and *The Younger Evangelicals: Facing the Challenges of the New World*. Webber also directed the Institute for
Worship Studies in Orange Park, Fla., and maintained the Web site AncientFutureWorship
.com.

[6] John Piper is pastor of Bethlehem Baptist Church in Minneapolis, Minn., author of many
best-selling books, and director of Desiring God Ministries (see www.desiringgod.org).

and saying something relevant to emerging church concerns. But wait. Not so fast. Let's back up a little.

Scot McKnight, author, blogger, keen observer, and friend of the emerging church phenomenon, agrees that we are dealing with a protest movement.[7] But clearly, the emerging church is moving beyond its birthing in protest and nursing in discontent. Increasingly, its attention and energies are being drawn away from what it left to the actual work of building what it wants. Still, a brief examination of its original discontent illuminates much of what the movement has become and where it might be headed.

Much of the dissatisfaction experienced by the eventual leaders of the emerging church is indicated by reference to these four terms: *authenticity, community, mission,* and *mystery.* Each of these terms points to facets of discontent that would spawn the emerging church. Three additional terms, *culture, narrative,* and *the arts,* must also be included among the defining marks of the movement.

Where effective and relevant church planting is concerned, the emerging church considers culture of supreme importance, the significance of which can hardly be exaggerated. Narrative points to a prevalent re-thinking and exploration both of the proper way to approach the Bible and of the most adequate means for comprehending and communicating about ourselves and about history, especially the history of God's relationship to the world. Along with the element of protest or discontent, these six terms will provide the framework within which I shall attempt to provide an overview of the emerging church movement, offer sporadic critique, and suggest ways Evangelicals might think about and perhaps even engage this alternately fascinating and disturbing but also promising phenomenon. But first I will make a comment about the state of Evangelical engagement with the emerging church and attempt to define a handful of important terms.

ONE HAND CLAPPING

One of the most respected contemporary Evangelical voices has already spoken on the subject of the emerging church. D. A. Carson's publication of *Becoming Conversant with the Emerging*

---

[7] Scot McKnight's Web site is www.jesuscreed.org.

Church provides what I believe should and will remain a permanent contribution to Evangelical comprehension of the movement.[8] Anyone who has read Carson's treatment with care cannot fail to recognize how significantly my own understanding of the emerging church overlaps with and sometimes depends upon his insight and reasoning. So why another major treatment of the subject by Evangelicals? Because since 2005 the movement has grown, diversified, and shown itself composed of more dimensions than Carson recognized and capable of transmutations and trajectories Carson does not address.

My own contribution to the discussion involves less a correction of Carson than a call for an expanded view of what makes up the emerging church movement. I find little to dispute in Carson's treatment when he comments upon the *slice* of the emerging church his book examines. It is a big slice, an enormously influential slice, but a slice nonetheless. The result is that a major stream of the emerging church goes unnoticed. Especially important for our purpose in this volume is that the unacknowledged stream shares much more in common with Evangelicalism than the one Carson ably critiques and questions. The result is that widespread reading of Carson's treatment as a comprehensive examination of the entire emerging movement injects enormous confusion and miscommunication into discussions that inevitably include emerging church folk for whom the Carson critique just won't fit. These "other" emerging church believers read Carson and respond thus: "We agree and that's not us!"

My own attempt to comprehend the emerging church is depicted schematically in figure 1. I use the term *emerging* to designate the broad movement, the phenomenon as a whole. So *emerging* is the umbrella heading on the schematic. Within the broader movement I identify two major streams, the doctrine-friendly stream[9]

---

[8] D. A. Carson, *Becoming Conversant with the Emerging Church: Understanding a Movement and Its Implications* (Grand Rapids: Zondervan, 2005).

[9] Those associated with the doctrine-friendly stream include Tim Keller (Redeemer Presbyterian Church, New York), Mark Driscoll (Mars Hill, Seattle), Darrin Patrick (The Journey, St. Louis), Ed Stetzer (LifeWay Christian Resources and the North American Mission Board of the Southern Baptist Convention, the Acts 29 Church-planting Network, www.acts29.org), Matt Chandler (The Village Church, Denton, and two other locations

EMERGING

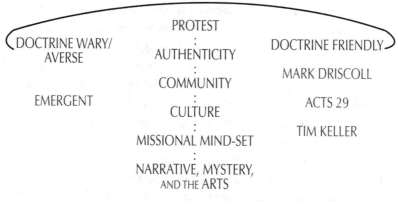

Figure 1

and a stream that presents along a range running from doctrine-wary to doctrine-averse.[10] Under the doctrine-friendly stream I have included two additional headings: Acts 29 and Tim Keller. Acts 29 is the name of the church-planting network founded by Mark Driscoll, also founding pastor Mars Hill Church in Seattle, Washington, and author of several best-selling books. Tim Keller, as mentioned above, is pastor of Redeemer Presbyterian Church on Broadway in Manhattan.

I highlight Keller, Driscoll, and Acts 29 not because the doctrine-friendly stream of emerging is reducible to these men and the ministries they lead. Many other names and ministries could be mentioned.[11] I give special prominence to these particular

in Texas), and Rafael Erwin McManus (Mosaic, Los Angeles). It seems that John Burke (Gateway Community Church, Austin, Tex.) may not fit neatly within either stream but seems much closer to the doctrine-friendly stream than doctrine wary/averse. Dan Kimball (Vintage Faith Church, Santa Cruz, Calif.) seems involved in a heroic attempt to keep one foot planted within both streams. The same might apply also to Rob Bell (Mars Hill, Grandville, Mich.).

[10] Those associated with the doctrine wary/averse stream include Brian McLaren (formerly of Cedar Ridge Community Church, Washington, D.C. area), Doug Pagitt (Solomon's Porch, Minneapolis), Tony Jones (Emergent Village, www.emergentvillage.com), Eddie Gibbs and Ryan K. Bolger (Fuller Seminary).

[11] Among Southern Baptists, for example, Ed Stetzer, a contributor to this volume, and Darrin Patrick, lead pastor of The Journey in St. Louis, deserve special recognition. Stetzer is the best sympathetic interpreter of the doctrine-friendly stream to Southern Baptists and The Journey provides perhaps the most vibrant ministry among Southern Baptists that epit-

ministries and men because I believe both of them epitomize the doctrine-friendly stream and seem likely to exert continuing and growing influence within it, and because close examination of their writings, Web sites, and ministries provides an excellent introduction of this stream of the movement for anyone willing to take the time to look and learn. For those who know Carson's book, the justification for a new attempt at Evangelical engagement of the emerging church should be obvious—Carson's treatment passes over the doctrine-friendly stream of the movement.

Included on the doctrine-wary/doctrine-averse side of figure 1 is the term *Emergent*. Emergent refers to the Web site www.EmergentVillage.com operated by Tony Jones. Throughout this paper, *emerging* will designate the movement as a whole while *Emergent* will be employed synonymously with the doctrine-wary/doctrine-averse stream. Though this contingent of the movement includes a fairly significant diversity of voices, EmergentVillage.com probably provides the best single portal through which the major influencers within this stream can be accessed.[12]

I have already introduced the column of terms situated in the center of the schematic. Each of these terms indicates a defining area of interest and concern shared by the entire movement. When pastors, church planters, and writers from both streams articulate who they are as Christians and how they understand the nature and mission of the church, they do so in great measure through the employment of these terms along with concerns associated with them. Do the terms mean exactly the same thing on both sides of the divide 100 percent of the time? No, but the extent of shared meaning is certainly very strong and does, I believe, justify inclusion of both streams within the same emerging movement.[13]

omizes the doctrine-friendly contingent within emerging. Also among Southern Baptists, one might mention Erwin Rafael McManus, lead pastor of Mosaic in Los Angeles, Calif., which holds the Baptist, Faith, and Message 2000 as its confessional statement.

[12] Other significant Web sites that facilitate conversation within the emerging movement as a whole include: www.tallskinnykiwi.com; www.theooze.com; and www.internetmonk.com.

[13] An important next step in the comprehension of the emerging church should involve the testing of the extent of shared meaning these terms retain on either side of the divide.

But make no mistake; from an historic Evangelical standpoint (or even an orthodox Christian standpoint, for that matter), what separates the two sides is greater, or at least more fundamentally decisive, than what they share in common. Simply put, Christians for whom doctrine serves as an essential vehicle for Christian confession, a protection against heresy, a guide to the interpretation of Scripture, a connector to the historic church, an anchor for congregational stability, and a means for the nurture of Christian faith and practice, can never view its neglect, loss, rejection, or marginalization without alarm.[14] So evident has this difference between the two streams become that some doctrine-friendly leaders now hesitate to self-identify as "emerging" at all, preferring instead the term *missional*—a term we will examine more fully in due course. It is my contention that, notwithstanding the very real and unavoidable division that separates the two streams, too much of what defines the emerging church penetrates the thinking, outlook, self-understanding, and practice of the two streams to avoid the recognition that they are part of a single movement, not so much, as Scot McKnight has perceptively noted, a theological movement but an ecclesiological one.

THE PARTICULARS OF PROTEST

"Why I Hate Us," the heading of a category of posts on Southern Baptist Steve McCoy's heavily trafficked Web site, expresses the conflicted sentiments of many who are attracted to the emerging church but have maintained denominational affiliation.[15] Several recurring dimensions of dissatisfaction surface when emerging believers explain their quest for a new way of being and doing church.

COMMUNITY WITHIN AND WITHOUT

One set of concerns centers around what happens at church and what happens outside the walls of the church. Within the church,

[14] For an excellent exploration of the marginalization of doctrine among Evangelicals see David Wells, *No Place for Truth; or, Whatever Happened to Evangelical Theology* (Grand Rapids: Eerdmans, 1993).

[15] Steve K. McCoy, pastor of Calvary Baptist Church in Woodstock, Ill., is a significant Christian blogger who provides on his Web site "Reformissionary" (www.stevekmccoy. com) a helpful portal for engagement of the emerging movement.

emerging Christians lament the absence of genuine community characterized by authentic relationships. Tim Keel of Jacob's Well (Kansas City) longed to recover the relationship-rich community he had enjoyed in college that was lost once he settled into megachurch life. For many emerging Christians, church culture invited a certain mask-wearing artificiality while discouraging transparency and confession of brokenness and doubt. At the same time, the atmosphere of church struck many as disturbingly inhospitable to spiritual seekers who confront immediate pressure to conform to doctrinal statements without sufficient opportunity to explore, question, and reflect. The emerging church insists that the embodiment of the gospel be reflected both within the community of believers and in Christian presence and investment in the outside community, in the world, where Christ the Lord is also present and at work. Emerging churches attempt to provide safe places for unbelievers and spiritual seekers to consider the claims of Christ in an atmosphere characterized by patience and openness.

Though both streams share this two-directional pursuit, Emergent churches, in particular, decry what they call the us-versus-them mentality they find among Evangelicals. Some even reject formal demarcation between believers and nonbelievers, eschew formal church membership altogether, and assume a belonging-before-believing posture toward all comers. Conversely, many doctrine-friendly emerging churches attempt to provide a safe place for unbelievers while maintaining covenant-shaped, church discipline-regulated membership within their congregations. On a given Sunday at one of The Journey's (St. Louis) three worship sites, unbelievers may constitute up to 40 percent of those gathered, with some having maintained regular attendance for more than three years!

CULTURE AND MEANING

Disagreement between the two streams of the emerging movement is profound and covers many critical areas of concern that range from the ideological to the practical. Critics of the Emergent stream question their orthodox Christian credentials. For a time, the Emergent community dealt with these tensions mainly by conversing among themselves and dismissing their Evangelical critics as either "Fundamentalists" or at least as trapped within supposedly outmoded modern categories of thought. Over the last three years or so, the antipathies between the two streams have sharpened and gone more public while, of late, signs of renewed dialogue and even cross-pollination between significant leaders on the two sides have also become evident. This should not surprise us, since the affinities and continuities shared by the two streams cover a wide range of issues important to both groups.

One significant and widely shared pattern of thinking centers around a cluster of linked convictions related to culture and meaning. The first is the conviction that the North American landscape is increasingly defined by identifiable and multiple subcultures. These subcultures may present geographically (e.g., urban, suburban, rural) but may just as well present in other ways (e.g., YUPPIES, DINKS,[16] artists, lawyers, the homeless, the working poor, online chatters, and gamers of various sorts). Second is the conviction that recognition of these subcultures and adaptation to them usually has profound, even determinative effects upon attempts to evangelize or plant churches within them. Why? Because culture exerts considerable effects upon the conveyance of meaning—meanings conveyed by both words and actions and thus bearing upon meanings conveyed in preaching, personal evangelism, worship style, and ministry strategies. Culture provides an essential key for anticipating the meanings conveyed where Christian ministry is pursued and the planting of churches is attempted.

This insight is not new. Effective international mission agencies long ago faced the futility of missionary efforts where culture is ignored or otherwise by-passed in the training of missionaries and the shaping of mission strategies.

Upon landing in Bangkok, Thailand, my entire family learned over the course of many weeks of orientation that about 85 percent of everything we naturally say and do either would or could be received as an insult to the Thai people we hoped to reach for Christ. Cross your legs and point your toe at the wrong angle in

---

[16] Young urban professionals (YUPPIES); dual income, no kids (DINKS).

the wrong place at the wrong time and chances for genuine communication collapse. Inadvertently, you may have just given the equivalent of "the finger" to the host population. Don't know the age or status of your neighbors and want to have significant influence among them? Forget it. Thais exist within highly intricate and complicated relational terrain shaped by ancient history and culture. One learns culture, adapts to it, or loses all possibility of even conveying an intended message, much less winning someone to Christ. But note this well! Before missionaries understood these things, gospel tracts were presented to smiling, nodding Thais who were counted as believers and recorded back home in the States as converts. Culture and meaning are inextricably linked. The certainty of this link is a defining conviction of the emerging church movement.

Third is the conviction that all authentic and effective Christian ministries are, whether consciously or unconsciously, contextualized within the culture they inhabit. They are indigenous to their cultural contexts. When genuine cultural contextualization takes place, real communication and authentic practice of Christianity becomes more likely, not least because shared meanings are conveyed; folks understand one another. Such indigenous ministry can arise in various ways. Ironically, highly effective and sustainable church planting tends to take place where little or no self-conscious attention is given to the need for contextualization. For example, leaders shaped from birth by the culture within which they minister do not require cultural orientation. As missionary consultant Ben Hess once told me, "the most successful church plants tend to be the easiest." While ministers already indigenous to a cultural context say and do things that are "just right" without even realizing it, an outsider must negotiate a treacherous cultural landscape to avoid giving offense left and right.

In Bangkok the optimal goal was to reach and train Thais who would then lead their own congregations with diminishing oversight from missionaries. Thus were missionaries taught by the International Mission Board of the Southern Baptist Convention. The sooner a ministry becomes indigenous to its culture the sooner it could spread like wildfire. Part of the explanation for the amazing rise and sustained strength achieved especially by Southern Baptists, but also by other Evangelicals in the South, was the utterly and unconsciously indigenous character of the ministries they planted within that cultural context. The leaders and those they evangelized were all of the same soil, and so the ministries produced proved organic to the wider culture—a recipe for just the kind of exponential advance of the gospel that occurred in the South. Indeed, as Martin Marty has noted, Southern Baptists became the Catholics of the South.

But with the increasing replacement of broad-based and deeply rooted cultural continuity in the South and elsewhere with multiple subcultures, no longer can the same words and actions or the same culturally conditioned ministries convey anticipated meanings as efficiently across great swaths of geography as before. Now evangelists and church planters must become "missionaries" in a new way right here in the good ol' US of A. The emerging church sees itself as attempting just this transition to a culture-aware and culture-sensitive approach to the spread of the gospel.

POSTMODERN OR POST-CHRISTIAN?

Informed by impressive primary source research and driven by admitted sympathy with the Emergent stream of emerging, Ryan K. Bolger and Eddie Gibbs articulate the convictions, values, and goals of that stream very well. All the more significant, then, is their frank use of the terms *postmodern* and *post-Christian* to describe changes that help explain and justify significant features of the emerging church. As Christendom gives way to post-Christendom, they contend, religion "is understood in terms of its sociological and psychological significance, discounting any claims to divine revelation and absolute truth." Coinciding with this change is the shift from modernity to postmodernity, representing "a challenge to the main assertions of modernity, with its pursuit of order, the loss of tradition, and the separation of the different spheres of reality, expressed, for example, in the separation of the sacred and the profane at every level."[17]

[17] Eddie Gibbs and Ryan K. Bolger, *Emerging Churches: Creating Christian Community in Postmodern Cultures* (Grand Rapids: Baker Academic, 2005), 17–18.

Proof of the alienation emerging generations feel toward church structures shaped by modernity are the growing numbers of self-identified Christians as well as other spiritual seekers who opt to pursue God or spirituality outside the church, viewing existing modes of church largely as hindrances to their faith.[18] Denominational disaffiliation among Christians, combined with increased disinterest in and ignorance of Christianity by nonbelievers, all contribute to the final dying out of the last vestiges of Christendom-like cultural characteristics and the deepening de-Christianization in the West. The profound cultural transformation taking place all around us, the emerging church contends, demands equally profound transformation of evangelistic method, strategies for church planting, and the overall mind-set of churches that hope to grow. Tim Keller, pastor of Redeemer Presbyterian Church in New York City and a major influencer of doctrine-friendly emerging church planters and pastors, identifies three problems the postmodern context either creates or intensifies:

> First, there's a *truth* problem. All claims of truth are seen not as that which corresponds to reality but primarily as constraints aimed to siphon power off toward the claimer. Second, there's a *guilt* problem. Though guilt was mainly seen as a neurosis in the modern era (with the reign of Freud), it was still considered a problem. Almost all the older gospel presentations assume an easily accessed sense of guilt and moral shortcomings in the listener. But today that is increasingly absent. Third, there is now a *meaning* problem. Today there's enormous skepticism that texts and words can accurately convey meaning.[19]

One might add that, where the world of the arts and the world of spirituality are concerned, texts are increasingly approached as vehicles for the construction of meanings driven by the varied

---

[18] See Gibbs and Bolger, 21, but also George Barna, *Revolution* (Carol Stream, Ill.: Tyndale House, 2005), 1–38.

[19] Keller, "The Gospel and the Supremacy of Christ in a Postmodern World," in *The Supremacy of Christ in a Postmodern World*, ed. John Piper and Justin Taylor (Wheaton, Ill.: Crossway, 2007), 108.

interests brought by the consumers of those texts. It could be
that one of the most defensible claims to postmodern uniqueness
relates to the notion of the constructability of meaning.

Is it true that growing numbers of artists of all kinds, including
writers, bring less and less interest in conveying definite meanings when they create? Is it also true that growing proportions
of the art and text-consuming population reflexively, and therefore unashamedly, construct meanings of their choosing? Would
not widespread habituation to such construction of meaning justify employment of the term *postmodern* or some other term to
account for such a watershed cultural transformation?[20] Audacious
assumption of the prerogative to construct one's own meanings
from another's "speech" (conveyed through whatever medium),
whether in cahoots with author intent or not, marks a striking
subjective appropriation of the objective denial of absolute truth.
Seen in this light, the step from reflexive assumption of the constructability of meaning to the constructability of truth seems a
short one indeed. That such phenomena would not result in deep
and far-reaching implications for the proclamation of the gospel
seems fantastic!

On the other hand, though considerable agreement characterizes descriptions of the contemporary cultural terrain by those
who take postmodernism seriously, once attention turns to exploration of the implications of the postmodern context for evangelism, church-planting, and church renewal, consensus collapses.
From the standpoint of Evangelicalism and orthodox Christianity,
Emergents seem more anxious to affirm what they find in culture than they are protective of the gospel message where conflict
between culture and gospel arises. The result is that the gospel
itself must change, become less message and more way of life.
Emergents, when viewed through Evangelical eyes, seem prepared
to pretty much genuflect before the ostensibly irresistible proclivi-
ties and antipathies embedded within the postmodern psyche as

---

[20] In this regard, one of the most intriguing introductions to postmodernism continues
to be Walter Truett Anderson's *Reality Isn't What It Used to Be: Theatrical Politics, Ready-
to-Wear Religion, Global Myths, Primitive Chic, and Other Wonders of the Postmodern
World* (San Francisco: Harper, 1990).

they define it. For many Evangelicals, Emergent reasoning runs something like this: "Don't want absolute truth? Fine. Out it goes. Had enough of Evangelical fixation on Paul's straight talk regarding homosexual behavior? Don't worry; whenever Evangelicals are the offenders, count on a heap of affirmation from us and a fresh re-thinking of those issues."

Such surrender recalls the response of the great father of Protestant Liberalism, Friedrich Schleiermacher, to similar challenges. The Enlightenment, which found its apex and the beginning of its self-correction in the thinking of Immanuel Kant, denied the knowability of a metaphysical referent such as "God" by the human mind. Schleiermacher, in the face of this radical challenge, hoped to salvage as much of Christianity as possible. Thus he attempted to inoculate Christian theology against Enlightenment critique by abandoning any suggestion that Christian doctrine means to describe metaphysical objects of inquiry, including God. Instead, Christian doctrine would describe the content of the Christian self-consciousness, confident that what it found there necessitates acknowledgment of the truth of Christianity in much the same way as Kant's categorical imperative demanded acknowledgment of a moral divine being and an afterlife.

The ease with which some Emergents equivocate on an array of traditional readings of Scripture and either question the use of doctrine or abandon doctrine altogether is astounding. From comparative disinterest in the historicity of Scripture to dispassion for the doctrine of justification by grace through faith alone to congenital vagueness regarding homosexual behavior, Emergents evidence little answerability to either Bible or tradition. Emergent adjustment to postmodernism combined with distaste for the Enlightenment seems strikingly uncomfortable with major dimensions of the Christian past that predate Modernity and the Enlightenment.

Meanwhile, doctrine-friendly emerging pastors such as Mark Driscoll, Tim Keller, and Darrin Patrick manage to maintain intense interest in the implications of a postmodern, post-Christian West *and* commitment to fully orbed doctrinal statements, unashamed

embrace of both orthodox theology and Christology, protectiveness of Reformation recovery of bold objective notions of atonement, clear identification of homosexuality as sin, and opposition
to abortion on demand. And they do this without alienating the
twenty- and early thirty-somethings Emergents insist will not find
doctrine-heavy ministries relevant.

Doctrine-friendly emerging types tend to treat postmodernism as a fluid phenomenon that offers guidance for the shaping of
Christian ministries but that also uncovers new opportunities for
the conveyance of ancient Christian truth. Emergents often treat
postmodernism as some hegemonic cultural force that determines
what growing proportions of the population can and cannot find
meaningful. For them, postmodernism just rules out truckloads
of traditional Evangelical ways of acting and speaking as irrelevant—especially where doctrine, propositional truth, exacting
language, and demands for certitude are concerned. Such suggestions appear ludicrous as large numbers from the so-called thoroughly postmodern generations continue to find relevant what
Emergents insist they cannot. It is amazing how weak commitment to the elasticity of meaning becomes (no matter when or
where one was born) when a lawsuit or medical report or financial document crosses one's desk. No, all God's children remain
capable of nuzzling up to warranted linguistic exactitude and the
category of absolute truth.

POSTMODERN, POST-CHRISTIAN EVANGELISM

Both streams of emerging identify profound implications of the
postmodern, post-Christian context for evangelism. The enormity
of the effects of cultural change upon evangelistic effectiveness is
illustrated by the experience of one particular (now-failed) church
plant of which I am aware. This congregation, passionate for the
conversion of sinners, made evangelism the core commitment that
would shape the church's identity from its founding. Accordingly,
members, over the course of just a few years, knocked on upwards
of seven thousand doors to share the gospel and literature from
their church. The result? Some tiny percentage of the contacts

resulted in visits to the church. Of thousands encountered in the massive, labor-intensive door-knocking campaign, a total of three persons joined the church. And they were believers beforehand!

How should we account for such meager results from such a massive investment of time, energy, prayer, and actual verbal witnessing? Passionate defenders of such methods of evangelistic outreach may comfort themselves with various explanations. "Our responsibility is to share the gospel, plant seeds, not to convert sinners. Only God the Holy Spirit can convert the lost." Undoubtedly, such explanations do, to *some* extent, account for the apparent wholesale rejection of the gospel encountered by these dedicated witnesses. But the emerging church wants to go further and ask, "To *what* extent?" What if cultural factors render such approaches far less likely to be effective with increasing portions of the unbelieving population? What if the investment of time and energy in alternative approaches could have resulted in many more authentic gospel-sharing encounters? By authentic gospel-sharing encounter I do not mean only those in which conversion occurs. Rather, I mean one in which the gospel call to repentance and faith is actually understood and responded to one way or another.

The strength of the problems produced by postmodern culture varies greatly according to geography and subculture. This exacerbates potential miscommunication between emerging and nonemerging pastors, scholars, and church planters. The strength of post-Christian and postmodern cultural transformation is much greater in Europe than in the United States, greater in cities than in smaller towns and rural areas, greater in the Northeast and West Coast of America than in the flyover states, and greater among younger than among older demographics. When Tim Keller warns of the waning usefulness of some traditional evangelistic methods that Mark Cahill, leader of an evangelistic ministry based in Georgia, still finds effective, Keller's suggested changes may be misconstrued as a call to retreat from evangelistic zeal.[21]

Descriptive accounts of the character of postmodernism overlap significantly between the two streams of the emerging church.

---

[21] See www.markcahill.org.

Both welcome insights from Leonard Sweet, Alan Hirsch, Leslie Newbigin, and Stanley Grenz. But the import given and use made of these insights often diverges. Emergent thinkers are much more likely to argue that our actual comprehension of the gospel itself must change in a postmodern world. Thus, the Synoptic Gospels and parenetic passages come to rule the hermeneutical roost, while the apostle Paul with all his head-heavy theologizing becomes marginalized, and objective views of the atonement are displaced with subjective ones. For some, the doctrine of justification by grace through faith itself is viewed as either irrelevant or as an actual threat to the gospel. Famously, Steve Chalke characterized the substitutionary atonement as a case of cosmic child abuse.[22] And while Chalke's radical view does not characterize the entire spectrum of Emergent thinking, attitudes ranging from nonchalance to marked resistance to Reformation views of the atonement are the order of the day among them.

What are we to make of shared emerging interest in postmodernism juxtaposed with divergent assessments of the implications precipitated by postmodernism for ministry? Emergent thinking seems to repeat one of the fatal errors endemic to Protestant Liberalism from its inception in Schleiermacher's theology—the reflexive conflation of description with prescription. Both streams of emerging welcome accurate description of the terrain Christian ministry must traverse. But description must be distinguished from prescription. The content of the gospel cannot be read off the cultural milieu. God reveals it in His Holy Word. Divine diagnosis of the patient is already complete! Complete by none other than the Great Physician. Again, description is not prescription. Emergents seem to allow their comprehension of culture to dictate the shape relevant ministries must assume in ways the doctrine-friendly types do not. Thus, where Emergents are concerned, one learns to expect more politically correct approaches to culturally controversial issues.

Thus, on the homosexuality question, one encounters responses ranging from nonchalance to acceptance of homosexual behav-

---

[22] See D. A. Carson's treatment in *Becoming Conversant*, 182–87.

ior as an alternative lifestyle. And under the pressures of relativism and pluralism, one finds retreat from the exclusive claims of Christ and a bad conscience for proselytizing. Prophetic critique among Emergents seems welcome mainly where Fundamentalism and Evangelicalism are the targets.

Conversely, doctrine-friendly emerging churches display a marked willingness to confront and offend cultural norms where the truth of Scripture, as they see it, is at stake. Clear identification of homosexuality as sin, proclamation of the exclusive claims of Christ, conversion-seeking evangelism, and restriction of eldership to males characterizes many of these congregations. So, ministry-shaping alertness to culture? Yes. Reflexive accommodation of ministry and message to culture? No.

DIRECT EVANGELISM DELAYED?

One feature of much emerging church approach will likely raise concerns for many Evangelicals, namely, an increasing acceptance of a new kind of patience with those targeted for evangelization. The reasoning is as follows: Where a uniform culture replete with shared meaning prevails, perhaps sermons and disciple-seeking conversation should dovetail quickly into urgent pleas for saving repentance from sin and faith in Jesus Christ. But what if no such obvious shared terrain of meaning can be assumed? What then? Is there ever justification for delaying direct, conversion-seeking evangelistic appeal? Haven't we seen this all before? You know, the gospel is essentially reduced to matters of morality with perhaps a pinch of tolerance for idiosyncratic personal spirituality, but any insistence upon the need for faith in the saving death of Jesus and new birth are left behind.

But there are other strategic reasons for the delay. Many Evangelical mission-sending agencies have been so impressed by the methods and materials of New Tribes Mission that they have adopted them as their own. And the justification for delay of direct evangelistic appeal in some contexts by the doctrine-friendly emerging stream overlaps significantly with the New Tribes sensibility.

Remote peoples targeted by New Tribes share little in terms of worldview and conceptual framework with the missionaries seeking their conversion. Given such wide cultural and conceptual distance, immediate appeals to convert proved impossible. But New Tribes found that patient teaching, beginning with the book of Genesis and moving through the Pentateuch and the Prophets and only then to the New Testament over a period of weeks and even months, could lay a foundation for conversions on a spectacular scale. But they had to wait. Emerging churches may not face equivalent radical cultural disparity, but they still find that patience, leaving time for teaching and the development of a certain level of relational comfort and trust, often serves the interest of evangelization. Attempts to evangelize remote village-dwellers in Asia may call for a considered and cautious approach, but does prudent patience in Papua New Guinea commend similar patience in Pittsburgh? I think the answer of the emerging church is, sometimes.

AVERSION TO CONVERSION?

Such acceptance of delayed evangelism leaves many Evangelicals uneasy and not without reason. The Emergent, doctrine-wary stream of emerging does display some of the conversion-averse tendencies that liberal Christianity lapsed into with such devastating consequences to itself and to the advance of the gospel generally. Scot McKnight has recognized this anti-evangelistic posture and sees it as a threat to the movement:

> I offer here a warning to you and to the emerging movement: any movement that is not evangelistic is failing the Lord. We may be humble about what we believe and we may be careful to make the gospel and its commitment clear, but we better have a goal in mind—the goal of summoning everyone to follow Jesus Christ and to discover the redemptive work of God in Christ through the Spirit of God.[23]

[23] Page 26 of McKnight's address at Westminster Theological Seminary, October 26–27, 2006, as http://www.foolishsage.com/wordpress/wp-content/uploads/McKnight%20-%20What%20is%20the%20Emerging%20Church.pdf. See also his article "Five Streams

Again we see a major difference between the two streams of the emerging church movement. Surely few indicators herald the weakening, decline, and potential demise of a would-be church movement so certainly as the development of a bad conscience for proselytizing. Meanwhile, doctrine-friendly emerging churches have displayed an impressive ability to reach particularly gospel-resistant demographic sectors in cities, in the arts community, and among twenty- and thirty-somethings.

MISSIONAL VS. ATTRACTIONAL

Associated with the cluster of ideas related to culture and meaning within the self-identity of emerging leaders is a commitment to what they call *missional* ways of being and doing church. Though the term missional is not new, emerging church leaders employ the terminology in specific ways expressly intended to distinguish their way of being the church from alternate models. By *missional*, emerging church leaders communicate two inter-related ideas, one negative and one positive.

First, the negative. Missional models of church contrast with attractional models. Attractional congregations attempt to draw seekers to their churches by establishing and advertising relevant ministries within their target communities. Convinced that, upon wooing seekers across the worship center threshold, much of the task of reaching them is finished, disproportionate energy is invested in what goes on within rather than without the walls of the church. Some emerging leaders reject such strategies as a departure from the outward-focused, "go-ye-therefore" imperative of our Lord, while others argue merely that such attractional models cannot draw seekers from the subcultures they wish to target.

As a positive term, *missional* conveys at least one ontological conviction related to the church and one methodological consequence of that conviction. "I am the church" replaces the notion "I go to church." And just as significant, the notion "I send missionaries" is displaced by "I am a missionary." Missional thinking suspects that patterns shaping many current models of church

of the Emerging Church: Key Elements of the Most Controversial and Misunderstood Movement," in *Christianity Today*, vol. 51, no. 2 (February 2007), 35–39.

have lost sight of the "go ye into the world" dimension of the Great Commission and may have drifted into a distorted, exaggerated comprehension of that other mandate, "be ye separate." Rather than encourage a pattern of activity in which believers flock to a location many miles from their homes where they "do church" and "are discipled," missional churches focus much more on the world outside the church, within the neighborhoods where members live, with a keen awareness of and jealousy for the lordship of Christ already operative there. They look not so much to "reach" the community for Christ in the sense of involving some slice of the community in their programs within the walls of their churches. Rather, they look to see the community transformed as believers engage those with whom they work, study, and play. Member-led missional-minded groups meet in homes and target the immediate neighborhood.

Emerging leaders contend not only that this missional mind-set coincides more faithfully to biblical patterns of following Jesus and being church, but also that it is vital for effective church-planting in a post-Christian, subculture-shaped landscape. Prospects under the age of 35, they insist, are largely immune to the kinds of attractional and program-configured ministries to which so many Baby Boomers have responded with such eagerness.

THE GREEK PHILOSOPHICAL BOGEYMAN

Some emerging church thinkers point to pernicious philosophical influences of Western philosophy upon Christianity visible already in the first and second centuries among Gnostic Christian sects. They argue that Greek philosophy in the West, running from Plato and Aristotle through Neo-Platonism, provided hermeneutical filters through which the Bible's message often suffered tragic distortion.

We can identify two major areas precious to the emerging church where the overcoming of Greek categories matters. First is the metaphysical disparagement of matter and thus of physicality so endemic to certain strands of Western philosophy. As opposed to the Greek philosophical dualism between flesh and spirit, Christianity, they argue, can distinguish between flesh and spirit while affirming both as dimensions of God's good creation.

The prologue of John's Gospel provides an excellent model. It unashamedly assumes and manipulates a given philosophical and linguistic tradition for the purpose of separating wheat from chaff within that tradition while also expressing something new. Thus the apostles' audience is first lulled into docility through reflexive agreement with these assertions:

> In the beginning was the Word, and the Word was with God, and the Word was God. He was with God in the beginning. All things were created through Him, and apart from Him not one thing was created that has been created. Life was in Him, and that life was the light of men. That light shines in the darkness, yet the darkness did not over-come it (John 1:1–5).

Given the shaping bequeathment of a fundamentally Platonic metaphysic and cosmogony, all this (and for that matter, vv. 10–13 as well) could be asserted without the slightest fear of ruf-fled feathers among the intended first-century audience. But then, in an Amos-like turning of the tables, verse 14 must fall like a thunderclap upon Greekified and either Gnostic or at least proto-Gnostic psyches—"The Word became flesh!"

In addition, the Platonic doctrine of the immortality of the soul did not provide the best linguistic vehicles for the articulation of the Christian hope of bodily resurrection. The resurrected Jesus ran roughshod over large swaths of Greek conviction when He "took [broiled fish] and ate it in their presence," and when, in the face of doubts, He bade the disciples, "Look at My hands and My feet, that it is I Myself! Touch Me and see, because a ghost does not have flesh and bones as you can see I have."[24] Ancient streams of disdain for the physical body present in the Greek tradition appear also in Paul's writings. Juxtaposed against Platonic yearn-ing for release of the soul from the tomb of the body, the contrast with Christian sensibility seems striking indeed. The italicized words in the following Pauline excerpt amount to a direct assault upon such Platonic sensibilities:

---

[24] Luke 24:39–43.

For we know that if our temporary, earthly dwelling, is destroyed, we have a building from God, an eternal dwelling in the heavens, not made with hands. Indeed, we groan in this body, desiring to put on our dwelling from heaven, since, when we are clothed, *we will not be found naked*. Indeed, we groan while we are in this tent, burdened as we are, because *we do not want to be unclothed but clothed*, so that mortality may be swallowed up by life.[25]

All authors, including those who produced the New Testament, cannot but employ the philosophical and linguistic tools at hand, fraught as they are with the peculiarities attaching to time, space, and culture. But this inevitability did not trap the apostles John and Paul within the received field of meaning of words such as *logos*, for example. John exploits the anticipated meaning his audience attached to this word precisely in order to affirm, deny, and transcend aspects of that given field of meaning and thus have his way with it in order to teach something new, namely, the truth of God, not the outgrowth of any philosophy, including Platonism. That communication within any culture must employ the philosophical and linguistic tools available does not lead to inevitable genuflection before the ideological presuppositions admittedly embedded within that philosophico-linguistic machinery.

Emerging reading of Holy Scripture finds much justification for the affirmation of the human body and all things physical and earthly. Such affirmation coincides, they insist, with orthodox confession of the doctrine of the incarnation and points to profound implications touching the Christian life and, more specifically, the nature and mission of the church. These implications become conspicuous within the emerging church as two distinctive quests: (1) the quest to recover respect for the physical dimension of life in all its facets and (2) the quest to overcome strict distinction between the sacred and the secular.

---

[25] 2 Cor 5:1–4 (emphasis added).

LORDSHIP AND THE SECULAR REALM

Gibbs and Bolger's identification of "transforming secular space" as one of only three core practices of emerging churches highlights a defining feature of the movement.[26] They consider the sacred/secular split as a child of modernity tracing back to fourteenth-century scholastic philosopher/theologians William of Ockham and Duns Scotus. Sharp separation between ostensibly secular and sacred realms fails to take seriously both the lordship of Jesus Christ over the entire world and the kingdom living that lordship justifies and invites.[27]

Against politically correct relegation of spirituality to personal piety and private practice, emerging churches insist, along with Madeleine L'Engle, that "there is nothing so secular that it cannot be sacred, and that is one of the deepest messages of the Incarnation."[28] Thus, emerging churches, not unlike Dietrich Bonhoeffer, call for a "Christian worldliness" and insist that true disciples of Jesus will "plunge into the tempest of living," recognizing that our God's concern extends to the nooks and crannies of everyday life along with its problems and struggles. Where the interests of the poor, sick, imprisoned, and indigent (the least of these!) are ignored or trampled upon, faithful Christian witness depends upon both word and deed. But surely collapse of the spiritual into the physical or the loss of any distinction between the sacred and the secular cannot easily assimilate major strata within the biblical witness where miracles occur, where Jesus prays "not for the world" and bids us "render to Caesar what belongs to Caesar."

Nevertheless, when Jesus said "I give you a new command: love one another. Just as I have loved you, you must also love one another. By this all people will know that you are My disciples, if you have love for one another," He connected the credibility of Christian witness to observable love. Thus Francis Schaeffer could contend that "we as Christians are called upon to love *all* men as

---

[26] Gibbs and Bolger, *Emerging Churches*, 43.

[27] Ibid., 65–88.

[28] L'Engle, *Walking on Water* (Colorado Springs: Harold Shaw, 1980), quoted in Gibbs and Bolger, 65.

neighbors, loving them as ourselves" and "that we are to love all the Christian brothers in a way that the world may observe."[29]

In response to emerging church re-thinking of the relationship between the secular and sacred realms, Ray Anderson commends the writings of Karl Barth and Dietrich Bonhoeffer as resources that could undergird their commitment to be in the world, take responsibility for the world, and love the world in the name of Jesus Christ.[30] That the church's image in the eyes of the world needs addressing and that God lays obligation upon the church for the world has been noted by Evangelical theologians with no organic connection to the emerging church. Given the frequent expressions of suspicion toward doctrine and theology so prevalent within the Emergent conversation, Anderson's attempt to provide, as the title of his book indicates, *An Emergent Theology for Emerging Churches* is certainly welcome. And it is noteworthy that a significant array of influential Emergent leaders have provided endorsements of Anderson's volume.[31]

Yet Anderson, by referencing Barth and Bonhoeffer, offers a needed corrective to the collapse of the distinction between the secular and the sacred so often encountered within the Emergent conversation. Affirmation of Christ's lordship over the whole world and recognition that the church's responsibility for the world is grounded in and informed by that lordship does not require and need not result in the utter collapse of the distinction between the sacred and the secular in the Christian mind. When this collapse does result, Christian witness is threatened.

The Emergent conversation evidences genuine discomfort with the notion of Christian witness for several reasons. One such reason shares much with an insight Rick Warren has articulated, namely, that the world has come to view conservative Christianity as a BIG MOUTH shouting about what everybody is doing

---

[29] In Timothy George and John Woodbridge, *The Mark of Jesus* (Chicago: Moody, 2005), 19.

[30] Ray S. Anderson, *An Emergent Theology for Emerging Churches* (Downers Grove, Ill.: InterVarsity, 2006), 194–95.

[31] Especially noteworthy are Brian McLaren, Dan Kimball, Eddie Gibbs, Doug Pagitt, and Tony Jones.

wrong and screaming about hell.[32] Meanwhile, liberal Christianity is viewed as disproportionately focused upon meeting the social and physical needs of the world. A 2006 *Wall Street Journal* study indicates that, by almost any measure, conservative Christians outstrip liberals by a long shot in ministry to hurting people.[33] Still, in the popular perception at least, a division of labor seems to operate in which one branch of the church concerns itself with souls while the other branch attends to the body. The corrective, Warren believes, must involve keeping the proclaiming "mouth" but also reclaiming the "hands and feet" eager to respond to those in physical, economic, and social need.

Emergents also advocate the recovery of a warranted humility before the world where Christian proclamation is concerned. Pounding pulpits and shouting from street corners that we and we alone are the possessors and purveyors of the most precious truth known to humankind strikes Emergent sensibilities as somehow incompatible with a Savior who washes feet and keeps silent before a perplexed Pilate holding power to punish or set free. But the pursuit of humility in proclamation can go too far. It can lead to the toleration of a diversity too expansive to remain compatible with a Jesus who, though a servant *par excellence*, also knows Himself to be Lord, could say of Himself, "Before Abraham was, I am," and offered Himself as the *only* way to the Father. Note this from Ben Edson, leader of the Sanctus1 community in the UK and featured in Gibbs and Bolger: "We had a guy from the Manchester Buddhist center come to Sanctus1 a couple of weeks ago and talk about Buddhist approaches to prayer. We didn't talk about the differences between our faiths. We didn't try to convert him. He was welcomed and fully included and was really pleased to have been invited."[34] Gibbs and Bolger account for the mind-set thus: "Christians cannot truly evangelize unless they are prepared to be evangelized in the process."[35] Never mind that Buddhism

---

[32] David Kinnaman and Gabe Lyons, *unChristian: What a New Generation Really Thinks about Christianity . . . and Why It Matters* (Grand Rapids: Baker, 2007), 245; also "Interview with Rick Warren," *Larry King Live*, March 22, 2005.

[33] Arthur C. Brooks, "A Charitable Explanation," *Wall Street Journal*, Nov. 27, 2006.

[34] Gibbs and Bolger, 133.

[35] Ibid., 131.

is formally god-less—there is no god to pray to—but for Emergents so often critical of the seeker church, Sanctus1 sounds pretty seeker friendly for Buddhists!

Surely a quest to reclaim the church's responsibility for "loving in a way the world can see," and a posture that bespeaks a humility appropriate to all who know themselves to be blood-bought sinners, need not shirk its duty to proclaim the gospel. And the reduction of witness to nonverbal means cannot suffice. Jesus, Paul, Stephen, and who knows how many other "martyrs" (witnesses!) across the millennia, could have spared their lives if only they could have kept their mouths shut. But they could not do so and neither can we. Jesus was not divinely designated "the Word" for nothing. Yes, recognition of the duty to proclaim the gospel message remains politically incorrect and bound to bring offense where diversity and pluralism have become unquestioned behavioral pillars of polite society. But the content-full character of Christian witness as the proclamation of an unchanging message cannot be avoided.

Undoubtedly, the credibility of the gospel message depends upon walking the walk and not just talking the talk. But the truth of the gospel does not so depend. Ultimately, the church does not bid unbelievers "look at us" but "look at Him."

Christian loving care and service are not the thing itself but, as Barth would say, serve as parables that point to the true caregiver. The church must point away from both itself and the world. The true soteriological resources reside outside both. Proper acknowledgment of the sacramental potential of earthly things never imagines the capture-ability or dispensability of God's power and grace at the disposal of a church with its hands on the heavenly faucets.

Where a pronounced gap separates the witness of the church from her walk, the credibility of her message is proportionately undermined. And that is as it should be. Thus the unavoidable privilege and burden of witness serves as a constant call to repentance. Whatever else it might mean that we take up the ministry of our Savior and serve, in Luther's memorable terms, as "little Christs" to one another, woe unto us if we extrapolate too much from this unity with Christ—so much that our unity with the Savior results in a displacement of the one mediator between God and man and identifies His body with the Head. There are vital dimensions of Christ's work with which we have no share. Luther could also say of Christ's model, "the example is too high. We cannot follow!" There are stations along the way of Jesus we cannot, were not meant to, and should not attempt to follow. However faithfully our lives together in community reflect our "having been with the Lord" (and He deserves to have this reflection be perfect), our burden remains that of reflection and witness. The world needs us, but it needs Him in ways that we cannot help.

RECOVERY OF NARRATIVE

Initially, the higher critical methodologies that traced back to the nineteenth century seemed to hold much promise for biblical theology. But ultimately, higher critical attempts to go behind the best extant manuscripts and reconstruct something more "original" foundered. The initial incentives that shaped the rise of both the canonical hermeneutic advanced by Brevard Childs and narrative theology associated with Hans Frei included exhaustion and frustration with "the loss of the Bible" amidst the labyrinthine, fanciful, and often speculative contortions of higher critical attempts to reconstruct Holy Scripture. The recovery of an intact Bible allowed for a fresh focus upon the literary genre most prominent within it—narrative.

The emerging church brings a heightened appreciation and protectiveness of the narrative form that shapes so much of the biblical witness. Faithful exposition of biblical texts should remain true to that narrative shape. Might not those who hold dear the authority of the Scriptures, who confess the Reformation *sola scriptura*, find much here to celebrate? At least formally, do not conservative Christians mean to test all things, including every sermon, every commentary, and every systematic theology by Scripture? The Bible is not a puzzle to be deciphered and decoded by either systematic theology or three-point sermons. Ought not the study of the exacting minutiae of background and archaeological materials, the intricacies of grammar and syntax and systematic theology itself prove their Christian viability by the power to illuminate the meaning of the text, rather than by their displacement of the text or by becoming some permanent authoritative grids through which the text is to be read? Whenever systematic theology or loyalty to any particular tradition of interpretation results in the exaltation of a pantheon of approved interpreters or interpretations, the Reformation *sola scriptura* has been lost. Now, rather than assuming the proper posture of all true Protestants under the Word, we find a "standing-above-the-Word" that supposes to tame but may inadvertently silence it.

The critique and sometimes even rejection of propositional truth along with disinterest in the rise and development of doctrine and of systematic theology by some within the Emergent church goes too far. But both systematic theology and adherence to doctrine, when they do not function as they should, do pose certain risks to the very Word they should illuminate and defend. The emerging church phenomenon invites a needed exploration of the proper nature and limits of doctrine and systematic theology among Bible-believing Christians.

HISTORY OR STORY?

Certainly much of the talk about *story* among emerging leaders must strike the ears of many as quite vague and strange. What does it mean to "live into God's story"? I suspect it means something akin to what Edward Farley had in mind when he insisted that "in living out of the inherited symbols and narratives of one's faith, one isn't just applying dead truths to a living situation. Instead, one is embodying or incorporating oneself into a living tradition. That's a creative act and an interpretive act, an act of theological understanding."[36] The word *embodying* is important to emerging models of church. Where this desire expresses a quest to break out of head-heavy, scholastic modes of Christian identification into more holistic comprehension of the Christian life where theology and praxis go together, well and good.

---

[36] See the interview with Edward Farley at http://www.religion-online.org/showarticle.asp?title=366.

However, Emergent talk of *narrative, authenticity, story,* and *mystery* often seems to involve radical forms of retreat and reductionism vis-à-vis anything recognizable as historic, biblically grounded Christianity. I mean retreat from the inescapably historical dimension and consequent historical vulnerability of the Christian witness to the world. Inescapable because the church's witness has always known itself as anchored to the actual, sometimes visible in-break of God into history. Vulnerable because, for example, "if Christ has not been raised, your faith is worthless."[37] Such urgent concern for the historical accuracy of the biblical witness strikes many Emergent ears as a leftover irrelevancy of a modernity suffused with Enlightenment sensibilities. But for the church across the ages, such concern belongs to faithful preservation of the concrete intention of the apostle Paul, who predated the modern world by almost two millennia and who fairly represents attitudes prevalent within the earliest Christian communities.

Claims of first-century nonchalance regarding historicity cannot bear too close scrutiny. Modest exploration of the institution of slavery in the first century alone suffices to disabuse fair-minded inquirers of such notions. What one finds is a world replete with meticulous record-keeping and disputes about who said what when and to whom and when this or that happened or this or that document was sealed or transaction occurred and on and on.[38] So, no. Breezy, effortless assertions that New Testament authors were content with the community-nurturing power of history-disinterested "story" are fantastically ill informed concerning that world. While a post-Enlightenment mentality might insist that nothing less than a camcorder at the tomb could justified belief in the resurrection, current inability to reach back the two thousand years and set-up the camera tells us nothing about the intentions of the first-century authors who recorded what they witnessed.

---

[37] 1 Cor 15:17a.
[38] See for example, K. R. Bradley, *Slaves and Masters in the Roman Empire: A Study in Social Control* (Oxford: Oxford University, 1987) and *Slavery and Society at Rome* (Cambridge: Cambridge University, 1994) and William L. Westermann, *The Slave Systems of Greek and Roman Antiquity* (Philadelphia: The American Philosophical Society, 1955).

PREFERENCE FOR PILGRIMAGE AND PROGRESSIVITY

Fascination with narrative and periodic overuse of the word *story* attracts emerging types for another reason: the desire to recover the "pilgrim" language of the Bible in the comprehension of both the Christian life and life as the body of Christ within the world. Tension between the "already" and "not-yet" aspects of salvation as well as between punctiliar and durative dimensions of the Christian life has proven endemic to Christianity because biblical authors employ the language of all four. The same apostle Paul who "runs a race" also insists that Christ "makes us alive" and "is" our sanctification. Peter can speak frankly of the "resident alien" status of believers making their way through this world, but also of their inheritance, undefiled, unfading, "kept in heaven for you." The same Jesus who bids us follow also knows that Nicodemus lacks and needs re-birth—an inconvenient concept where the durative language of journey and story are expected to carry the entire freight of meaning where the Christian life is concerned.

Grappling with these alternate conceptions of divine redemption and the Christian life surfaces periodically within the church. Various attempts to relate durative and punctiliar dimensions of the Christian life range from Eastern Orthodox fixation upon durative, progressive ascent toward perfection to Martin Luther's grace-protective fascination with the punctiliar, forensic, declarative heart of salvation. Lutheran apologist Gerhard O. Forde aptly captures something of the spirit of Luther when he defines sanctification as "simply *the art of getting used to justification.*"[39] Such views exhibit zealous protectiveness of the grace-character of the whole of redemption. "To progress is always to begin again," Luther could say.[40] Here the Christian life is viewed more as a series of "starting all over" junctures characterized by repentance and faith than as a trackable progressive sanctification process that invites the notions of measurability, love-threatening comparison with others, and lapse into Christianized works of righteousness.

---

[39] *Christian Spirituality: Five Views of Sanctification*, ed. Donald L. Alexander (Downers Grove, Ill.: IVP, 1988), 13.

[40] Martin Luther, *Lectures on Romans*, The Library of Christian Classics, trans. and ed. Wilhelm Pauck (Philadelphia: Westminster, 1961), 15:128.

In some cases emerging attraction to the imagery of pilgrimage marks a welcome attempt to recover biblical witness to the ongoing work of the Spirit within believers and the church. In other cases, we find conspicuous discomfort with the God who is pleased to break into our world and our lives vertically, in a flash as it were, calling sinners to definite and temporally locatable repentance and faith. That the response to the call of Jesus involves a bridge-burning, risky, whole life-committing act of repentance and faith was not invented by Evangelicals but spoken by the Savior and Lord with whom we have to do. Where fixation upon a past conversion experience yields disinterest in holy living, it is the conversion experience that is called into question, not conversion as such or in itself.

MYSTERY AND THE ARTS

In his best-selling book *A Generous Orthodoxy*, Brian McLaren lets Walter Brueggemann give expression to widely shared views within the emerging church:

> The gospel is . . . a truth widely held, but a truth greatly reduced. It is a truth that has been flattened and trivialized, and rendered inane. Partly, the gospel is simply an old habit among us, neither valued nor questioned. But more than that, our technical way of thinking reduces mystery to problem, transforms assurance into certitude, revises quality into quantity, and takes the categories of biblical faith and represents them in manageable shapes. . . . There is then no danger, no energy, no possibility, no opening for newness! . . . That means the gospel may have been twisted, pressed, tailored, and gerrymandered until it is comfortable with a technological reason that leaves us unbothered, and with ideology that leaves us with uncriticized absolutes.[41]

This from a book whose title identifies the pursuit to which Brueggemann calls the church—*Recovery of Poetry in a Prose-Flattened World*. As it stands, this challenge from Brueggemann should find a welcome among many Evangelical Christians. Where

---

[41] McLaren, *A Generous Orthodoxy*, 162.

theology and doctrine treat the Bible as a puzzle to be solved and
is, thus, by implication, superseded and displaced by systematic
theology and doctrinal construction, faithfulness to the Bible has
been abandoned and the authority of the Bible has been skirted.
Where sermons and worship and prayers instruct but fail to inspire,
provoke wonder and awe, and stir up surprising convulsions of
confession and repentance, biblical Christianity cannot flourish.

But clearly, the emerging quest for the recovery of mystery
seems to be driven by more than one interest. Where very long
lists of doctrines are asserted with equally high confidence,
emerging church leaders tend to be skeptical. They suspect that
more humility and nuance should attend declarations of Christian truth—humility and nuance in keeping with both the limits of what can be known on the basis of Holy Scripture and in
keeping with author intention where narrative, poetry, and song
provide vehicles for divine revelation. Certainly, Bible-believing
Christians should welcome such quests for more appropriate pro-
portionality between confidence and recoverable author-intended
meaning. Welcome also is the realization that narrative, poetry,
and song intend nothing less than the conveyance of not only historical, moral, and ontological truth, but also more.

The ransacking of biblical texts for the extraction and construction of context-devoid doctrinal assertion often does violence
to God's Word. Left within their inspired contexts, many biblical passages retain their intended power not only to inform (and
this power should by no means be minimized or gainsaid!) but
also to evoke and inspire in ways that transcend the power of language to express directly. Might not divine employment of poetry,
song, and narrative derive precisely from the fact that He intends
to convey both effable and ineffable dimensions of truth? When
one reads a sermon Charles Spurgeon once preached, no doubt
much is there to be gained. But how much is missed to which only
those in attendance had access? It is this kind of thing the emerging church is trying to get at in its hankering after the arts. This
need not imply that ineffable dimensions of meaning are superior

to or might be happily detached from the effable, but rather confesses that what believers gain from the Bible (and this by divine intention) includes more than they can tell with words alone.[42] Exhibit A from the Bible: the Psalms! Similar interests account for emerging concern for the aesthetic features of worship spaces and a new hunger for liturgy. Both can serve to facilitate the sense of transcendence and antiquity appropriate to the Christian faith and connection within a global and historic body of Christ.

Still, concerns arise when the category of mystery becomes a haven for doubt and denial at odds with ascertainable certainty provided by the biblical witness. Christian proclamation must attempt to avoid going beyond what is written, but also to avoid falling short of what the Bible makes clear where dogmatic assertion and covenant-defining confession are concerned. When narrative theologians assure us that the "story" of Christ's bodily resurrection retains its community-creating and hope-nurturing power regardless of its historicity, the sphere of healthy humility and warranted doubt has been left behind. Instead we are confronted with excessive and spineless post-Enlightenment-intimidated retreat from requisite Christian confession.

Do we not see in the Emergent stream of emerging a fairly recognizable, presupposition-heavy agenda shaped by the values and aims we have identified and largely praised? To what extent does the Emergent church bob and weave where direct biblical critique calls into question various dimensions of their vision? Do they not lapse into vague appeals to postmodernism and mystery suffused in an elasticity of language and meaning that the greatest artists eschew as strongly as the most unreconstructed Fundamentalist one could find?

The two great and indispensable mysteries of Christianity are explored in the doctrines of the Trinity and of the person of Jesus Christ. But these mysteries find their ground and justification in certainties, not in doubts—certainty that God is both three and one, certainty that Christ is both fully divine and fully human. Anchoring in what is revealed and thus certain justifies, directs,

[42] For an excellent treatment of ineffable knowledge see Michael Polanyi, *The Tacit Dimension* (Gloucester, Mass.: Peter Smith, 1983).

and regulates believing comprehension and enjoyment of the mysteries to which they point.[43]

Aversion to doctrine arises periodically in the history of the church and usually with good reason. When a community's list of nonnegotiables extends beyond a certain point, even Jesus appears too liberal to gain admission! But doctrine-averse movements often fall victim to a particular blind spot—blindness to the truism that the depth of all communal fellowship (whether Christian or not) is to some significant degree proportional to the depth of shared conviction. Current depths of fellowship within the Emergent stream are not rooted only or even especially in their "openness" but in the shared convictions that already operate like doctrines among them. These Emergent nonnegotiables are imbedded in the central column of terms that appear in figure 1. And this dogmatism is nothing to be ashamed of. What is needed is acknowledgment of these subterranean dogmas without which no rich and vital fellowship can endure.[44]

QUESTIONS, CONCERNS, AND CONCLUDING THOUGHTS

As we have seen, overlap between the two streams of the emerging church movement includes a wide array of convictions and goals touching matters of both identity and practice. Shared readings of culture and common instincts about the significance of culture result in extensive areas of agreement. Yet divergences in theology and mission between them may prove more profound and enduring than the affinities that bind them. And in case after case, the doctrine-friendly contingent appears much more recognizable as a development within the historic, orthodox stream

[43] A helpful treatment of the nature of language in this connection is found in C. S. Lewis, *The Seeing Eye: And Other Selected Essays from Christian Reflections*, ed. Walter Hooper (New York: Ballantine, 1967), 171–88.

[44] Moderates and liberals of the late controversy in the Southern Baptist Convention designated themselves as the freedom party and conservatives as the party of doctrinaire intolerance. Helpfully, Nancy Tatom Ammerman, an unashamed Baptist liberal, called for acknowledgment that both sides of the debate bring nonnegotiable conviction to the fray and that neither side (including the liberals) would knowingly hire professors to teach at SBC seminaries who could not affirm a hefty chunk of those beliefs. See Ammerman's *Baptist Battles: Social Change and Religious Conflict in the Southern Baptist Convention* (New Brunswick, N. J.: Rutgers University, 1995).

of Christianity and thus also as a likely partner for Evangelicals. Undoubtedly, the Emergent, doctrine-wary/doctrine-averse contingent should and will disturb the sensibilities of Evangelicals who cherish both their own historic theological formation and their unashamed commitment to conversion-seeking evangelism.

I would encourage Emergents to consider whether the original discontentments that shaped their quest for a new paradigm of church-planting might be functioning in ways at odds with their stated desire to root themselves within historic Christianity and to welcome help from any quarter in the Christian tradition. Do we not see a bit of a baby-out-with-the-bathwater reflex among them? Are the goals pursued by the Emergent church—community, authenticity, culture-sensitive church planting of missional churches, and recovery of narrative, mystery, and the arts—truly threatened by clear confession of the substitutionary atonement, conversion-seeking evangelism, and enjoyment of the vital service doctrine has provided to the church from its inception? Does not the effectiveness of the doctrine-friendly stream among twenty- and thirty-somethings call into question Emergent recoiling at these features of conservative Christianity in the name of postmodern culture and relevance?

Emergent leaders, freshly freed up from the restrictive confines and heresy-hunting exclusivity they experienced among Evangelicals, now relish the opportunity to seek spiritual resources within Roman Catholicism and Eastern Orthodoxy. Well and good. But if you don't like doctrine, watch out! Back up the truck! These traditions are up to their necks in dogma. Where do we find models of rich, biblical, sustainable ways of doing church devoid of doctrine or lacking the building of institutional structures able to preserve gains won during spiritual awakenings and theological watersheds? Nowhere.

I suggested to one prominent Emergent pastor that, from an historical standpoint, his community of faith, given its despising of doctrine, might not merit the designation of *church*. I wondered whether what he had on his hands might turn out to be more of a way station—a safe place for spiritual seekers of a certain age and imbedded within a particular cultural matrix to consider whether they wish to pursue biblical Christianity or not. This pastor did not disagree and indicated that such a notion did not bother him in the least. But it is interesting to see some of the Emergent congregations (especially those that have enjoyed significant growth) move from a doctrine-devoid existence to mere doctrine-wariness, nervously taking on the Apostles' or the Nicene Creed. The most influential thinkers within the Emergent church often identify the dangers of doctrine in convincing fashion. But can they account for the felt need for doctrine exhibited by some churches who also share the sensibilities most prized by the Emergent church?

MOVING FORWARD BY LOOKING BACK

One very hopeful and potentially self-correcting feature observable among many of the leaders across the entire spectrum of the movement is the declared openness to the whole Christian tradition, the desire to learn from the witness of the body of Christ extended in both time and space. They wish to avoid a lapse into one theological ghetto or another that would threaten to shut them off from fellowship with other Christians and destroy the unity of Christ that must concern all Bible-loving believers.

It seems that significant segments of the Evangelical world, perhaps disproportionately Reformed Evangelicals, are susceptible to such unhealthy separatist tendencies. The expansiveness of vision that informs emerging church identity could bespeak a warranted modesty and teachableness appropriate to us sinners who serve as undershepherds of God's little flocks. Willingness to learn from all Christian voices, testing all things by Scripture, also seems especially welcome, given the great shift of Christian vitality to the Southern hemisphere, together with the ever-increasing post-Christian character of the Western world.[45] We Bible-believing Christians need each other, and we need all the help we can find as we attempt to respond to the Great Commission of our Lord in these changing, complicated times.

That the entire spectrum of emerging leaders and influencers evidences serious interest in the history of the church is striking,

---

[45] See Phillip Jenkins, *The Next Christendom: The Coming of Global Christianity* (Oxford: Oxford University: 2007).

refreshing, and surprising, given that the very heart of the emerging movement centers around the desire to plant and nurture viable and relevant communities of faith here and now. One hopes that this willingness to move forward while looking back can save the emerging church from the pitfalls endemic to what Timothy George has called "the cult of contemporaneity." Past efforts by the church to achieve felt-relevance through myopic analysis of the present with no anchor within the "whole story" of God's activity through the centuries have caused the church to lose its depth and often even its connection to the living but ancient gospel it wishes to propagate.

The doctrine-friendly stream of the movement appears uniquely poised to benefit from serious engagement with the history of the church. This seems true not least because so much of this wing of the movement knows itself to be anchored within a part of that tradition, typically the Reformed tradition. Mark Driscoll, Tim Keller, Ed Stetzer, and Darrin Patrick evidence unashamed gratitude for and indebtedness to Reformed theology and its impressive contribution to the Church. But they also exercise great freedom to dialogue with a variety of traditions and to learn and find resources from a wide array of believing voices from the past. Such rootedness combined with openness bodes well for the future of this stream within the emerging movement.

On the other hand, the pattern of engagement with the Christian past on the Emergent side of the movement raises red flags on several fronts. To a significant degree, Emergent openness to Christian tradition appears to be grounded in its rejection of the strong us-versus-them attitude encountered in Evangelical churches. Upon leaving these separatist-inclined contexts, many are anxious to break free from the tendency to, as Scot McKnight has expressed it, "other" or in contemporary parlance "diss" so many confessing Christians from so many segments of the Church, both past and present.

It should be said that, despite this fresh zeal for happy fellowship and conversation within a global and historic Christian family, Evangelicals present targets for caricature, condescension, and lecturing from many among the Emergent contingent of the movement. All too often, one encounters a reflexive dismissiveness of Evangelicals as Pharisees. Indeed, it is sadly ironic that, within a community that sometimes prides itself on its openness and its insistence that humility be recognized as a distinctive mark of genuine discipleship, the "othering" of Evangelicals functions a bit like a badge of identity for some.

Nevertheless, Emergent engagement of Christian tradition is not limited to a rebellious, protest-inspired plunge into all things once denied to it. That the past is viewed as a rich resource for contemporary Christian leadership seems clear from review of Emergent books and blogs and is perhaps best epitomized by the widespread appreciation of Robert E. Webber's writings and the "Ancient Future" note they strike.

But while Emergents are happy to make eclectic, discriminating use of the Bible and the tradition, they display little awareness of being answerable to either. One gets the sense that, for Emergents (as for some "numbers-equals-success" practitioners within the church growth movement) values and goals are presupposed—the Bible, tradition, or whatever other sources may appear promising are exploited according to their usefulness for the advance of an agenda birthed elsewhere.

We touch here probably the crux of the antipathy not only between the two wings of the emerging movement, and not only between Emergent and Evangelicalism, but between Emergent and the whole stream of orthodox Christianity stretching back at least to Nicea but arguably to the earlier controversies involving Montanus and Marcion. The discomfort with doctrine within Emergent may well signal a more fundamental attempt to break free from authority as such.[46]

I say "may," first of all, because Emergent resistance to doctrine might be a result of an unnecessary and unconscious baby-out-with-the-bathwater tendency to look askance at most everything attaching to the faith communities from which they emerged and

---

[46] See perhaps the most formidable effort to discredit and call to move beyond categories of authority in Edward Farley, *Ecclesial Reflection: An Anatomy of Theological Method?* (Philadelphia: Fortress, 1982), 3–165.

now wish to critique. If so, their sometimes naïve dismissal of the importance of doctrine may prove less central to their identity than it now appears. Secondly, does not the history of the church suggest that some sort of historically recurring pendulum swing back and forth between head-heavy, doctrine-loving, scholasticizing Christianity and heart-enamored, community-centered, doctrine-wary, Christian-life-fixated Christianity is inevitable? And are not many of the Emergent critiques of the contemporary church needed? I think so. But unless Emergent can give a coherent answer to the question, "By what authority do you teach and live thus-and-so?" the specter and threat of not only human-centered but also human-constructed idolatry looms.

GO YE VS. BE YE SEPARATE

Faithful response to the gospel includes both world-denying and world-affirming impulses. Given the Bible's inclusion of both, it is not surprising that the demand to discern the true nature, extent, and relationship between these impulses has thrust itself upon the Church from the beginning. The same Yahweh who elects and separates out for Himself a peculiar people for covenant privilege also promises to make them a light and blessing to all the nations. The same Jesus who came not into the world to condemn the world but to save it also encouraged his disciples to lay up treasure in heaven where moth and rust do not corrupt and thieves do not break in and steal. The same New Testament that bids believers "be ye separate" also enjoins "go ye."

Sympathetic readings of the emerging church movement should detect within it a fresh prophetic call to fulfill the "go ye" dimension of the divine imperative. When emerging leaders survey contemporary models of church in the West, they notice certain tendencies toward retreat from the world, the presence of a kind of embattled, frightened, and escapist mind-set that too often keeps proclamation of the gospel bottled up behind the walls of the church and person-to-person engagement with the culture and the lost world to a minimum. Driven by zeal for the advance of the gospel and church-planting and undergirded theologically by a renewed emphasis on the lordship of Christ, the emerging church looks for every possible means to engage this world with the message of its Lord. Surely this is a good thing.

CONCLUDING THOUGHTS

To the extent that Phillip Jenkins's extraordinary findings and prognostications published in his 2007 book *The Next Christendom: The Coming of Global Christianity* prove accurate, they probably provide some of the most vital data we Evangelicals should consider as we look to the future. Relocation of the center of gravity of global Christianity to the Southern Hemisphere, combined with a North America composed of proportionately fewer Evangelicals, herald profound transformation of the cultural landscape where ministry must occur—transformation that proclaimers of the gospel and planters of churches can ill afford to ignore. Does not a landscape thus altered commend a shift away from remaining vestiges of Christendom-thinking to something very much like the kind of missionary or "missional" mind-set called for by the emerging church?

Underlying motivations of doctrine-friendly emerging leaders coincide significantly with one of the original motivations of the seeker- and purpose-driven tributaries within the wider church-growth movement, namely, the impulse to see the gospel advance within communities, neighborhoods, and segments of the population largely untouched by or impervious to existing models of church and evangelistic approaches. Yet having gained from observance and consideration of these efforts, these doctrine-friendly emerging churches seem comparatively more protective of core orthodox, evangelical theological commitments than either seeker or purpose-driven models.

In a 1989 attempt to discern the most pressing challenges facing Southern Baptist theological educators, Timothy George also uncovered two of the most pressing concerns raised by the emerging church from an Evangelical standpoint. The first is a concern that confronts Evangelicals by the Emergent stream within the movement: "A church which cannot distinguish heresy from truth, or no longer thinks this is an important thing to do, has lost its right to bear witness to the transforming gospel of Jesus Christ who declared Himself to be not only the Way and the Life, but also the only Truth which leads to the Father."[47] Emergent attitudes toward the value and significance of doctrinal truth range from striking disinterest to patronizing condescension to acute aversion in which doctrine is viewed as a pernicious threat to the "gospel" they wish to advance. Unless and until the concern George raises is satisfactorily addressed, Evangelical interest will likely remain restricted to matters touching the analysis of culture, while calls for a theological awakening among Emergents will remain appropriate.

But where the doctrine-friendly emerging church world is concerned, perhaps Evangelicals should ask themselves a few questions related to the obverse side of George's first contention, addressed to Southern Baptists but relevant also to all Evangelicals as they examine the emerging church:

> For Southern Baptists, at this stage in our history, the burning theological need is the ability to distinguish the central affirmations of the faith from the peripheral, adiaphorous issues which have become so divisive in our time. . . . [A] church which has become obsessed with the marginalia of the faith will soon find itself shipwrecked on the shoals of a fractured fellowship.[48]

Of course one man's marginalia is a another man's nonnegotiable truth, but the first point here is to acknowledge, precisely for the defense of the gospel, the common interest all Evangelicals have in achieving optimal success in the distinguishing of primary, secondary, and tertiary issues. This task of discrimination is rarely easy and is never fully completed. But surely the desire to remove every unnecessary stumbling block to the advance of the gospel should be a goal all would share.

---

[47] From George's paper "The Future for Theological Education Among Southern Baptists," presented to the Southeast regional meeting of the National Association of Baptists Professors of Religion, March 10, 1989, 18.

[48] Ibid.

How should Evangelicals respond to emerging church pastors and planters who combine exemplary zeal for the conversion of souls with crystal clear confession of core theological commitments ranging from the doctrine of the Trinity to the Christological consensus spanning Nicea and Chalcedon to the justification by grace alone through faith alone in Christ alone? Should not unashamed confession of core doctrines combined with evident zeal for church-planting and conversion-seeking evangelism justify an assume-the-best posture and a measure of patience where emerging church speech and practice raise concerns among Evangelicals? I think so. Albert Mohler's advice to Southern Baptists who would contemplate partnership with the wider Evangelical world could just as easily apply to Evangelicals who contemplate engagement with the emerging church. Thus, let us engage the emerging church with "an irenic, bold, and convictional posture which combines concern for orthodox doctrine with a spirit of engagement with the larger world and a missionary mandate."[49]

---

[49] From Mohler's chapter, "A Call for Baptist Evangelicals & Evangelical Baptists: Communities of Faith and a Common Quest for Identity," in *Southern Baptists & American Evangelicals: The Conversation Continues*, ed. David S. Dockery (Nashville: B&H, 1993), 239.

THE EMERGENT/
EMERGING CHURCH:
A MISSIOLOGICAL
PERSPECTIVE[1]

ED STETZER

WHILE RECOUNTING HIS RETURN to the West after serving as a
missionary in India for decades, the late Lesslie Newbigin was
unsettled by the accommodation of the gospel to "existing plausibility structures." Therefore, he set out to "rescue" the gospel from
perpetual inefficacy as defenders of the faith continued to give
ground in debate.[2] Newbigin called on defenders of the "message"
to resist domestication of the gospel: "It is plain that we do not
defend the Christian message by domesticating it within the reigning plausibility structure."[3] Newbigin borrowed from Peter Berger
in order to explain "plausibility structures" as "patterns of belief
and practices accepted within a given society, which determine
which beliefs are plausible to its members and which are not."[4]

The Emergent/Emerging Church (E/EC)[5] often stands as something of a collective voice intent on calling attention to the ways

---

[1] This chapter was originally presented at the Baptist Center for Theology and Minis-
try conference entitled "The Emerging Church, the Emergent Church, and the Faith Once
Delivered to the Saints" held on April 4, 2008. It was later published in the *New Orleans
Baptist Journal.*

[2] Lesslie Newbigin, *The Gospel in a Pluralist Society* (Grand Rapids: Eerdmans,
1989), 3.

[3] Ibid., 10.

[4] Ibid., 8.

[5] I am using "Emergent/Emerging" as this was the title of the conference where I presented this chapter. Increasingly, some are making a distinction between the two. Some

in which contemporary expressions of Christianity have been
domesticated. In doing so, it often provides a helpful critique. At
the same time, like all movements before, it runs the risk of itself
domesticating the gospel to "emerging plausibility structures"—
repeating the same error but in a new expression. This chapter
will explore its history and pertinent nuances stemming from the
development of Emergent Village as one expression of the E/EC. I
will provide some observations as to its current state, particularly
in relation to how the gospel engages culture. These interactions
will lay the groundwork for offering a way to engage the positive contributions of the E/EC movement as well as avoid what
I believe to be overly contextualized features of some within the
movement.

Therefore, the perspective of this chapter will be chiefly based
on the work of a missiologist. Thus, the history, the values, and
the practice of contextualization by those in the E/EC movement
will provide a framework to suggest bridges and boundaries for an
Evangelical engagement with the E/EC movement.

LEAVING THE OLD COUNTRY[6]

While speaking at Westminster Seminary, Scot McKnight, of
North Park College, offered an evaluation of the Emergent/Emerg-
ing Church movement (ECM).[7] In his introduction he noted, "To
define a movement, we must let the movement have the first word.
We might, in the end, reconceptualize it—which postmodernists
say is inevitable—but we should at least have the courtesy to let

Evangelicals are indicating that they are comfortable with Emerging, but uncomfortable
with Emergent.

[6] Tony Jones, *The New Christians* (San Francisco: Jossey-Bass, 2008). The subheading
here is taken from Jones's own telling of the E/EC story.

[7] Scot McKnight may well be considered one of the theologians of the Emergent
Church. At the very least, Scot carries on a good many conversations with the more prominent members of Emergent Village discussing theology and praxis in relationship to the revisioning of theology often present among "Emergents." The following biographic information comes from his blog, www.jesuscreed.org. "Scot McKnight is a widely-recognized
authority on the New Testament, early Christianity, and the historical Jesus. He is the Karl
A. Olsson Professor in Religious Studies at North Park University (Chicago, Ill.). A popular and witty speaker, Dr. McKnight has given interviews on radios across the nation, has
appeared on television, and is regularly asked to speak in local churches and educational
events. Dr. McKnight obtained his Ph.D. at the University of Nottingham (1986)."

a movement say what it is."[8] McKnight challenged critics to let those in the movement speak for themselves or at least engage in conversation until those being criticized would be able to say, "You've got it."

Tony Jones, national coordinator for Emergent Village, gives what many see as the best inside look at the ECM. In fact, Scot McKnight asserts all conversations about Emergent Village must now go through Tony Jones's book: "I admit to some weariness with folks mischaracterizing emergent and emerging when we have had so many good studies mapping the whole thing. Well, now, the major debate is over. If you want to know what 'emergent' (as in Emergent Village) is all about, here's the only and best firsthand account: Tony Jones, *The New Christians*."[9] McKnight's characterization of Tony Jones's work as definitive is not without detractors within the E/EC. As I have researched and written this chapter, I have found that some differ (often strongly) with some of Tony Jones's conclusions. Others have written (and are writing) other histories.[10] And not all see *The New Christians* as the definitive history. For example, well known E/EC leader Andrew Jones does not list *The New Christians* among his top five E/EC books.[11]

However, due to chapter length limitations, my analysis will be truncated and will rely on Tony Jones's work, with some modification. A broader treatment of the ECM would have to draw from sources outside of the United States, which I have passed up in order to limit the scope of the chapter. Furthermore, it would look back further than I have done. For example, Andrew Jones contends the beginnings of the ECM in Europe predate the same

[8] Scot McKnight, "What Is the Emerging Church?" Westminster Seminary Audio presentation (http://www.wtsbooks.com/product-exec/product_id/4959/nm/ What_Is_ the_Emerging_Church_and_Misnomers_Surrounding_the_Emerging_Church), 2006. The transcript of the audio may be found with the referred quote found on p. 2 at http://www. foolishsage.com/wordpress/wp-content/uploads/McKnight%20-%20What%20is%20 the%20Emerging%20Church.pdf.

[9] Scot McKnight, http://www.jesuscreed.org/index.php?s=conspirators.

[10] See for example, Becky Garrison, *Rising from the Ashes: Rethinking Church* (New York: Seabury Books, 2007) and Phyllis Tickle, *The Great Emergence: How Christianity Is Changing and Why* (Grand Rapids: Baker Books, 2008).

[11] Andrew Jones, http://tallskinnykiwi.typepad.com/tallskinnykiwi/2008/06/emerging-chur-1.html#more

movement in the United States,[12] and he also interprets counter-cultural church movements beginning in the 1960s to be precursors to the E/EC rather than the organizations and movements that become Emergent Village.[13]

That being said, we have used Tony Jones's history for several reasons. First, Tony Jones admits his telling of the story is indeed just one story and that it is part memoir, part explication of the ECM as he has experienced it. Second, D. A. Carson raised the level of focus on the ECM in his book, *Becoming Conversant with the Emerging Church*. Carson critiqued Brian McLaren and Tony Jones, among others, and their identification with Emergent Village alerted many Evangelicals to the ECM. Thus, for many, the ECM has been identified with Emergent Village.[14]

Finally, Brian McLaren represents one of the most public figures in the ECM. Brian's association with Emergent Village raised its visibility as a key voice (particularly in the United States) for the ECM. Thus, for the focus and intent of this chapter I have chosen to follow the story of the ECM as Jones tells it (with some revisions as detailed below).

Thus, *The New Christians: Dispatches from the Emergent Frontier* bears the weight of its endorsers as "the" definitive "explication and explanation" of Emergent.[15] In the first section, entitled "Leaving the Old Country," Jones offers his perspective on the history of the ECM. Tony helps the reader think through the reigning plausibility structures questioned by the group that eventually became Emergent Village and that also shaped the ECM.[16] The ECM reaches around the world, having a significant presence in the UK, Europe, Australia, and around the world years before

---

[12] Andrew Jones, http://tallskinnykiwi.typepad.com/tallskinnykiwi/2006/10/my_history_of_t.html. Jones writes, "I didn't realize at the time that in the UK there were new models of church far more advanced than ours. But more about that another time."

[13] Andrew Jones, http://tallskinnykiwi.typepad.com/tallskinnykiwi/2005/03/emergent2_count.html.

[14] This conclusion will be dated as Dan Kimball, Scot McKnight, and several others are discussing additional collaborations even as this chapter is published.

[15] Tony Jones, *The New Christians;* the quotation is attributed to Phyllis Tickle on the dust cover.

[16] Ibid., 1–22.

what we witness in the United States. However, again, I will focus on the expression of the ECM in the United States.

A brief lexicon may help the reader. This material is taken from Jones's work:

> **Emergent Christianity:** the new forms of Christian faith arising from the old; the Christianity believed and practiced by the emergents.

> **The Emergent Church:** the specifically new forms of church life rising from the modern, American church of the twentieth century.

> **The Emergents:** the adherents of emergent Christianity.

> **Emergent:** specifically referring to the relational network that formed first in 1997; also known as Emergent Village.[17]

Prior to the release of Jones's book, others had offered lexicographic help for understanding terms used by those considered "in" the E/EC. For example, Darrin Patrick of the Journey in St. Louis gave a presentation at Covenant Seminary in which one session was dedicated to a lexicon for conversations about emergent.[18] There is more than one good option for the vocabulary.

---

[17] Ibid., xix-xx. Following McKnight's conviction that to understand a movement is to let it speak until those who engage it hear, "You've got it," I will use the lexicon found in Jones's book. With that in mind, it is important to note the use of "The Emergent Church" may be a bit confusing to the readers, as old patterns would consider such a description to include something of a denominational structure. In this sense, there is no "Emergent Church." Instead, there are those in existing denominational structures who practice Emergent Christianity. Their network is a loose connection of people who share what will be referred to as an "ethos." Scot McKnight is helpful at this point when he notes,

> There is no such thing as the emerging "church." It is a movement or a conversation—which is Brian McLaren's and Tony Jones's favored term, and they after all are the leaders. To call it a "church" on the title of his [D. A. Carson's] book is to pretend that it is something like a denomination, which it isn't. The leaders are determined, right now, to prevent it becoming anything more than a loose association of those who want to explore conversation about the Christian faith and the Christian mission and the Christian praxis in this world of ours, and they want to explore that conversation with freedom and impunity when it comes to doctrine. (McKnight, "What Is the Emerging Church?" delivered at Westminster Seminary, October 2006.)

[18] Darrin Patrick, "Popular Terms of the Emerging Church," Covenant Seminary, October 22, 2007. The audio file may be found at http://www.journeyon.net/sermon/ session-

However, this chapter will follow Jones's terminology when the context relates to Emergent.

I will use the term *emerging* to describe the wider movement. One key difference rests with organizational expressions of the ECM, where Emergent Village would represent a more formal expression with events, local cohorts, and publishing agreements. On many occasions, I will use the combination *Emergent/Emerging Church* (E/EC) when the distinction between Emergent and Emerging is less helpful and the context is the wider movement that takes in Emergent and Emergent Village in particular.

GENERATIONAL THEORY AND A NEW CHRISTIAN MARKET

The nexus for the story of the E/EC may be tied to generational theory and the market approach to church growth/planting, at least in its expression in the United States.[19] In 1986 Dieter Zander planted New Song in California as one of the first Gen X churches in the United States.[20] It would be another ten years before talk of Gen X churches gained traction. At the time, "targeting" for church planting referenced "Busters" or in Zander's terminology, "The People in Between." Ten years after the start of New Song, Zander wrote one of the first books on Gen X ministry, *Inside the Soul of a New Generation: Insights and Strategies for Reaching Busters*.[21]

Dieter Zander attended the first Gen X forum at Colorado Springs in 1996 sponsored by Leadership Network.[22] Those in

two-popular-terms-of-the-emerging-church/.

[19] Andrew Jones included Zander and generational ministry in his telling of the history, but also adds that there were other early expressions of the ECM present in the 1980s that were not widely reported. Jones wrote me, "My first emerging church effort was a coffee shop environment in 88–89 at an Evangelical Free Church in Portland. . . . There were others in the 1980s but these people did not have book deals . . . so the history is skewed and inaccurate."

[20] Keith Matthews, conference call recording with Dieter Zander obtained from ETREK Collaborative Learning Journeys, 2007. Information about Dieter Zander and New Song may be found at http://www.newsongsd.org/253217.ihtml.

[21] Tim Celek, Dieter Zander, and Patrick Kampert, *Inside the Soul of a New Generation: Insights and Strategies for Reaching Busters* (Grand Rapids: Zondervan, 1996).

[22] Dave Travis (of Leadership Network) sent me an e-mail noting the timeline for the general meetings sponsored by Leadership Network, clarifying some perceived inaccuracies.

attendance at the Gen X forum discussed a number of issues. The following year, Doug Pagitt interviewed with Leadership Network to become the Young Leader coordinator. In addition, a group of about five hundred met at Mount Hermon Conference Center in California as one of the key early meetings.

The third conference in this series took place at Glorieta, New Mexico, and was dubbed the Re-evaluation Forum. Pagitt planned this event, which offered a variety of tracks and speakers. However, Travis contends (and Andrew Jones confirmed) that "the Group of 20" that became the seedbed of "Emergent" was actually post-Glorieta.

During and between these larger meetings, it appears from Jones that smaller informal meetings or networking sessions took place. From these developing friendships "emerged" what Travis calls "the Group of 20." Jones's telling of the story places the development of this group prior to Glorieta. Our research team confirmed the planning of the first "Gathering" at Glorieta by this small group was announced via a flier at the very first Emergent Convention in San Diego. Further, a reference to a "Group of 20" is applied by those outside that network.

The small group bore more resemblance to a G8-type group representing various smaller networks sharing "Emergent" sensibilities. Leadership Network concerned itself with facilitating a variety of "affinity" groups into networks. One of those networks included young leaders with an "Emergent" ethos. Though their perceptions in timing differ as to the emergence of a small "leadership" group, Travis's and Jones's accounts illustrate that the roots of what would become the E/EC developed through Leadership Network gatherings and the organization's goal of facilitating various networks for ministry.

Emergent Village represents the most organized iteration of a movement that initially sought to raise up the next Bill Hybels or Rick Warren. Tony Jones offers brief details of a meeting at Glen Eyrie Mansion just outside of Colorado Springs.[23] The name chosen for the gathering of about a dozen young leaders, orchestrated

[23] Jones, *The New Christians*, 42–43. Tony acknowledges others would tell the story differently and notes he was not present at any of the early meetings. "The timeline is really

by Doug Pagitt representing Leadership Network, was "Gen X
1.0."

Several years would pass before the term *Emergent* would signal a significant move on the contemporary Christian landscape.
The meeting in Glen Eyrie would eventually give rise to a project
referred to as "The Young Leader Network" and later "The Terra
Nova Project." Conversations occurred to purposefully identify
ways to connect with the Gen X generation. From these discussions considerations regarding cultural shifts developed, which
created new challenges and opportunities for the church.

Moreover, these conversations led the group to conclude that
Evangelical theology was in need of "revisioning." Questions
arose as to the success of the "Evangelical" project.[24] However,
when Emergent Christianity sets its critical gaze toward the state
of the Church, it often finds left and right categories polarizing,
whereas at times I find these categories clarifying.

This desire to critique modern expressions of Christianity was
often directed at Evangelicals. However, some in the emerging
church are even-handed in their critique of the church. Not only
do those in the Evangelical tradition face scrutiny, but also mainline churches do not get a free pass. As recently as last fall at
the American Academy of Religion/Society of Biblical Literature (AAR/SBL) meeting in San Diego, Tony Jones sparred with
Diana Butler-Bass over his frequent assertion that the "Mainline
Church" is "dead."[25] This has led to some controversy within the
emerging expressions of some mainline denominations, as many
E/EC movements are a part of those structures.

Some characterize the prophetic call of Emergent Christianity
to be nothing but angry rhetoric. I believe that a closer look at the
unarguable decline of Christianity in the United States gives cause

only relevant as it pinpoints certain participants" at a given meeting. A number of streams,
threads, or influences contributed to "Emergent Village" and that is chiefly Jones's point.

[24] I would agree with the need to evaluate the Evangelical movement and to conclude
that it falls short of its promise, hence my affirmation of efforts such as "The Gospel Coali-
tion."

[25] Scot McKnight, Tony Jones, and Diana Butler-Bass, "AAR Panel," Podcast, 2007,
http://www.emergentvillage.com/podcast/aar-panel-part-1 and http://www.emergentvil-
lage.com/podcast/aar-panel-part-2.

for us to reconsider the Emerging Church's call rather than dismiss it out of hand because we do not like the tone. Responsibility for the loss of Christian influence in American culture must be born by all expressions of the faith, particularly denominations who fail to take into account the changing cultural milieu while dreaming of a bygone day. As I have said of our own denomination, should the 1950s return we will be ready. Can it really be argued the issue is simply a matter of ecclesial structures? The E/EC suggests otherwise, and I believe that here they are at least partly right.

BEYOND CONSUMER CULTURE AND THE "HERMENEUTIC OF DECONSTRUCTION"

The framework for evaluating current practices and theology, by what would become the E/EC, came during that Glen Eyrie meeting. After some discussion focused on marketing to Gen X, the meeting shifted. As Brad Cecil listened, he found the conversation lacking.[26] At a point where his body language indicated that he had not embraced the tone and direction of the conversation, he was asked for his input. Brad suggested that the issues were deeper than looking for style points with Gen X. Deep cultural shifts indicated a need to look beyond matters of marketing to a new iteration of Christian consumer culture.[27]

Cultural analysis combined with ecclesiological, missiological, and theological responses led Cecil to refer to his reading and interaction with John (Jack) D. Caputo.[28] For Cecil, the way forward would be led by Caputo's "hermeneutic of deconstruction."[29] Caputo sought to put forth a way to retain orthodoxy while at the same time exposing the attachments and accommodations that

---

[26] Brad Cecil, "Axxess," Web page background of ministry led, at times, by Brad Cecil, http://www.axxess.org/?page_id=2. Also view the Power Point Cecil put together on the subject, http://www.slideshare.net/knightopia/ministry-in-the-emerging-postmodern-world.

[27] Jones, *The New Christians*, 42–43.

[28] Caputo retired from Villanova University and is now at Syracuse University, http://religion.syr.edu/caputo.html.

[29] J. D. Caputo, *What Would Jesus Deconstruct?: The Good News of Post-Modernism for the Church* (Grand Rapids: Baker, 2007), 19–34. Caputo considers healthy deconstruction to be a "hermeneutic of the Kingdom of God."

existing forms of Christianity make to conform to the reigning plausibility structures. At a pivotal break in the meeting, a few soon-to-be prominent figures would look around the room and wonder just "who got it."

The turn this new group would make led to the early label, "angry young white children of Evangelicalism." Many who found the hermeneutic of deconstruction helpful for recovering the gospel from the clutches of a consumer culture had not yet learned to temper their discontent with grace. Many popular message boards contained scathing words directed at what was and is referred to as the "Institutional Church."[30]

One of the early places for those working through the critique of the Church was "TheOoze." Spencer Burke left Mariner's Church convinced that ecclesial structures needed to be evaluated. One key issue was the disproportionate financial commitment to the "Sunday event," creating more of a consumer construct than a place for spiritual transformation and building community. Again, the entrance into theological conversations proved to be ecclesiology.

TheOoze community grew, and many of the interactions on the message boards in the early days demonstrated much of the angry Evangelical rhetoric. However, it became a key gathering point and connection place for leaders in the emerging conversation. It would also be the place where I first researched the movement. In 2001, I conducted a survey on TheOoze that focused on churches reaching postmoderns. That research was published in my book *Planting New Churches in a Postmodern Age* (2003).

Recently TheOoze celebrated its ten-year anniversary with the release of *Out of the Ooze*. In the introduction, founder Spencer Burke noted,

> In 1998, I decided to launch TheOoze.com as a place
> where people could come and share their questions, long-
> ings, and musings about the body of Christ. My desire

---

[30] For example, TheOoze message boards offered a place for the discontented to engage in conversation around themes questioning the future of the Church as institution, http://www.theooze.com.

was to create a place where honest and transparent dialogue about faith, culture, and ministry could happen.

Since that time, TheOoze.com has grown to over two
hundred and fifty thousand visitors a month from more
than one hundred countries around the world. Who are
these people? They are people who love the church and
desperately want to see her become the essential, life-
giving-community that God designed her to be. They
come from a wide variety of traditions, viewpoints, and
cultures.[31]

Over time, the early phase of grumblings and complaints faded
and the early conversations changed direction. Only offering critique would no longer be sufficient; it was now time to consider
what contributions could be made to see the Church become God's
"essential, life-giving-community."

ORGANIZATIONAL TURNS

What would be the next steps? The organization of TheOoze
illustrates a shift. Hierarchies are often anathema for those in
emerging Christianity. The disdain is not against order as much
as a conviction that responsibility be shared across a network. For
example, TheOoze is maintained by a number of volunteers. Each
area of content is managed in a way to include nearly anyone who
would commit to participate.

Discontent with ecclesial structures represents a significant
turn in the history of the E/EC. From the collaborative structure of
TheOoze to the loose network created by Doug Pagitt, the need to
gather the growing group into more of a formal network began.

As noted, Leadership Network was the early sponsor of what
would become the emerging church. I recently spoke with Bob
Buford about his "sponsorship," and he was unhappy with what the
movement had become. The gerund "emerging" showed up in one
of the many taglines supplied on Leadership Network materials. In

---

[31] Spencer Burke, *Out of the Ooze: Unlikely Love Letters from Beyond the Pew* (Colorado Springs: Navpress, 2007), 14.

one iteration of the many taglines Leadership Network described itself as "advance scouts for the emerging church." The reference to "emerging church" by Leadership Network is more coincidence than endorsement for any movement, more descriptive of Leadership Network's development of "emerging networks" rather than "emerging church." However, those who would eventually become leaders in the E/EC developed their network out of relationships forged via Leadership Network "networks." That gerund (emerging) would eventually become a noun (emergent), and from relationships fostered by Leadership Network, a future movement would find its moniker.

Jones writes of the faltering relationship between the Young Leaders and Leadership Network. In a conference call, this fractured relationship was discussed and the group determined to create a more formal organization to promote constructive ways to live the way of Jesus in a postmodern age. The label "Emergent" rose to the fore as a metaphor for new growth on the forest floor "emerging" beneath the old growth.[32] The idea was to maintain the connection with Christian history and at the same time develop new forms to engage the postmodern shift in culture.

Leonard Sweet offered a similar conception with the "swing."[33] In this image statement found on his Web site, Sweet borrowed from research that suggested when a person swings he or she simultaneously leans back and presses forward. Application of this image called for a reaching back into church history and a pressing forward into the future. The issue of contextualization would be an important component in analyzing this movement. Sweet became a popular church historian/futurist in the early days of the E/EC and, in many ways, encouraged the "Emergent Turn."

It should be noted here that Sweet recently offered the criticism that the "turn" may have gone too far with Emergent. So far, he asserts, rather than reach back into two thousand years of

---

[32] The metaphor of new growth emerging from the forest floor represents a common explanation of the attractiveness of "emerging" used in talks by many "leaders" in the E/EC.

[33] Leonard Sweet, "Image Statement," http://www.leonardsweet.com/imgstatement.asp.

church history, Emergent stopped at the "liberal turn" wherein the gospel became all social and no gospel. Sweet e-mailed me:

> The emerging church has become another form of social gospel. And the problem with every social gospel is that it becomes all social and no gospel. All social justice and no social gospel. It is embarrassing that evangelicals have discovered and embraced liberation theology after it destroyed the main line, old line, side line, off line, flat line church.[34]

Interestingly, in response to similar concerns, Brian McLaren responds on Andrew Jones's Web log to the charges of embracing liberation theology and accompanying criticisms.[35]

Dan Kimball, one of the early members of the Emergent Village "coordinating council," chronicled the use of the term *emerging* on his blog in April 2006. The irony lies in the title of Kimball's book, *The Emerging Church*.[36] Kimball notes he first heard the reference to "emerging" from Leadership Network, which inspired him to use the term in the title of his book, published in 2003. Kimball notes that the domain names emergingchurch .com, emergingchurch.net, emergingchurch.org were all purchased between 2000 and 2001. (I registered postmodernism .net in April 2000 to be used as a resource for those seeking to reach this emerging culture. But, unlike Dan Kimball, I never used the domain.)

The Young Leaders Theology Group that became Emergent Village purchased emergentvillage.com and emergentvillage.org in June of 2001. These moves indicate an interest to "ramp up" public interest and the networking of and for those self-identifying with the "emergent/emerging conversation."

These networks coalesced into the formation of Emergent Village. Early on Emergent Village functioned as a loose network

---

[34] Personal e-mail from Len Sweet.

[35] Andrew Jones, "Brian McLaren Responds to *Everything Must Change* Concerns," March 25, 2008, http://tallskinnykiwi.typepad.com/tallskinnykiwi/2008/03/brian-mclaren-r.html.

[36] Dan Kimball, "Origin of the terms 'Emerging' and 'Emergent' church—part 1, http://www.dankimball.com/vintage_faith/2006/04/origin_of_the_t html."

under the leadership of a "coordinating council." Those who participated did so voluntarily and without remuneration. The first "event" for this group took place at Glorieta Conference Center in New Mexico and was dubbed "The Emergent Gathering." Those who gathered for this event paid a small registration fee. Once again, the collaborative nature of the event found expression in the breakout sessions. Anyone who traveled to Glorieta could offer to host a session around the topic of their choice. The feel of the gathering was more fellowship than conference.

The Gathering was a small event but spurred a desire for larger conferences and more focused events. The need for partnerships to facilitate conferences and book publishing became apparent, and the first partner to step forward was Youth Specialties (YS). Not only would YS offer a proven event-planning team, but they also presented a viable publishing partner. YS and its founder Mike Yaconelli cosponsored the first National Pastor's Convention in San Diego. Soon a parallel convention, referred to as "The Emergent Convention," provided an alternate "track" for National Pastor's Convention attendees. The partnership was short-lived as YS re-focused their energies on their core ministry to youth workers. The separation was amicable. For example, Mark Ostreicher often writes of his continued friendship with Doug Pagitt, as well as Tony Jones and others he met during the YS-Emergent partnership. As evidenced by the most recent event in February 2008, many connected with Emergent still make presentations at the National Pastor's Convention.[37]

ORTHODOXY OVER ORTHOPRAXY?

For many in the E/EC, calls to rethink historic bipolarities figure prominently into conversations, whether in conference talks or books written. Without question one of the marks that frames the values of the E/EC and, as already noted, provides the door to

[37] Scot McKnight, Phyllis Tickle, and Tony Jones have all been associated with the Emergent Church on some level. Others at the conference could also be considered sympathetic. For example, Sarah Cunningham's book *Dear Church* (Grand Rapids: Zondervan, 2006) expresses the ethos of the Emergent Church. An argument could be made that Erwin McManus also has written in a vein familiar to the Emergent Church "mood."

theological revisioning is ecclesial discontent. The heart of this issue turns on the practice of faith in Jesus and its relationship to right belief. For many in the E/EC, the question of orthodoxy or orthopraxy is a false dichotomy. At the same time, they would be quick to note their experiences have witnessed a disconnect between right belief (orthodoxy) and right practice (orthopraxy). They often come across sounding as though right practice trumps right belief. I would contend that this is in itself an unnecessary bipolarity. Yet, for those in the Emergent Church, practice is often considered a first order spiritual matter while doctrine is second order.

Donald Miller may be a popular example of the emerging church's desire to emphasize orthopraxy. In *Blue Like Jazz: Nonreligious Thoughts on Christian Spirituality*, he tells the story of the "confessional." In an attempt to connect with what was considered one of the most secular college campus populations in the United States at Reed College, Miller and others set up a confessional during a week of festivities around the campus referred to as Ren Fayre.

Dressed in monastic attire, they waited for students to approach the booth. Upon inquiry, students learned the group was not accepting confessions but making them. Miller and his band of confessors apologized to students for the bad practices they had endured at the hands of Christians. The group confessed by referencing events in Christian history that seemed to contradict the ethic of Jesus. While Miller and his group had not directly participated in the actions, they understood the perception created by these events, which often left non-Christians questioning the veracity of a faith that, for example, forced conversions at the point of a sword.[38] They graphically demonstrated the difference between orthodoxy and orthopraxy.

Brian McLaren provides another example. He considers himself something of an anomaly when it comes to the ECM. Rather than an early participant as a "young leader," Brian instead responded to the invitation to participate though a full ten years or

[38] Donald Miller, *Blue Like Jazz: Nonreligious Thoughts on Christian Spirituality* (Nashville: Thomas Nelson, 2003), 113–27.

more older than the group assembled by Pagitt. His book *A New Kind of Christian* struck an early chord. The experiment in "fiction/nonfiction" gave voice to many young people who found their experience of life and faith in Jesus formed in more conservative, even fundamentalist, church settings. If *A New Kind of Christian* became the entry point for many to consider what would be the E/EC Movement, Jones's *The New Christians* serves as a description of how the movement developed along those lines. In that sense, the connection between McLaren's *A New Kind of Christian* and Tony Jones's *The New Christians* is unmistakable.

In 2006, McLaren published *The Secret Message of Jesus.* In the first chapter, titled "Excavation," Brian notes a deepening disconnect between what he learned as a young Christian, and also preached as a pastor, and his reading of the Scriptures. He explains,

> For me, these aren't theoretical questions. I grew up in the church and heard wonderful stories about Jesus that captured my imagination throughout my childhood. Then in my teenage years, after a brief but intense period of doubt, I became intrigued by Jesus in a more mature way, and I began wondering what it means to be an authentic follower of Jesus in my daily life. In college and graduate school, although I went through times of questioning, skepticism, and disillusionment, I retained confidence that Jesus himself was somehow right and real and from God—even if the religions bearing his name seemed to be a very mixed bag of adherents like me who often set a disappointing example.[39]

Here, a prominent figure in the Emergent Church points up not simply the dissonance between orthodoxy and praxis as an observer but also as a participant in the life of the church.

"-MERGENTS": THE BREADTH OF THE MOVEMENT AND THE MISSIONAL INFLUENCE

The movement has clearly grown in influence. For some, they believe that influence will grow dramatically over the coming

---

[39] Brian McLaren, *The Secret Message of Jesus* (Nashville: W Publishing, 2006), 5.

years. Phyllis Tickle, currently contributing editor in Religion and former religion editor for *Publishers Weekly*, offered some reflections on her forthcoming book, *The Great Emergence*, in an Emergent Village podcast.[40] During the conversation Tony Jones points up the interesting advocacy Tickle has demonstrated toward the E/EC. For two consecutive years, in 2004 and 2005, Tickle spoke to those who gathered at the Emergent Convention. A quote from her forthcoming book offers her rationale:

> While no observer is willing to say emphatically just how many North American Christians are definitively emergent at this moment, it is not unreasonable to assume that by the time the Great Emergence has reached maturity, about 60 percent of practicing American Christians will be emergent or some clear variant thereof.[41]

Once the ECM gained national prominence as a movement or conversation, observers and critics have attempted to determine the theology of the E/EC. There are certainly diverging opinions on the theology of the emerging church. Scot McKnight contends there is no theology of Emergent.[42] On the other hand, Don Carson considers Emergent to have left orthodoxy behind.

If Scot McKnight's admonition to let Emergent speak for itself is followed, then it may do well to consider the stated values of Emergent Village. The result would be the expression of an ethos assimilated into a variety of denominational, and so in many ways theological, constructs. The breadth of the Emergent Church ethos found in nearly every denominational setting makes it hard to consider the movement expressly theological. It may well lead to "revisioning" theological formulations, but this appears to often be done in the context of one's faith tradition. In a recent Emergent/C

---

[40] Emergent Village Podcast, 07/14/07, http://www.emergentvillage.com/podcast/phyllis-tickle-interviewed-by-tony-jones.

[41] Phyllis Tickle, *The Great Emergence* (Grand Rapids: Baker Books, 2008), 139.

[42] Scot McKnight, "What Is the Emerging Church?" Westminster Seminary Audio presentation (http://www.wtsbooks.com/product-exec/product_id/4959/nm/What_Is_the_Emerging_Church_and_Misnomers_Surrounding_the_Emerging_Church), 2006. The transcript of the audio may be found at http://www.foolishsage.com/wordpress/wp-content/uploads/McKnight%20-%20What%20is%20the%20Emerging%20Church.pdf.

e-mail newsletter, National Coordinator Tony Jones and Webmaster Steve Knight note,

> We're not sure how it started to happen exactly, but people from many different streams of Christianity started finding some inspiration, hope, and community through Emergent Village—and then they started to find each other. Well, it's grown dramatically over the past couple years, thanks in large part to the Internet. We're thrilled about this, as people explore how the emergent experiment might take hold in the Petri dish of their own traditions/denominations.[43]

They go on to note "-mergent" groups Lutheranmergent (Lutheran), Methodomergent (Methodist), Presbymergent (Presbyterian), Reformergent (Reformed), Submergent (Anabaptist), Anglimergent (Anglican/Episcopal), Convergent (Quaker), and AGmergent (Assemblies of God/Pentecostal).[44] The Emergent Village Web site describes itself as "a growing, generative friendship among missional Christians seeking to love our world in the Spirit of Jesus Christ."[45]

Applying adjectives to forms of Christianity may help understand nuances, but it often proves to limit the breadth of a movement. Embedded in the E/EC ethos one will find a distinct missional thread. Some find confusion when examining current Christian movements. Is it "missional"? Is it "Emergent"? Is it "Missional Emergent"? Is it "Emergent Missional"? Or, "What does missional have to do with Emergent?"

The E/EC cannot ignore the influence of the Gospel and Our Culture Network (GOCN) and its accompanying "missional conversations." Alan Roxburgh has served as an interesting conversation partner for both the Emergent Church and the GOCN. He served as a contributor to *Missional Church: A Vision for the Sending of the Church in North America* published by Eerdmans in 1998. Roxburgh was also invited to some of the pre-Emergent Village con-

---

[43] Tony Jones and Steve Knight, "Emergent Hybrid Synergy: The Rise of the –Mergents," March 28, 2008, http://www.emergentvillage.com/weblog/emergent-hybrid-synergy-the-rise-of-the-mergents.

[44] Ibid.

[45] Emergent Village, "Home Page," www.emergentvillage.com.

versations and to be a breakout session leader for at least one of the Emergent Conventions sponsored by Youth Specialties.

Biblical Seminary may provide a helpful example of how missional and emerging have blended. Alan Roxburgh served as consultant to Biblical Theological Seminary (BTS) as they were reimagining their role as a place to offer theological education. His association with GOCN and the "missional conversation" bears a significant mark on the language and move BTS has taken. At the same time, John Franke represents one of the young theologians many in the E/EC became familiar with at the release of *Beyond Foundationalism: Shaping Theology in a Postmodern Context* that he coauthored with the late Stanley Grenz.[46] There is little doubt that Grenz's conviction that Evangelical theology needed to be "revisioned" has influenced those in the E/EC.

Another figure offering input and consultation with BTS has been Tim Keel, pastor of Jacob's Well in Kansas City, Missouri. Tim has served on the coordinating council of Emergent Village since the early days. His church has been considered by some to really capture the ethos of the Emergent Church and, at the same time, carry on the missional thread with great intention. Tim tells his story in his recent book, *Intuitive Leadership: Embracing a Paradigm of Narrative, Metaphor, and Chaos* published under the "emersion" imprint. Today, Tim serves as a trustee of BTS.

WALKING THE TIGHTROPE: A CASE IN POINT

When the edges of the E/EC garnered both attention and harsh critique, BTS made a conscious decision to maintain a place in the middle between the extremes of the Emergent Church and the Missional Conversation. Todd Mangum, associate professor of theology and Dean of the Faculty, helped craft a statement expressing the place Biblical would stand. The statement reads in part,

> "Emergent" is a loosely knit group of people in conversation about and trying experiments in how the people of God can forward the ministry of Jesus in new and different

---

[46] Westminster John Knox, 2001.

ways. From there, wide diversity abounds. "Emergents" seem to share one common trait: disillusionment with the organized, institutional church as it has existed through the 20th century (whether fundamentalist, liberal, mega-church, or tall-steeple liturgical).

. . .

Biblical is seeking to come alongside the emergents as an evangelical friend that understands the disillusionment and wants to help. We're trying to supply training that capitalizes on the strengths and helps emergents mature beyond the weaknesses. We're unapologetically evangeli-cal in our theology (not all emergents are), but because we're generous and value the relationship (two virtues that trump everything else typically for emergents), we can get along with emergents even with whom we dis-agree vigorously in theological conviction.[47]

While some view it as flirting with danger, BTS attempts what others consider the impossible. Their conviction rests with the need to explore the value of the "Missional Turn" in concert with those healthy prophetic voices in the Emergent Church for the good of the church. In fact, Mangum presented a paper to the Theology and Culture Study Session of the Evangelical Theological Society in November of 2007 in San Diego titled "Has Our Culture Changed So Much Really? (An Apologia for the 'Missional Turn')." It is hard to escape the same sentiment expressed by Scot McKnight when he notes that Emergent Christians are seeking to live out the way of Jesus in a postmodern context—a clear missional concern.

The text of the BTS statement given by Todd Mangum does appear to distance the seminary in some sense from the Emer-gent Church. Other examples also illustrate the point. The Center for Emerging Church Leadership (CECL) has undergone a name change to Catalyst for Missional Leadership (C4ML). My own role at BTS, leading their 2007 faculty retreat and serving as an adjunct faculty member, was expressed around their desire to be

---

[47] Todd Mangum, "Q & A with Todd Mangum," October 6, 2007, Catalyst for Mis-sional Leadership at BTS's Web site, http://www.c4ml.com/wandering-off-course/10/.

more "missional" and less "emerging." Thus, some want to be missional but are cautious about being "emergent."

The ethos of Emergent Village characterized by their identity statement cannot be viewed as anything other than an attempt to express the melding of "emerging" and "missional." One could argue that "generative friendship" illustrates the move from hierarchical models of networking acutely important to the Emergent Church. And "missional Christians" retains the understanding of the work of God in the world in existing cultural contexts. The impulse to contextualize the gospel marks the Emergent Church as a "missiological turn" as much as it does a "theological turn."

VALUES AND THE EMERGENT CHURCH

While the Emergent Church continues to speak for itself through those with platform and voice, it becomes increasingly important to see how its values reflect a framework for contextualization and create an agreed-upon "rule of life" out of which Emergents seek to live the way of Jesus. The values of the E/EC illustrate a clear emphasis upon practice, which they believe is missing in the more conservative forms of the faith. For instance, Tony Jones identifies traits that he found as he visited a number of Emergent churches across the United States. He begins laying these out by writing,

> As a result of those category-defying characteristics, many emergents feel homeless in the modern American church. In 2006 I visited eight emergent congregations across the country. At each, I performed one-on-one interviews and facilitated focus groups, listening for articulations of just what emergent Christianity offered these people.[48]

Three traits emerged during the interviews and conversations Jones conducted. First, he found a remarkable disappointment with

[48] Jones, *The New Christians*, 70. One of the "category-defying characteristics" is illustrated by an e-mail Tony received wherein a Christian manager at Starbucks responds in a conversation by saying, "You know what I hate about those emergent people? They love everyone." This was in response to learning a group of Christians had befriended a lesbian barista in the store he managed, even offering a church to attend.

modern American Christianity grounded in the polarizations experienced in the left-right divide. Second, these people evidenced a
tortured desire for inclusion that transcended the warnings they
would fall on the slippery slope into liberalism. Instead they gave
themselves to the ideal of considering the "other" as valuable
human beings—even the enemy is in need of forgiveness. Third,
despite the condition of the world, those with whom Tony talked
shared a relentless hope-filled orientation. The good news of Jesus
is believed to be just that: good news of hope that brings an end to
war, poverty, and hunger. And Emergents believe that they should
actively participate in sharing this hope for the good of the world.[49]

One may readily recognize the connection to the kinds of sentiment Jones discovered with the values given on the Emergent
Village Web site. Each value is supported by both explanation
and suggested practices that also call attention to the unnecessary
disconnect between orthodoxy and orthopraxy. The values given
on the Emergent Village Web site are a commitment to God in
the way of Jesus, a commitment to the church in all its forms, a
commitment to God's Word, and a commitment to one another. It
would be a mistake to assume what these mean without reading
the practices and actions supporting these commitments.

The illumination of these values takes many forms. For example, one may argue Scot McKnight's recent book, *A Community
Called Atonement*, serves both as polemic and apologetic for the
conversations about the atonement among emerging Christians. In
terms of apology, McKnight calls the reader to the various ways
the atonement has been viewed in history and so emphasizes its
breadth. As a polemic, McKnight reminds the reader of the necessity of the various perspectives on the atonement, lest in throwing
out one view a person may develop as truncated a view of the
atonement as they critique others of having.

One cannot deny the interplay between orthodoxy and praxis.
Great risks are run when seeking one over the other. The Emer-

---

[49] Jones, *The New Christians*, 70–72. Jones concludes this brief section with a paren-
thetical caveat, "lists are dangerous, and emergents are rightly suspicious of them. These
three characteristics of emergent Christians are not conclusive, nor are they necessarily
provable—or disprovable. They are simply my intuitions based on scores of conversations
with emergents, and I expect—and hope—that they will provoke much debate."

gent Church considers it obvious that contending for doctrinal precision has not necessarily produced an embodied ethic—and I believe few would disagree with them. They would assert that the critics dissect words quickly in an attempt to ensure "orthodoxy," but that for them orthodoxy has not been compromised in favor of being relevant.[50] The curious, like the critics, look for marks by which to evaluate the Emergent Church.

PRACTICES, TAXONOMIES, STREAMS, AND LAKE EMERGENT—UNDERSTANDING THE DIVERSITY OF EMERGENT CHRISTIANITY

Eddie Gibbs and Ryan Bolger set out to identify the E/EC in their book *Emerging Churches: Creating Community in Postmodern Cultures*. The title of the book points the reader to consider the E/EC in terms of its practices. Gibbs and Bolger identified nine characteristic practices:

> Emerging churches are communities that practice the way of Jesus within postmodern cultures. This definition encompasses nine practices. Emerging churches (1) identify with the life of Jesus, (2) transform the secular realm, and (3) live highly communal lives. Because of these three activities, they (4) welcome the stranger, (5) serve with generosity, (6) participate as producers, (7) create as created beings, (8) lead as a body, and (9) take part in spiritual activities.[51]

---

[50] D. A. Carson, *Becoming Conversant with the Emerging Church* (Grand Rapids: Zondervan, 2005). Carson chiefly interacts with his reading of Brian McLaren. He includes Steve Chalke in the conversation. Those familiar with Emergent-UK note Chalke is not considered part of the movement there. In his famous line, "Damn all false antitheses," Carson asserts that rather than deconstruct polarities offensive to the gospel, McLaren creates false dichotomies that lead to a move away from, if not denying, the gospel. Scot McKnight suggests Carson rightly contends "hard postmodernism" runs contrary to the gospel (in "What Is the Emerging Church?"). But McKnight goes on to illustrate there is no evidence Brian McLaren or others leading Emergent Village, for example, are indeed "hard postmodernists." Rather, they are likely "soft postmodernists." While the intent of this chapter is not to debate the level to which some or all Emergents have embraced a philosophy of postmodernism, the contextual move will be important for understanding "taxonomies and streams" suggested by those hoping to engage Emergents and the Emergent Church.

[51] Eddie Gibbs and Ryan Bolger, *Emerging Churches: Creating Community in Postmodern Cultures* (Grand Rapids: Baker Academic, 2005), 44–45.

Based on their research, Gibbs and Bolger appear to indicate the formation of an "Emerging Church" tends toward these practices rather than an exclusive theological framework.

Even with the identification of nine practices observed by Gibbs and Bolger, the diverse expressions among E/ECs frustrates the curious and the critic alike. Engagement with one emerging church does not necessarily stand for the evaluation of another.

MY TAXONOMY OF THE EMERGENT CHURCH

In January of 2006 I wrote "Understanding the Emerging Church."[52] I laid out a three-layered taxonomy originally written for my own denominational context. I hoped that it would help my codenominationalists to understand the diversity in the E/EC. Unashamedly, part of my objective was to create "space" for young pastors who considered themselves emerging but still held to the denomination's theological statement.

My observation noted the diversity of this amorphous movement:

It's been interesting to watch the emerging church conversation over the last few months. Important issues are being discussed. Unfortunately, like many conversations, good things are lumped together with bad and important conversations are lost in more heat than light.

My own observation as one who speaks at some events classified as "emerging" is that there are three broad categories of what is often called "the emerging church." Oddly enough, I think I can fairly say that most in the emerging conversation would agree with my assessments about the "types" of emerging leaders and churches—and just differ with my conclusions.[53]

I dubbed the three groupings of the E/EC as the Relevants, Reconstructionists, and Revisionists. The article received surprising attention not, I believe, because it was brilliantly written, but

---

[52] "Understanding the Emerging Church," *Baptist Press* article, January 6, 2006, http://www.baptistpress.org/bpnews.asp?ID=22406.
[53] Ibid.

because it stated what others already saw: there was a wide diversity of what was called "emerging." Andrew Jones, at the time the most prominent emerging church blogger, commented on the article saying, "Ed Stetzer gets it."[54] I think it was simply a statement that there are levels "emerging" that need to be recognized.

To my knowledge, this was the first widely distributed analysis, but it was not the last—some were better than mine. Some borrowed and expanded on the article. Others created new approaches. But new taxonomies emerged from Wes Daniels, Darrin Patrick, Mark Driscoll, Scot McKnight, and Andrew Jones[55] as noted on the Web site, "Who in the World Are We?"[56] C. Michael Patton offers one of the most recent taxonomies of the E/EC.[57]

Two years later I see a few different nuances and might add an additional subcategory, but I still believe these categories helped provide a much-needed catalyst for those hoping to understand this movement or conversation and not be so quick to dismiss any positive contributions.[58] In a recent presentation to the Evangelical Free Church of America Mid-Winter Ministerial, I remarked,

> Ultimately there is such diversity in what is called the emerging church from inerrantists, complementarians, verse-by-verse preaching of evangelicals to basically post-evangelicals whose faith would be unrecognizable to those who would be firmly in the evangelical movement.

[54] http://tallskinnykiwi.typepad.com/tallskinnykiwi/2006/01/ed_stetzer_gets.html

[55] Andrew Jones, http://tallskinnykiwi.typepad.com/tallskinnykiwi/2008/01/models-of-emerg.html. Jones recently reminded me that he had written an earlier analysis and notes on his blog, "No one has ever quoted mine because no one has ever read it, at least not in the last 8 years. It was never published online, only in a Leadership Network magazine called *Next Generation*."

[56] Laura, "Hunting for Taxonomies," January 15, 2008, http://whointheworldarewe.blogspot.com/2008/01/hunting-for-taxonomies.html. Identified as a student at Talbot Seminary, Laura lists the noted taxonomies. Others have been offered, and a Google search reveals many "posts" or "articles" on the subject. Also, McKnight's contribution, to be used in this work, takes a different shape than, say, my taxonomy and so will be used to illustrate the "streams" contributing to "Emerging Lake."

[57] C. Michael Patton, "Would the Real Emerger Please Stand Up?", February 15, 2008, http://www.reclaimingthemind.org/blog/2008/02/15/would-the-real-emerger-please-stand-up/

[58] "Understanding the Emerging Church," September 21, 2007, http://blogs.life way.com/blog/edstetzer/2007/09/understanding_the_emerging_chu.html. In this blog post I admit, "I'd probably change a bit of it now. Yet, even though it was imperfect, I think it was helpful because it helped people to see that the Emerging Church has many 'streams' to it."

And yet they would all consider themselves emerging.
Now the challenge is, how do you have a conversation
without understanding from where people come?[59]

Though taxonomies are limited and limiting, I believe they
provide helpful frameworks for participating in the kinds of conversations needed when engaging any reform movement.

RELEVANTS

The first category of people associated with the Emergent
Church, "Relevants," is an admitted neologism.[60] These people
attempt to contextualize music, worship, and outreach much like
the "contemporary church" movement of the 1980s and 1990s.
Their methodology may be considered by critics to be progressive.
However, their theology is often conservative and evangelical.
Many are doctrinally sound, growing, and impacting lostness.

RECONSTRUCTIONISTS

"Reconstructionists" describe the second category. Largely
concerned about existing church structures, these people emphasize an "incarnational" model and may find a home in the "house
church" movement. My main concern with this group has been
noted: "If reconstructionists simply rearrange dissatisfied Christians and do not impact lostness, it is hardly a better situation than
the current one."[61] The move appears to be one step beyond the
Relevants, who maintain existing structures while innovating in
worship and outreach.

REVISIONISTS

Those in the third category are the "Revisionists." Most of
the harsh critique is reserved for this group. I noted that some in
this group have certainly abandoned Evangelicalism. (And I do
not think that statement would be either "news" or "offensive" to
those in this category.)

For this group, both methodology and theology may be revisioned. My concerns include that some might dispense with the

---

[59] Evangelical Free Church MidWinter Ministerial.
[60] Stetzer, "Understanding the Emerging Church."
[61] Ibid.

substitutionary atonement, the reality of hell, views of gender, and the very nature of the gospel. It is at this point that many believe the move is similar to the mainline denominations years before, and I agree.

Writing in a limited word count *Baptist Press* article requires some simplification of the subject. The writing requirements do not allow for a research piece. However, in my presentation to the Evangelical Free Church of America MidWinter Ministerial event, I had occasion to illustrate these categories by suggesting where some people may be in the taxonomy. Mark Driscoll would fit in the Relevant category. Driscoll himself borrowed my taxonomy and added a category for those who are Reformed.[62] Darrin Patrick modified the categories to include a different subcategory into which he felt more comfortable. Patrick and Driscoll participate in the Acts 29 Network and believed a further bit of distinction necessary for those who express their emerging impulse from a Reformed theological framework.

I talked with Dan Kimball about this taxonomy, and he agreed that he would fit the Relevant category. He quickly noted his understanding of the category was not merely an aesthetic issue—not about candles and coffee, a caricature largely pejorative and unhelpful.[63] Brian McLaren, Tony Jones, and Doug Pagitt would fall in the "Revisionists" category. Having talked to these men personally, I do not think they would object to the idea they were "revisioning," though all have indicated their disapproval of the article. It is my conclusions and evaluations that concerned them.

These extremes leave a large "middle," which once again points out the diversity among those generally classified as Emergents. When I first wrote this piece, Tony Jones objected to the categorization in the *Christianity Today* blog, Out of Ur.[64] However, I believe it helps the rest of us gain some understanding of the diversity in the Emergent Church.

---

[62] Mark Driscoll, "A Pastoral Perspective on the Emerging Church," *Criswell Theological Review*, 3(2) 2, 87–94.

[63] Evangelical Free Church of America MidWinter Ministerial, 2008.

[64] http://blog.christianitytoday.com/outofur/archives/2006/05/is_emergent_the.html

STREAMS CREATING LAKE EMERGENT

In a 2007 article written for *Christianity Today*, Scot McKnight took a different approach describing the E/EC. McKnight acknowledged he would himself fit in the broad movement. Rather than list a series of categories, McKnight wrote about "Five Streams of the Emerging Church."[65] The metaphors of "streams" and "lake" may create more clarity regarding the difficult task of drawing out the features of the E/EC, making it possible to understand the breadth of the movement by noting its themes.

According to McKnight, the five streams flowing into Lake Emergent are Prophetic (or at least provocative), Postmodern, Praxis-Oriented, Post-Evangelical, and Political. In his introduction, McKnight elaborates,

> Along with unfair stereotypes of other traditions, such are the urban legends surrounding the emerging church—one of the most controversial and misunderstood movements today. As a theologian, I have studied the movement and interacted with its key leaders for years—even more, I happily consider myself part of this movement or "conversation." As an evangelical, I've had my concerns, but overall I think what emerging Christians bring to the table is vital for the overall health of the church.
>
> In this article, I want to undermine the urban legends and provide a more accurate description of the emerging movement. Though the movement has an international dimension, I will focus on the North American scene.
>
> . . .
>
> Following are five themes that characterize the emerging movement. I see them as streams flowing into the emerging lake. No one says the emerging movement is the only group of Christians doing these things, but together they crystallize into the emerging movement.[66]

[65] Scot McKnight, "Five Streams of the Emerging Church," January 19, 2007, *Christianity Today*, http://www.christianitytoday.com/ct/2007/february/ 11.35.html?start=2.
[66] Ibid.

The metaphor of streams and a lake help underscore the sensibilities informing and giving shape to the Emergent Church.

THE PROPHETIC

The Prophetic, or provocative, draws parallels to the Old Testament prophetic voice, according to McKnight. The intent is to trigger an understanding within the hearer that things need to change. In the case of the Emergent Church, it is the church that is in need of such change. McKnight acknowledges the rhetoric is exaggerated, including his own on occasion, but the hope is that the particular use of language will make the point and not cause divisions.

One illustration of an "over the top" use of rhetoric came in the 2003 Emergent Convention in San Diego. In one main session, a series of presenters were featured that declared some familiar features within the church "dead." The intent was to point out that the way of doing youth ministry, children's ministry, and even preaching needed to undergo radical change in most churches.

Another example would be Doug Pagitt's "Preaching Re-Imagined." Pagitt contends that the day has come for old forms of preaching to radically change. No longer should we depend on one person to formulate a message. The community of faith preaches the message. One person may lead this "preaching" time, but the message flows from the organic movement of the people of God living out the way of Jesus today. Solomon's Porch, the church Doug planted in Minnesota, attempts to live out this "re-imagined" way of preaching.

POSTMODERN

In a witty turn of phrase, McKnight describes the Postmodern stream:

> Mark Twain said the mistake God made was in not forbidding Adam to eat the serpent. Had God forbidden the serpent, Adam would certainly have eaten him. When the evangelical world prohibited postmodernity, as if it were fruit from the forbidden tree, the postmodern "fallen" among us—like F. LeRon Shults, Jamie Smith, Kevin Vanhoozer, John Franke, and Peter Rollins—chose to eat

it to see what it might taste like. We found that it tasted
good, even if at times we found ourselves spitting out hard
chunks of nonsense. A second stream of emerging water
is postmodernism.

Postmodernity cannot be reduced to the denial of truth.
Instead, it is the collapse of inherited metanarratives
(overarching explanations of life) like those of science
or Marxism. Why have they collapsed? Because of the
impossibility of getting outside their assumptions.

While there are good as well as naughty consequences
of opting for a postmodern stance (and not all in the emerging movement are as careful as they should be), evangelical Christians can rightfully embrace certain elements of
postmodernity. Jamie Smith, a professor at Calvin College,
argues in *Who's Afraid of Postmodernity?* (Baker Academic,
2006) that such thinking is compatible, in some ways, with
classical Augustinian epistemology. No one points the way
forward in this regard more carefully than longtime missionary to India Lesslie Newbigin, especially in his book
*Proper Confidence: Faith, Doubt, and Certainty in Chris-
tian Discipleship* (Eerdmans, 1995). Emerging upholds
faith seeking understanding, and trust preceding the appre-
hension or comprehension of gospel truths.[67]

McKnight values a description given by Doug Pagitt that allows
three possibilities for those wishing to engage postmoderns: some
minister to postmoderns, some minister with postmoderns, and
others as postmoderns. The last group tends to be the most heavily
critiqued.

PRAXIS-ORIENTED

Another stream suggested by McKnight, Praxis-Oriented,
illustrates the ecclesiological concern. Worship, orthopraxy, and
missional make up the three areas where McKnight suggests
"Praxis-Oriented" is on display.[68] From the call for sacred spaces,
to a solid understanding of missional practice as a holistic redemp-

[67] Ibid.
[68] Ibid.

tive move among Christians, the Emergent Church seeks to live out a consistently robust faith. Again, Solomon's Porch provides an example. Rather than a pulpit with hard pews and everyone facing forward, those who gather for worship do so in the round— seated on couches and chairs scattered around the room.

For example, IKON, an emerging group from Ireland, provided a modern Tenebrae service at the Emergent Convention in Nashville.[69] Those who attended shared worship in a Presbyterian church. IKON created a sacred space for worship with candles, video, and original music. One may find a description of this service in Peter Rollins book, *How [Not] to Speak of God*.[70] The second part of Rollins's book contains contemporary liturgies illustrating "Praxis-Oriented" worship.

POST-EVANGELICAL

McKnight describes Post-Evangelical as a move that dissents from current practices of Evangelicalism in the same way that neo-Evangelicalism was post-Fundamentalist. However, as McKnight remarks, it is not a move away from theology: "Frankly, the emerging movement loves ideas and theology. It just doesn't have an airtight system or statement of faith. We believe the Great Tradition offers various ways for telling the truth about God's redemption in Christ, but we don't believe any one theology gets it absolutely right."[71]

Post-Evangelical in this vein is "post-systematic theology." McKnight also notes a concern for the "in versus out" exclusivity practices of Evangelicals. On the one hand, the concern is related to no one single Christian theology getting everything right. On the other hand, McKnight warns against a move to globalize this sentiment applying it to theology itself. He warns,

> This emerging ambivalence about who is in and who is out creates a serious problem for evangelism. The emerging movement is not known for it, but I wish it were. Unless you proclaim the Good News of Jesus Christ, there is no

---

[69] http://wiki.ikon.org.uk/wiki/index.php/Main_Page
[70] Brewster, Mass.: Paraclete Press, 2006, 77–85.
[71] Scot McKnight, "Five Streams."

good news at all—and if there is no Good News, then
there is no Christianity, emerging or evangelical.

Personally, I'm an evangelist. Not so much the tract-
toting, door-knocking kind, but the Jesus-talking and
Jesus-teaching kind. I spend time praying in my office
before class and pondering about how to teach in order to
bring home the message of the gospel.

So I offer here a warning to the emerging movement:
Any movement that is not evangelistic is failing the Lord.
We may be humble about what we believe, and we may
be careful to make the gospel and its commitments clear,
but we must always keep the proper goal in mind: sum-
moning everyone to follow Jesus Christ and to discover
the redemptive work of God in Christ through the Spirit
of God.[72]

Does this post-Evangelical turn lead some further than others?
Certainly. For example, Spencer Burke wrote *A Heretic's Guide
to Eternity*, in which he asserts that all may be born "in" and
some "opt out" in regards to their eternal destiny.[73] In this case
the "in versus out" noted by McKnight is applied to evangelism
for Burke.

The beginning point for Burke is that human beings are born
"into" the family of God by grace and "opt out" by walking away.
He maintains a commitment to total depravity but believes grace
is the gift of God to all people who cannot do anything to overcome their sinful condition. The decisional commitment is to
embrace grace and be faithful to it or to walk away from grace and
be condemned. Burke would indeed consider it a danger to ignore
the call to follow Jesus. And yet, he re-formulates the lines along
which that call is made. Rather than call for a decision to follow
Jesus from the position of being "out," the call is to embrace grace
as someone already in and part of the covenant community.

Burke is just one illustration of how some are willing to go
further than others in making the post-Evangelical turn. Burke's

---

[72] Ibid.
[73] Spencer Burke, *A Heretics Guide to Eternity* (San Francisco: Jossey-Bass, 2006), 61.

view is not the view of all Emergents. In fact, Burke hints, it may not be his view in the future. He often notes, "If I am not embarrassed about something I said I believed yesterday, then I have not learned anything today."[74] The oft-used retort indicates the intention to dialogue without coming to a particular conclusion and remaining open rather than closed to conversation, a trait noted by McKnight. However, this tact can be challenging and troublesome, as McKnight rightly warns.

POLITICS

Politics describes the last theme in McKnight's five streams. His autobiographical insertion in the piece is a helpful description:

> I have publicly aligned myself with the emerging movement. What attracts me is its soft postmodernism (or critical realism) and its praxis/missional focus. I also lean left in politics. I tell my friends that I have voted Democrat for years for all the wrong reasons. I don't think the Democratic Party is worth a hoot, but its historic commitment to the poor and to centralizing government for social justice is what I think government should do. I don't support abortion—in fact, I think it is immoral. I believe in civil rights, but I don't believe homosexuality is God's design. And, like many in the emerging movement, I think the Religious Right doesn't see what it is doing. Books like Randy Balmer's *Thy Kingdom Come: How the Religious Right Distorts the Faith and Threatens America: An Evangelical's Lament* (Basic Books, 2006) and David Kuo's *Tempting Faith: An Inside Story of Political Seduction* (Free Press, 2006) make their rounds in emerging circles because they say things we think need to be said.[75]

His words do not come without warning. Just as Leonard Sweet comments about the Emerging Church making the same mistakes

---

[74] Spencer Burke, an oft-repeated mantra by Burke in keynote addresses, breakout sessions, and radio interviews. Used in conversation for an ETREK Collaborative Learning Journeys Course at Biblical Seminary based on his book, *Making Sense of Church: Eavesdropping on Emerging Conversations About God, Community and Culture* (Grand Rapids: Zondervan, 2003).

[75] Scot McKnight, "Five Streams."

that leading mainline denominations have made in the past (which
leads to a social gospel that is all social and no gospel), McKnight
also sounds a word of caution.

Brian McLaren writes about, and in many ways represents,
this stream in *Everything Must Change*.[76] His association with Jim
Wallis and Sojourners regularly earns critique as trading the gospel
for politics. McLaren desperately wants Christians to consider the
"big questions" people are asking today because he believes that
the gospel of Jesus Christ speaks to these issues. McLaren cajoles
the religious right for forsaking these larger matters. (McKnight's
warning about exaggerated rhetoric may apply here.) Speaking at
the Emergent Convention in Nashville, McLaren commented that
sometimes extreme moves in thinking and exaggerated rhetoric
become useful means—something of a spiritual chemotherapy for
the perceived cancer of modern accommodations to the gospel.[77]

Categories and themes noted by observers and insiders help
those hoping to engage the Emergent Church. One underlying
issue gleaned from the variety of taxonomies, streams, and critiques centers on the practice of contextualization by those in the
Emergent Church. McKnight chose to describe this matter in terms
of a prepositional relationship to a postmodern culture with "to,"
"as," and "with." Another way exists to broaden this spectrum—a
missiological contextualization framework.

FROM TOO LITTLE TO OVERDONE— A CONTEXTUALIZATION SCHEME

A key missiological question as it relates to the Emergent
Church regards contextualization. I believe it is unfair to say that
the emerging church jettisons theology. I have found emerging
churches to be more theologically shaped than traditional and
contemporary churches that came before them. This is not to say
that I agree with all the theology, but it is disingenuous not to
acknowledge this as a theological movement. The missiological
perspective offers a way of seeing any movement as it carries the
gospel to a given cultural context. The missiological question may

---

[76] Nashville: Thomas Nelson, 2007.
[77] Brian McLaren in a breakout session at the Emergent Convention in Nashville, 2004.

well offer an evaluation of the Emergent Church from an angle creating better differentiation than taxonomies and streams.

C– WHAT?

Gregg Allison presented a paper titled "An Evaluation of Emerging Churches on the Basis of the Contextualization Spectrum (C1-C6)" to the Evangelical Theological Society on November 17, 2006. Allison takes the categories I wrote of—Relevants, Reconstructionists, Revisionsists—and applies them to the spectrum of contextualization. The place of beginning for Allison was the contextualization spectrum posed by John Travis (a pseudonym) in 1998 published as, "The C1 to C6 Spectrum: A Practical Tool for Defining Six Types of Christ-Centered Communities ('C') Found in the Muslim Context." He writes,

> At the heart of my proposal is the conviction that the emerging church phenomenon is, in part, a contemporary attempt at contextualizing the gospel and the church of Jesus Christ in a changing (postmodern) world. If this is the case, then the emerging church phenomenon (1) bears some similarities with contextualization efforts carried out in the past, and (2) manifests a spectrum of embodiments that are contextualized from a lesser to a greater degree.[78]

Allison may well have captured the missiological interest in the Emergent Church.

The abbreviations of the C1-C6 were modified by Allison to reflect the application to the British and North American contexts.[79] The spectrum offered by Allison suggests the following distinctive characteristics, which may be applied to the Emergent Church. I will discuss Allison's modification represented by Cm1-Cm6 where "m" represents "modified."[80]

"Cm1" represents Christ-centered communities that would be described as traditional using outsider language. The use of the

---

[78] Greg Allison, "An Evaluation of Emerging Churches on the Basis of the Contextualization Spectrum (C1-C6)," paper presented to the Evangelical Theological Society, 17 November 2006, 1.
[79] Ibid., 3.
[80] Ibid.

terms *insider* and *outsider* in this context relates to the peculiar culture surrounding a given Christ-centered community. Therefore, outsider language would be those talking about life and faith in "churchy" terms, the language of Zion. For example in Allison's matrix a Cm1 faith community would include churches where some people may be very entrenched in a postmodern worldview but use language outside that (postmodern) culture. Allison writes, "These churches are very traditional and reflect traditional Christian culture, liturgy, activities, etc. A huge cultural chasm, especially because of (but not confined to) linguistic distance, exists between these churches and the surrounding community."[81]

The Cm2 category describes a traditional church using insider language. This level of contextualization may pair with the Relevant category in my taxonomy and in the "to" spectrum for those wishing to engage postmoderns as noted by Doug Pagitt. These people use language from a postmodern worldview, but the religious vocabulary is still distinctively Christian.

Contextualization in Cm1 and Cm2 categories takes on predominantly traditional forms. A shift begins to occur at the Cm3 level. Those in the Cm3 category exhibit a Christ-centered community using insider language and religiously neutral insider cultural forms. Religiously neutral forms may include folk music, ethnic dress, artwork, etc. The aim is to reduce the foreignness of the gospel and the church by contextualizing to biblically permissible cultural forms.

If Cm1 and Cm2 reside in the Relevant category, then the Cm3 level most certainly describes this group. These people engage in postmodern culture—it is the water in which they swim. It is the lens through which they see the world. At the same time, they are only using certain permissible cultural forms. They are careful about issues where there might be confusion. Allison places Mars Hill in Seattle, where Mark Driscoll is the pastor, and Apostles Church in New York City in the Cm3 category.

The next level, Cm4, moves further. These people form Christ-centered communities using insider language and biblically permis-

---

[81] Ibid.

sible cultural forms as well as postmodern forms. Each of the first three levels refers to believers as Christians. In this group, the common Emergent idiom "followers of Jesus" or "Christ followers" is prevalent. This level may parallel the Reconstructionist category that I created and the "with" focus noted by Pagitt. Those in this category are deconstructing and reconstructing in postmodern culture, being careful in most cases to use only biblically permissible forms. Many conservative Evangelical mission agencies (including the International Mission Board[82]) view Cm4 as the limit of contextualization. Allison places Vintage Faith Church in Santa Cruz, where Dan Kimball is the pastor, in the Cm4 category.

For myself and many Evangelicals, the next two levels cross the line into overcontextualization. The Cm5 level forms Christ-centered communities where participants see themselves more as postmoderns who are Christians rather than as Christians living in a postmodern milieu. Allison places ReImagine in San Francisco, led by Mark Scandrette, in the Cm5 category.

The high end of the spectrum, Cm6, encompasses small Christ-centered communities of secret underground believers. Allison notes Cm6 communities "eschew many/most of the activities, attitudes, traditions, even doctrines of the Cm1-Cm5 communities."[83] Allison places Monkfish Abbey in Seattle and IKON in Ireland, mentioned earlier, in the Cm6 category.

The Emergent Church began with a cultural consideration, "How will we reach Gen X?" Existing forms would not be able to capture this generation, even if there were a "boomerang" experienced like the "Boomers" returning to church years earlier. The turn came about when Brad Cecil observed that the cultural shifts were too dramatic to simply adjust the aesthetics of worship styles and outreach methodologies. The ecclesiological question gave way to exploring the theological foundations for existing forms and structures. The Emergent Church set out to contextualize the gospel by taking apart old forms (deconstructing) and implementing new forms (reconstructing) to facilitate the advancement of

---

[82] http://imb.org/main/news/details.asp?StoryID=6197.
[83] Allison, "An Evaluation," 6.

the gospel during a period of erratic, discontinuous change.[84] On occasion, these moves have left some in the Emergent Church perilously close to "abandoning the Gospel," as noted by D. A. Carson. I believe the move, in some cases, may be more a "neglect of the gospel" than abandonment. It is often not a denial, but in my opinion, often a dangerous lack of emphasis.

EVALUATION

Can anything good come from the E/EC? What boundaries should be set when considering engagement with the E/EC?

BRIDGES, CONTRIBUTIONS, BOUNDARIES, AND GUIDELINES

Christians always engage new cultures—whether they cross an ocean in the case of foreign work, or the culture changes around them in the case of the postmodern shift. The E/EC movement may be more than, but it is not less than, a contextualization movement. Care must be taken when considering this movement from a missiological perspective—such engagement has some bridges and some boundaries.

BRIDGES FACILITATING ENGAGEMENT

Bridges that engage the E/EC may be developed through a consideration of important lessons from early engagement with the movement. Evangelical leaders may wish to write off all things "emerging" and proclaim that Brian McLaren is wrong because he uses the title "Everything Must Change" (a statement made by one well-known apologeticist, demonstrating he had not read beyond the title). However, young Evangelical pastors do not write off all things emerging. I have spoken to young leader gatherings in many denominations (Southern Baptist, Evangelical Free, Church of God, Wesleyan, Assemblies of God, and others)—and they are talking about the Emerging Church. At the Evangelical Free Midwest Ministerial, a third of those attending indicated they use the term *emerging* to define themselves—and yes, this is Don Carson's

---

[84] The phrase "discontinuous change" is described by Alan Roxburgh in *The Missional Leader: Equipping Your Church to Reach a Changing World* (San Francisco: Jossey-Bass, 2006).

denomination. Thus, some principles for responsible engagement should be considered.

First, the ECM cannot be ignored. As noted earlier, the E/EC finds expression within nearly every denomination in the United States. Some expressions may be more formal than others, but the movement has attracted attention widely.

Second, critics must be on guard against bearing false witness. When the contemporary church movement gained the same kind of traction across denominational boundaries, many critical words were spoken, many of them false. The E/EC has not been able to escape the same kind of criticism. In regards to the contemporary and the emerging church movements, it seems that many in Evangelicalism struggle with the ninth commandment—a shame when we Evangelicals hold to the inerrancy of Scriptures that list that very commandment. If you are going to speak out against a movement, learn about it. Then you can speak with wisdom and clarity—for there is much that needs critique in the church, including the emerging church.

Third, many have embraced the E/EC movement uncritically. If Evangelicals intend to remain Evangelical and hold to biblical fidelity, they cannot afford to embrace any movement without careful evaluation. There is much to be concerned about in the E/EC movement. For example, I have little disagreement with Don Carson's analysis of Brian McLaren. (One of the reasons I recently joined the faculty at Trinity Evangelical Divinity School was because of my appreciation of Don.)

Fourth, reading one book or hearing one speaker considered to reside within the Emergent Church does not constitute interaction. Too many have undertaken partial engagement. While D. A. Carson rightly evaluated Brian McLaren in his book *Becoming Conversant with the Emerging Church*, many would be quick to point out that McLaren does not represent the diversity that is present in the Emergent Church. In other words, you cannot become conversant with the emerging church by reading only Brian McLaren (with a little Steve Chalke), particularly when you only read about them and you do not read them.

CONTRIBUTIONS

Scot McKnight considers one of the streams of the Emergent Church to be the "Prophetic." Many believe that Evangelicalism has not delivered, and it would be difficult to argue against that point. The Prophetic aspect within the E/EC may provide needed correctives.

First, the emphasis upon authenticity cannot be overstated. Dishonesty about sin and our own failings leads most to believe all is well. Too often, the temptation is to clean up our history, heritage, and personal experiences. We find it difficult to abide the late Mike Yaconelli, who considered real spirituality to be messy.[85] Instead, we put on a façade to the world and to one another, hiding our own foibles and idiosyncrasies—our own sin.

Second, the E/EC emphasis on the kingdom of God may mark the recovery of a lost treasure in Evangelicalism. The covenantal-dispensational rift relegated conversation of the kingdom of God to the sideline. *Everything Must Change* by Brian McLaren offers a vision of the impact of the kingdom of God on what he sees as the key issues facing the world. While there may be disagreement on the extent of the kingdom of God and how it is expressed, one cannot escape the call to consider Jesus' obsession with the kingdom of God.[86]

Third, the missional turn in the E/EC provokes a regular reference to the *missio Dei*. The theological underpinning of the "God who sends" prompts those in the E/EC to pursue contextualization; understanding the *missio Dei* is larger than the *missio ecclesia*. This move does not exclude the Church but locates the missional turn in the very nature of God. Misused however, this contribution can also be weakness, as noted later.

Fourth, the E/EC rejects reductionism. Sometimes, emerging leaders have chosen interesting terminology to illustrate this contention. For example, the phrase *atonement only gospel* is a euphemism that the work of the atonement is broader than ensuring a person misses hell and gains heaven. Scot McKnight uses

---

[85] Mike Yaconelli, *Messy Spirituality* (Grand Rapids: Zondervan, 2002).

[86] Russell Moore's *The Kingdom of Christ* is an excellent look at the kingdom of God from a conservative Evangelical perspective.

the language of a "holistic" gospel, that is, a call to see Jesus' life, death, and resurrection as vital to our relationship with God, self, others, and the world.[87] Modern reductionism concerns only the personal relationship with God.

Fifth, similar to John Piper's call in *Brothers We Are Not Professionals*, the E/EC rejects pragmatism. The charge is often made that modern churches look more like businesses with CEOs than bodies of Christ with God-called pastors. Managing the church becomes akin to marketing goods and services to a Christian subculture.

Sixth, the E/EC promotes holistic ministry. Jesus not only asserted that He came to seek and save the lost (Luke 19:10), but He also drew attention to a ministry of justice (Luke 4). Some consider that the road the E/EC is taking to live out this second mandate may well become its undoing. Time will tell. However, Christians must find a way to join Jesus and His mission—to seek, to save, and to serve in such a way that also preserves theological integrity.

BOUNDARIES

Critical evaluation of any movement not only evaluates contributions, but it also requires the consideration of boundaries or areas of caution. The same is true for the E/EC. As an Evangelical, there are some areas that concern me and I would suggest boundaries are needed.

First, one of the risks run by those in the E/EC who press very close to overcontextualization appears to be an underdeveloped ecclesiology. Here, the concern relates to those who have an overdeveloped sense of the kingdom of God that in some writings all but eliminates the church. The apostle Paul makes it clear that the wisdom of God will be made known through the church, not without it.

Second, overcontextualization skews the necessary boundaries and, more often than not, gives way to syncretism and a loss of the uniqueness of Jesus, the Christ. The answer does not lie in resisting contextualization. Rather, maintaining the Scriptures as the "norming norm" militates against going too far in our desire

---

[87] Scot McKnight. *A Community Called Atonement* (Nashville: Abingdon, 2007), 9.

to bring the gospel to bear on the various cultures in which people minister—postmodern or Muslim. The accompanying danger of overcontextualization means one makes sin acceptable and calls it an attempt to engage culture.

Third, some seem to have an apparent fear of penal substitutionary atonement, a fear of the cross as understood by Evangelicals and other historic Christian traditions. Some in the E/EC point out that there are multiple theories of the atonement. However, it appears at times that this diminishes the import of substitutionary atonement. This criticism may not be universalized in the E/EC, but it is present nonetheless. And it has become an issue in broader Evangelicalism, as some in the E/EC have challenged existing views of the atonement. For example, in my interview with Brian McLaren, he indicated that he talks about the atonement as having many facets. When I pressed if the penal substitutionary atonement was one of the clubs[88] (views) in his bag (understanding of the atonement), he agreed. Yet, for most Evangelicals, the penal substitutionary atonement is the view they would mention first.

Fourth, the E/EC is not immune to promoting caricature. Those in the E/EC often resist caricatures assigned to them, but they seem willing to make exaggerations regarding those whom they critique. Wrestling with and through movements requires maintaining the integrity of the ninth commandment. Caricatures can be misrepresentations, and their use can border on lying.

CONVERSATION AND THEOLOGY

Acknowledging contributions and forming boundaries creates the need to establish "conversation" guidelines when engaging the Emergent Church or any reform movement. It is essential that we contend for the faith once delivered to the saints (Jude 3). Yet contending must be accompanied by contextualization, as Paul considers it important to become all things to all people so some might be saved (1 Cor 9:22–23). A biblically faithful church living in and contextualized to emerging culture will look different than a biblically faithful church that is living in and contextualized to

[88] Here the reference to "clubs" is found in Scot McKnight's analogy in *A Community Called Atonement.*

modern culture. If those ministering in the world deny the reality of contextualization, the gospel becomes more about the cultural norms used to transport the gospel than the gospel itself. In the end, we risk losing the gospel.

When the gospel becomes solely about the norms created around it, it leads to what missiologists call "nominalism." Nominalism is almost always rejected in the next generation. The gospel has to be reborn into, become indigenous in, a new culture. The nature of the gospel does not change. The language around the gospel may change, but the gospel does not change. Methodologies may change; our understanding of the gospel may even deepen; but the gospel does not change.

The E/EC provokes different ministry paradigms in new contexts, as alertness to cultural changes necessitates building new bridges to the lost. Evaluating those matters about which contentions will arise involves the hard work of differentiating between preferential matters and nonnegotiable issues. Too often, lines have been drawn along preferential patterns.

In a denominational context, the charge to contend also requires compassionate love intent on coming alongside those who may walk too close to the edge of orthodoxy. The missiological perspective gives aid to this process. Since many come close to the edge of orthodoxy via the route of contextualization, familiarity with the missiological perspective of any movement may create a humble orthodoxy or proper confidence. From this position, all can be strengthened to carry on the mission of God in the world, regardless of changing cultural milieus.

At the end of the day the incredible cultural shifts that exist require contextualizing the presentation of the gospel and how we live it out in culture. The narrative of the early missionaries in Acts reveals a number of small stories that support the larger story of the Church's growth and the expansion of the realities of the kingdom of God. Each of these stories illustrates an unchanging gospel contextualized within a particular context, from Jews and God-fearers to polytheists and philosophers. In each case the apostle Paul showed with great skill how the gospel proves itself powerful across cultures. As the Spirit gave life via the contextualization of the good news of Jesus the Christ in diverse arenas, lives were transformed.

The E/EC calls attention to the rapid cultural changes and the accompanying diversity that exists in our world and, without question, the United States. Yes, good has come out of the E/EC and its call to view the Church as something other than a purveyor of religious goods and services. The call to "be" the Church, to live an embodied ethic, and to engage the world by pointing to the King and the kingdom is always needed in any age and any day—it is the *semper reformanda* call.

But with any reform movement, history has demonstrated the perils of pressing too far. We cannot give up nor give away the gospel under the rubric or ruse of contextualization. We must contend for the faith once delivered to the saints. We must stand for biblical truth—truth that can be known, known through language, and believed. We cannot afford to waffle on doctrine, and we cannot refrain from the call to holiness.

New creations live in redemptive, healing relationships with God, others, and the world. The only way we may bring the reality of the King and the kingdom to bear on the world is by standing for the truth of the King and living as His subjects—without reservation.

CONCLUSION

To end where we began, Christianity always runs the risk of adopting the plausibility structures of the culture in which it is currently embedded. Contending for the faith and contextualizing the good news means always considering countercultural moves. Rather than becoming like the earthly powers, we must be in position to speak to the powers, whether they are structures in our culture, in our churches, or in our denominations. Building countercultural communities of faith who stand for the truth and contextualize the gospel would be the proper response to any reform movement in any age. May we follow the Spirit into the "emerging" day—where we who are new creations in Christ lovingly contend, faithfully contextualize, and authentically live as citizens of the kingdom of God.

PART ONE
BIBLICAL SECTION

A POSTMODERN VIEW OF SCRIPTURE

NORMAN L. GEISLER AND THOMAS HOWE

POSTMODERNS GENERALLY AFFIRM the self-defeating creed of being creedless. But one cannot avoid doctrine, if only for the reason that this is a doctrinal claim itself. Further, one need only survey their writings to find a multitude of doctrinal claims. Their doctrine of Scripture is no exception.

Since space will not permit discussing all so-called postmodern evangelicals on Scripture, two major proponents will be examined: Stanley Grenz and Brian McLaren. Grenz, now beatified and enlightened, was the philosopher of the movement; and McLaren is one of the foremost proponents of the emerging (postmodern) church.

STANLEY GRENZ ON SCRIPTURE

My friend Gordon Lewis was right when he told me that the Evangelical Theological Society would have done itself a great service by focusing on Professor Grenz's deviant view of Scripture and not just that of Clark Pinnock. As it turned out, Pinnock slipped through their net, and Grenz slipped off into eternity. Nonetheless, Grenz's view is still alive and is the best effort to provide philosophical underpinning to their doctrine of Scripture, and it is therefore one of the best ways to understand the foundation of the Emerging Church movement.

CLASSICAL ORTHODOX VIEW OF SCRIPTURE

Grenz summarizes well the classical view he rejects: "Evangelical theologians begin with the affirmation that God has revealed himself. This self-disclosure has come through general revelation and more completely in special revelation." Further, "The Holy Spirit preserved some of this special revelation by inspiring biblical writers [really, writings] to inscripturate it. The Bible, therefore, is God's Word. Because the Bible is the inspired Word of God, it is dependable, even inerrant."[1] Unfortunately, Grenz rejects this approach, claiming, "the construction of bibliology in this manner, 'from above' as it were, has certain shortcomings."[2] He adds, "we can no longer construct our doctrine of Scripture in the classical manner."[3]

REJECTION OF CLASSICAL ORTHODOXY

The postmodern rejection of the classical orthodox view of Scripture is sweeping. It includes a rejection of the correspondence view of truth, a rejection of objective truth, absolute truth, propositional truth, and the inerrant truth in Scripture. This is done in favor of antifoundationalism, relativism, subjectivism, constructionism, nonpropositionalism, Barthianism, and fallibilism.

ANTIFOUNDATIONALISM

Grenz approaches the Bible out of a postmodern antifoundationalism perspective. Like others, however, he wrongly sees all foundationalism as rooted in Cartesian (and Spinozan)[4] deductivism, which attempted to deduce absolute truth from self-evident principles. He ignores a legitimate Thomistic foundational reductivism, which grounds all truth in irreducible and self-evident first principles like the basic laws of thought.[5] Along with this, Grenz rejects the traditional rational apologetics based on God's general revelation that Augustine, Anselm, Aquinas, Calvin, and modern

---

[1] Stanley Grenz, *Revisioning Evangelical Theology* (Downers Grove: InterVarsity, 1993), 116.

[2] Ibid., 116.

[3] Ibid., 118.

[4] Spinoza in particular had a deductive system built on the model of Euclid's geometry wherein he began with allegedly self-evident axioms and attempted to deduce from them absolutely certain conclusions about his entire worldview.

[5] For Thomas Aquinas there were certain undeniable first principles (like the laws of logic) on which all thought was based and to which all rationally valid thinking could be reduced. But contrary to modern foundationalism (like Spinoza), one could not deduce from these principles alone any truth about the real world. All knowledge of the real world begins in sense experience.

followers held.[6] He chides "twentieth-century evangelicals [who] have devoted much energy to the task of demonstrating the credibility of the Christian faith."[7] But without a rational and evidential apologetic, one is left swimming in the sea of subjectivism. Indeed, Grenz contends, "we are in fundamental agreement with the postmodern rejection of the modern mind and its underlying Enlightenment epistemology."[8] While there is sufficient reason to disagree with some aspects of "enlightenment epistemology," classical foundationalism and a rational apologetic is not one of them, nor is a basic trust in the reliability of sense knowledge about an objectively real world.

Grenz, however, throws out the "baby" of proper foundationalism, which is the basis of the historic evangelical view of Scripture, with the "bathwater" of rationalistic deductive foundationalism. This leads to relativism and subjectivism, which Grenz renames as "post-rationalistic."[9] He does not explain how one can justify using reason to pronounce reason passe.

RELATIVISM

Once the foundation for absolute truth is destroyed, relativism and subjectivism follow. Grenz is a victim of this logic. He expresses this relativism as follows: "The Bible is seen, then, not as a finished and static fact or collection of facts to be analyzed by increasingly sophisticated methods, but as a potentiality of meaning which is actualized by succeeding generations in the light of their need."[10] This he sees as the proper understanding of 2 Tim 3:16–17, which Grenz grossly misinterprets as meaning that God breathed *into* Scripture like He did breathe *into* Adam. In fact, *theopneustos* ("inspired") means to breath out, not to breathe in. Just as Jesus said, every word of Scripture "comes *out of* the mouth of God."[11]

---

[6] For a discussion of general revelation, see N. L. Geisler, *Systematic Theology: Introduction and Bible,* vol. 1 (Minneapolis: Bethany House, 2002), chapter 4.

[7] Stanley Grenz, *A Primer on Postmodernism* (Grand Rapids: Eerdmans, 1996), 160.

[8] Ibid., 165.

[9] Ibid., 167.

[10] Grenz, *Revisioning Evangelical Theology,* 120.

[11] Matt 4:4, literal translation (emphasis added).

Grenz falls into the self-defeating trap of disclaiming the possibility of objective knowledge of the world or the past. He contends that "we ought to commend the postmodern questioning of the Enlightenment assumption that knowledge is objective and hence dispassionate."[12] He adds, "we affirm the postmodern discovery that no observer can stand outside the historical process. Nor can we gain universal, culturally neutral knowledge as unconditioned specialists."[13] Grenz seems blissfully unaware of his self-defeating claim to have objective knowledge of this allegedly subjective condition.

SUBJECTIVISM

The next of kin to relativism is subjectivism. Grenz couches his subjectivism in warm-sounding words like "community" and "the voice of the Spirit" in communal illumination. He wrote: "we can more readily see the Bible—the instrumentality of the Spirit—as the book of the community."[14] Grenz criticizes classical orthodox Christians who "often collapse the Spirit into the Bible. . . . [They] exchange the dynamic of the ongoing movement of the Spirit speaking to the community of God's people through the pages of the Bible for the book we hold in our hands."[15]

Grenz's self-labeled "functional" approach "starts with the role of Scripture within the Christian communities and then draws conclusions from the Bible's normative value."[16] He even reinvents the Trinity in terms of his communal model, declaring that "God is the social trinity—Father, Son, and Spirit."[17] But God is far more than a society of persons. There is only one God, and He has only one essence. He is essentially one, not just functionally one as a human community is.

In his communal subjectivity, Grenz also confuses the inspiration of the objective text of Scripture with the subjective illumination of believers to the objective Word. Indeed, he says, "the

---

[12] Grenz, *A Primer on Postmodernism*, 166.
[13] Ibid.
[14] Grenz, *Revisioning Evangelical Theology*, 115.
[15] Ibid., 117.
[16] Ibid., 119.
[17] Grenz, *A Primer on Postmodernism*, 168.

confession of the inspiration of the Bible is closely intertwined with the experience of illumination."[18]

Likewise, Grenz's rejection of general revelation and reason based on the noetic effects of sin contributes to his subjectivism. He misquotes Pascal's famous statement about the heart having reasons which reason does not know in a fideistic manner contrary to Pascal's own use of evidence to support the Christian faith.[19] While Grenz notes that "following the intellect can sometimes lead us away from the truth,"[20] he seems oblivious to the fact that following experience can be even worse. After all, the fall affects the whole person. Further, sin may efface the image of God, but it does not erase it. And the misuse of reason does not mean there is no proper use of reason.

CONSTRUCTIONISM

Grenz speaks of the postmodern move from realism—which claims: (1) there is an objective world, and (2) it can be known—to constructionism, which denies both.[21] This, he said, leads to rejecting a correspondence view of truth (that statements are true if they correspond to reality). Of course, if there is no knowable objective reality to which our thoughts can correspond, then the correspondence view of truth must be rejected. But in this case one must construct his own truth, since there is no objective standard by which one can measure the truth of his statements. One is left swimming in a sea of subjectivism. He is lost in the subjectivity of his community. And there is no way to adjudicate between conflicting truth claims of different Christian communities, to say nothing of those of other religions. Grenz and Franke make their position clear in their book *Beyond Foundationalism.*[22]

While Grenz does not wish to totally give up belief in all objective reality,[23] nonetheless, he does reject the knowability of a pres-

---

[18] Grenz, *Revisioning Evangelical Theology,* 118.

[19] Blaise Pascal, *Pascal Pensee,* sect. 1, chaps. 14–15; Sect. 2, chaps. 11–12, 16–18.

[20] Grenz, *A Primer on Postmodernism,* 166.

[21] Grenz, *Renewing the Center: Evangelical Theology in a Post-Theological Era* (Grand Rapids: Baker Academic, 2000), 169.

[22] *Beyond Foundationalism* (Westminster John Knox, 2001).

[23] Grenz, *Renewing the Center,* 245–46.

ent world by the senses and reason.[24] Without any serious analysis
or argumentation,[25] Grenz rejects the "Thomistic model" of realism and opts for a postmodern reconstruction that focuses on an
"eschatological realism" of the world to come. He wrote, "the only
ultimately valid 'objectivity of the world' is that of a *future,* eschatological world, and the 'actual' universe is the universe as it one
day will be."[26] Thus, our task is that of "constructing a world in the
present that reflects God's own eschatological will for creation."
In a Witgensteinian fashion, Grenz opines that "because of the
role of language in the world-construction task, this mandate has a
strongly linguistic dimension. We participate with God as, through
the constructive power of language, we inhabit a present linguistic
world that sees all reality from the perspective of the future, real
world that God is bringing to pass."[27] Of course, Grenz offers no
answer to the criticism that affirming the unknowability of present
reality is something he claims to know about present reality.

NONPROPOSITIONALISM

Along with his rejection of realism, Grenz discards the traditional orthodox view, that the Bible contains propositional revelation, in favor of what he calls a more "dynamic" view. He rejects
the venerable creedal and confessional view that we can make
propositionally true statements about God. He insists that "our
understanding of the faith must not remain fixated on the propositional approach that views Christian truth as nothing more than
correct doctrine of doctrinal truth."[28] One wonders whether Grenz
realizes the propositional nature of his doctrinal claim in that
statement. Indeed, elsewhere he admits that "right beliefs and correct doctrine are vital to Christian living."[29] But how can we have
these without a rationally knowable and propositionally statable
objective reality? Grenz's answer seems to lie in his subordination
of the propositional to the experiential. He claims that "sound doc-

[24] Ibid., 199f.
[25] Ibid., 230–31.
[26] Ibid., 246.
[27] Ibid.
[28] Grenz, *A Primer on Postmodernism*, 170.
[29] Ibid., 172.

trine is a servant of the Spirit's work in the new birth and transformed life."[30] Doctrine is like a Wittgensteinian language "game"
based in the changing experience of the community.[31] But here
again we are in the quagmire of subjectivism, for reason should
be the judge of experience, not the reverse. As Alister McGrath
noted, experience is something that needs to be interpreted, rather
than something which is capable of interpreting.[32]

Grenz also claims that, "Transformed in this manner into a book
of doctrine, the Bible is easily robbed of its dynamic character."[33]
He insists that "the inspiration of Scripture cannot function as the
theological premise from which biblical authority emerges."[34]
So, in place of the historic belief in the essential authority of the
inspired text of Scripture, Grenz proposes a "functional approach
[that] moves in a somewhat opposite direction from the canonical" approach.[35]

BARTHIANISM

Indeed, Grenz's view is not essentially different from that of
the Neo-orthodox theologian Karl Barth. Grenz seems to recognize
the similarity of his view in posing the very question, "Is this not
simply the older neo-orthodoxy dressed up in new garb?"[36] While
he attempts a qualified "no,"[37] the essence of his view of the relation of revelation and the Bible does not differ significantly from
that of Karl Barth, for he denies the identity of the Bible with God's
revelation. Rather, like Barth, he holds that "the Bible is a divinely
appointed channel, a mirror, or a visible sign of revelation."[38] The
Bible is not God's words in and of themselves. Rather, "the human
words of the Bible are God's Word *to us*."[39] In support of this, he

---

[30] Grenz, "Nurturing the Soul, Informing the Mind" in *Evangelicals Scripture, Tradition, Authority and Hermeneutics*, ed. Vincent Bacote et al. (Downers Grove: InterVarsity,
2004), 39.

[31] Grenz, *Renewing the Center*, 246.

[32] Alister McGrath, "Theology and Experience" in the *European Journal of Theology*
2, no. 1 (1993): 67.

[33] Grenz, *Revisioning Evangelical Theology*, 114–15.

[34] Ibid., 118.

[35] Ibid., 119.

[36] Ibid., 124.

[37] Ibid., 125.

[38] Grenz is citing Bloesch with approval in *Revisioning Evangelical Theology*, 131.

[39] Grenz, *Revisioning Evangelical Theology*, 130 (emphasis added).

mistakenly argues that the Bible nowhere claims that it is the Word of God.[40] This is clearly not the case, as an examination of only a few texts will illustrate. In John 10:34–35 Jesus uses "word of God," "writings" (*grapha*), and "cannot be broken" interchangeably. Second Timothy 3:15–16 does the same by saying all the writings *(grapha)* are "God-breathed" and are identical with the "sacred Scriptures" that Timothy knew from a child, namely, the Old Testament. In Matt 5:17–18 Jesus described the Old Testament Law and Prophets as the imperishable Word of God. Peter declared that the Old Testament prophetic writings find their ultimate source in God, not in human invention (2 Pet 1:20–21).

FALLIBILISM AND BARTHIANISM

Citing Berkouwer with approval, Grenz affirms, "Our listening to God's voice [in Scripture] does not need to be threatened by scientific research into Holy Scripture,"[41] for errors in the Bible are only part of the "skandal" it bears as a human instrument. The Bible is not the Word of God in and of itself, but only "to us." Grenz wrote, "the Bible is revelation in a functional sense; it is revelatory." Also, "Scriptures are revelation in a derivative sense."[42] Like Barth, the Bible is only a fallible record of or witness to God's revelation in Christ. "The Bible is revelation because it is the *witness* to and the *record* of the historical revelation of God."[43] The historic view of inspiration holds that the Bible is without error on whatever topic it touches: science, history, or psychology. Grenz demurs, insisting that "the Bible therefore may not be the kind of authority on the various branches of modern learning that many believers want to maintain."[44] Rather, it is an authority only on matters of salvation.

BRIAN MCLAREN ON INSPIRATION OF SCRIPTURE

In his book *A Generous Orthodoxy*, Brian McLaren claims to have a high view of Scripture. He says,

[40] Ibid., 131.
[41] Ibid., 110.
[42] Ibid., 133.
[43] Ibid. (emphasis added).
[44] Ibid., 135.

I have spent my entire life learning, understanding, reappraising, wrestling with, trusting, applying, and obeying the Bible, and trying to help others to do the same. I believe it is a gift from God, inspired by God, to benefit us in the most important way possible: equipping us so that we can benefit others, so that we can play our part in the ongoing mission of God. *My regard for the Bible is higher than ever.*[45]

CLEARLY AMBIGUOUS

McLaren gives the following as his explanation of "What the Bible Really Is":

The Bible is an inspired gift from God—a unique collection of literary artifacts that together support the telling of an amazing and essential story. The artifacts include poetry, letters, short histories, and other genres that we don't have labels for. Even a familiar category like history needs to be used carefully, because we must avoid imposing modern biases and tastes on these ancient documents: they need to be taken and appreciated on their own terms. The stories these artifacts support cover the amazing career of the descendents *[sic]* of a Middle Eastern nomad named Abraham. It traces their beginnings, growth, settlement, and resettlement through various social structures and economies, through many political arrangements, through good times and bad. This collection is uniquely profitable for teaching, rebuking, correcting, training, and equipping people so they can do good works for God.[46]

One of the more difficult aspects of McLaren's writings is his seeming unwillingness to say anything definitive about what he believes. He seems to want to be able to present his understanding of a given doctrine, but he doesn't want to say anything that might give others a basis upon which to critique his views. He wants to retain the right to say what he thinks is the correct way to

---

[45] Brian McLaren, *A Generous Orthodoxy* (Grand Rapids: Zondervan, 2004), 159 (emphasis in original).
[46] Brian D. McLaren, "Missing the Point: The Bible," in *Adventures in Missing the Point*, ed. Brian D. McLaren (Grand Rapids: Zondervan, 2003), 69–70.

depict a doctrine or belief, but he doesn't want to express himself in a manner that others can challenge. Consequently, it is virtually impossible to find a definitive statement of what he means by the term "inspiration." Those who attempt to critique his doctrines are vilified as "Modern" and "polarizing." The fact of the matter is, McLaren's view of inspiration is simply not orthodox.

UNDEFINITIVE DEFINING OF INSPIRATION

McLaren sets forth his view of inspiration by the use of an analogy:

> I am a human being with a name (plus an assortment of numbers that certify me as a citizen, driver, credit-card holder, phone owner, etc.). Like every other human, I am both a creation of God and a pro-creation of parents who, in partnership with friends and teachers and authors and culture in general, helped make me all I am today. The way God willed to create the "me" I am today, then, like every other human, is through a complex synergy of biology and community and history (plus my own will, choices, and the like). These parental origins, these organic means, these social and historical contexts, do not decrease in any way the reality of God as my ultimate Creator, the One who through all these many instrumentalities says, "Let there be a Brian," and here I am. In the same way Scripture is something God has "let be," and so it is at once God's creation and the creation of the dozens of people and communities and cultures who produced it. One doesn't decrease the other. One doesn't lessen the other. One doesn't nullify the other.[47]

The notion that the Scripture is God-breathed is not simply the notion that "God has 'let be'" the Scripture similar to the way God "let be" Brian McLaren. The orthodox doctrine is that the very words that compose the Scripture were the very words that God chose for His revelation. The biblical metaphor, "God-breathed," is designed to indicate that God spoke these very words—they

---

[47] McLaren, *A Generous Orthodoxy*, 161–62.

were breathed out by God.[48] McLaren argues that a more effective communication pattern in the postmodern matrix is "the power of story."[49] It was not at all clear in that context, but it seems here that power of story involves manipulating the facts to suit one's point.

PROPOSITION ABOUT A PROPOSITIONLESS BIBLE

McLaren is emphatically vocal about his opposition to what he characterizes as Modernism. He believes that modern, Western Christians have actually misrepresented the nature of the Bible: "because modern Christians loved the Bible, they paid it four compliments, which have damaged as well as enhanced the Bible's reputation."[50] One of the four "compliments" by which modern Christians have misrepresented the Bible is, according to McLaren, *"We presented the Bible as a repository of sacred propositions and abstractions."*[51] He gives the following as an explanation of what this means:

> Which was natural, for we were moderns—children of the 18th-century European Enlightenment—so we loved abstractions and propositions. Our sermons tended to exegete texts in such a way that stories, poetry, and biography (among other features of the Bible)—the 'chaff'—were sifted out, while the 'wheat' of doctrines and principles were saved. Modern Western people loved that approach; meanwhile, however, people of a more postmodern bent (who are more like premodern people in many ways) find the doctrines and principles as interesting as grass clippings.[52]

---

[48] It is interesting how McLaren skews the facts to fit the point he wishes to make. In an earlier chapter he criticizes the conservatives for their conflicting and fallible interpretations (ibid., 134ff), but in this context he applauds the "Christian community" of "Catholic, Protestant, and Orthodox" Christians for *always* having a "deep feeling and understanding for this integrated dual origin (human and divine) of the Scripture" and for holding on to "both dimensions of the origin of Scripture" (ibid., 162). This certainly does not sound like a group of "shrill, quarreling voices" who "constantly labeled the interpretations of the fellow Protestants grossly errant" (ibid., 134).

[49] Brian D. McLaren, *The Church on the Other Side: Doing Ministry in the Postmodern Matrix*, 2nd ed. (Grand Rapids: Zondervan, 2000), 90.

[50] McLaren, "The Bible," 70.

[51] Ibid., 71.

[52] Ibid.

That this "compliment" is perceived by McLaren to be a misrepresentation is not a misrepresentation. He says, "These misrepresentations were not malicious,"[53] clearly stating that he perceives the notion that the Bible is a repository of propositions to be a misrepresentation.

REASONS AGAINST REASON

This approach leads to the advice: "Drop Any Affair You May Have with Certainty, Proof, Argument—and Replace It with Dialogue, Conversation, Intrigue, and Search."[54] He apparently sees no inconsistency in his own clarion call against clarity. Apparently, God is not as capable in His Word as McLaren is. He advocates that Bible studies and sermons should not seek clarity because reality is, according to McLaren, "seldom clear, but usually fuzzy and mysterious; not black-and-white, but in living color."[55] The congregation should not aim to capture the meaning of the text, but aim for "a text that captured the imagination and curiosity of the congregation."[56] Of course, this is a false dichotomy. Nothing says that it cannot be both, clearly and accurately capturing the meaning while at the same time stimulating the imagination and curiosity of the congregation. And whether reality is seldom clear is no basis upon which not to be clear. If reality is fuzzy, someone needs to clarify it, and if God cannot clarify reality for us, what hope do we have? Whether reality is fuzzy is no grounds for the claim that God's Word is fuzzy.

THE BIG QUESTION ABOUT THE BIG QUESTION

Contrary to the apostle Paul's claim in the classic text on inspiration that Scripture was God-breathed to instruct us for salvation (2 Tim 3:15–17), McLaren indicates that the "Big Question of the whole Bible" is not the salvation of man. He says,

> Without focusing on the Big Story, we are tempted to impose alien readings on the Bible. For example, if we reduce the Bible to an elaborate answer to the question,

---

[53] Ibid., 72.
[54] Ibid., 78 (emphasis in original).
[55] Ibid.
[56] Ibid.

"How does a person go to heaven after he dies?"—if we think this is the Big Question the whole Bible is answering—we'll be prone to misunderstand major parts of the Bible that were written before that question was on anybody's mind (like the entire Old Testament). The Old Testament people were far more concerned about being the people of God *in* this life, not *after* this life. So when they performed sacrifices, for instance, they weren't seeking to get a clean slate so they could die forgiven as individuals and go to heaven after they died. To the contrary, they were seeking to remain pure enough as a community to participate in God's twofold promise to them: being blessed by God, and being a blessing to the whole world.[57]

According to McLaren, Old Testament saints did not ask the question, "How does a person go to heaven after he dies?" He says that in the entire Old Testament, this question was not on anyone's mind. For McLaren, the focus of the Bible is not salvation but service—not getting right, but doing good. But how can a person be "blessed by God" or be a "blessing to the whole world" unless this means first and foremost being saved by His grace? Is man inherently able to do good—good by God's standard? How can men do good if they do not get right?

AN ERRANT READING OF INERRANCY

According to McLaren, modern Western Christians use certain words to talk about Scripture: "For modern Western Christians, words like *authority*, *inerrancy*, *infallibility*, *revelation*, *objective*, *absolute*, and *literal* are crucial."[58] He then declares, "Hardly anyone realizes why these words are important,"[59] and his next assertion indicates that he must be one of those persons who does not realize why they are important: "Hardly anyone knows about the stories of Sir Isaac Newton, Rene Descartes, the Enlightenment, David Hume, and Foundationalism—which provide the context

---

[57] Ibid., 78–79 (emphasis in original).
[58] McLaren, *A Generous Orthodoxy*, 164.
[59] Ibid.

in which these words are so important."[60] Once again McLaren misrepresents the case. All of these terms with the possible exception of the term *infallibility* have been used by authors throughout history at least from Augustine. Augustine held to the concept of inerrancy even when it was necessary to resort to allegorical interpretation to avoid what he perceived to be a contradiction. None of these words was invented or found any substantively new connotations during the Enlightenment. Additionally, how does McLaren know what "hardly anyone" knows? And how can he be absolutely certain we should avoid absolutes?

McLaren also declares, "Hardly anyone notices the irony of resorting to the authority of extrabiblical words and concepts to justify one's belief in the Bible's ultimate authority."[61] Of course in one sense, all of the words that we use are extrabiblical since the Bible was not written in English. But McLaren does not merely claim that the *words* are extrabiblical. Rather he claims that the *concepts* are extrabiblical. McLaren proposes that it is more reasonable to include a statement like "The purpose of Scripture is to equip God's people for good works" than to use "statements with words foreign to the Bible's vocabulary about itself (inerrant, authoritative, literal, revelatory, objective, absolute, propositional, etc.)."[62] But not a single one of the words in the statement McLaren proposes is in the Bible. The Bible does not contain a single English word. Now of course someone will object, "Of course the Bible doesn't contain these English words! He's not saying the Bible must contain these exact English words. What he's saying is that it's more reasonable to use statements that contain the particular meanings, whether expressed in English or in the languages of the Bible, that are actually found in the Bible." But if that's what he is saying, then what's the problem? Every single one of the "meanings" of the words he lists as "extrabiblical" are also found in the Bible! The meaning of the term *authoritative* is found in Isa 46:9–10: "for I am God, and there is no other; I am God, and no one is like Me. I declare the end from the beginning, and from long ago

---

[60] Ibid.
[61] Ibid.
[62] Ibid., 164–65.

what is not yet done, saying: My plan will take place, and I will do all My will." Hebrews 6:18 says "it is impossible for God to lie." If the Bible is the Word of God, then the concept of inerrancy is in the Bible. We cannot allow the import of what McLaren has said to escape us. He not only said words like *authority, inerrancy, infallibility, revelation, objective, absolute,* and *literal* are extrabiblical. He said the concepts are extrabiblical: "Hardly anyone notices the irony of resorting to the authority of extra-biblical words and *concepts* to justify one's belief in the Bible's ultimate authority." What he is saying here is that the concepts of authority, inerrancy, infallibility, revelation, objectivity, absoluteness, and literalness are not concepts that we find in the Bible!

THE ISSUE OF OTHER ISSUES

There are simply too many misrepresentations, equivocations, *ad hominem* arguments, straw men, and outright falsehoods in McLaren's chapter on "The Bible" to attempt to address them all. Many of these take the form of innuendos and insinuations, but the blatantly false characterization of Gandhi as someone "who sought to follow the way of Christ without identifying himself as a Christian" reveals either an astonishing lack of understanding of both Gandhi and Christ, or an even more astonishing willingness to distort both for rhetorical effect. Gandhi was an enthusiastic adherent to the Hindu caste system that was originally designed as a tool of racial discrimination. Gandhi slept with nude teenage girls under the pretext of "testing his vow of chastity." Gandhi allowed his wife Kasturba to die of pneumonia when she could have been saved. Gandhi refused to allow her to be given a shot of penicillin because it was an "alien [British] medicine." Yet when Gandhi contracted malaria he took the alien medicine Quinine, and when he had appendicitis he allowed alien British doctors to perform an appendectomy. Contrary to the movie depiction, when Gandhi was shot, his last words were not "Oh, God!" Rather, he muttered, "Oh, Buddha." These are hardly the kinds of beliefs and actions that Jesus would have commended.[63]

---

[63] See Richard Grenier, *The Gandhi Nobody Knows* (Nashville: Thomas Nelson, 1983).

The title of his chapter in *A Generous Orthodoxy* ought to be changed from "Why I Am Biblical" to "Why Would Anyone Think I Am Biblical?" McLaren certainly has the privilege to express his beliefs. The disingenuous character of his writings is that McLaren presents his beliefs as if they are orthodox Christian beliefs. He either purposely or inadvertently misrepresents the facts in almost every case, yet he presents these distortions as if these are generally accepted and in complete conformity with the teaching of the Bible.

CONCLUSION

Postmoderns in general are in denial. They even deny making denials. This is true of the postmodern view of Scripture as well. They deny that they are denying an orthodox view of Scripture, but it is undeniable that they have. The orthodox view of Scripture is rooted in numerous premises denied by postmoderns. They deny absolutism, objectivism, foundationalism, propositionalism, correspondence, and infallibilism—all of which a genuine evangelical view entails, even though these are not always consistently acknowledged or applied. The Evangelical Theological Society, which is the largest group of evangelical scholars in the world, following the landmark "Chicago Statement" (1978) on inerrancy, has heralded this as the standard for understanding the inerrancy of the Bible.[64] Grenz and McLaren definitely fall seriously short of the standard on all major counts. The so-called emerging church is the diverging church, since it diverts from orthodoxy on one of its fundamental pillars—the one on which all the others rest.

Scripture is the most fundamental of all the fundamental doctrines, since it is the fundamental on which all the other fundamentals rest. And on their view of Scripture, Grenz and McLaren are not only postmodern but they are also post-Christian. Their rejection of the classical orthodox view of Scripture is sweeping. It includes a rejection of the correspondence view of truth, a rejection of objective truth, absolute truth, propositional truth, and

---

[64] R. C. Sproul, *Explaining Inerrancy: A Commentary* (Oakland, Calif.: International Council on Biblical Inerrancy, 1979).

inerrant truth in Scripture. This it does in favor of antifoundationalism, relativism, subjectivism, constructionism, and Barthianism,
nonpropositionalism, and fallibilism.

The so-called emerging church is not emerging; it has already
emerged. And what it has emerged into is not Christian in any
traditional, historic, or orthodox sense of the words. Indeed, it
has emerged from orthodoxy to unorthodox, from infallibilism to
fallibilism, from objectivism to subjectivism, from absolutism to
relativism, and from realism to agnosticism.

BIBLIOGRAPHY

Carson, D. A. *Becoming Conversant with the Emerging Church.* Grand Rapids: Zondervan, 2005.

Geisler, Norman L. *Systematic Theology: Introduction and Bible.* St. Paul:
Bethany, 2002.

Geisler, Norman L., and Thomas Howe. *When Critics Ask.* Grand Rapids:
Baker, 1992.

Geisler, Norman L., and William E. Nix. *General Introduction to the Bible,
Revised and Expanded.* Chicago: Moody, 1986.

Grenz, Stanley. *Renewing the Center: Evangelical Theology in a Post-
Theological Era.* Grand Rapids: Baker Academic, 2000.

_____. "Nurturing the Soul, Informing the Mind," in *Evangelicals,
Scripture, Tradition, Authority and Hermeneutics*, ed. Vincent Bacote et
al. Downers Grove, Ill.: InterVarsity, 2004.

_____. *A Primer on Postmodernism.* Grand Rapids: Eerdmans, 1996.

Howe, Thomas. *Objectivity in Biblical Interpretation.* Longwood, Fla.:
Advantage, 2005.

McLaren, Brian. *A Generous Orthodoxy.* Grand Rapids: Zondervan, 2004.

McLaren, Brian, and Tony Campolo, ed. *Adventures in Missing the Point.* El
Cajon, Calif.: Emergent Books, 2003.

Pascal, Blaise. *Pascal Pensees.* Baltimore: Penguin, 1966.

Sproul, R.C. *Explaining Inerrancy: A Commentary.* Oakland, Calif.: International Council on Biblical Inerrancy, 1979.

A NEW KIND OF INTERPRETATION: BRIAN MCLAREN AND THE HERMENEUTICS OF TASTE

DOUGLAS K. BLOUNT

What is now decisive against Christianity is our taste, no longer our reason.

– Friedrich Nietzsche[1]

Nature has all sorts of phenomena in stock and can suit many different tastes.

– C. S. Lewis[2]

Our interpretations reveal less about God or the Bible than they do about ourselves. They reveal what we want to defend, what we want to attack, what we want to ignore, what we're unwilling to question.

– Brian D. McLaren[3]

THE FOLLOWING CONCERNS itself with Brian McLaren's hermeneutics. In so doing, it focuses not on the *fruits* of his reading

---

[1] *The Gay Science,* trans. Walter Kaufmann (New York: Vintage, 1974), § 132, p. 186.
[2] *The Discarded Image* (Cambridge, England: Cambridge University Press, 1964), 221, quoted in Brian D. McLaren, *A New Kind of Christian: A Tale of Two Friends on a Spiritual Journey* (San Francisco: Jossey-Bass, 2001), 35.
[3] McLaren, *A New Kind of Christian,* 50.

of Scripture but rather on the *seeds* out of which that reading emerges. In short, it concerns not the end-result of his interpretive approach but rather its starting point, the assumptions that drive it. I argue that McLaren's interpretive starting point—and, consequently, *both* his interpretive approach *and* the readings that it generates—cannot be properly called Christian. As this suggests, there are such things as *distinctly Christian* readings of Scripture. So also there are *distinctly Christless* readings of it. What distinguishes the former from the latter are the assumptions that drive them; distinctly Christian readings of Scripture arise out of assumptions that are themselves distinctly Christian. In what follows, I argue that the assumptions underlying McLaren's reading of Scripture run contrary to the faith and thus yield interpretations of the sacred text that are themselves contrary to the faith. Before so arguing, however, I first discuss the role of taste in explanation generally and textual interpretation specifically.

I. EXPLANATION, INTERPRETATION, AND TASTE

In asserting that nature "can suit many different tastes," C. S. Lewis underestimates the situation. For, as philosophers of science have long recognized, a finite and explainable set of data has infinitely many possible explanations.[4] This fact presents would-be theorists with what has come to be known as "the problem of underdetermination": from the radical multiplicity of explanations available for any given data set, it follows that *data always underdetermines theory*.[5] No data set ever *entails* a particular explana-

---

[4] As this indicates, infinite or unexplainable data sets constitute special cases. Since, however, no one reading this article is likely ever to deal with an infinite data set and unexplainable data sets pose no threat to my argument, I shall worry no further about such sets. So, in the remainder of this article, "data sets" shall refer only to finite, explainable data sets. On the implications of having infinitely many explanatory options available for any given data set, see Michael J. Murray, "Reason for Hope (in the Postmodern World)," in Michael J. Murray, ed., *Reason for the Hope Within* (Grand Rapids: Eerdmans, 1999), 1–19. For a distinctly Christian perspective on science, see J. P. Moreland, *Christianity and the Nature of Science: A Philosophical Investigation*, 2nd ed. (Grand Rapids: Baker, 1999).

[5] As Robin Le Poidevin states, "The *problem of underdetermination* concerns the relationship between theory . . . and the empirical data. For any given theory, the evidence will never determine the choice between that theory and some rival theory. The problem then is

tion. However much data one gathers, one *always* has infinitely many possible explanations available for one's data set; it thus follows that data sets alone *never* lead inexorably to particular explanations.[6] So, to put Lewis's point differently, infinitely many explanations can accommodate the data with which nature presents us; consequently, nature can suit *infinitely* many different tastes.[7]

Suppose, for instance, that Alvin returns to his car after a long day of work at a local recording studio, only to find the car's front passenger's side window broken and his copy of Bob Dylan's *Modern Times*—which he had left in the front passenger's seat— gone. In short, Alvin faces a data set that includes the following two bits of information:

(δ_1) the front passenger's side window is broken, and
(δ_2) *Modern Times* is missing.

Let this modest data set be Δ. If Alvin restricts himself to Δ, a number of explanations might present themselves to him. Perhaps in his view the most plausible one involves theft; he thus explains Δ in terms of a thief's having broken into the car by way of the front passenger's side window and stolen the CD. While this explanation accounts for Δ, so also do other possible explanations.[8]

So perhaps, as Alvin's sensitive friend Theodore believes, the window was broken not by a thief but rather by a friend of Alvin's seeking to remove the CD in order to protect it from the heat of a long summer's day. Such an account also explains Δ.[9] Or perhaps, as

---

to show how theory choice can ever be rational." *The Oxford Guide to Philosophy*, ed. Ted Honderich (New York: Oxford University Press, 2005), s.v. "underdetermination."

[6] One sometimes hears talk of "following the data [or, perhaps, evidence] wherever it leads." Strictly speaking, such talk is twaddle, for *data never leads anywhere of its own accord*. Only in company with assumptions, biases, and the like does data or evidence ever go anywhere; and in such cases, it follows as much as it leads.

[7] This does *not* mean that all explanations are equal. Nor does it mean that, explanatorily speaking, *anything goes*. I shall return to these points below.

[8] Let Δ be true just in case all of its members are true. Alvin's explanation accounts for Δ because the latter's truth follows from the former's truth. In other words, it accounts for Δ because the following conditional holds: *if* Alvin's explanation is true, *then* Δ is true. Notice that this conditional holds even in cases where Alvin's explanation is false; in other words, Δ's following from Alvin's explanation does *not* entail that explanation's following from Δ.

[9] Like the one put forward by Alvin, Theodore's explanation accounts for Δ precisely because Δ's truth follows from it.

the brainy Simon would have it, alien spaceships happen magneti-
cally to attract audio CDs; if so, Δ can be explained by a spaceship's
having flown too close to Alvin's car, causing *Modern Times* to fly
out its front passenger's side window and thus break it. Or perhaps,
by way of explaining Δ, Dave suggests the following: Unbeknownst
to most of us, audio CDs are animate objects possessing an extraordinary and heretofore unnoticed ability to respond to their environ-
ments. Alvin's copy of Dylan's *Modern Times* was incensed that
its owner would be so insensitive as to leave it locked in a car on a
long, hot summer's day. So, in keeping with its extraordinary ability to respond to its environment, the CD sprouted appendages, beat
on the front passenger's side window with those appendages until it
broke the window, exited the car, and made its escape in search of a
more enlightened owner of audio CDs. Now, however implausible
such an account might seem, it *does* explain Δ.[10]

So each of our would-be theorists explains Δ. But of course
they offer us only a taste of the vast array of possible explanations
that could be put forward for that data set. Indeed, the only limit
to the explanations one can advance for Δ is the limit that arises
from one's own imagination. Were one sufficiently creative, there
would be no end to the explanations one could offer for Δ.

Of course, some of the explanations thus far examined might be
eliminated by gathering more data and thus augmenting Δ. So perhaps all of the glass from the car's broken window happens to be
inside the car. Since breaking the window from within the car would
presumably cause glass to fall outside the vehicle, such additional
data would eliminate explanations according to which the window
was broken from within the car.[11] Both Simon's and Dave's explanations would thus be eliminated. From this one might conclude
that, were enough data gathered, a single explanation could be isolated from the plethora of possible ones. Such a conclusion would,
however, be ill-drawn. For as long as only finitely much data is

[10] It does so because its truth implies Δ's truth.

[11] Things are not quite this simple. For, as astute readers will realize, one can envision
circumstances in which, though the force breaking the window comes from within the
car, all of the glass nonetheless falls inward, thus ending up inside the car. But since it has
no bearing on the present discussion, I shall ignore this complication and assume that the
glass's ending up in the car rules out the window's having been broken from within it.

gathered, only finitely many possible explanations are eliminated; and as long as only finitely many possible explanations are eliminated, *infinitely* many possible explanations remain.[12] So, unless one gathers infinitely much data, there remains no end to the possible explanations that could be put forward for Δ. And as things go here for Δ, so they go for any other data set.

Of course, possibility does not entail plausibility; and while the former does not come in degrees, the latter does. So not all of a given data set's possible explanations are equally plausible. But plausibility is largely a function of taste. On this point, consider, for example, the data of human consciousness. Those with a taste for, say, metaphysical naturalism—according to which nothing exists except matter and its effects—explain consciousness in accordance with that taste. On their view, consciousness arises out of various physical processes involving material objects acting in accordance with purely natural laws. Metaphysical naturalists thus explain consciousness by appealing to such laws and processes.[13] Those, however, whose taste runs toward some form of supernaturalism—such as, say, orthodox Christians—explain consciousness by way of nonphysical entities such as minds, souls, and spirits; ultimately, of course, such Christians account for such entities— and the phenomena connected with them—by appealing to God's creative activity. So both metaphysical naturalists and orthodox Christians accommodate the data of human consciousness; each group explains such consciousness on its own terms. In short, then, the data of human consciousness can accommodate either taste. And as things go in this regard for human consciousness, so they go more generally. *Whatever* one's tastes, the data of the natural world can be explained in a manner that accommodates those tastes.

None of this means that all explanations are equal. On the contrary, some explanations are superior to others.[14] Indeed, some are

---

[12] As Billy Preston might say, "Finite from infinite leaves infinite." Although this merits further discussion, I shall, in the interest of space, let it be.

[13] If specific laws and processes cannot be pressed into such service, the appeal becomes more general. But the explanation still goes forward, albeit with blanks in the appropriate places and promises that those blanks will in the fullness of time be filled.

[14] So, for example, J. P. Moreland argues that theism handles the data of human consciousness far better than metaphysical naturalism. See his *Consciousness and the Existence*

true, others *false*. Even so, one's *estimate* of a given explanation depends on the tastes with which one approaches the data in question; the data alone can never force one to regard the explanation as plausible or implausible. The explanation is either true or false independent of what any mere mortal thinks of it; one's estimate of its plausibility, however, is not. That estimate depends on the assumptions, biases, preferences, and such with which one considers it.[15] In short, then, one's estimate of an explanation's plausibility depends on one's tastes.[16]

Now the problem of underdetermination and the role that taste plays in explaining data bears significantly on interpretation. For, of course, texts constitute data sets; interpretation involves making sense of those sets. So interpretation amounts to a kind of explanation; to interpret a text *is* to explain it.[17] It thus follows that, for any given text, there are infinitely many possible interpretations of it. Moreover, as a theorist's estimate of the plausibility of a particular explanation of a given data set depends on that theorist's tastes, so also a reader's estimate of the plausibility of a particular interpretation of a given text depends on that reader's tastes. As with *any* data set, a text never leads inexorably to a particular interpretation. Theorists move from data to explanation only by way of their tastes; so also readers move from text to interpretation only by way of their tastes.

For example, some who profess Christ—motivated by distaste for the God portrayed in the Old Testament—distinguish that God from the God of the New Testament. Scot McKnight sees such a tendency within the Emergent movement, noting that

> emergents sometimes exercise a deconstructive critique
> of the Bible's view of God. Sometimes I hear it in ways
> that are no more interesting that [sic] Marcion's old (and

---

of God, Routledge Studies in the Philosophy of Religion (London: Routledge, 2008).

[15] While truth is objective, rationality is not. See Murray, "Reason for Hope."

[16] See Thomas S. Kuhn, "Objectivity, Value Judgment, and Theory Choice" in *The Essential Tension: Selected Studies in Scientific Tradition and Change* (Chicago: University of Chicago Press, 1977), 320–39.

[17] Or perhaps the point should be put the other way round and explanation construed as a kind of interpretation. Such a construal would, for example, view scientific explanation as interpretation of the natural world.

heretical) critique of the violent God of the Old Testament. Yet upon close inspection, the rumblings are subtler
and more sophisticated, and the struggle is palpable and
genuine. For some emergents, the Bible includes portrayals of God that cannot be squared with their understanding of a God of love.[18]

Needless to say, no understanding of divine love on which the God
of the Old Testament fails to count as "a God of love" deserves the
label "Christian." The continuity of the Old and New Testaments
is something to which the church has been unswervingly committed since its earliest days; those who deny that continuity thus
reject one of the fundamental commitments of Christian orthodoxy, thereby placing themselves at odds with the community in
whom the Spirit of truth dwells.[19]

My point here is not to charge the Emergent movement with
Marcion's heresy, though against some of its members such a
charge would be well-aimed; my point rather is that, given the
church's historic commitment to the continuity of the two testaments (especially with respect to their portrayal of God), those
who deny that continuity cannot rightly claim simply to be reading the sacred text objectively and without bias.[20] As McKnight
suggests, their denial of theological continuity across the testaments arises from a particular conception of love. In short, they
have a taste for a certain understanding of love as well as its atten-
dant understanding of divine love—of what it means for God to
be "a God of love"—and this taste leads them to reject not only
readings of the Bible with which it cannot be squared but also to
deny the truthfulness of those *passages* that cannot in their view
be interpreted in harmony with it. In their hands, such passages
"are interpreted as the way ancients talked about God, with later

[18] Scot McKnight, "The Ironic Faith of Emergents," *Christianity Today,* September
2008, 63. However subtle and sophisticated the view or genuine and palpable the struggle
of those about whom McKnight writes may be, those who dismiss the Old Testament portrayal of God as simply "the way ancients talked about God," a way inconsistent with the
New Testament presentation of "a God who is altogether gracious and loving," are no less
heretical than Marcion himself.

[19] See John 16:13.

[20] Much less can they claim to be reading it Christianly.

biblical revelation seen as clearly presenting a God who is altogether gracious and loving."[21]

Given that data sets alone never lead to particular explanations,
it follows that texts alone never lead to particular interpretations.
Only in company with assumptions, biases, preferences, and such
do texts lead to interpretations. So those who dismiss the Old
Testament's portrayal of God as untenable do so *not* because the
Bible taken by itself demands such a conclusion.[22] Rather, they
do so because their assumptions, biases, preferences, and such
demand it. In short, they do so because their taste—*not the sacred
text*—demands it.[23]

Or consider the service into which texts like Jonah 3:10 have
been pressed by open theists. According to that text, despite having
sent Jonah to pronounce judgment on Nineveh, God responded to
the repentant Ninevites by refraining from destroying them. Open
theists conclude from this that God lacks comprehensive knowledge of the future.[24] Their conclusion rests on the assumption that,
if God had known the future comprehensively, He would not have
sent Jonah to announce Nineveh's impending destruction. After
all, the argument goes, an all-knowing God would have known
that such destruction was not in fact forthcoming; that He sent
Jonah to pronounce a destruction that would not in fact take place
thus implies that God did not know precisely what the Ninevites'
future held. When He sent Jonah to Nineveh, God did so expecting
that the city would be destroyed. But when the Ninevites followed
their king's wise decree and repented, God then adjusted His plans

---

[21] McKnight, "Ironic Faith," 63.

[22] If the Bible alone demands such a conclusion, whence comes orthodoxy? Let no one
suggest the popular but Christless view that orthodoxy arose in an early church that was
unduly influenced by Greek philosophy. On this, see my "Togas, Tulips and the Philosophy
of Openness," *Southwestern Journal of Theology* 47 (2005), 177–89.

[23] I do not suggest that historic Christian orthodoxy takes a better path because it approaches Scripture *without* assumptions, biases, preferences, and such. Rather, it takes a
better path because it approaches the sacred text with the *right* assumptions, biases, preferences, and such—i.e., assumptions, biases, preferences, and such that are in fact *true*. As
this suggests, not all tastes are equal.

[24] Prominent among such theists are Gregory A. Boyd, Clark H. Pinnock, and John
Sanders. See Boyd's *God of the Possible: A Biblical Introduction to the Open View of
God* (Grand Rapids: Baker, 2000), Pinnock's *Most Moved Mover: A Theology of God's
Openness* (Grand Rapids: Baker, 2001), and Sanders's *The God Who Risks: A Theology of
Providence*, 2nd ed. (Downers Grove, Ill.: InterVarsity, 2007).

accordingly. Surely, the argument goes, this shows that God *did not know* that the Ninevites would repent and their destruction would be canceled.[25]

However impressive it might seem, such an argument misunderstands the text that it seeks to explain. For, as Jer 18:7–10 clearly indicates, divine declarations of judgment are *always* to be understood as opportunities—opportunities for repentance for those to whom destruction has been declared and for obedience for those to whom blessing has been declared. In short, divine declarations of judgment are always contingent. They indicate how God *would* act toward a nation *if that nation were to make no relevant change in its behavior.* But when a nation responds to such a declaration with such a change, God deals with it not according to that declaration but rather according to its changed behavior.[26]

So Jonah 3:10 does not demand the conclusion that open theists draw from it. Not surprisingly, in fact, it can be understood in ways quite consistent with the traditional Christian understanding

---

[25] This line of reasoning suggests not merely that God failed to believe a truth (to wit, that the Ninevites would not be destroyed) but also that He believed a falsehood (to wit, that the Ninevites would be destroyed). Now the suggestion that God fails to believe a truth is itself troubling; far more troubling, however, is the suggestion that He believes a falsehood. For in that case, God Himself errs. Moreover, since God cannot possibly err, this suggestion amounts to a *reductio* of open theism's reading of Jonah 3:10 and similar texts.

[26] Jonah's declaration to the Ninevites must thus be understood in light of God's fixed intention to deal with the nations à la Jer 18:7–10. In calling his subjects to repent before God, Nineveh's king recognizes the possibility that the declaration is contingent (Jonah 3:7–9). Even before attempting to flee to Tarshish to avoid going to Nineveh, Jonah himself had taken the declaration to be contingent (Jonah 4:1–3). What Jonah and the king of Nineveh thus understand, open theists apparently do not. Divine declarations of judgment should not be construed as committing God to particular courses of action *no matter what their recipients do in response to them* anymore than parental declarations of judgment should be construed as committing parents to particular courses of action *no matter what their children do in response to them.*

More to the point, a divine declaration that destruction is coming *when in fact it is not* no more implies that God lacks knowledge of how the relevant events will play out than parental declarations that punishment is coming *when in fact it is not* implies that parents lack knowledge of how the events relevant to their situations will play out. Parents sometimes use declarations of impending punishment as tools to facilitate repentance in their children; in so doing, they aim ultimately not at making punishment inevitable but rather at making it unnecessary and thus forestalling it. So also God sometimes uses declarations of impending destruction as tools to bring His creatures to repentance; in so doing, He aims not at making their destruction inevitable but rather at making it unnecessary and thus forestalling it. In neither case does the use of such a declaration demonstrate a lack of knowledge on the part of the one making it.

of God according to which He enjoys comprehensive knowledge of the future. Those who draw from it the conclusion that God lacks such knowledge do so *not* because the text itself demands such a conclusion, but rather because they bring to the text certain assumptions, biases, preferences, and such that stand at odds with the tradition.[27] In short, they draw that conclusion not because the text alone demands it, but rather *because their tastes demand it.*

II. *CREATIO EX* MCLAREN

"The old way [of being a Christian] was, as an old Bob Dylan lyric puts it, 'rapidly aging,' and I needed to disembed and reevaluate and begin a journey toward a new home—for my sake, for the sake of the people I was called to lead, and perhaps even for God's sake. But the new way hadn't been created yet."[28] Thus Brian McLaren describes the critical juncture in his spiritual journey when he began extracting himself from "modern Christianity." This self-extraction came in response to a deep dissatisfaction with such Christianity, a dissatisfaction that for McLaren culminated in a crisis of faith. As he explains it, *something* had to give: "Either Christianity is itself flawed, failing, untrue, or our modern, Western, commercialized, industrial-strength version of it is in need of a fresh look, a serious revision."[29] Hoping to arrive at such a revision, McLaren cast off his modern moorings and set sail in search of a brave, new Christianity—a Christianity appropriate to the postmodern milieu in which we find ourselves.

Chief among the reasons for his dissatisfaction with modern Christianity is McLaren's perception that it lacks authenticity. About a radio preacher "absolutely sure of his bombproof answers and his foolproof *biblical* interpretations," McLaren writes, "And the more sure he seems, the less I find myself wanting to be a

---

[27] Interestingly, just as a particular conception of divine love drives some within the Emergent movement to deny the continuity of the Old and New Testaments, so also a particular conception of divine love drives open theists to their view. This can be seen in, e.g., William Hasker's argument against the doctrine of divine timelessness. See "Is God Timeless?" in his *God, Time, and Knowledge,* Cornell Studies in the Philosophy of Religion (Ithaca, N. Y.: Cornell University Press, 1989), 171–85.

[28] McLaren, *New Kind of Christian*, xi.

[29] Ibid., xv.

Christian, because on this side of the microphone, antennas, and speaker, life isn't that simple, answers aren't that clear, and nothing is that sure."[30] About his own ministry, he writes,

> I preach sermons that earn the approving nods of the life-long churchgoers, because they repeat the expected vocabulary and formulations, words that generally convey little actual meaning . . . but work like fingers, massaging the weary souls of earnest people. Meanwhile . . . these very massaging messages leave the uninitiated furrowing their brows, shaking their heads, and shifting in their seats. They do this sometimes because they don't understand but even more when they do understand—because the very formulations that sound so good and familiar to the "saved" sound downright weird or even wicked to the "seekers" and the skeptics. These people come to me and ask questions, and I give my best answers, my best defenses, and by the time they leave my office, I have convinced myself that *their questions are better than my answers.*[31]

Despite having "a lot of Bible knowledge, Christian background, theological astuteness, and 'pew time,'" many of the Christians whom McLaren counsels lead lives insufficiently distinguishable from those of unchurched people. Counseling such believers leaves him "troubled, wondering, 'Shouldn't the gospel of Jesus Christ make a bigger difference than this? *And does pew time have to result in spiritual pride and inauthenticity?*'"[32] So a desire for authenticity underlies McLaren's search for "a new kind of Christian," an authenticity true to life's complexities, difficulties, and doubts; honest in response to the questions of "seekers" and skeptics; and proven to have transforming power.

Sadly, however, McLaren provides no examples of "the expected vocabulary and formulations" that comprise those "words that generally convey little actual meaning" to which he refers. So whether his concerns on this front merit attention remains a

---

[30] Ibid., xiii.
[31] Ibid. (emphasis added).
[32] Ibid., xiv (emphasis added).

matter of conjecture. Let us nonetheless assume that his concerns are well-founded.[33] Even so, to warrant—as he puts it—*creating a new* kind of Christian, and thus a new kind of *Christianity*, it is not enough that these concerns are well-founded; to warrant *revising* that faith once for all delivered over to the saints, they must be endemic not just to American evangelicalism in the early twenty-first century but also to Christianity itself.

Here it seems helpful to distinguish *revision* from *reform*. As I understand it, *reform* involves *return*; to reform the church is to call her back to the beliefs and practices constitutive of historic Christian orthodoxy, to return her to the faith of the apostles.[34] Of course, understood in this way, reform involves departure as well as return. Returning to the apostolic faith obviously requires departing from those present beliefs and practices that stand at odds with it; if we have wandered away from historic Christian orthodoxy, we return to it only by leaving the ground where we are presently entrenched. So too *revision*, as McLaren seems to envision it, involves *departure*. Like reform, it involves leaving the ground where one is presently entrenched. Rather than returning to the apostolic faith, however, revision repudiates current beliefs and practices in order to enshrine new ones in their place.

True to its postmodern provenance, the revision recommended by McLaren deconstructs present beliefs and practices. In so doing, it does *not* seek to recover the faith of our ancient Christian forebears; instead, it prepares the way for novel beliefs and practices to replace old ones. So revision departs from the pres-

---

[33] And what Christian would quibble with McLaren's desire for greater authenticity within the church? Who among God's people does not resonate with calls for greater integrity, honesty, and godliness within the church?

[34] So, as I understand reform, its supreme example remains the Protestant Reformation of the sixteenth century. For, of course, the Reformers did not seek changes simply for the sake of doing so; rather, the changes they sought were intended to return the church to the apostolic faith. The Reformation, as A. Skevington Wood tells us, "was a reform, not a revolt. Continuity was preserved, so that the Reformers could justifiably claim that what seemed to be the new church was indeed the old church." *Baker's Dictionary of Theology*, ed. Everett F. Harrison, Geoffrey W. Bromiley, and Carl F. H. Henry (Grand Rapids: Baker, 1960), s.v. "Reformation." See *Pocket Dictionary of Theological Terms*, ed. Stanley Grenz, David Guretzki, and Cherith Fee Nordling (Downers Grove, Ill.: InterVarsity, 1999), s.v. "Reformation," according to which Martin Luther, Ulrich Zwingli, and John Calvin "protested against what they perceived as the overall degeneracy of the Roman Church and its departure from . . . the faith of the apostles and early church fathers."

ent not in order to return to the faith of the apostles but rather to carve out a new and distinct faith.[35] Both reform and revision à la McLaren would thus have us depart from modern beliefs and practices; once underway, however, they would chart radically different courses—one ancient, one postmodern.[36]

That the Christianity McLaren seeks amounts to a new and distinct faith follows from his admission that, when he began to extract himself from modern Christianity, "the new way hadn't been created yet." Although he names *modern* Christianity as the incumbent to be defeated, his quest for a new kind of Christian arises from the perceived inadequacy of *all* that has gone before us. "I realize, as I read and reread the Bible," he writes, "that many passages don't fit *any of the theological systems I have inherited or adapted*. . . . My old systems . . . can't seem to hold all the data in the Bible, not to mention the data of my own experience, at least not gracefully."[37] These comments say less about the data than about McLaren himself. For, as he himself writes, "Our interpretations reveal less about God or the Bible than they do about ourselves. They reveal what *we want* to defend, what *we want* to attack, what *we want* to ignore, what *we're unwilling* to question."[38] Now if the apostolic faith counts as one of the options that does not fit the data, then McLaren's new kind of Christian must be *post*-apostolic; so also if that faith does *not* count as an option to

---

[35] McLaren nonetheless describes his view as "orthodox," though he uses that term in what he himself admits is an *un*orthodox way. See Brian D. McLaren, *A Generous Orthodoxy* (Grand Rapids: Zondervan, 2004), 28:

Many will agree: the choice of the word *orthodoxy* in the title [of this book] is a terrible mistake. For most people, *orthodoxy* means right thinking or right opinions, or in other words, "what *we* think," as opposed to "what *they* think." In contrast, orthodoxy in this book may mean something more like "what God knows, some of which we believe a little, some of which they believe a little, and about which we all have a whole lot to learn." Or it may mean "how we search for a kind of truth you can never fully get into your head, so instead you seek to get your head (and heart) into it."

However warm the sentiment expressed by these words seems, they fail to define orthodoxy. And while McLaren is free to use the word *orthodoxy* anyway he chooses, using it in such an unusual way and then insisting that, contrary to appearances, his view is "orthodox" seems somewhat disingenuous—even, one might say, *inauthentic*.

[36] That McLaren parts company with ancient (or *apostolic*) ways of faith is quite clear: "Similarly, to be postmodern . . . is certainly different from being premodern." McLaren, *New Kind of Christian*, 13.

[37] Ibid., xiv (emphasis added).

[38] Ibid., 50 (emphases added).

be considered, then that Christian must be *post*-apostolic. Either way, then, it follows that *both* his new kind of Christian *and* the Christianity that she professes are post-apostolic.[39]

McLaren ostensibly affirms the faith of the apostles. By his lights, the "generous orthodoxy" that he commends to his readers "consistently, unequivocally, and unapologetically upholds and affirms the Apostles' and Nicene Creeds."[40] He thus *appears* to stand within the stream of historic Christian orthodoxy. But this appearance of fidelity to the apostolic faith is belied by McLaren's reading of certain biblical passages, a reading that he sets forth less than 150 pages after the affirmation quoted above.[41] Since I take up this issue below, here I am content simply to reiterate a point made above: *No* reading of Scripture according to which the God of the Old Testament—that is, *God as the Old Testament portrays Him*—is distinct from the God of the New deserves the label "Christian"; the apostolic faith is fundamentally committed to the continuity of the Old and New Testaments, *especially with respect to their portrayals of God.*

Neo—the protagonist of *A New Kind of Christian*—says, "We're talking about *a* new kind of Christian, not *the* new kind or a *better* kind or *the* superior kind, just a new kind."[42] While this points to the novelty of that for which McLaren seeks, it also hints at its transitory nature. On his view, "one must anticipate a time when the new liberating paradigm itself becomes confining and old."[43] This suggests that no "version" of Christianity—*not even that of the apostles themselves*—transcends the particular cultural setting in which it arises. "No model—no matter how resplendent with biblical quotations—can claim to be *the* ultimate Christian worldview," McLaren writes, "because every model is at the least limited by the limitations of the contemporary human mind, not to

---

[39] I take this to constitute a *reductio* of McLaren's view.

[40] McLaren, *Generous Orthodoxy*, 28.

[41] Ibid., 166–71.

[42] McLaren, *New Kind of Christian*, 47.

[43] Ibid., xi. This obviously evokes Thomas Kuhn's discussion of scientific revolutions. See Thomas S. Kuhn, *The Structure of Scientific Revolutions*, 3rd ed. (Chicago: University of Chicago Press, 1996).

mention the 'taste in universes' of that particular age."[44] Like the
faith of any other age, then, the apostolic faith was so shaped by
the culture in which it arose that it counts as only one of many possible versions of Christianity—first *pro tempore* but not *in aeter-
num*. The "orthodoxy" of any age deserves adherence only so long
as that age's "taste in universes" endures. But as culture changes,
so also must the faith.

In short, then, revising the faith involves repudiating not just
those beliefs and practices associated with it in our particular cultural setting but also those beliefs and practices constitutive of the
apostolic faith and in virtue of which Christians of any given era
rightly claim continuity with those of other eras. But in what sense
can a position that repudiates such beliefs and practices be called
Christian?

Here McLaren faces a dilemma: *Either* the authenticity he
seeks can be found in the faith of our ancient Christian forebears
or it cannot. If it can, then we need reform, not revision; if it cannot, then we need not only to cast off the moorings that presently
hold the church in the port of modernity but also to set course
for waters well beyond the coast of Christendom. In other words,
McLaren's attempt to revise the faith goes *either* too far *or* not far
enough. If it remained within the confines of the apostolic faith, it
could safely hug Christendom's coast; and if it gave up the pretense
of being Christian, it could enter the open waters of a pluralistic
sea. But insofar as he seeks to revise the faith without relinquish-
ing his claim to being Christian, the Good Ship McLaren risks
being pounded by the winds of pluralism into oblivion upon the
rocks of truth.[45]

Perhaps McLaren will respond by reiterating his commitment
to Scripture. "I have spent my entire life," he tells us, "learning,
understanding, reappraising, wrestling with, trusting, applying,
and obeying the Bible. . . . I believe it is a gift from God, inspired

---

[44] McLaren, *New Kind of Christian*, 36–37. By "the limitations of the contemporary
human mind," he clearly means "the limitations of the human mind contemporary with
that model," not "the limitations of the human mind contemporary with the writing of this
sentence."

[45] I suspect that, in order to prevent the ship from going down, its captain will be
obliged ultimately to let her loose in open waters.

by God. . . . *My regard for the Bible is higher than ever.*"[46] Even
so, at his hands various biblical texts receive treatment at odds
with this stated commitment; in fact, McLaren reads certain Old
Testament passages in ways that minimize their authority.[47] So,
for instance, "passages in Exodus or Joshua where the God of
love and universal compassion to whom Jesus has introduced me
allegedly commands what today we would call brutality, chauvin-
ism, ethnic cleansing, or holocaust" cause McLaren to cringe.[48]
He therefore interprets such passages in a manner influenced more
by contemporary cultural mores than by the faith of the apostles.

God, he tells us, must dance with those He brought. We miser-
able humans tend toward violence. In the ancient Middle East,
this tendency made survival unlikely for a people inclined to deal
gently with potential enemies. In short, the Jews faced a situation in which violence was the norm; their survival as a people
thus necessitated a willingness to fight. So, McLaren concludes,
"if God is going to enter into a relationship with people, then God
has to work with them as they are in their individual and cultural
moral development. And back in those days, that meant that any
group of people, if they were to survive, had to fight."[49]

Here the point is not far to seek: God only *allegedly* commanded
the Jews to commit these atrocities; God met them where they were,
gradually moving them where He wanted them to be. Thus understood, the passages from Exodus and Joshua that cause McLaren

---

[46] McLaren, *Generous Orthodoxy*, 159.

[47] McLaren deemphasizes Scripture's authority in favor of its usefulness. "When we
let [the Bible] go as a modern answer book, we get to rediscover it for what it really is: an
ancient book of incredible spiritual value for us, a kind of universal and cosmic history, a
book that tells us who we are and what story we find ourselves in so that we know what to
do and how to live." McLaren, *New Kind of Christianity*, 52. On his view, then, the Bible
functions as a useful tool for helping us to orient our lives. But, the question still remains,
does it speak *truly*? For, of course, its usefulness cannot be separated from its truthfulness.
William Abraham is correct that Scripture's primary function involves spiritual transformation; it does *not* function first and foremost as an epistemic criterion. Still, the Bible's
transformative power is inextricably linked to its absolute authority and utter truthfulness.
See William J. Abraham, *Canon and Criterion in Christian Theology* (New York: Oxford
University Press, 1998).

[48] McLaren, *Generous Orthodoxy*, 166 (emphasis added). *Cringe* is the word McLaren
himself uses here: "The more I learn from Jesus, the more I cringe when I read passages
in Exodus or Joshua."

[49] Ibid., 167–68.

to cringe give us a snapshot of Jewish understandings of God at the time of their writing. We should *not*, however, construe such passages as indicating that God actually commanded such atrocities. While ancient Jews may have believed otherwise, the Lord of heaven and earth—the God to whom Jesus Christ introduces us—is far too compassionate and loving ever so to act. "The Bible is a story," McLaren tells us, "and just because it recounts (by standards of accuracy acceptable to its original audience) what happened, that doesn't mean it tells what should always happen or even what should have happened."[50] The Jews committed ethnic cleansing in the *mistaken* belief that God commanded it, a belief that found expression in the sacred text. Given Christ's teaching, however, we see this belief for what it is—a horrible, though perhaps understandable, mistake. Still, as outraged as God must have been at the atrocities committed in His name, He cannot be faulted for nonetheless refusing to forsake His people.[51] Or, at least, so suggests McLaren.

Now, as mentioned above, the apostolic faith emphatically affirms the continuity of the Old and New Testaments. In so doing, it categorically and explicitly rejects *any* suggestion that the portrayal of God in the one stands at odds with the portrayal of God in the other. So while McLaren's interpretation of texts that make him cringe may soothe the postmodern conscience, it does so in defiance of historic Christian orthodoxy. However much one reads and rereads Scripture—however often one seeks to learn, understand, reappraise, wrestle with, trust, apply, and obey the Bible—one who approaches the sacred text with tastes unformed by the apostolic faith will *not* read it Christianly.

As this implies, taking the Bible as one's starting point does *not* guarantee arriving at an authentically Christian destination. For, of course, it matters not just *what* one reads but also *how* one

[50] McLaren, *Generous Orthodoxy*, 167. Although one hears it trumpeted with much fanfare as a great and recent discovery, the view that *Scripture is a story* is simply false and, ironically, ignores the subtleties of literary genre that its advocates allegedly champion.

[51] "If God blesses anyone," we are told, "he must bless the violent and the children of the violent because there is no one else to bless. This is not an excuse, but it is reality. We can't remove ourselves from this equation. There is no other raw material with which for God to work but this ugly, violent, primitive raw material. If God wants a nonviolent and kind humanity in the future, God must enter into heartbreaking relationship with violent and cruel humanity in the meantime" (McLaren, *Generous Orthodoxy*, 168–69).

reads. The struggle between orthodoxy and heresy has *never* been a struggle between those who read Scripture and those who do not. On the contrary, heresy *always* appeals to Scripture to support itself. What distinguishes orthodoxy from heresy, then, is not *whether* each reads the sacred text; rather, what distinguishes them is *how* each reads it. Orthodoxy reads the Bible with tastes thoroughly formed by the apostolic faith; heresy reads it with tastes formed by something other than that faith.[52]

Ironically, then, the reading of Scripture that McLaren puts forward in his quest for an authentic Christianity takes him to a destination not itself authentically Christian. More surprisingly, perhaps, it turns out to be untrue even to his own interpretive principles! About safeguarding authentic Christianity against corruption, Neo says,

> I guess the first protection that comes to mind is the Bible. This is why I think we must always keep coming back to the Bible and doing our best to let it form and unsettle us when necessary. A friend of mine who now pastors back in Jamaica once told me that the parts of the Bible that bother you most are the ones that have the most to teach you. He said that instead of minimizing your discomfort and trying to explain those parts away, you should bear down on those passages and maximize how different they are, really wrestle with those parts. That sort of wrestling is good for us. It would have been nice if American and Jamaican Christians in the eighteenth century had wrestled a little harder with Paul's letter to Philemon, for example, while they were importing my ancestors from Africa and enslaving them on plantations.[53]

Here Neo is right. Our understanding of Christianity needs to be driven by Scripture, not by the mores of the broader culture in which we find ourselves; the tastes that guide our interpretations

---

[52] Here I do *not* charge McLaren—or anyone else—with heresy; I *do*, however, charge those of us who claim Christ to allow the affections that drive our reading of Scripture to be formed by the apostolic faith to which His Spirit calls us—not by the present *Zeitgeist*, whether modern or postmodern.

[53] McLaren, *New Kind of Christian*, 78–79.

of the sacred text need to be distinctively Christian ones. It would indeed be nice if those American and Jamaican Christians to whom he refers had read the Bible in a way less informed by the broader culture in which they found themselves and more informed by the faith of the apostles; and it would also be nice if so-called post-modern Christians did likewise.[54]

McLaren recognizes that one's reading of the sacred text will be significantly influenced by the culture in which one finds oneself, that one tends to read the Bible through the lens of one's culture. "That's why," Neo says, "we need the church itself—not just our little local church or our denomination . . . but more, the whole church, now and through history." So one's reading of Scripture needs to be informed by the community of God's people. But even when that community speaks univocally—about, say, the continuity of the two testaments and the harmony of their portrayals of God—one apparently has license to ignore its counsel if it conflicts with the tastes of the present age, if it makes one cringe.

On what led him to conclude that modern Christianity lacks authenticity, McLaren writes, "My data is my experience—my general experience as a committed Christian and my specific experience as a pastor."[55] Out of that experience arose the crisis of faith in response to which he has sought to revise the faith. For McLaren, revising the faith amounted to a *via media*—a middle way—between two equally untenable alternatives. "At the time [of the crisis of faith]," he tells us, "I could only see two alternatives: (1) continue practicing and promoting a version of Christianity that I had deepening reservations about or (2) leave Christian ministry, and perhaps the Christian path, altogether. There was a third alternative that I hadn't yet considered: learn to be a Christian in a new way."[56]

But of course there is a *fourth* alternative, which McLaren apparently does not consider—namely, to reform, to return to the apostolic faith, to leave modern Christianity in favor not of a

---

[54] I criticize "postmodern Christianity" *not* in order to praise "modern Christianity"—a pox on both their houses; let each of them be accursed! Like the Reformers, I hope to see Christ's people return to a distinctively *apostolic* Christianity.

[55] McLaren, *New Kind of Christian*, xii.

[56] Ibid., ix-x.

brave, new postmodern faith but rather of an ancient one. McLaren
assumes that the way forward is a postmodern one. He fails to
consider the possibility that, paradoxically, the way forward might
involve a reversal of sorts, a move backward, a return. Neo says to
his friend, "You have a modern faith, a faith you developed in your
homeland of modernity. But you're immigrating to a new land, a
postmodern world."[57]

But why *assume* that leaving modernity means moving to
postmodernity, that abandoning a modern faith means embracing
a postmodern one? No doubt the experiences that drive McLaren
away from modern Christianity can be interpreted in ways that
accommodate postmodern tastes. Data can, after all, accommodate
any taste. Just as surely, however, his experience can be interpreted
in ways that accommodate tastes formed by the apostolic faith.

Why, then, favor a postmodern way over an ancient one?
Sadly, McLaren does not say. *Perhaps* he simply prefers the postmodern way; perhaps his taste simply runs in that direction. *Perhaps* ancient assumptions, biases, preferences, and such make
him cringe, though postmodern ones do not. If *that* serves as its
basis, then McLaren's choice of a postmodern Christianity over an
apostolic one rests on precisely the same foundation as Friedrich
Nietzsche's choice to abandon Christianity altogether. Whether
such tastes can lead ultimately to a choice other than Nietzsche's
remains to be seen; in any case, they cannot sustain an authentically Christian reading of Scripture.

---

[57] Ibid., 13.

"EMERGENTS," EVANGELICALS, AND THE IMPORTANCE OF TRUTH: SOME PHILOSOPHICAL AND SPIRITUAL LESSONS

R. SCOTT SMITH

FOR EVANGELICALS LIKE MYSELF, truth is very important, and rightly so.[1] In our masters of arts program in Christian apologetics at Biola, we give reasons why we can know the truth of Christianity, and we think there are many good reasons for believing it to be true. After all, Jesus said that if we abide in His word, we will know the truth, and it will make us free (John 8:31–32).[2] In His high priestly prayer, He asked the Father to sanctify us in the truth; "Your word is truth" (John 17:17). Moreover, Scripture is God-breathed (2 Tim 3:16), and God has spoken in the prophets and His Son (Heb 1:1–2). These are but a few passages that Evangelicals have understood to mean that in Scripture, God has given us His very Word, and His Word is truth, so we have the truth revealed by God in Scripture. Furthermore, the Holy Spirit, the Spirit of truth, will lead and guide us into all the truth (John 16:13), so that we can know the things freely given to us by God (1 Cor 2:12). So,

[1] I even titled one of my books *Truth and the New Kind of Christian: The Emerging Effects of Postmodernism in the Church* (Wheaton, Ill.: Crossway, 2005). Then, and now, I see truth as central to the issues raised by proponents of the emerging church. It is not the only issue, but a very important one.

[2] Unless otherwise noted, all Scripture references and quotes are from the *New American Standard Bible* (Anaheim, Calif.: Foundation Press Publications, for the Lockman Foundation, 1977).

if we apply good principles of interpretation, in reliance upon the Holy Spirit, we can know the proper interpretation of Scripture.

Furthermore, for Evangelicals, God's revealed truth is objective, in the sense that truth is a correspondence, or matching up, of a proposition with how things are in reality, regardless of whether anyone believes that proposition to be true.[3] For instance, that Jesus was crucified, dead, and buried, and rose again on the third day is objectively true; it is the way things are in reality, even if some people do not believe (accept) that proposition to be true.

No wonder, then, it strikes many Evangelicals as strange, even heretical, when today some Christians, many of whom come from evangelical backgrounds, challenge this received view of truth, as well as our ability to know it as it really is. I have in mind some key, higher-profile proponents of the emerging church, particularly those who participate as part of Emergent, as well as those who write in support of such views, such as James K. A. Smith and others.[4] For these individuals, an emphasis upon knowing *objective* truth is utterly misguided.

In a series of posts and responses I had with Alan Hartung, who reviewed my *Truth* book on his blog, this very different understanding became apparent.[5] While in that book I tried to defend a view of truth itself as objective, in terms of what truth *is*, at first

---

[3] And a proposition would not be the same as a sentence. Propositions are the contents that are expressed in declarative sentences, and they are the contents of thoughts. E.g., see J. P. Moreland and William Lane Craig, *Philosophical Foundations for a Christian Worldview* (Downers Grove: InterVarsity Press, 2003), 184.

[4] *Emergent* and the *emerging church* are not identical. According to Mark Driscoll, in his essay, "A Pastoral Perspective on the Emergent Church" (*Criswell Theological Review* 3:2, Spring 2006, 87–93), *Emergent* is the term given to a leadership group that formed out of a Leadership Network conference in the mid-1990s. It shifted focus from reaching a generation to being the church in an emerging postmodern culture. Emergent has included people such as Doug Pagitt, Brian McLaren, Tony Jones, Andrew Jones, Chris Seay, Dan Kimball, and Driscoll. On the other hand, the *emerging church* is a broad umbrella term for a wide range of churches that are engaged in "a missiological conversation about what a faithful church should believe and do to reach Western culture" (90).

Alternatively, Scot McKnight suggests that Emergent is "an official organization in the U.S. and the U.K. . . . . While Emergent is the intellectual and philosophical network of the emerging movement, it is a mistake to narrow all of emerging into Emergent Village." See his "Five Streams of the Emerging Church," http://www.christianitytoday.com/40534, accessed March 27, 2007.

[5] See our exchange at http://www.alanhartung.com/blog/index.php/2006/03/14/truth-and-the-new-kind-of-christian-by-r-scott-smith/, accessed January 10, 2008.

he interpreted my use of "objective" in a very different way, as meaning that none of *us* can be objective. That is, he argued that no one is neutral, disinterested, or unbiased. For Tony Jones, we *cannot* be objective.[6] For him, there simply is no neutral place to stand and interpret anything—any event, any text, etc. We are subjects who are trapped in human skin, and we necessarily have subjective viewpoints. Each of us brings our biases and socially formed perspectives with us when we consider any truth *claims*. So, how could anyone know an objective truth (in my sense) for what it really is, and what it really is about, since we cannot shed these biases, interests, etc.?

Here, then, are two distinct issues: what truth *is*, which is an ontological question; and how we *know* truth, which is an epistemological one. But if we cannot know objective truths as they are, but only from the standpoint of our biases, interests, etc., then inevitably we cannot "transcend" our interpretations of those truths and arrive at knowing the pristine, unadulterated truths of how reality actually is. Though one can maintain that there are objective truths (e.g., that there is a God who created the universe), in effect they *become* what we interpret them to be. In this case, the epistemology drives the ontology. But that view runs contrary to the evangelical view that in Scripture God has revealed objective truth and that we can know it as such (i.e., we can have the proper interpretation of Scripture and even know what the authors, even God, had in mind). Moreover, our *knowing* such truths does nothing *to* them; the epistemology does not drive the ontology.

So, there can be philosophical reasons raised against the traditional evangelical view that we can know truth as it really is. But various proponents of the emerging church also have offered other, very influential explanations of why Evangelicals tend to adopt such a view of truth. Perhaps the foremost person is Brian McLaren, who offers more sociological and ethical reasons, drawn from his understanding of how "modernity" has influenced not only broader culture, but also the church. McLaren and others suggest that if Evangelicals have the truth, why then are so many

---

[6] E.g., see his *Postmodern Youth Ministry* (Grand Rapids: Zondervan, for Youth Specialties, 2001), 74 ("no one . . . objectively approaches a text").

living hypocritically? Moreover, why are they often so adverse
to their own people having doubts about their faith? McLaren, as
well as others, suggest that it is due to the influence of modernity
that Evangelicals have embraced their views about truth, but that
means perhaps we should rethink them in light of our living now
in more postmodern times.

In essence, then, there are at least two broad kinds of reasons
that we will consider, which are offered by these proponents of the
emerging church, that as Christians we should change our concept
of truth. One reason is philosophical and the other is more sociological and ethical. What then should Evangelicals conclude from
these very different points of view? And what should emerging
Christians who are inclined toward these proponents' standpoints
make of all the discussion going on? To help answer these questions will require that we look at these reasons. But first, I will try
to explain their view of truth along with our abilities to know it,
starting with their sociological/ethical reasons and then their more
philosophical one(s). Second, I will assess one main philosophical issue they raise in support of their contention that we need to
change our concept of truth.[7]

I believe there also is a third kind of issue at work here, one
that I think surfaces spiritual implications of this philosophical
view. Moreover, as we unpack this issue, we will be able to see
that it has implications not only for emerging Christians but also
Evangelicals. It involves the relationship of our hearts and minds
to the Lord. To examine this issue, we will need to dive into Scripture, to try to see the Lord's heart (and mind) on this topic. I think
the issues are far deeper than some of the very good insights some
of these emerging church proponents have brought to the surface.
In turn, this study will help highlight why truth is so important, but

---

[7] Due to the limits and focus of this essay, I am not going to address in any detail a
tendency I see in some leaders (e.g., James K. A. Smith, Nancey Murphy, and Tony Jones)
toward physicalism. But if creation is physical, and if we are basically physical beings,
without souls as a substance, then truth, and our concept thereof, most likely will need to
change too. For what would a concept of truth be, if it must, in the end, be physical? And if
creation is physical, then what would truth itself be? I am not suggesting that there might
not be some answers that someone like Nancey Murphy might make, but I do think that
truth, and our concept thereof, most likely will be forced to change. See also note 48 for
some more details and another source to consider.

also why it is something that must not merely be assented to by the mind, but embraced by the truly humble heart before God.

AN "EMERGENT" VIEW OF TRUTH

So far, in describing this set of views, I have written rather broadly. But as we attempt to describe this overall "view," it immediately becomes difficult, in that I need to try to define more clearly whose views I have in mind. For instance, Scot McKnight distinguishes three categories of emerging Christians.[8] First, there are those who are ministering *to* postmoderns, to rescue them from relativism. Second, there are others who minister *with* postmoderns, in that they accept postmodernity as the reality of present-day life, "into which we are called to proclaim and live out the gospel."[9] According to him, "the vast majority of emerging Christians and churches" fit into these two categories; that is, "they don't deny truth, they don't deny that Jesus Christ is truth, and they don't deny that the Bible is truth."[10] But the third category is the one in which various Christians "minister *as* postmoderns. That is, they embrace the idea that we cannot know absolute truth, or, at least, that we cannot know truth absolutely."[11] These Christians also speak of the "importance of social location in shaping one's view of truth."[12]

Alternatively, Mark Driscoll describes three types of emerging Christians.[13] The first are the "relevants," who are conservative Evangelicals who want to update worship and preaching styles and address church structures, rather than reshape theology. Second are the "reconstructionists," who generally are theologically evangelical. Dissatisfied with seeker, contemporary, and purpose forms of churches, they emphasize life transformation of Christians. Third are the "revisionists," who are theologically liberal and criticize evangelical doctrines in terms of appropriateness

---

[8] McKnight, "Five Streams of the Emerging Church," 3.
[9] Ibid.
[10] Ibid.
[11] Ibid.
[12] Ibid.
[13] Driscoll, "A Pastoral Perspective on the Emergent Church," 89–90.

for the emerging postmodern world. For them, core doctrines of
Christianity are open to reconsideration, even if their formulations
were developed at major councils or the Reformation.

In this essay, then, my concern is not with either of McKnight's
or Driscoll's first two categories. Rather, I am looking to examine
those leaders who would be the ones ministering *as* postmoderns,
who largely have accepted these core philosophical positions, and
who (thereby?) seem to consider doctrines to be open for reconsideration. They are the ones who, as McKnight says, attract the
most attention, often since they are the ones writing and speaking
the most on these topics. In need of a term, I choose *Emergent*,
not because it necessarily is a perfect fit for everyone who is part
of that leadership group, but because many such leaders and advocates (e.g., Pagitt, McLaren, Jones, etc.) are part of that group. So,
I also will use *Emergents* hereafter to refer to people who hold this
Emergent view.

SOCIOLOGICAL-ETHICAL REASONS

McLaren addresses the more practical influences of modernity
upon the church in several places.[14] Just as in modernity Western
cultures sought to conquer and control, whether that be through
imperialistic efforts, technology, or the attempt to subjugate every
aspect of life under science's dominion, so the church has tended
to adopt similar attitudes and even terminology. In evangelism,
he says we often have tended to reduce the gospel message to a
simple tract, in which the whole message has been packaged as

---

[14] "Modernity" might be characterized, roughly, as the period from the 1660s (the Enlightenment) through perhaps 1945 (the end of WWII), though its influences are being
experienced even today. Modernity has philosophical, scientific, ethical, sociological, and
other dimensions. While we can glean various values and attitudes from McLaren's descriptions that I have included here, others might be the optimism and confidence in human
reason, apart from revelation, to know universal truths; and the goodness of knowledge, in
particular that of science, which would be used (supposedly) for the betterment of humankind. But one reason for suggesting WWII's termination as an ending date for modernity
is that it marks two major events that undermined peoples' confidence in the goodness of
science. One was revelation of the Nazi death camps and their use of scientific experiments
upon Jews and other people. The other was the use of the atom bomb. Now science could
be used, even under the guise of experiments for the supposed good of people, as an instrument of death, oppression, and gross evil. The confidence in the goodness and inevitable
progress of science started to give way to the more postmodern attitude of suspicion.

simple laws and steps.[15] Just as science supposedly has given us the absolute truth about the realm of nature and physical laws, so we have distilled and packaged the essential, absolute spiritual truths. But if so, where is any room for someone to discuss those laws with us? They are presented as absolute truths, so in witnessing, someone is left either with simply accepting or rejecting them, with no room for discussion. This mind-set also treats peoples' questions, which may be rooted in profoundly difficult life experiences, as being subject to easy, simple answers.

McLaren also thinks we tend to view evangelism as encounters that should try to convert the person by winning an argument, without really valuing a genuine friendship. Thus the methodology is coercive, not loving. Moreover, it is as though rational acceptance of the truths as presented is all that is needed for the person to become a follower of Jesus. So, Christianity tends to be treated as a rigid belief system that must be rationally accepted, instead of a unique, joyful way of living, loving, and serving.[16]

Accordingly, apologetics should be defensive, which implies that there is a war going on, so we tend to not pursue a friendship with people, whether or not they ever become His disciples.[17] It also implies that we become defensive. That is, we expect that apologetically we should give irrefutable arguments designed to win a debate. But that expectation fosters a position from which we must make our case, provide evidence, all of which are to lead up to the verdict that Christianity is absolutely true.[18] But in addition to truth, postmodern people want to see that the followers of a particular religion are good and authentic. They have seen too many hypocritical leaders, whether religious, political, or other. So when we preach that God loves people, postmoderns want to see that our lives embody that message. Instead, according to McLaren, what they often see is that Christians are angry, reacting

[15] Brian McLaren, *More Ready Than You Realize* (Grand Rapids: Zondervan, 2002), 25. Also, per Tony Jones, this is "a natural outgrowth of foundationalism; that is, foundationalism begets reductionism," from private e-mail correspondence, June 22, 2004.

[16] Ibid., 41–42.

[17] Ibid., 48.

[18] Ibid., 148.

against pressures and challenges posed by those who disagree with them.[19]

Furthermore, McLaren thinks that Christianity itself has come to be seen as mechanistic and deterministic.[20] In modernity, people have tried to categorize everything into systematic, tidy categories by analyzing things down to their constitutive elements. Christians have treated God similarly, he thinks. By thinking we can convey the whole truth of the gospel in simple laws, and that we can understand our discipleship to Jesus similarly, we tend to remove God's mysteriousness. We lose our sense of wonder and awe at who God is, as well as the joy and freedom in living in a vital relationship with Him.[21]

Modernity's influences also have tended to leave Evangelicals with a view of God as controlling, who requires utter certainty in our intellectual assent to doctrinal truths. If we have doubts, then there is something wrong with us, which we should confess. The Christian life is a belief system, a transmission of information,[22] which we should intellectually accept fully. But if we have doubts and struggles, that is a reflection upon our lack of faith or some other sin. For McLaren, the result of treating Christianity as a "belief system" that focuses upon the transmission of certain, indubitable truths found in Scripture, is that we ought to be able to analyze and systematize all truths into clear-cut categories. Thus, modern Christians expect us to have systematic theologies, which impose an analytical outline on the Bible, to mine it for all absolute truths.

McLaren thinks modernity's influence on the church has been so great that we have tended to become arrogant, rigid, defensive, and legalistic. We have tended to become defensive when challenged, to keep our beliefs pure, safe, and sanitized, being afraid of heresy and wrong beliefs. That arrogance in thinking that our

---

[19] Ibid., 158.

[20] Ibid., 116. See also *The Story We Find Ourselves In* (San Francisco: Jossey-Bass, 2003), 83, where Neo and Kerry discuss a modern view of God as controlling and manipulative. See also the passage in *More Ready*, 63–64, where McLaren discusses modern Christians' view of God as being uptight, rigid, and controlling.

[21] McLaren, *More Ready*, 148.

[22] Ibid., 167.

system of belief is utterly true has had the effect that we do not tend to love others if they do not believe our message.

But for him, there are more than just sociological and ethical implications of modernity's influences, which impact his view that we need to find a new way of being Christians in postmodern times. There also are some more philosophical implications that he hints at.[23] But others have given fuller exposition to those views, so here I will consider, for sake of space, those of two major authors in the field, James K. A. Smith and Nancey Murphy.

PHILOSOPHICAL REASONS

In my earlier writings, including my contributions to *Christianity and the Postmodern Turn* and my *Truth* book, I had understood McLaren and Christians who embrace more postmodern philosophical views as advocating that we are somehow "inside" language and cannot escape those limitations to know the reality as it is. James K. A. Smith (hereafter Jamie), however, replied in the *Postmodern Turn*, where he helpfully pointed out that I understood them to mean that we are somehow "imprisoned in language—that there is a world 'out there,' but it is like a noumenal realm we can never reach, because we are confined by the strictures of language that come 'between' us and the world."[24] On that interpretation, I concluded that we have to "construct" the world according to our use of our community's language. But he argues that my criticisms are misguided because I have a "restrictive understanding of language."[25] Rather, language is part of the world, just as we, the language users, are. Moreover, the world we inhabit is "always already *interpreted* within a framework of signs or a semiotic system."[26] But these points do not entail the "kind of stilted Kantianism that Scott paints."[27]

Instead, Jamie argues that interpretation is inevitable, even to experience reality, but that does not mean it is something we must

---

[23] I discuss some of these in *Truth and the New Kind of Christian*, 59–65.

[24] James K. A. Smith, "Who's Afraid of Postmodernism? A Response to the 'Biola School,'" in *Christianity and the Postmodern Turn*, ed. Myron B. Penner (Grand Rapids: Brazos Press, 2005), 221.

[25] Ibid., 222.

[26] Ibid. (emphasis in original).

[27] Ibid.

overcome. Modern views tried to get us to believe that we can (and should) transcend our particularity, as well as our bodies and our finitude, to gain a pure, immediate gaze into reality itself, from a God's-eye viewpoint. But these views are mistaken, he suggests. First, by trying to escape from the "prison" of our bodies, we betray the fact that we are created, embodied beings. But as creatures, our finitude is one aspect of God's good, creative work, and even in eternity, we still will be finite and embodied.[28]

Second, Jamie rejects the view that reality can be immediately and directly present before us in conscious awareness. We are finite, embodied, and historically situated creatures; thus, we cannot shed these mediating influences and somehow "arrive" directly to things in themselves (i.e., in an unmediated way).[29] Language is a key mediating influence, even of our experience of things themselves. Hence, interpretation is inevitable, since all our knowledge, even experience, is mediated.

Moreover, for him, "as finite human beings we never have (nor ever will have) access to the thoughts of another as immediately present. . . . Instead, I always hear another or read a text from 'where I am,' translating the other's discourse into where I am. . . . To use a more popular metaphor, I always read a text or see the world through the lens of an interpretive tradition from which I cannot extricate myself for it is part of what it means to be human."[30] Because human beings do not share identical languages, vocabularies, or thoughts, "interpretation is inescapable."[31]

Thus, even when we come to "clear" passages of Scripture, and "someone promises to deliver 'the Scriptures alone,' he or she has always already delivered an interpretation that is carried out within an interpretive tradition."[32] Even the New Testament books are "interpretations of a person and an event."[33] In reference

---

[28] See James K. A. Smith, *The Fall of Interpretation* (Downers Grove, Ill.: InterVarsity Press, 2000), 144.

[29] James K. A. Smith, *Who's Afraid of Postmodernism? Taking Derrida, Lyotard, and Foucault to Church* (Grand Rapids: Baker Academic, 2006), 42.

[30] Smith, *The Fall of Interpretation*, 150.

[31] Ibid., 150–51.

[32] Ibid., 43.

[33] Ibid.

to Abraham Kuyper, Jamie suggests our "interpretive glasses are 'cemented to our face.'"[34]

Jamie also follows Derrida when he argues that "there is nothing outside the text," i.e., "we can't get beyond or behind the text to a referent (or signified) that is outside language."[35] We never get beyond interpretation to an immediate experience of things themselves. Even more importantly, Jamie thinks Derrida means that "there is no reality that is not always interpreted through the mediating lens of language . . . everything is a text."[36] That is, "everything must be interpreted in order to be experienced."[37]

That does not mean that for Jamie there are not real objects in a real, material reality that we all can experience. Still, those experiences have to be interpreted. Consider the "material reality" in the crucifixion. Jamie says that "not everyone sees what the centurion sees. Of course, they all see and encounter the same material realities—crosses, bodies, and eventually corpses—but these material phenomena are texts that need to be interpreted."[38] Even so, he claims that what these various people see "is not immediately clear. So the very fact that both the centurion and the chief priests are confronted by the same phenomena and yet 'see' something very different would seem to demonstrate Derrida's point: the very experience of the things themselves is a matter of interpretation."[39]

Nancey Murphy takes a very similar position. For her, there is a real world, but our experience of it is always theory-laden.[40] For instance, in philosophy of science, there are no data that are simply given; rather, all "facts" are made "by means of their interpretation" in light of other theoretical assumptions.[41] Like Jamie, we do not have direct access "into the nature of reality, putting

[34] Ibid., 53.

[35] Smith, *Who's Afraid of Postmodernism?*, 38.

[36] Ibid., 39. See also his "Who's Afraid of Postmodernism? A Response to the 'Biola School,'" 225.

[37] Smith, *Who's Afraid of Postmodernism?* 39.

[38] Ibid., 49.

[39] Smith, "Who's Afraid of Postmodernism? A Response to the 'Biola School,'" 218.

[40] Nancey Murphy, *Beyond Liberalism & Fundamentalism: How Modern and Postmodern Philosophy Set the Theological Agenda*, Rockwell Lecture Series, ed. Werner H. Kelber (Harrisburg, Penn.: Trinity Press International, 1996), 92.

[41] Nancey Murphy, *Anglo-American Postmodernity* (Boulder, Colo.: Westview Press, 1997), 27.

us in a position to compare reality itself with our favored way of conceiving and talking about it."[42]

McLaren, as well as Tony Jones, also has embraced this position.[43] For McLaren, there is no neutral place to stand to interpret anything. As subjects, we all have limited perspectives.[44] We cannot "shed" or "escape" our perspectives, backgrounds, and historically situated, conditioned experiences; no one is purely objective, or neutral.[45] We also cannot know absolute, certain truths. Instead, all truth is contextual, and all meanings find their place within a story and community.[46] I shared Jamie's criticisms of my views with McLaren, to which he replied that he resonated deeply with Jamie's view that everything is interpretation.[47]

There are other philosophical views we could consider, such as a tendency I see in some leaders toward physicalism in anthropology (i.e., roughly, the view that human beings are not a unity of body and soul, but that we are, essentially, bodies, without souls as a substance). I think there are major issues that surface from that position alone.[48] However, for space considerations, as we turn to assessment, I am going to focus upon just the view that everything is interpretation.

ASSESSING THE EMERGENT VIEW
OF TRUTH PHILOSOPHICALLY

On this view, we must keep in mind that there is a real world;

---

[42] Ibid., 127.

[43] In his *Postmodern Youth Ministry,* Jones also supports this view by drawing upon Murphy (under whom he studied at Fuller), W. V. O. Quine, and Alasdair MacIntyre.

[44] McLaren, *More Ready*, 76.

[45] Ibid., 94.

[46] Brian McLaren, *A New Kind of Christian* (San Francisco: Jossey-Bass, 2001), 106.

[47] E-mail correspondence from Brian McLaren to myself, July 17, 2006.

[48] I have detailed much of my concerns with the apparent "Christian materialism" of Jamie Smith, as well as the nonreductive physicalism of Murphy, in my "Where Is the Emerging Church Heading?" presentation at the Evangelical Theological Society annual meeting, Nov. 2007, in San Diego, Calif. For instance, I raise concerns over several core doctrines that would seem to need to be reinterpreted, such as the nature of sin, and accordingly, the nature of Christ's work on the cross, as well as the doctrine of the eternal destiny of believers and unbelievers. I argue that by following physicalism, we also would need to reconsider the doctrine of the incarnation of the Son of God, and even the doctrine of eternal life for all who trust Christ as Savior.

no author in this discussion that I have read denies that that is so. Yet, we are told, our access to it always is conceptualized or interpreted; to even *have* an experience requires conceptualization. Clearly there is some truth implied by this view, for what we experience in the real world needs to be conceptualized if it is to become knowledge. Factual knowledge, or knowledge of reality, involves justified true beliefs, and beliefs involve concepts. Without concepts, we would not have such knowledge. Furthermore, we are subjects who are influenced by a number of factors, including our biases, historical location, and so forth. But the key question will be if nonetheless we can know reality directly, immediately. That is the key position that these authors deny.

Suppose we look at a red delicious apple. What is it we see? One thing is clear: on this view, we cannot see the apple directly, but we surely see something. Suppose, then, that we see its round shape. But following this view consistently, the reply then can be made that we cannot see *that* directly. If so, then what are we seeing? If the answer is a red color, then the same reply can be made again. Suppose instead we see a stem. Still, the same problem represents itself all over again, for we cannot see the stem directly. For that matter, regardless of which quality we experience, the same problem arises. Now we are in a position to see a key problem with this view: any quality (not to mention wholes—objects, persons, etc.) whatsoever we try to experience always eludes our abilities to experience and know. In the end, there is nothing left we can experience. In effect, the real world (whatever that really is) vanishes, becoming inaccessible to us altogether.

If so, how is it possible for us to begin to form concepts? Early on, I taught my daughter several concepts, such as "apples." I would show her many pictures of different kinds of apples, as well as real ones in our refrigerator or the grocery store. Here is what I think happened: she was able to observe these apples for what they are, and from many noticings and comparisons between what she noticed she was able to form the concept of an apple. She also could hear me utter the word "apple" as I pointed to these various examples and learn to associate that word with the apples themselves and even the concept she formed. We went together to the store one night when she still was pretty young and there were some new kinds of apples from Australia on display, ones even I had never seen before, though I had worked for over five years in the grocery business. She had no problem identifying them as apples. How? I think she could see the new ones for what they are, compare them with her concept of what an apple is, and see these new ones *as* apples.

Now let us take a different case: how could she learn to correct her concept of an apple if, for instance, she saw a small red ball and thought it was an apple? I could tell her that no, it is a ball, and then she could look at it, see it for what it is, and then compare what is represented in her experience with her other noticings, and even with her concept of an apple, and adjust her concept accordingly.

Notice, however, that all this would be impossible if any experience already is conceptualized. Actually, our situation seems even worse, for how could we ever get started to form our concepts, much less correct them, if all our experiences already come conceptualized?

If the real world in effect "disappears" from us, so that we cannot experience or know it at all, then theologically we are left with a very problematic position. For now all doctrines, even the most central ones of Christianity, must be the result of only our interpretations. That is, *all* our theological beliefs (that there is only one God; that He has spoken; that Jesus is God incarnate; that He arose bodily from the dead; etc.) must be our constructs, but as far as their having anything to do with reality, we could not know. Nor could we know Jesus as He is, and we thereby lose any hope of knowing the authentic Jesus. But if we cannot know Him veridically, nor any truths about Him, then how could we become like Him? We thereby lose any hope of being authentic Christians, which is one of the central (and well-taken) admonitions of the proponents of the emerging church.

But this view is surely false, and not just for reasons I have given thus far. Consider Saul of Tarsus, whose conceptual scheme was that of a "Pharisee of Pharisees." When Jesus appeared to him on the Damascus road, who, or what, did he experience? If all experience is a conceptualization, then Saul could not have experienced Jesus Himself directly. Moreover, he could not have experienced Him *as* Lord; that concept was not even possible in his conceptual scheme. But the text indicates that Saul was radically, even instantly, changed from a persecutor into a Christ follower, and the best explanation for that is what he claimed—that Jesus Himself appeared directly to him. This strongly suggests that our God can reveal truth directly to us.

Other Scriptures also seem to indicate this, such as Ps 19:8b (the word of God enlightens the eyes), and Heb 4:12 (the word of God is sharper than any two-edged sword, and it is able to judge all our thoughts and intentions). In 1 Samuel 16, God sends Samuel to anoint a new king in place of Saul. When Samuel sees the eldest son, Eliab, he thinks that surely he will be God's anointed. But the Lord intervenes and teaches Samuel a valuable lesson: "Do not look at his appearance or his stature, because I have rejected him. Man does not see what the LORD sees, for man sees what is visible, but the LORD sees the heart" (v. 7 HCSB). Then God makes His decisions known regarding all of David's other brothers as Samuel has to listen to God's voice, and finally God reveals His anointed is David. But Samuel had a very different conception of who would be God's choice, and God needed to (and could) make His choices clearly known to Samuel. But how could that be if Samuel could not know what God's choices were in themselves but only his conceptualizations of them? Moreover, if we cannot experience reality directly, despite God's efforts, then this implies that God is limited and lacks the ability to enable us to know truth as it really is.

Before moving on, let me suggest a further, significant implication of this philosophical view. As I have argued, if we cannot know anything as it truly is, or anyone as that person truly is (including God), then a major implication is that reality (including God) becomes unknowable, being inaccessible to us *altogether*. But that is *not* how reality presents itself to us; nor is it how persons, even God, present themselves to us. We do not live in a world that has no apples, rocks, rivers, machines, people, thoughts, or God. Nor does it seem that we could live in such a world; even we would be inaccessible to ourselves, and to others. Suppose that this core epistemological principle is correct. Then somehow, someway, those things must be *made* to be what they are, which is similar to what I argued before in my Ashgate book. All these things, and even God, must be *made* into how we experience them. In regards to God, plainly that would be an idolatrous position to take. I will suggest below that the most likely candidate for who (or what) does this making would be us.

Thus, there are serious problems with a core philosophical contention of this Emergent view, that everything is interpretation. But now let us move on to consider what I think is a further set of issues. Here I will address some spiritual implications of this view. Then, in the following section, I will see what implications there might be for Evangelicals.

SOME SPIRITUAL IMPLICATIONS FOR "EMERGENTS" ABOUT THE HEART-MIND CONNECTION

If we believe we have access to reality only through our interpretations, such that all access requires interpretation, I am afraid that we cannot avoid silencing God's Spirit. Why? We will be unable to access God's intended meaning in His revelation, whether in Scripture, creation, or the witness of the Spirit in our lives. Put differently, if we cannot know reality directly, as it truly is, then we cannot access His self-disclosure directly, but only as we interpret it. When we also take into account the depravity of every human heart, even our own, and the desire to overthrow God's authority over our lives, we can see that we make ourselves susceptible to the suggestion the serpent whispered to Eve: "You will be like God." From the garden story, we will see that our hearts and minds were disconnected from God and separated instead to Satan. We also will be able to see that God needed to send His Son, for He is fully connected to the Father's heart and mind. Furthermore, as a human being, Jesus was connected to us in our hopelessness in order to break this disconnect of our hearts and minds from God.

Let me start with Jesus, to focus on the intimate relationship between the Father and the Son, even in terms of the mind of Christ. In Jesus we see a deep unity with the Father, and not just in purpose. Rather, there is the deep love relationship between the Father and the Son, which shows their strong connection of both heart and mind. The Son is fully connected to the Father's will, and He knows the beauty and fulfillment of what it is to have the Father's love. We see that intimate relationship throughout the Gospels, but especially in John 17, where Jesus' intimacy with and devotion to the Father are showcased for us to observe. His heart is set on doing the Father's will, thereby glorifying the Father (vv. 1–4), whom He knows so intimately that He would call Him Abba, Daddy (Mark 14:36). There is a deep relationship of love, trust, intimacy, and obedience, for Jesus knows that the Father's will is indeed completely pure, loving, holy, and good. Thus, when the Father asks Him to lay down His life, there is no fear of obeying the Father, even though Jesus fully knows the horrors and agony that await Him. Importantly, then, *the mind of Christ is not merely a set of all true beliefs; rather, it is defined by His love for the Father.*

But in stark contrast, consider the hearts and minds of the rest of human beings. Fundamentally, due to the fall, our hearts and minds have been severed from God and are bent on usurping Him by worshiping ourselves. To help us see that, I will give a brief meditation on Gen 3:1–13, along with some connections to a few other passages. There, Satan denies that Adam and Eve will die if they eat from the tree of the knowledge of good and evil, thereby claiming that God lied to them. Moreover, he accuses God of a will to power and of withholding something good from them: "In fact, God knows that when you eat it your eyes will be opened and *you will be like God*, knowing good and evil" (v. 5 HCSB, emphasis mine). God cannot be trusted and does not want them to rival Him. They would "know" (i.e., define, choose) good and evil, independently of God. In essence, they could become their own gods.

It seems that Eve was mesmerized (1 Tim 2:14 tells us that she was deceived), but flat out, Adam was disobedient by eating. Yet both were united in their will to become powerful over God Almighty by escaping the death sentence (2:17) and diminishing His absolute love. God did not truly love them absolutely, they thought, for He was withholding something good from them, and they could act in such a way as not to suffer God's stated consequences. Interestingly, they did not even consider asking God about the serpent's claims.

God gave them opportunity to choose freely to obey unto life, to enjoy a closer relationship with Him. Instead, they chose to listen to deception and let Satan provide a definition of God and what He is like. They sold their souls for a moment of perspective (of being like God) from their own thoughts. The key point of contention was to choose death or life, even in terms of who would be God.

They chose to silence God's Spirit by refusing to listen to and obey God, instead giving heed to the serpent's appeal and the desires of their own hearts. But in that, they became afraid of God's voice and of being seen by Him, out of fear of His being able to override their desires for power and authority. Like Lucifer, they fell due to their arrogance and attempt to usurp God.

Thus, the core of sin is the attitude and willful choice to usurp God and worship a god of our own making, even ourselves. These attitudes are replete throughout Scripture. For instance, the chief priests delivered Jesus up out of envy (Mark 15:10). Moreover, along with the scribes and elders, they had decided to reject and kill Him, thus prompting His warning and declaration that He knew their intentions (Mark 12:1–12). In that parable of the vine-growers, Jesus exposes their hearts as intent on usurping the inheritance of the son of the owner, even by killing him (v. 7). Like Adam and Eve, the chief priests, scribes, and elders exhibit the same willful heart to usurp God by grabbing for power and control, by rejecting Jesus, whose words and miracles clearly attested to His being the

Son of God (cp. v. 29, where Jesus exposes their duplicitous hearts by their unwillingness to admit that John clearly was a prophet; so too they were unwilling to acknowledge the clear witness of His identity).

The human heart, therefore, is deeply rebellious, intent on idolatrous self-worship. So God, being perfectly holy and just, had to remove Adam and Eve from His presence in the garden. Likewise, our sins have separated us from God. There is nothing we can do to control God or that will suffice for our salvation. Our hearts and minds, which originally were connected to God's heart and mind, were disconnected from Him and instead separated unto Satan.

With that backdrop in place, we can see something very important for our present purposes.[49] That is, we can see that God needed to send His Son, who is fully connected to the Father's heart and mind, and yet who also, as a human, was connected to us in our hopelessness, in order to break this disconnect of our hearts and minds from God. We can see the stark contrast between Adam and Eve on the one hand and, on the other, the last Adam, Jesus, in a few vignettes in His life, in addition to His prayer in John 17. In Gethsemane, Jesus felt the coming horror of bearing the sins of the world, yet He also so intimately knew the reality, beauty, and fulfillment of the Father's love that He could embrace the Father as Abba. So, unlike Adam and Eve, He prayed and entrusted Himself and submitted to the Father, even to die on a cross. Not only that, He prayed and endured all that the Father had ordained for Him to accomplish, whereas His disciples caved in to temptation not to be watchful and pray, and due to the weakness of their flesh, abandoned Him.

At Golgotha, He was so intent on abiding in the Father's love that even after He had endured the agony of atoning for sin, He still fulfilled even one last Scripture (John 19:28, where He said, "I'm thirsty"). Indeed, down to the last details, He obeyed fully.

[49] Not only this, but we also can see that Jesus' penal substitutionary atonement on the cross was necessary if God were to redeem humans, for He is perfectly holy, and our hearts are deeply disconnected from God and intent on usurping Him. This has important implications for any proponents of the emerging church who might deny, or sell short, the importance of this view of His sacrifice.

He also fulfilled His stated purpose for coming to earth: "For even the Son of Man did not come to be served, but to serve, and to give His life a ransom for many" (Mark 10:45). So when He was crucified, and the rulers and soldiers mocked Him, sarcastically calling on Him to save Himself, they did not understand that no one had taken His life from Him; instead, He laid it down on His own initiative (John 10:18). Why? Because of the Father's deep love for us, He sent His Son, who would atone for our sins and break the disconnect of our hearts and minds from God and supersede all our efforts at our control.

The crucifixion thus presents a stark contrast to the garden of Eden experience. There Adam and Eve gave in to sin, thereby corrupting themselves and the rest of humanity out of a desire to replace God. Unwittingly, they became like their father, the devil, whose heart and mind are bent on usurping God's throne.[50] But unlike Adam, Jesus does not usurp the Father's rightful authority. Instead, He humbles Himself and fully obeys the Father, thereby fulfilling all the righteous requirements of God's holiness and providing the necessary sacrifice, so that we could be reconciled to God.

Jesus walked and lived upon earth with human abilities to see and hear, yet with a heart and mind fully connected and attuned to the Father's will. As a man it seems He could know reality directly, as it truly is, and not simply due to His divinity. To suggest otherwise, that as a man He could not know reality directly, yet as God He could, would strongly imply that Jesus would have experienced a radical, unlivable disconnect in His own person. For that reason, I do not think this position is an option. In that light, as well as others we have surfaced above, it seems that the view that "everything is interpretation" is mistaken.

Now we can start to explore some further connections, even in regards to our own hearts and minds. A crucial issue presents itself. If we *desire* (from the heart) to interpret God by our limita-

---

[50] It is no wonder then that in John 8:44 Jesus would tell the Pharisees that they were of their father the devil, for they had their desires set on his, to murder and to lie, for there is no truth in him. Just like him, we, too, set our hearts on usurping God's throne, and a chief example is that of the rulers' killing of His Son.

tions, then it surely seems that we will create a god who, in reality, is no god at all. For if everything is interpretation, then we cannot know God as He truly is; somehow, it seems God would have to be *made* into what He is.

Therefore, this discussion suggests a crucial question: What is in our hearts? Are we willing to humble ourselves and really seek to know God? If so, He will be found, like He spoke through Jeremiah (29:12–14). Similarly, He promised to disclose Himself to those who love Him (John 14:21), and promised that He would come, dine, and manifest Himself to the one who hears His voice and opens the door to Him (Rev 3:20).

We need humble hearts for a number of reasons, but most of all because otherwise we will keep living out of our fallenness, with hearts bent on usurping God's throne. And it is nothing that we can do for ourselves; in light of the utter desperation of our heart's condition (see Jer 15:9–10), and how our hearts and minds have been severed from God's, we are utterly dependent upon God to reconcile us to Himself through Christ, thereby enabling us to have renewed hearts and minds. But just because we may be justified before God, it does not follow that we are thereby walking by that new heart and renewed mind under the Spirit's direction and power. As is abundantly clear, we still can be seduced and live in our flesh, according to the old Adamic desire to control and usurp God's throne. In that case, it is crucial that we realize that it is not sufficient for one to be a true follower of Christ simply to have knowledge of truth. Demons know the truth about God but reject it as rebels; likewise, the Pharisees had a clear witness of the truth of who Jesus is yet rejected it. So only those who humbly submit to the Lord—in all their thoughts and ways and with all their hearts—can stand in the place of truth.

With that in mind, we can see that the art of persuasion predominately by way of reason is not the essence of truth, unless the persuasion comes by way of His infilling of the entirety of our being—all our hearts, souls, minds, and strength. Anything less is prone to deception, due to the weakness of our thoughts and our flesh and the deceptiveness of the devil. For the devil will seek to have us welcome indirectly his suggestions, which will enforce our own assumptions, thereby attempting to bind us into their accuracy as being even the very word of God. And this appeals to us with our hearts' fallen condition. Therefore, it is crucial that we love the Lord with all our hearts, souls, minds, and strength, lest we be like Solomon who, although he was granted wisdom by God unlike anyone else, still had, at best, half a heart, for we see early on an example of a pattern that would mark his life: he married foreign women who eventually would turn his heart away to their gods. He stands in marked contrast to David, who, despite his great sin and lack in parental disciplinary skills, still was a man after God's own heart. David would repent after being confronted with his sin (e.g., 2 Sam 12:13 and 24:10), but not Solomon, who did not repent after God confronted him with his great sin (1 Kgs 11).

Importantly, then, there is a danger for all of us, including the proponents of the Emergent view as I have defined it above. Still, we are told by authors, such as Merold Westphal, that our inability to access truth and reality as they are should lead us to a humility of knowledge, as opposed to the modern pretensions to gain absolute certainty and a gaze directly into the nature of reality.[51] Wouldn't that kind of humility help mitigate this danger?[52] For sure, Westphal and Jamie Smith are right to emphasize our predilection to self-deception due to our fallenness. But I think they also seriously underestimate the depths of the effects of sin. That is, if all we have to work with are our perspectives on the truth of reality, but not the truth as it is in itself, then we also need to consider that perspectives change not only with circumstances, *but also with the whims of our hearts*. Based on those whims, and our hearts' tendency to usurp God, even Christians can create untruth as an elevated, arrogant thought to explain (or rationalize) things in a way that fits with our

---

[51] E.g., Westphal characterizes the modernist view as one in which "neither inference nor interpretation separates us from immaculate, immediate, infallible intuition . . . the object is totally here and at no distance that might dim or distort our view of it." See his "Postmodernism and religious reflection," *International Journal for Philosophy of Religion* 38:1–3 (1995), 129.

[52] Ironically, if we cannot know reality as it is, how can we know we are being truly humble? For that seems to require that we have an accurate view of ourselves. Thanks to my colleague, Joe Gorra, for this suggestion, as well as many others he provided on an earlier draft of this essay.

desire to control all things. Their own view is not immune from self-deception and the heart's desire to usurp God. Unfortunately, their core philosophical position plays right into that desire to have authority and power over God, and it seems it plays into the trap of worshiping ourselves and our own minds.

We may see this very real danger illustrated in Scripture in Acts 4:14–20, where the council called before them Peter, John, and a lame beggar who had been healed through them (3:1–9). The council members could say nothing against the fact that a miracle had taken place through Peter and John, and this fact was *evident* to all. But then we read their action: "But, so this [the report of the miracle, and the turning of people to trust in Jesus] does not spread any further among the people, let's threaten them against speaking to anyone in this name again" (v. 17 HCSB). Their perspective was driven not by evidence, which was clearly available to them (and to all) of the Spirit's miraculous work, but by their hearts' desire to silence the disciples as well as God. Out of that desire the council members willfully suppressed the truth.

So by believing that we only have access to reality through our interpretations, we simply cannot avoid silencing God's Spirit. According to this core epistemological principle, we cannot access His self-disclosure directly but only as we interpret it. Thus we cannot access God's intended meaning when He has given us revelation, whether that be in Scripture, creation, or the inner witness of the Spirit in our lives. When we couple this with the depravity of our hearts and our flesh's bent to overthrow God's authority over our lives, we set ourselves up for listening to the same whispered suggestion that the serpent made to Eve: "You will be like God."

There is grave danger in interpreting God according to our limitations, for inevitably we will create our own god, which is why it is so important to check our ideas against Scripture. But it seems the Emergent view *requires* that we create our own god. Indeed, if we cannot know anything that is real as it truly is, then it seems to me that we end up determining (defining) it according to our own interpretations.[53] Truth (not to mention reality) in itself would be

---

[53] The same result holds just as much for knowing persons.

indeterminable. But we should beware the danger of those who think their own thoughts will put a *universal* determination (that *any*thing or *any*one that *any* human may experience or know *inescapably* requires interpretation) to what is supposedly the "indeterminable" truth. Why? They repeat the Eden experience, elevating their own thoughts over God's. But redemption in this kind of case comes only as we humble ourselves, agree with God that we have indeed sinned, and repent from any attempts to control and usurp Him. If instead we persist on this view in seeking to determine God Himself, then inevitably we will sin.

Moreover, this is suggestive; since God has sent the Spirit of Truth into the world, how can those who advocate the Emergent view proclaim that they do not know truth as it really is, unless it is because they have chosen like Adam to follow the father of lies? That implies that their love for God has grown cold, for just like Adam, they choose to blame God for whom they have become. After all, according to this view, all the problems that stem from everything being interpretation flow directly from how God has made us.[54]

SOME SPIRITUAL IMPLICATIONS FOR EVANGELICALS

If these problems attend the Emergent view, it is important that we *also* notice that Evangelicals are not immune to the same tendencies along with their dangers. It is not enough that Evangelicals would assent to true doctrine; the problems we are discussing are rooted in the heart, and if *anyone* does not humble his or her heart before the Lord, any one of us is capable of worshiping our own selves. But the forms that might take may differ from those I just discussed for those who follow the Emergent view. What might they look like for more traditional Evangelicals?

Here I will try to sketch a few dangers, and these results are ones that I think people like McLaren and others have been trying to bring to Christians' attention. First, subtly, I think some Evan-

---

[54] So it is not enough to reply, like Jamie, that being finite is part of God's good creation; that is true. But due to the implications that follow from the view that everything is interpretation, God would have to be the One to blame for those problems.

gelicals can be prone to a tendency toward a "Christian rational-
ism" in that they would elevate the use of their reason to the place
of authority in understanding and living out Scripture, such that
they do not really depend upon the Spirit. That implies that Christians would get skilled at living "out of their heads" without really
paying attention to their hearts' attitudes and condition.[55] This can
happen even unintentionally, such as when coming to some decision that needs to be made (e.g., should a church build onto its
existing facility, moving ahead in faith that God will supply, even
though the resources have not yet come in?), in which we study
all the options that we can discern, pray for a few minutes about
it in a meeting, and then make the decision as seems best to us.
Of course, we need to trust the Lord, but sometimes God does not
give us an immediate answer. Instead, He may want us to continue
to seek Him in prayer—perhaps also to fast and pray—and just
wait until He decides to speak and give us guidance. I am not saying that we should not use a sound mind rooted in Scripture and
good advice, but we also must listen to the Lord to be sure we are
not getting ahead of Him and justifying our own desired courses
of action.

Second, I do think Evangelicals are right to stress the importance of knowing the truth—after all, Jesus says true worshipers
are to worship God in spirit and truth (John 4:23)—but truth can
be used as a weapon in various ways, especially if it is not united
with compassion. It is good, for instance, to focus upon the mind's
needs for truth, but at the same time if we forsake the cries of the
hearts of those given to us to shepherd, in effect we send them to
look outside the body of Christ for the love they need, which is
where the evil one's affections will overtake them. In such cases,
knowledge becomes a weapon against their fullness of a future
and hope. Feeding knowledge above compassion encourages dis-
obedience, which repeats the Eden experience.

McLaren is onto something when he points out that too many
Christians expect that they should never have any struggles in
their faith, as though there are only two sources of problems in

---

[55] My thanks to Joe Gorra for this suggestion.

life—spiritual problems (which boil down to the effects of our sin) and physical problems. So, if they do struggle, woe to them! They must simply lack faith, and they need to confess their sin and just believe the truth. But too many Christians have been wounded by another source, others' sin against us, and the pain that can come from these actions may have profoundly deep, lasting effects.[56]

Instead, truth needs to be united with grace and God's love. After all, Jesus embodied these qualities, and so should we. Even speaking about love, without truly living it out sacrificially, will not build up and minister to the hearts of those He has entrusted to us. God wants to shepherd us, and one thing I am becoming very convinced is deeply on His heart now is that He wants to turn the hearts of the "fathers" (including dads, leaders in churches, professors, and more) to the hearts of the "children" (including, but not limited to, those in need of shepherding in our churches), and the hearts of the children to the fathers (maybe even as a result of the hearts of the fathers being drawn in genuine love to the children).

Third, well-meaning Evangelicals also can be overtaken by evil, in that they, too, can place their thoughts above the Lord's even when trying to defend the "truth." Those who have the truth, and are truly in Christ, still can elevate their own thoughts subtly above His, thereby becoming arrogant and engaging in the worship of their own minds. For instance, I think it is a temptation for apologists to rely on a particular kind of reasoning (e.g., philosophical), rather than humbling ourselves and submitting all our thoughts, ways, and hearts to the Lord, letting Him assess our ideas, especially before proclaiming them as truth. Evangelicals who do not humble themselves before the Lord set themselves up for being influenced by their flesh and even by demonic forces, perhaps by speaking "truth" as if they created it and in authoritative tones that put others to submission. Just as much as anyone else, Evangelicals can become arrogant, perhaps by proclaiming that their place to stand is without question.

McLaren has highlighted this attitude in his analysis of the influences of modernity upon the church. There he picks up on

---

[56] I discuss this topic somewhat more in *Truth*, 124–30 (especially 127–28), where I tell my own story.

things like the mistaken notion that we must have utter certainty in our beliefs and that we must prove others wrong who disagree with us, for we *must* be right. But even with acknowledging the impact of these cultural influences, there is a deeper story to be told, which is that the human heart, even if regenerated by Christ, still can exalt itself above Him in pride and arrogance, which thereby will harm many others around it.

Fourth, these factors can lead to another problem: the silencing of God's Spirit.[57] Since Evangelicals still are fallen, and thus can elevate arrogantly our hearts above God's rightful place over our lives, there can be a danger especially from stressing an intellectual assent to the truth that is not coupled with humble hearts before God. In such cases, there still is the disconnect of the heart from the mind and the heart from God, so that we are not loving God with all our being. Consider the Pharisees, who were the religious conservatives of their day. They thought they were strictly obeying what God wanted, but they also had hearts that were far from God. Indeed, their hearts were hypocritical, insincere, proud, and self-righteous, such that even when they were presented with clear evidence of Jesus' identity, they *would* not see the truth (e.g., Mark 3:1–6); it is as though they plugged their ears, being unwilling to receive the truth. Just like the Pharisees and everyone else, Evangelicals are not above temptations to "be like God," and we need to submit our ideas to the Spirit (1 Thess 5:19) and the test of Scripture. Having other trusted, respected followers of Christ check our ideas (especially against Scripture) also is very important. And how that attitude of trying to be like God might manifest itself could take subtle forms, because I think Evangelicals do have access to the truth revealed in Scripture.[58]

---

[57] As one source to look further into this idea, see Dallas Willard, *Hearing God: Developing a Conversational Relationship with God* (Downers Grove, Ill.: InterVarsity, 1999).

[58] I have not given so much a positive case for how we know reality directly as I have offered a critique of the view that everything is interpretation. But I make a brief positive case in chap. 9 of my *Truth* book.

CONCLUSION

The Lord desires truth in the innermost being, and it matters to Him and us. We cannot be a true worshiper if we do not stand in truth. We have examined a few kinds of errors, starting with the Emergent view that everything is interpretation. Unfortunately, we would not be able to know the created reality as it is, and we also could not know God as He truly is.[59] This entails that we could not know the authentic Jesus, which undermines a major point of these proponents of the emerging church. And it means that we would make a god, according to our interpretations. Though unintended, this conclusion repeats the Eden experience. Thus, this view cannot address the deepest, real need of humans, for instead of humbling ourselves before God, we would try to replace Him.

But truth also is not merely the art of persuasion by reason. The Lord must fill our entire being and not just the mind. Those who espouse the Emergent view are not alone in this; Evangelicals also must take heed to the Lord's admonition to humble our hearts before Him, to love Him with all our hearts, souls, minds, and strength, and our neighbors as ourselves; otherwise, we (myself included) also are prone to the same satanic deception that the devil used in the garden, and is using even today.

---

[59] Though we cannot know Him exhaustively, on this view we also could not know Him veridically.

PART TWO
THEOLOGICAL SECTION

EMERGENT/EMERGING CHRISTOLOGIES

DARRELL L. BOCK

THE EMERGENT/EMERGING MOVEMENT is not a singular movement but more like a spectrum. What they all share is a sense that the church needs reshaping and restructuring to work in the postmodern world of the twenty-first century. They are missionally driven and desire to pursue an authentic and deep experience of being a follower of Christ. It is the full divinely driven journey they seek. All of these are worthy goals.

Now for many people any change is seen as deviation, but biblically rooted people should know better. The gospel itself is about a process of change that starts with conversion and is not over until we are with God in glory. Glorification does not come in an instant; it is part of what God does to bring us into conformity with Him until He finishes the job. So change is not the issue.

Now some will say that when it comes to change, the circumstances surrounding doctrine are different than form or practice. In one sense this is true. The Bible teaches what it does about Jesus (or any other topic). What it teaches reflects the inspired Word. That teaching does not change. True. However, there are three other factors that make pursuing the goal of articulating doctrine more complicated than simply thinking it is what it is.

First, there is a difference between what the text is and my ability to determine what it says. The Bible is God's Word, but that does not mean I always read it correctly. One of the ways to "test" my reading is to interact with other Spirit-indwelt people to see if there is something missing in my reading. Second, the Bible is so rich and deep that it can allow us to look at the same doctrine from many angles or say things in a variety of ways. Let me use salvation as an example. When we share the gospel, we can tell people to believe, come, trust, turn, repent, receive, or rest in Him. Any of these descriptions is an adequate summary of how to respond. Each description is capable of representing a response of a faith that saves. This means that in teaching an area like Christology, saying something differently or emphasizing an aspect of Christological teaching is not in itself a problem just because something is said differently than the way another says it. So "different" in itself does not equate with "dangerous." Third, there is the issue of balance in the midst of a complicated and deep doctrine like Christology. As one looks across the Scripture for what it teaches on a doctrine, it can be important to consider how balanced the discussion of doctrine is. When dealing with Jesus this can get complicated because the mixture of his divinity and humanity is unique in the creation. Now combine these three factors with the variety of things being said about Christology in the Emergent/emerging movement (hereafter E/e), and one can see where the confusion enters in when assessing what is taking place.

People in the E/e movement are thinking through how to present Jesus in a changing world. They are looking for fresh angles and emphases. Part of the value of such newness is that presenting the gospel from a fresh angle can have a freshness that the retelling of a well-known version can lack. The question is not whether the story is different or has a different style (narrative versus didactic for example; sermon versus dialogical delivery); it is whether the difference still reflects the experience of knowing Jesus in a way that coheres with the depth and balance in scriptural teaching. Does the taking up of one kind of emphasis mean we are wise to leave behind or minimize other emphases? Might there actually be a benefit in thinking through how to rearticulate doctrine in fresh, biblically rooted and conceived ways for our time? When it comes to Christology, both of these questions are important.

In this chapter, I propose to look at the spectrum of E/e positions on Christology. I will use the grid of other chapters, pointing to the groupings of relevants, reconstructionists, and revisionists.

I have seen these categories used by people who are favorable to E/e concerns. Mark Driscoll has used this kind of classification.[1] He calls himself a "relevant." Some people in the Emergent movement decry the use of labels, but they are inevitable and can either be about power (which is why they are decried) or about description, which can be helpful. Scot McKnight, an Emergent enthusiast, has said it this way:

> It is nice and all to speak about not having categories and a linear arrangement, and I'm aware of emerging's desire to transcend such categories. Problem is that once one brings in a category like theological orthodoxy then it is impossible not to have a spectrum of some sort, or at least views. For instance, Tony [Jones][2]—who sometimes talks like getting beyond—has a book called the "new" Christians which, by its structure, means there are at least some "old" Christians. We may be trying to get beyond that in relationships with other Christians, but when one enters into that relationship some theological category, we have "yes, no, maybe, etc." and it is unavoidable.[3]

I am using these labels not as an attempt to separate or exercise power, but to describe and try to get a sense of the spectrum of views and emphases in movements that are saying several things at once as well as attempting to balance things in distinct ways. I will use the people associated with and representative of each grouping as a way of showing the spectrum of views within E/e. We shall consider (1) what is being highlighted, (2) what is being questioned, (3) is the fresh angle helpful, and (4) is there something missing or perhaps lacking in balance? In this way we hope to get a sense for what we can learn from and what we need to be aware of as believers discuss Christology in the E/e movement and what it can teach the church.

[1] Mark Driscoll, "A Pastoral Perspective on the Emergent Church," *Criswell Theological Review* 3/2 (Spring 2006): 87–93.

[2] Tony Jones complains about labels like Emergent and emerging in his blog on April 15, 2008. See http://tonyj.net/ entry: "Emerging" Vs. "Emergent." He is regarded as among the more avant garde in the movement.

[3] Response 12 on his blog, Jesus Creed, dated February 19, 2008 under the entry "Mapping Emerging." His site is: http://www.blog.beliefnet.com/jesuscreed/.

A LOOK AT CHRISTOLOGY AMONG RELEVANTS
(MARK DRISCOLL, DAN KIMBALL)

DRISCOLL'S TAKE ON JESUS

Relevants are those who take the traditional message of Scripture and are thinking through how to make it more relevant to today's postmodern culture in the context of variation in worship and preaching style, as well as leadership models.[4] Mark Driscoll, a self-confessed relevant, received the assignment of writing about theology in a book on multiple views within E/e churches.[5] In it he chooses to focus on three doctrines: revelation, the nature of God (i.e., the Trinity), and atonement. In introducing his chapter, he says, "The topics the publisher chose for this book are the essential elements of the Christian gospel according to the apostle Paul, who said the second person of the trinity, Jesus Christ, atones for our sins by his death and resurrection in fulfillment of the Scriptures."[6] Later he says in discussing resistance to the Trinity, "But the fact remains that Jesus Christ is distinct from and superior to all religious leaders and their religions, and philosophers and their philosophies."[7] Everything that Driscoll says here reflects a traditional and orthodox view of the gospel.

The chapter lacks the criticism of the development of doctrine in the early centuries that some E/e writers make. It also focuses on atonement in a way that some E/e writers hesitate to do. It also incorporates Paul in the doctrinal remarks in contrast to some E/e writers who discuss mostly Jesus and ignore Paul, which leaves the impression that Paul has little to offer about theological reflection on Jesus. All of these differences of emphasis I hope to show in what follows.

---

[4] Driscoll, "A Pastoral Perspective," 89–90. Other than those we discuss, he places Donald Miller and Rob Bell in this category.

[5] *Listening to the Beliefs of Emerging Churches: Five Perspectives*, ed. Robert Webber (Grand Rapids: Zondervan, 2007), 21–35.

[6] Driscoll, in *Listening*, 21.

[7] Ibid., 27.

THE REACTION OF OTHER E/E REPRESENTATIVES AND AN ASSESSMENT OF THEIR DISTINCT RESPONSES

The value of the *Listening* book is that it has other E/e leaders respond to the main essays in a dialogical format. John Burke says, "I think Mark just made the book worth buying."[8] He observes, "The Emerging church must find its way through the narrow straits of following truth in a postmodern world by holding to the most clear, compelling revelation from God available—that found in the Bible."[9] He simply urges that the church needs to go beyond propositional assent to practice, something all would affirm. Dan Kimball, often considered a reconstructionist, is similar, "I fully resonate with Mark's beliefs on core doctrine that aligns with the Nicene Creed."[10] He only questions the extent and detail of Mark's certainty, especially about some details of Calvinism. Doug Pagitt, one of the early, more visible leaders of the movement, is less receptive. He opens, "At times, I find it difficult to read Mark's chapter."[11] He calls Mark's approach to the Bible a "reference approach."[12] He questions Mark's sense of looking for a correct view of the text and a need to correct others, calling this a "ludicrous assumption" that Driscoll is correct on such matters. Raising other concerns whether most in church history have held such views, Pagitt concludes by noting that Mark's approach "seems to be filled with issues of power."[13] He closes by wishing for good things for Mark. One can appreciate Pagitt's candor here, but one can notice how his response is out of step with the other responses. It also seems out of step with biblical calls to be discerning, something Jesus (Matt 7:1–5,13–20; Luke 6:39), as well as Paul, taught of leaders especially (Acts 20:28–31). These texts, understood in the context of discussing central teachings about the faith, call us to think through the gospel carefully both individu-

---

[8] Burke, *Listening*, 36.

[9] Ibid., 36–37.

[10] Kimball, *Listening*, 40.

[11] Pagitt, *Listening*, 42.

[12] Ibid., 43.

[13] Ibid., 44. He goes on to speak of oppression and what makes Christianity unattractive. Near the close he says, "The offensiveness of this view may have little to do with the gospel and more to do with one view of the gospel in competition with all other understandings."

ally, as leaders, and as communities. Karen Ward, a minority representative of the movement, affirms Driscoll's read by noting his remarks about the Trinity showing "a loving community existing throughout eternity," as well as noting his remark that to lose the Trinity is to "lose the root system from which we nourish community, love, and friendship."[14]

A SUGGESTION ABOUT THE DEFINITION OF THE GOSPEL AND JESUS' WORK

Having said this, I want to return to Mark's definition of the gospel, a teaching that is rooted in Paul and Scripture as he notes. I want to connect Ward's observations about Driscoll's teaching with his Pauline definition of the gospel. I seek to deepen Mark's point and make it cohere more with the doctrinal-relational emphasis that he defends. My own read of Scripture is that Mark's statement of the gospel in terms of death for sin is one way to express the core gospel. In this expression, the emphasis is on *how* salvation is accomplished, through Christ's work of substitution and atonement that pays for sin. Using biblical imagery, this sacrificial work cleanses and makes a new life of being born again for the person who embraces it.

Now, I want to emphasize the relational part of this articulation because it goes back to Jesus and Paul as well. Jesus said it to Nicodemus. Paul says it when he affirms, "if anyone is in Christ, he is a new creation" (2 Cor 5:17), which is another way to speak about a new life. Romans 6–8 also pictures this idea because to experience no condemnation is to be brought into God's family and be indwelt by God's Spirit, enabling us to cry out, "Abba (Father)." John 17:3 makes this point affirming that eternal life means to know the Father and the Son. In the statements that I have just outlined, we have the *who* and *the product* of the gospel as well as the relational core to which forgiveness of sins leads. In other words, the gospel is not merely about forgiving sin; it is about what gets established as a result—a renewed, reconciled relationship with God through Jesus and His work that simply requires one embrace what God offers. This involves the choice

---

[14] Ward, *Listening*, 46.

of faith to enter into this relationship aware and appreciative of all that God has done in Christ. The Spirit (see how Trinitarian all this is) seals the deal by entering into our lives as a guiding and teaching presence, supplying the enablement God calls us to live in this new life. When one appreciates the greatness of the One making the sacrifice (Jesus), the initiative of the One who sent Him to do it (the Father), and the enablement that is the gracious gift of new life (the Spirit), then the Bible, the Trinity, and salvation come together into the core package that is at the hub of Christian faith. That lived-out life *rooted in gracious divine provision* is what E/e communities emphasize when they seek to live missionally and seek to be Christ-followers in practical everyday life in line with the exhortation and example that the Scriptures and God's inspired saints of the past provide.

Relevants are right to seek to be rooted doctrinally. They bring something very important to the E/e discussion: a commitment to search, understand, and live out the way God calls followers to live. In the pursuit of proper understanding, even of the gospel, it is important that the relational goal of the Scripture not be underemphasized. Christ died for sin so that I might know God and become an eternally reconciled child of God (2 Cor 5:20–21; John 1:12; 6:29–40). As Jesus prayed in John 17:3–6,

> This is eternal life: that they may know You, the only true God, and the One You have sent—Jesus Christ. I have glorified You on the earth by completing the work You gave Me to do. Now, Father, glorify Me in Your presence with that glory I had with You before the world existed.
>
> I have revealed Your name to the men You gave Me from the world. They were Yours, You gave them to Me, and they have kept Your word.

Here is the relational result of God's activity through Christ and the Spirit. It is rooted in Jesus' death and is seen as a glorification and lifting up of new life in the Spirit sent from above.

DRISCOLL IS NOT ALONE

Dan Kimball is another relevant. His chapter on Christology comes in his book *They Like Jesus But Not the Church: Insights from Emerging Generations.*[15] The chapter is entitled, in typical Emergent tongue-in-cheek style, "Jesus as Son of God and Plastic Action Figure." In this chapter, he reviews the ways that Jesus is marketed today and the fascination that surrounds Him. He discusses two ends of the spectrum about Jesus. In one, Jesus is treated informally, as a buddy and friend. On the other more extreme fundamentalist end, Jesus is an angry avenging figure.[16] There also are all of the variations in between, including a pop culture Jesus who stands up for the poor and needy and is a revolutionary for the oppressed.

Kimball contrasts these Jesus portraits with the "Vintage" Jesus. This Jesus is the second Person of the Trinity. He is a Jewish rabbi; a teacher who astonished; a figure full of compassion; an advocate of the poor, marginalized, and oppressed; One who opposed legalism; One who provided wine; One tempted but without sin; One who took on our sin; One who accomplished redemption by a substitutionary sacrifice; One who called followers to go out into the world and live missional lives; One who loves the church; and One who will come again to judge the living and the dead. He closes his description by saying, "Jesus is our friend and the friend of sinners, but he also is a righteous judge who will hold us all accountable one day for how we lived our lives. We must have a balanced view of Jesus, being careful not to swing to one extreme or the other."

I could not have said it better myself. Jesus is not a one-dimensional figure. He is multidimensional and comes in high-def. He

[15] (Grand Rapids: Zondervan, 2007), 50–59.

[16] In another article on "Humble Theology," as he argues for exploring fresh ways to express and think about theology, Kimball says, "It is interesting, however, that some of the more aggressive 'defend and attack' Christians out here, who generally won't openly discuss and explore theological beliefs besides their own, are the ones who hold more strongly to imputed sin and stress constantly how sinful we are. The irony, of course, is that if we are inherently sinful, how can we be so darn certain that our particular interpretation of the Scriptures and our own theological positions are the absolutely correct ones?" (*An Emergent Manifesto of Hope*, ed. Doug Pagitt and Tony Jones [Grand Rapids: Baker Books, 2007], 222).

touches every corner of our lives and challenges us at a variety of levels, not as a mere teacher or guide, but as Lord and Savior. He sees down to the pixels of our lives. Such an Emergent Christology is biblical. It not only sets Jesus in His ancient context but reminds us that the cultural Jesuses of our world are not reflections of a faith that appreciates Jesus as the uniquely sent and exalted One from God.

A LOOK AT CHRISTOLOGY BY RECONSTRUCTIONISTS (NEIL COLE, ALAN HIRSCH)

Reconstructionists are those who are generally seen as evangelical but are dissatisfied with current forms of the church. They have reacted against seeker or purpose-driven contemporary churches because they have failed a generation by not producing real life change, as statistics on divorce and other lifestyle issues show.[17] They are seeking to reconstruct the church with more informal, organic, and incarnational models of community. In this way, this grouping is more about a variation in forms of community and worship and less about theological discussion.

A LOOK AT NEIL COLE

One night, I spent over an hour working through sixteen Google pages on Neil Cole. I found numerous interviews and discussions dealing with the failures of the institutional church and with the desire for communities that are small, effective, and missional. I could not find any detailed discussion of beliefs in these Web discussions other than an affirmation of a commitment to Jesus. I note this at the start not as a complaint but as an observation. The primary concern is fostering growth and maturity through fresh structures that contribute to the mission of the church.

Coles's book *Organic Church* is similar in thrust. When Cole discusses Divine Truth he says,

> Truth comes from God. It is the revelation of God to humankind. It is best seen in the person of Jesus and the Scriptures. In both cases, there is a mysterious connection

[17] Driscoll, "A Pastoral Perspective," 90.

of the Divine and human. Jesus is both God and human. God authored the Scripture, but at the same time there were more than forty authors as well. Nevertheless, Jesus and the Scriptures are both without blemish. The indwelling Spirit of God is also Divine Truth. He brings the revelation of God and the frailty of humanity together. All of the Spirit's leading is infallible, though we must note that our understanding and application of His leading is often full of errors, just as our understanding and application of Scripture is not always correct.[18]

This divine truth is what Cole sees as part of the DNA of the organic church (along with nurturing relationships and apostolic mission). He goes on to say, "The simple idea—Jesus Christ coming to us in the flesh for our redemption—embodies the entire DNA."[19] Everything said here reflects the core beliefs of the faith about Jesus. There is not much elaboration, just a straightforward affirmation. The discussed concerns are elsewhere. Some reconstructionists are immersed in the pursuit of the practice of living out God's call, a wonderful cause to embrace.

A LOOK AT ALAN HIRSCH

Hirsch's book is a call to return to the "forgotten ways" of the earliest church.[20] His claim is that the church needs to turn away from being so institutional and become more missional. Many of its existing structures get in the way of the church meeting that calling. Much of his writing, like that of other reconstructionists, spends the bulk of the time treating issues of how the church can meet its calling as a dynamic, engaged group of believers. This means that topics like Christology do not get detailed attention. However, Hirsch does present in the midst of his book a chapter on Jesus called, "The Heart of It All: Jesus Is Lord."[21]

---

[18] Neil Cole, *Organic Church: Growing Faith Where Life Happens* (San Francisco: Jossey-Bass, 2005), 115.

[19] Ibid., 119.

[20] Alan Hirsch, *The Forgotten Ways: Reactivating the Missional Church* (Grand Rapids: Brazos Press, 2006).

[21] Ibid., 83–100.

The fusion of theology and life is very clear from the opening of his chapter. Hirsch discusses 1 Cor 8:4–6, where he treats the relationship between God, Jesus, and Christian movements. He says, "A God who is in the very moment of redeeming us claims us as his own through Jesus our Savior. If we fail to apprehend this spiritual center and circumference of the Jesus movements, we can never fully understand them nor reinvoke the power that infused their lives and communities."[22] Discussing a "white-hot faith," Hirsch goes on to note how persecuted churches operate underground, recovering a simple structure and Christology. A simple Christology involves "the capacity to rapidly transfer the message along relational lines. Freed from the philosophical density of the academy and from dependence on the professional cleric, the gospel becomes profoundly 'sneezable.'"[23] In other words, it takes on a form that allows it to spread easily. Now, it is important to recall when Hirsch treats the academy and the professional cleric, that he ministers in Australia where formal denominational churches are the traditional presence of the church.

This biblical simplicity is reflected in a confession of monotheism like Deuteronomy 6:4. Hirsch highlights the relational dimensions again when he says,

> When the New Testament people of God confess that "Jesus is Lord and Savior," it is not just a simple confession that Jesus is our Master and we are his servants. It certainly is that, but given the Hebraic context of that confession, and the fact that Jesus is the fulfillment of the messianic promises to Israel, the confession wholly reverberates with beliefs that go back to Israel's primal confession that "Yahweh is Lord." As such, this confession touches upon the deepest possible currents in biblical revelation: theses that take us directly to the nature of God, his relation to the world, and to his claim over every aspect of our lives, both individual and communal. It also relates to the defining encounter, the redemptive experi-

---

[22] Ibid., 84.
[23] Ibid., 86.

ence that forms the covenant relationship between God
and his people.[24]

In the context of polytheism and Jewish monotheism, this was
a penetrating statement. Hirsch again adds, "So in the Hebraic
perspective, monotheism is not so much a statement about God as
eternal being in essential oneness, as it was for the Hellenist theologians, but rather an existential claim that there is only one God
and He is Lord of every aspect of life."[25] Everything about this
confession impacts worldview and orients it toward life and faith.
It represents a "practical monotheism." When it comes to Jesus,
Hirsch says that when the early church confesses Jesus as Lord,
"it does so in precisely the same way, with the same exact implications, that Israel claimed God as Lord in the *Shema*."[26] This leads
to a Jesus-shaped monotheism and to the development of the Trinity. There is a "three-ness of sorts in the divine nature," but also
"the overall emphasis in the scriptures falls nonetheless on the
oneness of God."[27] Still, Paul notes that the function of lordship is
now passed on to Jesus.

When it comes to articulating the lordship of Jesus, Hirsch
affirms, "This redefinition of biblical monotheism around the role
of Jesus I will call christocentric monotheism, because it does
realign our loyalties to God around the person and work of Jesus
Christ. Jesus becomes the pivotal point in our relation to God, and
it is to him that we must give our allegiance and loyalty. Jesus is
Lord! And this lordship is expressed in exactly the same way that
it is in the Old Testament."[28]

Such a Christology takes us beyond a sacred-secular divide.
It prevents us from having one kind of life and faith on Sunday
and another during the week. After treating practical examples of
such strong faith in the context of South African apartheid and
genocide in Rwanda, Hirsch wraps up, "I have become absolutely
convinced that it is Christology, and in particular the primitive,

[24] Ibid., 87.
[25] Ibid., 89.
[26] Ibid., 91.
[27] Ibid., 92.
[28] Ibid., 93.

unemcumbered Christology of the NT church, that lies at the heart
of the renewal of the church at all times."[29]

ASSESSING HIRSCH

Virtually everything said here is solid theologically. Jesus is
affirmed as the Lord of all. His divinity is seen in relationship to
the confession of Him in 1 Cor 8:4–6, one of the key doctrinal
summary texts of the New Testament. Everything said of God as
Lord can be said of Jesus. The orientation of that teaching to life
and its practicality and relational dimension are highlighted.

The only small hesitation is the distance Hirsch implies between
this and the articulation of these ideas in Greek terms and concepts,
which the church quickly had to face, even in the times of Paul and
others who reached out to Gentiles. This more philosophical discussion does show up in key New Testament texts, such as 1 Cor
1–4 or Col 1:15–20, the later text belonging to a hymnic doctrinal
summary of the faith. As such, I see these alternative expressions
not as distractions or perhaps a complicating of the simple portrait
of Jesus, but simply as other appropriate ways to discuss Him in
contexts where more complicated questions about God, Jesus, and
Their relationship are raised.

This is in many ways a small quibble. However, it needs to be
made because often in suggesting the church must do things one
way, both sides in this discussion suggest other ways of doing
and saying are wrong, rather than just different or perhaps simply
more appropriate in certain contexts. The result is that each person
or group takes sides—and the church risks dividing on matters
and issues that reflect the very variety of practice and form the
early church permitted as it grew and developed. As the church
grew, it faced real practical problems in how to structure itself as it
was dealing with more people. These issues are starting to emerge
in a serious way at the end of the New Testament period, but the
principle of dictating very little when it comes to the forms of the
new community had already been established.

My assessment is wandering now from Christology into the doctrine of the church and ecclesiology, but I do so because the debate

[29] Ibid., 99.

among E/e churches and between them and other approaches has a kind of "gotcha" feel from each side of the debate. It is a point-counterpoint confrontation that risks descending into a 1 Corinthians 1 "I am of Paul, Cephas, or Apollos" experience that Paul rebukes in that letter. We need to get beyond that. We need to affirm clearly the practical oneness that all followers of Jesus as Lord are supposed to have. We may need to recognize that Christ can show Himself to be Lord in a variety of forms within His church.

We have seen that E/e representatives of the relevant and reconstructionist stripe are able to articulate a solid Christology. Their emphases have also raised potential minor questions of balance, something we all risk falling into. What of the revisionist take on Christology?

A LOOK AT CHRISTOLOGY AMONG REVISIONISTS (DOUG PAGITT, TONY JONES, BRIAN McLAREN)

A third group within E/e is called the revisionists. This approach is dissatisfied with the current forms of church and argues that new times (postmodern times) require new approaches, especially as our culture becomes less christianized in the West and more globalized overall. Doug Pagitt says it this way, "The faithful of the first century of Christianity found themselves needing to recalibrate the way they lived, believed, interacted, and reconciled in light of God's activity in Jesus."[30] Pagitt argues that what Christians did in the first century was innovate, so we have to be careful that religion's tendency to preserve and become immovable may not "serve the story of God's action in the world very well."[31] I have said elsewhere that such questions and the E/e analysis of the church's current state raise very fair, complex, and important questions for all believers.[32] Such questions and answers might suggest that there is a wider variety of ways to do church than we

---

[30] Doug Pagitt, "Communities of Hope: New Ways, Questions, and Outcomes for Church of Our Day," in *The Emergent Manifesto of Hope*, ed. Doug Pagitt and Tony Jones (Grand Rapids: Baker Books, 2007), 77.

[31] Pagitt, "Communities," 75.

[32] Darrell L. Bock, "Summary on Emerging and Emergent Church Movement," at www.bible.org/bock, October 6, 2006 entry, expanded January 12, 2007.

tend to consider. Sociological sensitivity is a healthy thing for the church. The questions surround how the message of the church is presented in such a context.

Now, even the issue about the message is more complex than we tend to think. Paul, as a first-century believer, can issue a scathing condemnation of first-century culture (Rom 1:18–32), and yet when he addresses that same culture can do so in a completely different tone and in a bridge-building manner even as he tries to educate the culture in religious perceptions (Acts 17:16–31). This kind of varied presentation points to a healthy contextualizing of the gospel message. Part of what concerns all involved with the E/e movement is a proper contextualization of the gospel message. Much of what the movement claims as "new" is motivated by these concerns.

The reaction against some strands of the E/e movement has been because these critics claim that some E/e leaders do more than contextualize the gospel message.[33] The message itself is being recalibrated in ways that actually no longer reflect the original message. This is a key criticism to make and, in fairness to all, needs to be carefully tested and examined. One of the crucial areas of the message involves Christology, although it is not the only area that is involved in such critiques. Generally speaking, it is the revisionists who have received the most criticism. How do revisionists, who often argue for the greatest degree of change, fit here? In this survey, I both present and assess simultaneously because it is these E/e presentations that are the most debated.

A LOOK AT TONY JONES

In his recent book, *The New Christians: Dispatches from the Emergent Frontier*, Tony Jones takes some time to talk about truth, a topic that leads us into the nature of the Christian message.[34] Dispatch 13 begins with the claim, "Emergents believe that truth, like God, cannot be definitively articulated by finite human beings."[35]

---

[33] Probably the most well-known critique here is by D. A. Carson, *Becoming Conversant with the Emerging Church* (Grand Rapids: Zondervan, 2005).

[34] Tony Jones, *The New Christians: Dispatches from the Emergent Frontier* (San Francisco: Jossey-Bass, 2008).

[35] Ibid., 153. Dispatches are what serve as chapters for Jones.

In one sense, this is not news. The key term *definitively* can mean that no expression of theology is exhaustive or completely reveals the depths of who God is and what He does. However, that is not the only issue. Coming at things from the other side of the spectrum revisionists can ask, "Is it possible for finite human beings to adequately approach proper theological expression?" The claim of the church, premodern, modern, and even postmodern, is that the church's commitment to revelation means that theology can be *both* adequately expressed *and* incarnated in life. This is precisely why revelation and the inspired Word of God exist, to be a completely sufficient source for theological expression of truth.

I stress the both/and here because Jones has a section later in this dispatch that plays these elements against each other to a degree. It reads,

> Yet "truth" is not the hinge on which the biblical narrative turns. The narrative turns, instead, on the way of life into which Yahweh in the Old Testament and Jesus in the New calls us. The preoccupation with "truth" among emergents has often been pushed on them by their conservative critics, primarily because truth is a central concern of theirs. And their preoccupation with truth is a symptom of their modernism. They want the Bible to be unswervingly factual (here *truth* equals *fact*), for if it is, then its claims about eternal salvation cannot be ignored.[36]

Casting himself as in the middle, Jones goes on to discuss the liberal Marcus Borg's claim that the tomb of Jesus was not empty. He notes that Borg has slipped into the gutter on one side of modernity's bowling alley, relying on reason. Jones then comes back to John Piper as a member of the opposite end of the spectrum, as one who emphasizes God's sovereignty. He closes this survey by noting,

> Each man is constricting God by forcing God to play by certain rules; the rules of physics or the rules of sovereignty. And each is attempting to squeeze all the para-

---

[36] Ibid., 154.

dox out of God. But emergents don't fear paradox; they embrace it. God can be the creator of the universe *and* the breaker of the rules of physics. God can be sovereign and *yet* not the author of evil. So again emergents are left to chart a middle course, one between the fideism (in human reason) of the left and the fideism (in the supernatural) of the right. As is so often the case, the "truth" lies in between, in a person (Jesus the Christ) who was *truly* human and *truly* divine in faith, not fideism.[37]

Now, these sentences can be read in a variety of ways. One way they can be read is that the narrative is ultimately about how we are called to live, not just what we believe. In this sense, the remark is fair and on target. Jones's later both/and leads me to think this is what he intends here. And yet, there is an uneasiness that truth here is being equated with a kind of exhaustive understanding and articulation that I do not recognize as the concern reflective of many conservative claims. The idea that truth is a modernist idea ignores the fact that the Bible itself, as a premodern book and as a trans-era book, discusses truth, whether one looks at the Psalter as the praise of God for giving truth or one thinks of Jesus Christ as "the way, the truth, *and* the life." In fact, John's prologue makes the point most emphatically by calling Jesus *the Word*, which is a way of saying Jesus is the revelation *and* revelator of God (John 1:1–18). Truth is both personal *and* propositional. The suggested opposition implied in Jones's treatment of truth and modernism detaches the two ideas a little too much.

Having been somewhat critical, let me seek to balance the criticism. Some conservatives are so fixated on truth as proposition that incarnating truth in the nature and tone of their living receives less than adequate attention. In fact, I suspect all of us are guilty of this to a degree for we all are sinners, even as the redeemed, and that process will undergo change and, hopefully, deepening until God completes the process and brings us to Himself in fullness one day. In other words, I share Jones's desire to have propositional truth and incarnational truth be in a "messy" dialogue that

[37] Ibid., 154–55.

moves toward the beauty of a lived life that honors God. What I do not share is his later statement that the

> contemporary North American version of Christianity rarely reflects these aspects of truth-God. The statements of faith that populate church Web sites truck almost exclusively in theory, making unembodied statements about God, the Bible and church government. You'll find declarations like "We believe that the Bible is the inspired word of God, without error in its original manuscripts" and "the Lord Jesus Christ is both true God and perfect man, a unique supernatural manifestation of God in the flesh." All theoretical, impersonal statements. On the contrary, you aren't likely to find something like this on a church Web site:

> "Statement of Faith

> "We at First Christian church acknowledge that God's coming to earth in the person of Jesus Christ and recounted in the gospels turns upside down what we used to think about concepts like 'truth.' For in him 'truth' walked around, talked to people, and even cried and bled. We're left with a faith that, while deep, is also paradoxical and difficult. As a result, we've committed to leaning on each other as we collectively try to follow Jesus. We're confident about some things: Jesus' coming to earth was good news, it's still good news, and there's good news to come. You are welcome to join us anytime."[38]

Now, I like what this "more personal" statement says, but I also have a concern about what it lacks. The good news is not merely that Jesus came and that He lived among us. It also was about who He was, what He taught, *and* what He did *for us*. The "impersonal statements" complained about above briefly describe (1) the source from which *we are able to know* about this Jesus and (2) remind us of who Jesus is in the *fullness of His person*. These doctrinal summaries are not the whole story by any means, but they

[38] Ibid., 161–62.

are important components, just as the things Jones wants to high-light are. More than that, when Jesus turned "truth" upside down, the sacred tables He was toppling were a kind of human autono-mous self-defined truth. What theology attempts to do, and some expressions do it better than others, is to articulate the "truths" God wishes to teach those He created, both conceptually as a mat-ter of worldview (what Proverbs called wisdom) *and* incarnation-ally as a matter of living (what Proverbs also called wisdom).

At the beginning of this chapter, I raised the issue of balance. I think what we see from revisionists is a call for better balance in our theology, a little more humility about its expression and com-plexity, embracing that we do not have all of the detailed answers, and a passionate pursuit of living out what Jesus and those close to Him called for from those who are His followers. This appeal is worth hearing. On the other side, conservative critiques to the revisionists are saying, the movement away from proposition toward incarnation carries great risk and harm *if it becomes too detached, so please, as brothers and sisters, tread carefully here.* Both proposition and incarnation are crucial, not just one or not even one more than the other, because even incarnated life is lived out from value, perspectives, and ideas that one holds as guiding and defining. Like DNA, the risk is tearing asunder things that belong so tightly together, and doing away with one strand of the double helix risks killing the life so passionately being sought.

A LOOK AT BRIAN McLAREN

Brian McLaren has written several books. I also have worked with him on *The Voice Project* as the academic consultant behind the volumes on Luke and Acts. I am going to focus on his most recent work, *Everything Must Change: Jesus, Global Crises, and Revolution of Grace.*[39] I cover this book because, as his most recent statement, it is made in light of past responses to him and has an overview on Christology.

McLaren considers key issues tied to Jesus as well as how con-ventionals and Emergents discuss this Jesus in *Everything Must*

---

[39] Nashville: Thomas Nelson, 2007.

Change.[40] This section reveals a great deal about the views some Emergents hold of the conservatives' (conventionals') and Emergents' framing of Jesus. I present McLaren's side-by-side explanations of the emphases of both camps in a series of sequenced comparisons he makes. Then I shall evaluate his presentation.

For McLaren, the conventional view of Jesus has to do with God's sovereign determination "that [in light of the fall of Adam and Eve after a perfect creation] the entire universe and all it contains will be destroyed, and the souls of all human beings—except for those specifically exempted—will be forever punished for their imperfection in hell." In contrast, McLaren says Emergents believe that God created the world good, but that human beings have rebelled and filled the world with injustice and evil. "God wants to save humanity and heal it from its sickness, but humanity is hopelessly lost and confused, like sheep without a shepherd, wandering further and further into lostness and danger. Left to themselves, human beings will spiral downward in sickness and evil."[41] The conventional view is that Jesus seeks to save people from eternal punishment in hell and help people be happy and successful until then. Emergents say Jesus seeks to deal with the "mess we're in . . . both in terms of the general human condition and its specific outworking among contemporaries living under domination by the Roman Empire and who were confused and conflicted as to what they should do to be liberated."[42]

For the conventional view, Jesus preached that one needed to "repent of your individual sins and believe that my Father punished me on the cross so he won't have to punish you in hell. Only if you believe this will you go to heaven when the earth is destroyed and everyone is banished to hell." Emergents contend that the good news is that "God loves humanity, even in its lostness and sin. God graciously invites everyone and anyone to turn from his or her current path and follow a new way. Trust me and become my disciple, and you will be transformed, and you will participate in the transformation of the world, which is possible beginning right

[40] McLaren, *Everything*, 77–147. These labels are his.
[41] Ibid., 78.
[42] Ibid.

now."[43] For the conventional view, Jesus solves the problem of original sin. They are saved from wrath as a free gift of God. To serve God leads to a happier life. For Emergents, Jesus came to be "the Savior of the world, meaning he came to save the earth and all it contains from its ongoing destruction because of human evil."[44] This seed of goodwill prevails over evil as they experience liberation from the fear of death and condemnation. McLaren notes that this goodwill is also seen as a free gift.

McLaren's evaluation of the consequences of the conventional story also is important.[45] There are six unintended negative consequences of the conventional story that contrast with Emergent emphases.

(1) The Emergent view sees Jesus as a "medicinal cure to a lethal infection that plagues humanity (diagnosing and treating the individual and societal sickness called *sin*)." However, "the conventional view sees Jesus primarily as the legal solution to a capital infraction against God (legally resolving the capital offense of imperfection and the eternal punishment it demands)."[46] The conventional view relegates Jesus to practical irrelevance in relationship to human social problems.

(2) "While the emerging view sees God's primary focus as the transformation and salvation of humanity within history, the conventional view offers relatively little hope for history, but rather anticipates its complete destruction and replacement."[47] He calls this historical hopelessness "an opiate of the masses."

(3) "From the emerging viewpoint, God's concern is more holistic or integral, seeing individual and society, soul and body, life and afterlife, humanity and the rest of creation as being inseparably related." The "conventional view, however, is more dualistic, with human souls and other 'spiritual' things in one category and human bodies and other 'secular' things in another."[48] This

---

[43] Ibid., 79.
[44] Ibid.
[45] Ibid., 80–83.
[46] Ibid., 81.
[47] Ibid.
[48] Ibid.

dualism steers people away from engagement and divides life into a less than productive set of categories.

(4) "Fourth, in the emerging view, God cares about all people, and special blessings that come to one person or one group are to be shared for the common good. . . . But in the conventional view, God offers blessings to an elect group and little or nothing (except condemnation) to everyone else."[49] This risks producing an us-versus-them kind of elitism, seeking self-interest and little common good.

(5) "In the emerging view God seeks to save us and our world from the suicidal machinery of a society driven by a destructive and false framing story. But in many versions of the conventional view, God must destroy the world and all it contains because of our sin, so it is *from God*—and specifically from God's wrath and eternal damnation—that we must be saved."[50] Because this account is oriented toward wrath, there is little effort to see God involved in transformation.

(6) The conventional view sees a deteriorating history and such deterioration as God's will and plan. This risks creating a self-fulfilling prophecy. One can be led to seek humanity's progress in self-destruction rather than seeking to turn it around.[51]

McLaren then goes on to mention that some people in both camps will treat the emphases of the other camp as legitimate but added that such claims of legitimacy work more like fine print. He also contrasts the gospel *about* Jesus (conventional) with the gospel *of* Jesus (Emergent).

Another chapter discusses key titles tied to Jesus. According to McLaren, Jesus the *Christ* presents Jesus as more than a prophet, a "liberating king promised by God."[52] The message is: "Risk everything, including your life, to stand up to Caesar and join me in revolution—not by fighting and killing, but by being willing to die with me."

---

[49] Ibid., 82.
[50] Ibid.
[51] Ibid.
[52] Ibid., 97.

The *Son of Man* title "evokes a dream of liberation from the book of Daniel."[53] Living unbowed within a hostile imperial narrative is the point of that Old Testament book. That is, Daniel's concern is how to stand up to imperial power. Similarly in Jesus' usage of the imagery from Daniel is the presence of Jesus' authority and the handing over of the kingdom to the saints as they fight a similar imperial existence in Rome.

The title *Lord* points to Jesus as "the ultimate 'sir,'" but it was also the term used for the emperor. "The earliest confession of the earliest followers of Jesus—Jesus is Lord—was not in this light primarily a theological confession of Jesus' divinity, as many assume today; it was a very earthly declaration that Jesus, not Caesar, was the ultimate authority."[54]

McLaren concludes emphatically, *"Believe this good news, and defect from all human imperial narratives, counternarratives, dual narratives, and withdrawal narratives. Open your minds and hearts like children to see things freshly in this new way, follow me and my words, and enter into this new way of living."*[55]

Later in the book, McLaren makes another key complaint: one that is against a Second Coming Jesus[56] that often reflects the conventional view he has described. He complains that Jesus coming with the sword is not an image of violence because the sword comes out of Jesus' mouth. Jesus' word overcomes the world. This is the message of the book of Revelation. Jesus and the saints conquer "with a message of justice" and "the blood on Jesus' robe."[57]

ASSESSMENT OF McLAREN

My first critique of this presentation is simply whether McLaren has caught correctly the heart of Jesus' gospel message and Jesus' role in it. Another way to phrase it is whether McLaren's center in liberation is Jesus' center of liberation.

[53] Ibid., 98.
[54] Ibid.
[55] Ibid., 99.
[56] Ibid., 144–45.
[57] Ibid., 145.

I have already suggested my own critique of a "death for sin"-only gospel in my remarks evaluating Mark Driscoll's summary of the gospel. McLaren labels an account like Driscoll's as conventional. *However, in contrast to both McLaren and Driscoll, notice that my own stress was not on a liberation battle with Rome but on a liberation of the human heart by the Spirit of God.* I find it fascinating how much McLaren can mention Rome by name when Rome hardly comes up at all as an exclusive source of critique in the New Testament. The New Testament uses "Rome" sixteen times, and all sixteen mentions of the name "Rome" are references to a location. (The treatment of the term *Caesar* follows next.) Now, I know there are indirect references to the nation and the pagan culture it fosters, and there is even much New Testament critique of such, especially alluded to in the book of Revelation as a sample of what the world is like. But what is amazing is that Rome is more a cipher for what the world is and what allegiance to Christ requires us not to identify with as we live our lives as Christ's followers. Christian lives lived in Rome are handled much more subtly and by more indirect kinds of allusions than the directness and emphases McLaren gives to Rome as the key concern.

A check in the New Testament of the word *Caesar* shows that Jesus' remarks about rendering to Caesar the things that are Caesar's (Matt. 22:21 and parallels); the Jewish charges of Jesus denying the paying of taxes to Caesar, of which the passion accounts say Jesus is innocent (Luke 23:2); the Jewish charge to Pilate that to release Jesus, who claims to be a king, is to be no friend of Caesar (John 19:12); Paul's remarks about not having done anything against Caesar (Acts 25:8,11); and the apostle's appeal to be heard by Caesar are the only texts that mention the office in time from Jesus' ministry on. Paul, whom McLaren calls one of Jesus' best theological friends,[58] tells Christians *not* to be revolutionary in the sense McLaren's language about Rome suggests (Rom 13:1–7). First Peter does the same, and Peter also knew Jesus well (1 Pet 2:11–17). Peter even says, "Honor the emperor." These points suggest that McLaren's teasing out of the gospel emphasis and of Jesus'

[58] Brian McLaren, *The Secret Message of Jesus* (Nashville: W Publishing Group, 2006), 91.

teaching does not fit that of Jesus' most contemporary followers and confidants.

Now who does Jesus spend most of his time criticizing? That question is not hard to answer. A concordance check of Pharisees, scribes, Sadducees, or Jews (often meaning the Jewish leaders) shows that Jesus directly criticizes them far more than the Romans. Why? It is because if the most religious people, even those oriented to the one God in a polytheistic world cannot truly walk with God, then who can? I think it is because there was a fundamental need for all people, even the most religious, to see their absolute need for God to provide what is lacking in us, not merely to give us moral calls and instructions but to say that the disease that eats at us consumes us most dangerously from within (Mark 7:1–23). This is the point of Romans 1–3, all (Jews and Gentiles) sin and fall short of God in terms of being able to live as He calls us to live. Paul spends far more time making the point to Jews than to Gentiles in Rom 1:18–3:20.

McLaren does not doubt this but "reframes" it. My take is that he reframes its emphasis incorrectly in a corporate and largely sociopolitical realm. I agree that Jesus did not come to merely die for sin. However, Jesus is working in a context that is individual *and corporate* (thus Jew and Gentile). This challenge aims more at religious affections and impure hearts that lead to the formation of destructive structures than at the structures themselves. He gets at the personal cause that leads to the structural fault. The cause is not Rome, but our own human hearts and then how those hearts work out injustice, evil, *and* unrighteousness in all sorts of corporate contexts, including religious corporate contexts, as well as national political ones.

Jesus came to reconcile us to God. John the Baptist said it early on: "Here is the Lamb of God, who takes away the sin of the world!" The picture of sacrifice and atonement in the new covenant's inauguration is the picture Jesus shows His disciples at the Last Supper. Jesus' death opens the way to reestablish a broken relationship with God, where God takes the gracious initiative to restore us. God acts out of His love and commitment to the human race. This I take to be the conventional story, whether one reads John the Baptist (Luke 3:15–17), Jesus (Luke 24:49; John 14–16; and the Comforter to come), Paul (Rom 3–8), or Peter (1 Pet 1:1–9). They all note that Jesus' death opens the way for His Spirit to be sent to those who respond or embrace this message.

In other words, I am not sure the contrasts McLaren builds with the conventional story and his story are the only stories to be considered. More importantly, the conventional story, even as McLaren presents it, is a key dimension of Jesus' emphasis. This key component risks being lost in the move to a more sociopolitical Jesus, *even though I absolutely agree that the teaching of Jesus at its ethical level has significant and important social implications for how Jesus followers are called to live in light of the gospel. My point would be not to pit the conventional and emerging story against one another as McLaren is prone to do but to consider how these features combine to do a better job of filling out the full scope of what the biblical call to experience the gospel means.*

My second critique of McLaren has to do with how the book of Revelation and judgment are read. I agree with McLaren that the Jesus and sword image is about what comes through the "sword" of Jesus' teaching. But what that observation ignores is the context into which Jesus' teaching speaks. It comes in the midst of the bowl, seal, and trumpet judgments at the end, in a word of final and decisive judgment. It comes as Jesus returns to exercise judgment not in an idealized "every moment" morality of the church's ongoing activity. Jesus is not teaching and judging through how the church lives morally from day to day. This teaching by Jesus and the exercise of His authority takes place in a return that culminates in the righteous vindication of God's people, who to this point have suffered even unto death. Many believers as pictured in the book of Revelation have experienced this suffering at the hands of some of the world's most powerful leaders, including the Roman rulers. However uncomfortable the idea, the Bible does teach that God will make distinctions one day, with some being accepted into his eternal presence and others tragically failing to do so. This judgment is something Christ performs. His word exe-

cutes it in the decisive victory over evil. It does come in the midst
of seemingly catastrophic self-destruction that Jesus compared to
the horrific fall of Jerusalem in AD 70.

Having said this, let me make another balancing remark. The
fact that the world is headed in this direction and is said to end
up there one day does not mean that believers should abandon
their call to represent God and reflect His righteousness in a needy
world.[59] In other words, Christ's arrival to bring decisive righteousness to the world in His coming kingdom does not nullify
the call of God to His saints today to serve and be light in the
world. Once again, my complaint is that McLaren's juxtaposition
of Second Coming theology in contrast to Emergent emphases is
not the only way to describe those two options.

In sum, my take on themes among revisionist Emergents is that
all of the church needs to hear and give reflection to some of what
they say in terms of being more comprehensively Christian in our
practice. However, elements of their emphasis again risk losing
key components of the package. This is done in one of three ways
to which all sides of the discussion need to give careful attention.

The first involves mistaking sociopolitical goals as the ends
when it is people's hearts that desperately need what God alone
can supply. No human effort on its own is able to take us there in
terms of mending a diseased heart—what the theology has correctly called sin, both individual and corporate.

The second danger involves highlighting practice while being
too critical of attempts to think precisely theologically. On the
other hand, those who do careful theological thinking also need to
pay attention to criticism from the other side that on some matters,
a touch of humility might be a healthy thing.

---

[59] I do not have space here to develop this idea, but I have questions about the church's
"cultural mandate" to change the world. Some think such a mandate reflects a social aspect
to the call of God. However, a key question is whether the burden of this call tells the
world how to live or functions best in how the church engages the world. Such engagement
does not come through exercises of competing power with the world (i.e., a cultural war).
It comes in the power of living righteously and pursuing righteous goals in all aspects of
life, including in forms of corporate persuasion that do not use the same methods of power
the world uses. This engagement by the church includes how we give and serve in our
world righteously (i.e., in efforts like those to meet needs during and after Katrina or the
Indonesian tsunami).

The third danger is related to the second. It comes in some Emergents' desire to shy away from theological affirmation beyond some of the most basic Christian claims. I agree with Emergents, even revisionists, that the church has often fought too hard with each other about in-house issues, in some cases being too quick to draw lines of those who are in and out. One way to handle this problem is to step back from such divisive theological debate and simply not go there. We need to be sure our differences on several issues are worth the destructive effects of certain types of debate. Nonetheless, in many cases care in theological reflection benefits the church and helps her from falling into emphases and ideas that take us from the central emphases of God's call.

CONCLUSION

It is important to ask why some of these theological debates, especially central ones, like Jesus' nature, person, and work, occupied the church and the Spirit of God in the church for as long as they did. The church must have sensed by the Spirit that something significant was gained as they sought carefully to explain God and His Person. Believers have tried to wrestle with the depths of God, His Son, and Spirit for centuries. I suspect much of what was done in the past that the church has affirmed as valuable for us was studied for good reason. We should be careful to not leave the impression that what the Spirit is doing through our generation, whatever generation that is, was not available to previous generations of saints who also sought to be faithful. Faithfulness, even in theological dialogue and fellowship, has been a key goal of this chapter, written by one who thinks the right type of theological dialogue helps all of us to grow and mature, a goal I believe we all share. I was asked to highlight a particularly contemporary expression of this area, Emergent Christology, which I have presented as Emergent Christologies. The church has been at such discussion for a very long time—and for good reason; Jesus stands at the center of what God is about. Our voices are but one set in a long line of such discussions.

It is important to appreciate why Jesus was not only followed
as a teacher but is worshiped with the Father. Interestingly, none
of the Emergent subgroups seems to have problems with the doctrine of the person of Jesus or even the Trinity, although some
could read some Emergents' complaints about Greek philosophy
in the church as criticism of attempts at careful theological formulation. More discussions between all the groups, conventional
and Emergent, wrestle with the center of Jesus' message and what
he was emphasizing to followers. My essay has not sought to say
who is in or out. It has tried to make an appeal to all sides of the
discussion for a balance, in which I believe there is more need for
some both/and thinking versus the either/or. I also question arguments that appeal for more of some components at the seeming
expense of other key components. What we all need to seek is
more consideration of genuine integration, rather than taking sides
with guns loaded.

THE EMERGING CHURCH AND SALVATION

ROBERT E. SAGERS

BILL BRIGHT, FOUNDER of the evangelical campus ministry Campus Crusade for Christ, once gave his famous evangelistic presentation—the "Four Spiritual Laws"—to a group of faculty members at Berkeley. When one of the professors asked him how he would alter the presentation for a more intellectually astute audience, Bright responded, "I would probably read it more slowly."[1]

More recently, my brother told me about something that had occurred at the small liberal arts college he attended. During a time of outreach to incoming freshmen, the Campus Crusade for Christ chapter at the school handed out not the "Four Spiritual Laws" gospel tract made so popular by the organization's founder, but instead Donald Miller's recent book, *Blue Like Jazz*.[2]

Was such a shift in evangelistic strategy just one campus ministry's recognition that the gospel cannot be diluted down simply to four propositions? Or was something else taking place? Even if salvation is more than merely, "Pray this prayer so that you can go to heaven when you die," then what is it? And can the recent phenomenon commonly referred to as the emerging church movement help to sharpen and hone an evangelical understanding of soteriology?

---

[1] John G. Turner, *Bill Bright and Campus Crusade for Christ: The Renewal of Evangelicalism in Postwar America* (Chapel Hill, N.C.: The University of North Carolina Press, 2008), 103.

[2] Donald Miller, *Blue Like Jazz: Nonreligious Thoughts on Christian Spirituality* (Nashville: Thomas Nelson, 2003).

SETTING THE TABLE: EMERGING AND EMERGENT

While walking in Central Park in New York City, a friend of mine stopped to ask a woman for directions—or at least to be pointed to the nearest way out. Her response? "Not all who wander are lost. Enjoy the wandering." At the time, such advice was not the most helpful to my friend, but a similar distinction may be made in the present discussion—that is, that not all who are "emerging" are "Emergent."[3] Beyond this basic distinction, several pastors and scholars involved in the movement have sought to further delineate those within the emerging "conversation," including Scot McKnight,[4] Mark Driscoll,[5] Ed Stetzer,[6] and Darrin Patrick.[7] This is to say, though emerging church leader Mark Driscoll and Emergent church leader Karen Ward are both church planters in Seattle, the two of them are quite different in their beliefs and practices.[8]

[3] Emerging is that which refers generally to the conversation taking place among many churches and their leaders about how best to minister in a world that is increasingly postmodern in its mind-set, while Emergent—or Emergent Village—is an official organization, headed up in the United States by theologian Tony Jones. The former group is fairly amorphous and has no official statement of faith or denominational affiliation, while the latter group is an organization with its own particular leadership structure, conferences, Web site, blog, and book series.

[4] Scot McKnight, "Five Streams of the Emerging Church," *Christianity Today*, February 2007, 34–9. McKnight writes of five alliterated "streams" of the emerging church that flow into the emerging "lake": prophetic (or provocative), postmodern, praxis-oriented, postevangelical, and political.

[5] Mark Driscoll, "A Pastoral Perspective on the Emergent Church," *Criswell Theological Review* 3/2 (2006): 87–93. Driscoll, citing the influence of Southern Baptist missiologist Ed Stetzer, divides the emerging church conversation into three camps: relevants, reconstructionists, and revisionists. While relevants are concerned not with changing orthodox Christian doctrine but only updating church practices, and reconstructionists are generally evangelical but are putting forth new ways of "doing church," revisionists "are theologically liberal and question key evangelical doctrines."

[6] Ed Stetzer, "Understanding the emerging church," *Baptist Press*, 6 January 2006; accessed 29 April 2008 at www.sbcbaptistpress.org/printerfriendly.asp?ID=22406. Stetzer—who like Driscoll divides the emerging conversation into three types of leaders and churches—is unequivocal about the theological malpractice performed by those in the revisionist camp. He proposes that evangelical Christians ought to engage and read the work of such revisionist leaders "as we read mainline theologians—they often have good descriptions, but their prescriptions fail to take into account the full teaching of the Word of God."

[7] Darrin Patrick, "The Emerging Church: Discerning a Missional Milieu"; accessed 5 July 2008 at http://www.journeyon.net/the-emerging-church-discerning-a-missional-milieu-audio-content/. I am grateful to my friend Blake Ring for pointing me to a series of lectures delivered by Patrick, in which the pastor divides the emerging church movement into three streams—emerging conversational, emerging attractional (which splits into two more substreams: neo-Reformed and neo-"seeker sensitive"), and emerging incarnational.

[8] A clear delineation of the differences in the theological views of Driscoll and Ward on issues such as Scripture, the Trinity, and the atonement of Christ may be found in *Listening*

Those across the emerging church spectrum have critiqued various aspects of the contemporary evangelical doctrine of salvation. This essay aims to discern those aspects of the emerging critique to which the broader evangelical community may do well to listen and take heed, and which aspects may—if embraced—do more harm than good to our churches. Such soteriological reflection is important. After all, the glory of our King, Jesus, is at stake—as are the lives of our neighbors.

SALVATION AND THE KING: NARRATIVE AND THE EMERGING CHRISTIANS

Anyone who has had any amount of exposure to evangelical churches is probably familiar with the event known as the "testimony." The testimony often takes place within a corporate worship service or in an evangelistic encounter and is dedicated to the Christian's recounting how Jesus saved him or her—typically in order to encourage other believers or in hopes that an unbeliever may similarly be drawn to faith in Christ. There is something powerful in hearing a Christian's testimony—the narrative of how he once was lost but now is found. Indeed, this is a key aspect of the emerging church movement—and of postmodernism as a whole—that is, that everyone has a story, a way of making sense of the things that happen to them.

Emerging church leader Brian McLaren encourages Christians to "rely on the power of stories" when sharing the gospel with an unbeliever, stories from one's personal experience and biblical

to the Beliefs of Emerging Churches: Five Perspectives, ed. Robert Webber (Grand Rapids: Zondervan, 2007). Ward appreciates the irony that "many think of [Driscoll and I] as 'yin and yang' poles on the 'emerging' continuum, so I smile with the knowledge that God, in wisdom (or perhaps in serendipity) has seen fit to locate our respective faith communities less than two miles apart within Seattle." Karen Ward, "Response to Mark Driscoll," in Listening, 47. There may be some indications, however, that it will not be long until Driscoll is nearly entirely eliminated from reference in such discussions, as he becomes more entrenched in the Reformed speaking circuit and isolates himself from—and is himself isolated from—the theological underpinnings driving certain aspects of this movement. Note, for example, that Robert Webber references the group of contributors to this book several times in his conclusion to the volume, yet writes something akin to "except Mark Driscoll" four times in only seven pages. Robert Webber, "Conclusion: Assessing Emerging Theology," in Listening, 195–201.

stories.[9] Elsewhere, McLaren urges Christian leaders to rejoice in postmodernism's focus on individual narrative (if not its skepticism of—and at times even disdain for—metanarrative), though it is never made clear what the Christian metanarrative is about, ultimately.[10] Tony Jones asserts that Christians "believe that there is, indeed, one story into which all humanity and the entire cosmos can be enfolded," though in a postmodern world "we are going to have to be creative in how we tell the story."[11] McLaren, responding to Jones, is a bit less "confident that any of us really understands that metanarrative very well."[12]

Doug Pagitt, a pastor in Minneapolis, wrote a book on spiritual formation with nearly every other page devoted to a journal entry from a church member—giving the reader insight into the personal lives and struggles of those within Pagitt's church.[13] Pagitt tells of the time in his church's corporate worship service in which various members of the community may share their "stories." "Telling and hearing these stories shapes us and forms us," Pagitt asserts.[14] Mike Yaconelli edited a book detailing the respective "stories" of fifteen

[9] McLaren writes, "Your stories—about how you came to faith, about how God has made a difference in your life—are important data for a questioning friend. Think of Paul in the book of Acts—he's constantly telling his own story. But don't stop with your own story: tell biblical stories, too. Jesus seldom taught without telling a parable." In Tony Campolo and Brian D. McLaren, *Adventures in Missing the Point: How the Culture-Controlled Church Neutered the Gospel* (Grand Rapids: Zondervan, 2003), 96.

[10] Jerry Haselmayer, Brian D. McLaren, and Leonard Sweet, *A Is for Abductive: The Language of the Emerging Church* (Grand Rapids: Zondervan, 2003), 205–7. According to its various prefaces, this book is to be a "beginner's guide" of sorts for emerging church leaders in a postmodern matrix, and includes definitions of words such as *Be-living*, *Fuzzy*, *Quest-ions*, and *Zending*. Missing from this beginner's manual containing nearly 150 entries are words and terms such as *Christ*, *death*, *evangelism*, *faith*, *God*, *gospel*, *heaven*, *hell*, *Holy Spirit*, *hope*, *preaching*, and *sin*, among others that might seem to be relevant to such a guide.

[11] Tony Jones, *Postmodern Youth Ministry: Exploring Cultural Shift, Cultivating Authentic Community, Creating Holistic Connections* (Grand Rapids: Zondervan, 2001), 209.

[12] Ibid.

[13] Doug Pagitt, *Church Re-Imagined: The Spiritual Formation of People in Communities of Faith* (Grand Rapids: Zondervan, 2003).

[14] Ibid., 74. Pagitt insists that these stories are different than testimonies, a distinction that seems somewhat artificial—as Kevin DeYoung has pointed out. After quoting this section from Pagitt's book, DeYoung responds: "So, let me get this straight. They aren't testimonies, just stories that serve as testaments to what God is doing in our lives. Sounds like a testimony to me." In Kevin DeYoung and Ted Kluck, *Why We're Not Emergent: By Two Guys Who Should Be* (Chicago: Moody Publishers, 2008), 154.

emerging church leaders, "the new journeys of those who are trying to define and find Church . . . a group of people who have rediscovered the power of story, who see the gospel as story, who believe quite simply that Church is the place where we share our stories."[15]

Karen Ward asserts that those in "authentic emerging churches" are able to "learn to see ourselves connected to God's story only in so far as we have opportunity to tell and reflect upon our own stories, as faith and transformation are birthed by the Spirit in the overlap where God's story and our own human stories meet."[16] These different "voices" in the community, then, inform and make a "from-scratch" theology of the community where Ward serves as a pastor.[17] Going even further than Ward, philosopher Peter Rollins recounts a story adopted from a Buddhist parable that insinuates that a woman's life of good works is even "more splendid" than the Bible itself.[18]

Everyone created in the image of God is designed to hear, tell, and find meaning in stories.[19] And just as there are many different saviors and many different kingdoms in which people—outside of Christ—find their hope and their future, there are many different narratives that people tell to make sense of the world around them. These stories, if not seen within the grid of the *story* told in Scripture, can become distractions—or worse, idols—even for those who are in Christ. Observing the consumerist tendencies found within some Christian churches, James B. Twitchell argues that even Mammon worship is a narrative through which consumers make sense of their world.[20]

[15] Mike Yaconelli, "The Illegitimate Church," in *Stories of Emergence: Moving from Absolute to Authentic*, ed. Mike Yaconelli (Grand Rapids: Zondervan, 2003), 21.

[16] Ward, "Response to John Burke," in *Listening*, 79.

[17] Ward, "The Emerging Church and Communal Theology," in *Listening*, 162.

[18] Peter Rollins, *How (Not) to Speak of God* (Brewster, Mass.: Paraclete Press, 2006), 126–27.

[19] "One of the most universal human impulses can be summed up in a familiar four-word phrase: Tell me a story," Leland Ryken notes. "The Bible constantly satisfies that demand. Narrative is the dominant form of the Bible. Despite the multiplicity of literary genres found in the Bible, it is above all a book of stories." Leland Ryken, *Words of Delight: A Literary Introduction to the Bible*, 2nd ed. (Grand Rapids: Baker, 1992), 35.

[20] According to Twitchell: "When we go shopping, be it for fast-moving consumer goods or slow-moving redemption goods, it is because we are seeking a narrative that makes us feel powerful and perhaps even makes the pursuit worthwhile. . . . It's time to stop fighting about religion and recognize that we are hardwired to seek its palliative effect

As with all stories, it matters greatly how one tells the Christian narrative, and whether he believes the story and its details are true. Pagitt admits as much when he asserts that he finds "God's hopes, dreams, and plans for the world to include the eradication of sin and freedom for humankind through Jesus, but those are not the primary points of the gospel."[21] Responding to Mark Driscoll— who presents a more historic Protestant view of individual salvation in terms of God's holiness, man's sin, and the need to believe in Christ for the forgiveness of such sin—Pagitt writes, "I think much of our difference comes from the fact that in many ways we are telling different stories of Christianity. We seem to be calling for different starting points and ending points."[22]

Of course, God Himself—as His Spirit-breathed Scriptures reveal—has already declared the starting point *and* the ending point of the story of Christianity. That beginning and ending, that Alpha and Omega, has a name: Jesus of Nazareth. Emerging church writer Donald Miller recalls giving a gospel presentation to a class of students at a Bible college. Stating beforehand that he would be leaving out a key component of the gospel, Miller spoke of man's sinfulness, the need to repent and believe in order to be saved, and that those who repent and believe could live lives that are "God-honoring and God-centered." However, according to Miller, not one of the forty-five students in the class was able to point out that the missing component—the missing *man*—from Miller's gospel presentation was Jesus Christ. "To a culture that believes they 'go to heaven' based on whether or not they are morally pure, or that they understand some theological ideas, or that they are very spiritual, Jesus is completely unnecessary," Miller writes. "At best He is an afterthought, a technicality by which we

and purpose. And it's time to admit that materialism and spiritualism—consumerism and religion—are not in opposition but simply part of the complex meaning-making equipment of being human." In James B. Twitchell, *Shopping for God: How Christianity Went from In Your Heart to In Your Face* (New York: Simon and Schuster, 2007), 94. Given this assessment, it is difficult to discern whether Twitchell has ever been exposed to a truly countercultural community of Christians committed to living according to the ethics of Christ the King—and not simply to the ethics of the prince of the power of the air, in whatever form the father of lies presents them.

[21] Pagitt, "Response to Mark Driscoll," in *Listening*, 42.
[22] Ibid.

become morally pure, or a subject of which we know, or a founding father of our woo-woo spirituality."[23]

Miller's point is well taken. It is much too easy for all people to focus on God generally, without focusing on God's glory as mediated through Christ. Conservative Evangelicals are not exempt from this temptation. In one sense, then, some emerging church devotees are right to be "suspicious" of systematic theology, at least in the way that they might define it.[24] After all, God did not reveal to us a systematic theology textbook. Instead, He gave us a *story*—a narrative that is good specifically because it is a narrative that is true. This is not to downplay the importance of systematic theology but only to augment its importance and vitality through the increase of focus on biblical theology.[25] Throughout the Scriptures God is moving toward a goal—a *man*—the One in whom all the Law and the Prophets find their fulfillment, Jesus Christ (Luke 24:27,44). A serpent who speaks, a global flood, a giant slain by a shepherd boy—even righteous pleas for infants to be dashed against the sides of rocks—only make sense in light of God's purposes in a Jewish carpenter from Galilee.

Soteriology, then, is radically Christ-centered. In speaking of salvation, theologians sometimes ask questions such as, "From what (or whom) am I saved? In what (or whom) am I saved? To what (or whom) am I saved? By what (or whom) am I saved?" The answer to each of the four questions above, ultimately, is the same: Jesus. The Christian is saved from his own sin and therefore Christ's just judgment of it in looking to Christ as the forgiveness of sin (John 3:14–15). To an inheritance that is his in Christ—the resurrected One sitting at the right hand of God—is the believer saved (Eph 1:11–14). In Jesus alone is forgiveness found, this One who was made sin on our behalf, "that we might become the righteousness of

---

[23] This anecdote and subsequent quote can be found in Donald Miller, *Searching for God Knows What* (Nashville: Thomas Nelson, 2004), 157–60.

[24] McKnight, "Five Streams of the Emerging Church," 38.

[25] For a succinct presentation of how biblical theology and systematic theology ought to inform one another, see D. A. Carson, "Systematic Theology and Biblical Theology," in *New Dictionary of Biblical Theology: Exploring the Unity & Diversity of Scripture*, ed. T. Desmond Alexander, Brian S. Rosner, D. A. Carson, and Graeme Goldsworthy (Downers Grove, Ill.: InterVarsity Press, 2000), 89–104.

God" (2 Cor 5:21). The Christian is saved by faith—not faith in the abstract, but faith in a person: Jesus Christ (Gal 3:20). And for what purpose is salvation granted in Christ? "So that at the name of Jesus every knee should bow—of those who are in heaven and on earth and under the earth—and every tongue should confess that Jesus Christ is Lord, to the glory of God the Father" (Phil 2:10–11).

Therefore, a recovery of the full-orbed gospel of Christ may necessitate a renewed emphasis on the *story* of the gospel as revealed in the Bible—a narrative that is focused on Christ. Even God's commands to His people Israel are rooted in His redemptive dealings with them in the past and in their hopes of His preservation of them in the future (Deut 6:20–25)—redemption that is seen not in the abstract but in God's delivering them from the bondage of slavery to Pharaoh, in plagues upon the people of Egypt, in bringing them through the Red Sea, and in providing for them food and water in the wilderness. The prophet Isaiah foresees a day in which an Anointed One of God will proclaim the year of the Lord's favor (Isa 61), looking forward to the day when the true representative of Israel (Matt 3:13–17) will provide salvation to all men who call on His name (Acts 4:12). The apostle Paul writes a letter to the church at Rome explaining the purpose of this narrative (Rom 1:1–7).

In telling this story, then, Christians—emerging or otherwise— must focus on the main character of the story, Jesus Christ, and the mission of this main character, the ushering in of the kingdom of God. Without this focus, there is no Christianity—there is no gospel. As important as the individual stories of those within our churches are, what is of ultimate importance is whether or not those individual stories—and the men and women who tell them—have been crucified, buried, and resurrected in the person and work of Jesus Christ.[26] Musician and author Michael Card is asserting biblical truth when he sings, "Life is a song we must sing with our days, a poem with meaning, more than words can say; a painting with colors, no rainbow can tell, a lyric that rhymes either

[26] Russell D. Moore, "Beyond a Veggie Tales Gospel: Preaching Christ from Every Text," *The Tie (Southern Seminary Magazine)*, Spring 2008, 14–15. Alan Jacobs recently published a proposal as to how Christians can properly understand and intertwine their own personal testimonies in light of the "One Story" of the Bible, a book entitled *Looking Before and After: Testimony and the Christian Life* (Grand Rapids: Eerdmans, 2008).

heaven or hell."[27] Those who find their identity in Jesus know that in Christ, their life finds meaning; in Christ, they have a story to tell—a testimony worth sharing.

SALVATION AND THE CROSS: ATONEMENT AND THE EMERGING CHRISTIANS

Since the biblical storyline—indeed, since all of the world's history—is centered on the Word of God who took on flesh, then Christians must make sense of the self-stated mission of this One who declared that He "did not come to be served, but to serve, and to give His life—a ransom for many" (Mark 10:45). But the question remains: if "the Son of Man has come to seek and to save the lost" (Luke 19:10), then what exactly does this mean, and how exactly did this happen? Why was the sinless Son of Man cruci-fied, and what did His death and resurrection accomplish?

In speaking of the atonement of Jesus Christ, not many emerg-ing church adherents are quick to defend the centrality of Christ's penal substitutionary death. Mark Driscoll contends that "it is the death of Jesus and what it accomplished that is the most contro-versial aspect of Jesus' life and ministry, because it is the most important."[28] He defends penal substitution based upon "four essential truths of Scripture": mankind is sinful; God is both holy and just; God hates sin; and God deals with both sinners and sin through the atoning work of Christ.[29] In fact, for Driscoll, Jesus' atoning work is at the heart of the gospel itself.[30]

Not all emerging church leaders are so accepting of the doc-trine of penal substitution. Doug Pagitt argues against the "judicial model" of the atonement, arguing that it "puts the law at the center

[27] Michael Card, "The Poem of Your Life," from the album *Poiema* (Sparrow, 1994).

[28] Driscoll, "The Emerging Church and Biblicist Theology," in *Listening*, 29.

[29] Ibid., 29–30. In a later work, Driscoll expands the significance of Jesus' death on the cross to seven biblical truths: "God is holy and without any sin"; "God made us holy and without any sin"; "[s]in results in death"; "Jesus is sinless"; "[w]e are sinful"; "Jesus be-came our sin"; and "Jesus died for us." Gerry Breshears and Mark Driscoll, *Vintage Jesus: Timeless Answers to Timely Questions* (Wheaton, Ill.: Crossway, 2007), 107–20.

[30] Driscoll contends that "the Bible is one story about the Trinitarian God who created us, mercifully endures our sin, and sent Jesus Christ to live and die in our place, thereby saving us from eternal wrath if we repent of sin and trust in him alone." Driscoll, "The Emerging Church and Biblicist Theology," 35.

of the story."[31] In one of his fictional works, Brian McLaren presents several different views of the atonement through the book's four main characters.[32] After one of the characters presents to her friends a truncated synopsis of the classic penal substitutionary view of the atonement, Kerry—a "seeker"—responds by declaring, uncontested, that such a view "sounds like divine child abuse. You know?"[33] New Testament theologian D. A. Carson points out that McLaren does not seek to provide any kind of biblical justification for any of these various theories of the atonement, and seems especially put off by any kind of substitutionary theory of the atonement of Christ.[34]

Others within the emerging church movement, such as Spencer Burke and Barry Taylor, write that it was not Jesus' intention to die as a propitiation of God's wrath for the sins of the world. Instead, Jesus died because He threatened the religious community by breaking their rules, which He did out of His sacrificial love for others. Christians, then, need to "balance" penal substitution—which "can reinforce a caricature of a God who is

---

[31] Doug Pagitt, *A Christianity Worth Believing: Hope-Filled, Open-Armed, Alive-and-Well Faith for the Left Out, Left Behind, and Let Down in Us All* (San Francisco: Jossey-Bass, 2008), 155. Pagitt writes of the "judicial view": "In this view, God is not a softy but rather a hard-nosed, immovable, infallible judge who cannot abide defiance of the law. And boy, did we defy it. When Adam and Eve broke God's law in the garden, they offended and angered God. So heinous was their crime that their punishment extended to all of humanity for all time. The antidote to this situation is the crucifixion of the Incarnate Son of God because only the suffering and death of an equally infinite and infallible being could ever satisfy the infinite offense of the infinitely dishonored God and assuage his wrath. Yikes!" Ibid., 154.

[32] Brian D. McLaren, *The Story We Find Ourselves In: Further Adventures of a New Kind of Christian* (San Francisco: Jossey-Bass, 2003), 100–108.

[33] Ibid., 102. Kerry's response here is an echo of the now-famous assertion from British theologians Steve Chalke and Alan Mann that penal substitutionary atonement is akin to "divine child abuse." In Steve Chalke and Alan Mann, *The Lost Message of Jesus* (Grand Rapids: Zondervan, 2003), 182. McLaren wrote an endorsement for *The Lost Message of Jesus*. McLaren not only writes little of penal substitution—except in a dismissive way—but at times he seems to drive a wedge between Christ's atonement as a demonstration of peace and a demonstration of victory. Brian D. McLaren, *The Secret Message of Jesus: Uncovering the Truth that Could Change Everything* (Nashville: W Publishing Group, 2006), 99. However, one might ask in response, what if God intended for Christ's death on the cross to be *both* a securing of victory over the principalities and powers (Col 2:15) and the means through which He would bring ultimate peace with God and neighbor (Eph 2:1–22)?

[34] D. A. Carson, *Becoming Conversant with the Emerging Church: Understanding a Movement and Its Implications* (Grand Rapids: Zondervan, 2005), 166–68.

angry, bloodthirsty, and judgmental"—with good works done in love. After all, they assert, "[w]hat counts is not a belief system but a holistic approach of following what you feel, experience, discover, and believe; it is a willingness to join Jesus in his vision for a transformed humanity."[35]

Biblically speaking, it is precisely this "vision for a transformed humanity" that necessitated Christ's substitutionary death on the cross.[36] Throughout the Old Testament, Israel is commanded to offer a sacrificial substitute to take on the penalty for sin incurred by the people's offenses against a holy God. Such sacrifices, then, are both penal and substitutionary. In the fullness of time, God sent One who would serve as the final sacrificial substitute, One who would take the sin of the world upon Himself: Jesus Christ. As John writes of Jesus, "He Himself is the propitiation for our sins, and not only for ours, but also for those of the whole world" (1 John 2:2).

As Jesus Christ is hanging on the cross—dying even for the sins of those standing at His feet in mockery—He cries out to God, "Father, forgive them, because they do not know what they are doing" (Luke 23:34). Blinded by the prince of darkness, men—if left to themselves—would never come to God; indeed, they cannot (Rom 8:7). Like the Pharisee who trusted in his own righteousness (Luke 18:9–14), the natural man will never recognize his need for another to die in his place—that God's holiness and wrath would be satisfied in looking upon Christ and pardoning all those who are found hid in Him. But John writes that the light came into the world not to condemn it, "but that the world might be saved through Him" (John 3:17). In becoming the cursed One by being nailed to a tree, Christ's dying cry of "It is finished" (John 19:30) means that the fulfillment to which the blood of bulls and goats

---

[35] Spencer Burke and Barry Taylor, *A Heretic's Guide to Eternity* (San Francisco: Jossey-Bass, 2006), 130–31. The story of Burke's evolution from megachurch pastor to emerging church leader is detailed in Spencer Burke, "From the Third Floor to the Garage," in *Stories of Emergence: Moving from Absolute to Authentic*, ed. Mike Yaconelli (Grand Rapids, Mich.: Zondervan, 2003), 27–39.

[36] For two recent defenses of the atoning work of Christ as both penal and substitutionary, see Steve Jeffery, Michael Ovey, and Andrew Sach, *Pierced for Our Transgressions: Rediscovering the Glory of Penal Substitution* (Wheaton, Ill.: Crossway, 2007), and Thomas R. Schreiner, "Penal Substitution View," in *The Nature of the Atonement: Four Views*, ed. James Beilby and Paul R. Eddy (Downers Grove, Ill.: InterVarsity Press, 2006), 67–98.

had pointed (Heb 9:1–10:18) has now come in this Lamb of God who takes away the sin of the world (John 1:29). The atonement, then, far from being a "verb," is something that has been accomplished by God within history—in Christ.[37]

It was not simply God's wrath or justice that held Jesus there on the cross—though such characteristics are necessary expressions of God's holiness toward sin. "We speak easily of Jesus as our pal—our friend who comes to us on bended knee to wash feet and bring hugs—but we forget, with little difficulty, that it was God's justice, the necessity of His holiness, that brought death to give life," emerging church worship leader David Crowder writes. "It is His holiness that required the shedding of blood, the losing of life, to be the only way to make things right. It was the turning of His back that darkened the sky as our Christ breathed finality."[38] God's holiness and justice, though, are not at odds with God's love (1 John 4:16). The Father's love for the Son, the Son's love for the Father, and God's love for the world drove Jesus' Spirit-empowered mission to be the propitiation for the sins of the world (1 John 2:2). Love is most clearly expressed in the Son of God being hung on a tree, dying, and being raised from the dead—all that He might be the Savior of the world.

Burke and Taylor are correct to assert that the atonement of Christ ought to lead Christians to perform good works done in love—but not as a "balance" to the crucifixion. On the contrary, the penal substitutionary death of Christ is the *grounds* for such good works and holy living. As the apostle Peter writes to the exiles, Christ's suffering and death on our behalf is the grounds for which Christians may endure suffering on Christ's behalf (1 Pet 2:18–25). And the apostle John writes that being found hid

---

[37] "For Mark (Driscoll), it seems that having a correct doctrine of atonement is absolutely critical, while my writing centers on atonement as more of a *verb*, a happening to and within God that invites a happening to and within us." Ward, "Response to Mark Driscoll," *Listening*, 46.

[38] David Crowder, *Praise Habit: Finding God in Sunsets and Sushi* (Colorado Springs: THINK, 2004), 69. Timothy J. Stoner makes a similar point about the relationship between God's judgment and His mercy: "At the cross, judgment triumphs over mercy in order that mercy may triumph over all. It is only this that makes sense of the most startling and offensive of all biblical statements." Timothy J. Stoner, *The God Who Smokes: Scandalous Meditations on Faith* (Colorado Springs: NavPress, 2008), 100.

in God by His love compels us to love our brother (1 John 4:19–21). Paul asserts that the reconciling work of God in Christ in His substitutionary death on the cross (Eph 2:1–10) is the grounds for reconciliation to one's brother (vv. 11–22).

The hope of the gospel in the finished work of Christ on the cross is the impetus behind persevering to the day that Christ will present all those in Him as "holy, faultless, and blameless before Him" (Col 1:21–23). Joel B. Green and Mark D. Baker, in a work that is cited often by some emerging church leaders, contend that penal substitutionary atonement "does not intersect with the day-to-day reality of actual people." In addition, they assert, "[e]thically this model has little to offer; it can do little more than serve as an example to point to when calling individuals to imitate Christ."[39] Very little could be further from the biblical truth.

Living holy lives and suffering for the sake of the gospel—in following the example of Christ (Isa 52:13–53:12)—are not just to be done because turning the other cheek is the "right" thing to do. Instead, Christians are to follow the example of Christ in humility specifically because they know that God, in the last day, will exalt them—just as He has exalted Jesus. The prophet Isaiah foretold of a righteous, obedient servant of Israel who nevertheless would be struck in His back, have His beard plucked out, and be disgraced and spit upon. However, this suffering servant is able to set His face like a flint because He knows that God will help and vindicate Him (Isa 50:5–8).

The disciples understood not why their Rabbi must be "mocked, insulted, spit on" (Luke 18:32) in order to accomplish all that was written about Him in the prophets, but Jesus knew that—though He would be killed—" He will rise on the third day" (Luke 18:33). In light of the awful death set before Him that caused Him to sweat even drops of blood, Jesus knows that His Father is with Him; He knows and trusts that Solomon spoke Spirit-breathed words when He recorded, "humility comes before honor" (Prov 15:33). This honor, then, is bestowed upon Christ for His humility and obedience

---

[39] Joel B. Green and Mark D. Baker, *Recovering the Scandal of the Cross: Atonement in New Testament and Contemporary Contexts* (Downers Grove, Ill.: InterVarsity Press, 2000), 149.

in His being raised from the dead by the Spirit of holiness (Rom
1:4), being given "the name that is above every name" (Phil 2:9)—
that He may be worshiped by all in His kingdom forever.

Emerging church adherents are right to emphasize the Christus
Victor theme of the atonement. Where they diverge from a holistic
picture of the atonement is emphasizing it to the deemphasis—
or often the dismissal—of the atonement's penal substitutionary
aspect. For a movement that is so sensitive to broad-brush criticism, the hypocrisy in presenting such a caricature of penal substitution—"cosmic child abuse"—is somewhat astounding. But even
the victory of Christ over the principalities and powers is rooted in
Christ's substitutionary death.

Beginning in Eden, the ancient, cosmic warfare that takes place
throughout history between the seed of the woman and the seed of
the serpent (Gen 3:15) is decisively won by the One who crushes
the head of the serpent at Golgotha, the Place of a Skull (Mark
15:22).[40] In the work of the cross, Jesus "disarmed the rulers and
authorities and disgraced them publicly; He triumphed over them
by Him" (Col 2:15). But this victory over the principalities and
powers takes place specifically because God has reconciled believers to Himself through the work of Christ on the cross: "He made
you alive with Him and forgave us all our trespasses. He erased
the certificate of debt, with its obligations, that was against us and
opposed to us, and has taken it out of the way by nailing it to the
cross" (Col 2:13–14). The Scriptures show that the cosmic bondage of all of creation is contingent on human sin and guilt (Gen
3:14–19; Rom 8:19–23)—sin and guilt that entered the world
through one man, Adam (Rom 5:12–14).[41] In Christ, this curse
has been reversed, for He has overcome the human enslavement to
sin and death "by bearing the punishment due to a humanity justly
accused by the satanic powers . . . thereby restoring humanity as

[40] For an overview of head-crushing in the Scriptures and how this biblical theme relates to Christ's defeating sin and death, see James Hamilton, "The Skull Crushing Seed of
the Woman: Inner-Biblical Interpretation of Genesis 3:15," *The Southern Baptist Journal
of Theology* 10/2 (2006): 30–54.
[41] Russell D. Moore, *The Kingdom of Christ: The New Evangelical Perspective*
(Wheaton, Ill.: Crossway, 2004), 114.

king of the cosmos in the person of the Second Adam"[42] (see Rom 5:15–17).

Through His death and subsequent resurrection and ascension to the right hand of the Father, Jesus Christ gives good gifts to men, the spoils of victory. Just as David sings to the God who "ascended on high, leading a host of captives in your train and receiving gifts among men" (Ps 68:18 ESV), so too "grace was given to each one of us according to the measure of the Messiah's gift" (Eph 4:7)—specifically, gifts for the building up of the body of Christ, the church (Eph 4:11–12). The indwelling Spirit of Christ, breathed out into the church at Pentecost (Acts 2), is given so that those in the church may encourage and edify one another in love—indeed, that those in Christ may take part in this love-driven warfare (1 Cor 12–14).[43]

Donald Miller may be leery of the "war metaphor," but the gospel is the declaration of God's victory over the principalities and powers in Christ.[44] Without the war, there is no victory; without the victory, the wrath of God remains on us (John 3:36). It was the will of God to crush Jesus (Isa 53:10), that in Him there would be forgiveness and righteousness. And the love of God demonstrated therein is about as far from child abuse as one can get.

SALVATION AND THE NEW BIRTH: INDIVIDUAL CONVERSION AND THE EMERGING CHRISTIANS

Many emerging church leaders point out that the gospel is bigger than just individual salvation. After all, they argue, Jesus came to bring a kingdom, not an evangelism tract. Therefore, it is deduced, what Christians should be about is "kingdom work"— that is, doing good works in Jesus' name. Too many Evangelicals today, some emerging church leaders assert, are too caught up in

---

[42] Ibid., 115.

[43] Though it is not without weakness, a recent work by Scot McKnight attempts to show that the death and resurrection of Christ was to create a Spirit-filled, justified *community* of believers—an admirable effort to provide some correction to an all-too-often individualistically-focused contemporary evangelical theology. Scot McKnight, *A Community Called Atonement* (Nashville: Abingdon Press, 2007).

[44] Miller, *Blue Like Jazz*, 132.

reading the words recorded by the apostle Paul instead of the "red letters" from the mouth of Jesus.[45] What is missed in such discussion, however, is that it is specifically this individual salvation that is necessary for one even to *see* this kingdom of God. "I assure you," Jesus says to Nicodemus, "unless someone is born again, he cannot see the kingdom of God" (John 3:3). Jesus did not divorce individual regeneration from cosmic regeneration, and neither should His followers.

Beginning with Adam and Eve, sin and death have pervaded the world. It seems that sin, however, is seldom discussed within some emerging churches—at times intentionally so. "We don't talk about sin very often," emerging church pastor Mike Yaconelli declares. That is because Yaconelli asserts that people already know what sin is, and therefore it's assumed that they don't need to talk about it. Instead, they come to church looking for answers to questions about their sin: "We don't have to talk about sin. It's a given. What we're all longing for is good news."[46]

At other times, original sin seems to have been completely discarded at the expense of a more beatific view of human nature. Steve Chalke and Alan Mann contend that far from teaching original sin, Jesus instead "believed in *original goodness!* God declared that all his creation, including humankind, was very good. That's not to suggest that Jesus is denying that our relationship with God is in need of reconciliation, but that he is rejecting any idea that we are, somehow, beyond the pale."[47] At a more popular level, Donald Miller—in ruminating on his love for Jesus—writes that "I think the difference in my life came when I realized, after reading those Gospels, that Jesus didn't just love me out of principle; He didn't just love me because it was the right thing to do. Rather, there was something inside me that caused Him to love me."[48]

[45] Or so argues Barry Taylor, who—in seeking "a fresh understanding of the gospel"—realized that he "needed to stop reading Paul for a while and instead focus on Jesus." As quoted in Ryan K. Bolger and Eddie Gibbs, *Emerging Churches: Creating Christian Community in Postmodern Cultures* (Grand Rapids: Baker, 2005), 48.

[46] Yaconelli, "The Illegitimate Church," 18.

[47] Chalke and Mann, *The Lost Message of Jesus*, 67.

[48] Miller, *Blue Like Jazz*, 238.

Christians throughout the centuries have affirmed the need to be forgiven of sin in order to be reconciled to the Father. However, emerging church pastor Rob Bell writes, with the coming of Christ now *everyone* has been forgiven.[49] In fact, he says, even hell is full of forgiven sinners. The difference between forgiven sinners in heaven and forgiven sinners in hell "is how we choose to live, which story we choose to live in, which version of reality we trust. Ours or God's."[50] While Bell's emphasis on the Christian's finding one's life hid in Christ is helpful, just where repentance of sin fits within this choosing to live God's story—in being brought into union with Christ—is somewhat unclear.

Spencer Burke and Barry Taylor go even further than Bell when they assert that "we are already in unless we want to be out."[51] The fact that grace and sin are linked together in the Christian tradition is a "problem," for "linking grace to sin detracts from its beauty and intensity."[52] Instead, grace is "not conditional on recognizing or renouncing sin, and it comes to us whether or not we ask for it. We don't have to do something to receive it, nor do we even have to respond to it in some way. It simply comes."[53] Unbiblical contentions such as these evoked an uncharacteristically stern response from Scot McKnight, who wrote to Burke on his blog: "Go back to church. Go back to the gospel of Jesus—crucified and raised. Let the whole Bible shape all of your theology. Listen to your critics. Integrate a robust Christology, a robust death-and-resurrection gospel, and a full Trinitarian theology back into your guide to eternity."[54]

Another central aspect of the emerging church movement is its renewed emphasis on living out one's salvation in the context of community. Spiritual formation, contends Doug Pagitt, is not merely being in accountability with others—though this is

---

[49] Though Rob Bell has seldom—if ever—publicly identified himself with the emerging church movement, his writings, sermons, lectures, and NOOMA videos are all very popular with emerging church adherents.

[50] Rob Bell, *Velvet Elvis: Repainting the Christian Faith* (Grand Rapids: Zondervan, 2005), 146.

[51] Burke and Taylor, *A Heretic's Guide to Eternity*, 61.

[52] Ibid., 62.

[53] Ibid., 63.

[54] Accessed 29 April 2008 at www.jesuscreed.org/?p=1319.

important. Rather, "We feel called to vulnerability. We are seeking
to move into relationships where we don't merely ask others to
hold us to living in the way of Jesus, but where we invite them to
participate in our efforts to do so."[55] Indeed, though he laments the
"sound byte" dissection of the gospel into isolated Bible verses
and proof texts, he makes much of the "sound byte" in Mark 1:15.
Commenting on these words of Jesus—" The time is fulfilled, and
the kingdom of God has come near. Repent and believe in the
good news!"—Pagitt questions whether the good news is found
in the life, death, resurrection, and promised return of Christ, or
whether it is instead an "invitation into Kingdom life."[56]

This emphasis on salvation within the context of community directly affects the evangelistic strategies of some emerging
churches. At times, confrontational evangelistic techniques are
replaced by "missional living."[57] Others attempt to convince people that following in the way of Jesus is merely "the best possible
way for a person to live."[58] McKnight laments the fact that the
emerging church movement is not known for evangelism—though
he wishes it was. "Unless you proclaim the Good News of Jesus
Christ," McKnight warns, "there is no good news at all—and if
there is no Good News, then there is no Christianity, emerging or
evangelical."[59]

Perhaps such a movement is not known for evangelism specifically because some of its leaders seem to lack clarity on the issue
of "who is in and who is out" when it comes to the Christian faith.

---

[55] Pagitt, *Church Re-Imagined*, 27.

[56] Ibid., 33, 35. In seeming to pit the gospel as a call to believe in Christ over against
"an invitation into Kingdom life," Pagitt partakes in the very kind of false dichotomy of
which emerging church leaders are so critical of evangelicals.

[57] Lauren Sandler has this to say about Mark Driscoll's church, Mars Hill in Seattle,
Washington: "Mark never views evangelism as a form of marketing. Because Mars Hill
members frown on the traditional techniques of Bible thumping on the street corner, begging on televangelism programs, and threatening eternal hellfire on talk radio, they've had
to consider missionary work of a different flavor, which they call 'missional living.' This
is the notion that living well in strict accordance with the Bible, while reaping the benefits
of a deeply supportive community, advertises the faith to the heathens by demonstration.
. . . That demonstration is what is known as relational evangelism, or simply, the act of
hanging out with an unbeliever until he or she is born again." Lauren Sandler, *Righteous:
Dispatches from the Evangelical Youth Movement* (New York: Viking, 2006), 50–51.

[58] Bell, *Velvet Elvis*, 21.

[59] McKnight, "Five Streams of the Emerging Church," 38.

In June of 2005, Emergent Village issued a statement—signed by such emerging church leaders as Tony Jones, Dan Kimball, Chris Seay, and Brian McLaren—clarifying that "yes, we believe that Jesus is the crucified and risen Savior of the cosmos and no one comes to the Father except through Jesus."[60] Despite such a statement, it remains unclear whether these leaders believe that personal faith in Christ—belief by the one crying out in repentance and faith before one's death—is necessary for reconciliation to the Father. It is one thing to say that salvation comes only through Jesus, but it is something else to affirm the necessity of personal belief in Him for one to be saved.

Karen Ward asserts that she remains undecided on the eternal fate of those who do not trust in Christ alone for salvation, but says she never downplays "the twenty-four/seven calling of Christians to make bold our witness to the gospel of Jesus Christ."[61] Likewise, McLaren recently wrote a book "dedicated to all who are seeking faith, spirituality, purpose, hope, and God." An apologetic work of sorts, McLaren seeks to answer some of the common objectives to "faith," including the question, "Don't all paths lead to God?" McLaren admits that there are many unknowns about God that do not bother him, including God's treatment of those in religions other than Christianity.[62] "Well, I wouldn't put it past God to be able to get through to people in (or out of) any religions," McLaren muses. "In my experience, God is amazingly merciful, so I wouldn't be shocked at all if God's mercy extends to surprising lengths, in unexpected directions, to people you never would have guessed."[63] At the end of the book, McLaren urges his readers to continue their journey for faith by—among other things— finding "a pastor, priest, rabbi, trusted friend, or other spiritual mentor to help me process my remaining questions."[64]

---

[60] Accessed 19 May 2008 at http://www.emergentvillage.com/weblog/our-response-to-critics.

[61] Ward, "Response to Mark Driscoll," 46.

[62] Brian D. McLaren, *A Search for What Makes Sense: Finding Faith* (Grand Rapids: Zondervan, 2007), 175.

[63] Ibid., 177.

[64] Ibid., 183.

Timothy J. Stoner recalls a conversation that took place among members of his theology discussion group. Stoner inquired as to whether Rob Bell really believed that sincere adherents of non-Christian religions—"they reject Jesus"—would be saved. After a moment of palpable silence, a man who had been a founding member of Bell's church and served in leadership roles there—and who was on a first-name basis with Bell—blurted out, "Of *course* that's what he believes!" In reflecting on that conversation, Stoner notes that he has not been able to confirm or deny the accuracy of this man's statement, but what troubled him was that "this is what a friend who really ought to know is convinced Rob believes. That's the danger of posing too many questions. You may wind up confusing your own friends, if not yourself."[65]

Many emerging church leaders are right to point out the fact that being found in Christ is not merely a one-time decision—a decision with few or no ramifications for the believer in terms of seeking to apply Jesus' lordship to every area of his or her life. McLaren likens such one-time decisional views of regeneration to runners who, in getting ready to compete in a race, stop to congratulate themselves after crossing the starting line, never to run any further.[66] At the same time, Tony Campolo's critique of McLaren on this point is equally valid, for there does come a time when the Spirit works to change a person's heart—a time that may be known only to the Lord, but a time of conversion nonetheless.[67]

This is not to take away from the need for continual faith and repentance, however. After all, the Christian's walk with Christ is to be characterized by ongoing faith and repentance, with continual cries of "Lord, I believe; help my unbelief!" and "Lord, have mercy on me, a sinner." When speaking to someone about his having trusted in Christ, the focus is not just on the past tense, but also on the present tense of the verb "trust." And the work of God through the power of the Spirit to draw people to faith in Christ is not merely a matter of the person deciding to live in a slightly different way. Rather, such a change of heart is of cosmic signifi-

---

[65] Stoner, *The God Who Smokes*, 36–39.
[66] Campolo and McLaren, *Adventures in Missing the Point*, 26–27.
[67] Ibid., 29.

cance, for God "has rescued us from the domain of darkness and transferred us into the kingdom of the Son He loves, in whom we have redemption, the forgiveness of sins" (Col 1:13–14).[68]

The believer in Christ is not saved simply to move on with life as usual, but rather "we are His creation—created in Christ Jesus for good works, which God prepared ahead of time so that we should walk in them" (Eph 2:10). Faith without works is dead, James tells us, and Christians are to "be doers of the word and not hearers only, deceiving yourselves" (Jas 1:22). Unfortunately, as Mark Driscoll points out, many Christians "wrongly believe that once they have trusted in Jesus they are free to have their own mission for their life, such as success or wealth, and they expect Jesus to serve their mission. That kind of thinking is completely inverted."[69] It is good to remember that even after being found forgiven in Christ, the Christian remains sinful, and sometimes horribly so. But as the follower of Christ—by the power of the Spirit—wages warfare against the passions of the flesh and seeks to take every thought captive for Jesus (2 Cor 10:5), he is declaring his allegiance to another, proclaiming that he has died to himself and been found hidden in Christ (Col 3:1–3).

Individual salvation, though, is meant to be displayed within the context of a community. Tony Jones rightly critiques the overly individualistic emphasis of contemporary evangelical youth ministry, asserting that "many of us have also changed 'For God so loved the world that he gave his only son' to 'For God so loved *Jimmy* that he gave his only son,' and in doing so we have *changed* Scripture's intent."[70] Similarly, some Evangelicals preach texts such as Christ's declaration, "Listen! I stand at the door and knock. If anyone hears My voice and opens the door, I will come in to him and have dinner with him, and he with Me" (Rev 3:20) as though Jesus is standing outside the "door" of an

---

[68] This is not to blur the traditional—and biblical—distinction between justification and sanctification, as Tony Jones proposes Christians ought to do. Jones, *Postmodern Youth Ministry*, 133. Rather, the Christian life is one in which faith is shown by works, and works are done in faith. The works themselves do not justify the sinner before God; faith does. But faith always shows itself by its works, lest the faith shows itself to be dead.

[69] Driscoll and Breshears, *Vintage Jesus*, 223.

[70] Jones, *Postmodern Youth Ministry*, 119.

individual's heart—just begging to come in.[71] In reality, Jesus is
sending a warning to a lukewarm community of God, the church
in Laodicea, commanding them to repent, for He loves them.

Joining in covenant fellowship with other believers, then, is
more than just an afterthought to becoming a Christian—something to think about "on down the road." Christ died to purchase
for Himself a church—a church made up of individuals but individuals from every tribe, language, people, and nation (Rev 5:9).
That is why even spiritual gifts, so often seen through an individualistic lens, are given to members of the church for building up
the body (1 Cor 14:26). Good works are to be done for all people
but "especially for those who belong to the household of faith"
(Gal 6:10). Through the Spirit the church serves also as a training ground for ruling and reigning authority in the coming kingdom. The way in which believers in the Lord Jesus live now will
have direct impact upon how they will rule with the King who has
come, and is coming. Jesus promises the churches in Thyatira and
Laodicea that to those who persevere in faith to the end, He will
grant them ruling authority over the nations (Rev 2:26–27; 3:21).
In other words, Jesus is training His subjects of the kingdom to be
kings and queens of the universe. Such training, as trivial as it may
seem at the time, is individual, and such training is also cosmic.[72]

But the church is not only the place where Christians are to do
good works, or to live out their salvation within the context of the
community. The church also declares salvation in Jesus to those outside the church, a declaration that should come with bold humility.
This declaration comes in word and in deed. Emerging church pastor Rick McKinley suggests the superiority of "being" as opposed
to "speaking" in witnessing to the kingdom of God: "What *would*
the world think if we loved our sisters in Cuba enough to take them
medicine? And how much could our lives say *without speaking* if
we were willing to suffer for the sake of the kingdom? The act alone

---

[71] Ibid.

[72] For more on how the church serves as the training ground for ruling in the coming
kingdom of Christ, see Russell D. Moore and Robert E. Sagers, "The Kingdom of God
and the Church: A Baptist Reassessment," *The Southern Baptist Journal of Theology* 12/1
(2008): 81–84.

would preach volumes."[73] However, the good news must be told in words for someone to know how to live by it; both the verbal proclamation of the gospel of the kingdom and performing good works in the name of Christ are called for from Christians.

The gospel, which is to be made available to all men, comes as an invitation—but an invitation with authority because the One giving it is a King (Matt 22:8–10). It also comes with a sense of urgency, for "everything is ready" (Matt 22:4). The gospel is a victory proclamation, for what Christ has accomplished in the past will be consummated in the future. And this good news is an invitation to partake in fellowship not only with King Jesus, but also with other subjects of His kingdom in the church (1 John 1:3). The preaching of the gospel of the kingdom is to bring men and women to salvation in Jesus Christ (2 Tim 3:15), urging people to repent of sin to be a part of the kingdom now—which all men may enter, if they respond to the gospel in obedient faith—even as the church prays for God's kingdom to come (Matt 6:10). "There is salvation in no one else, for there is no other name under heaven given to people by which we must be saved" (Acts 4:12), Peter preached, and such a truth should drive Christians to evangelism.

The gospel is not only for unbelievers, but for believers, as well. The pull of sin is ongoing and powerful, and therefore even Christians need constantly to heed the voice of their Shepherd-King. But this is not simply a matter of *hearing* God's voice, or even being able to discern the voice of Christ among all of the other voices that exist ubiquitously in a world fallen and held under the sway of the wicked one—a wicked one who, after all, has a voice as well (Gen 3:1–5). Indeed, our father Adam heard clearly the voice of God in the Garden—and shrunk back in fear because of his guilt and shame at his nakedness (Gen 3:8–11). The voice of Jesus will someday call from the grave both the just *and* the unjust (John 5:28–29), and those who stand justified and those who remain dead in their sins will both hear their final verdict from the same Judge (Matt 25:31–46).

[73] Rick McKinley, *This Beautiful Mess: Preaching the Presence of the Kingdom of God* (Sisters, Ore.: Multnomah Press, 2006), 154.

Rather, hearing the voice of Christ in the words of Scripture should bring with it an obedient response, a response characterized by repentance and faith. The plea of the knowingly sinful disciple of Christ to his King's voice is a continual cry: "I do believe! Help my unbelief" (Mark 9:24). The response of a sheep to his Good Shepherd's voice is to follow after Him as He leads (John 10:27). The church, then, as the covenant community of believers, is made up of those who hear the voice of the Holy Spirit of Christ and harden not their hearts but rather respond in belief (Heb 3:7–4:16).

It is true that God, in all of history, is working toward the summing up of *all* things in Christ (Eph 1:9–10). However, the question remains: just *how* does God work to redeem and restore all of creation? The apostle Paul gives us the answer when he tells the church at Rome that all creation groans "for God's sons to be revealed" (Rom 8:19–22). In other words, in Christ the Spirit is conforming those who have been adopted into the household of God to the image of the One who, unlike our father Adam, is able to put all things under His feet—including even sin and death. God is working toward a consummated kingdom in which Jesus Christ is exalted as rightful King over all the cosmos—an exaltation that is expressed in every knee bowing, and every tongue confessing, that Jesus is Lord (Phil 2:9–11). There can be no cosmic reconciliation without personal, individual salvation, without all of the redeemed of all of the ages crying out with one voice, "Blessing and honor and glory and dominion to the One seated on the throne, and to the Lamb, forever and ever!" (Rev 5:13).

SALVATION AND THE KINGDOM: COSMIC RECONCILIATION AND THE EMERGING CHRISTIANS

Evangelicals are often branded as being overly obsessed with the afterlife. Recognizing the biblical teachings about a literal heaven and hell, evangelical Christians often rightly emphasize being reconciled to God in Christ for the forgiveness of sins and an eternity spent with Him. Some emerging church leaders, on the other hand, rightly emphasize the reality of God's kingdom present in the world even now, and the ethical implications that such a reality should have on the lives of Christians. What if both groups are partly right in their assertions and emphases but end up missing the all-encompassing scope of the eschatological fulfill-ment that God is working toward—indeed, that God has already begun—in Christ?

"For people who come from evangelical and fundamental-ist backgrounds (as I do)," writes emerging church leader Brian McLaren, "life is about being (or getting) saved, and knowing it."[74] However, McLaren asserts, salvation isn't just about trust-ing Jesus and going to heaven when one dies, with the flames of hell licking at his heels. Instead, "salvation means being rescued from fruitless ways of life here and now, to share in God's saving love for all creation, in an adventure called the kingdom of God, the point of which you definitely don't want to miss." This is in addition to what seems to amount to an afterthought in McLaren's view, that is, "the wonderful gift of assurance that you will not perish after this life, but will be forever with the Lord."[75] Rob Bell speaks to the already realized nature of the kingdom of God by asserting, "For Jesus, this new kind of life in him is not about escaping this world but about making it a better place, here and now. The goal for Jesus isn't to get into heaven. The goal is to get heaven here."[76]

In a more recent work entitled *Everything Must Change*, McLaren laments that many of the world's most pressing crises are not being addressed because Christians are too concerned with getting people to believe a set of propositional statements about the work of Christ—so that they can "go to heaven when the earth is destroyed and everyone else is banished to hell."[77] In contrast to such a "conventional view" held by so many Christians today, the "emerging view" of Jesus and the message of the kingdom is more

---

[74] Campolo and McLaren, *Adventures in Missing the Point*, 19.

[75] Ibid., 25–26.

[76] Bell, *Velvet Elvis*, 148.

[77] Brian D. McLaren, *Everything Must Change: Jesus, Global Crises, and a Revolution of Hope* (Nashville: Thomas Nelson, 2007), 79. This, the "conventional view," "reflects a Calvinistic, evangelical, Protestant version of the message," writes McLaren in an endnote. Ibid., 308.

all-encompassing and hopeful—and Christians ought to consider deemphasizing their focus on the impending judgment of God in the afterlife and instead join Jesus in the work of the gospel in helping to solve global crises in the present.

The Scriptures declare that in the person and work of Christ everything has *already* changed.[78] "Therefore, having overlooked the times of ignorance, God now commands all people everywhere to repent, because He has set a day on which He is going to judge the world in righteousness by the Man He has appointed. He has provided proof of this to everyone by raising Him from the dead," Paul preached to the Athenian philosophers at the Areopagus (Acts 17:30–31). Earlier in Thessalonica Paul reasoned with the Jews from the Scriptures, "explaining and showing that the Messiah had to suffer and rise from the dead: 'This is the Messiah, Jesus, whom I am proclaiming to you'" (Acts 17:3). If Jesus is the Christ—the Anointed One of God—then such lordship has cosmic implications. Indeed, many were jealous of the fact that some were coming to follow after this Lord, pleading before the city authorities, "These men who have turned the world upside down have come here too. . . . They are all acting contrary to Caesar's decrees, saying that there is another king—Jesus!" (Acts 17:6–7) Such news, far from comforting them, disturbed the unbelievers who heard it.

Jesus' lordship over the cosmos has implications for how His followers live now, perhaps even in the way that they respond to HIV infections in Africa and global climate change and run-down city parks not four blocks from their homes. But over against McLaren's view of the message of Jesus as having more to do with "the world's global crises" than "our individual souls and their eternal postmortem destiny," can't it be said that the gospel of the kingdom has to do with both?[79] Not only this, but a deemphasis on the coming judgment of God robs Christians of the impetus for performing the kinds of good works done in Jesus' name for

---

[78] I owe this insight to a review article by David Fitch, "Review/Interaction: Everything Must Change," accessed 2 May 2008 at http://www.the-next-wave-ezine.info/bin/_print .cfm?id=35&ref=ARTICLES_FEATURED ARTICLE: SPOTLIGHT_507.
[79] Ibid., 83.

which He will someday reward them (Matt 25:31–40). In addition, focusing only on the "here and now" of God's justice takes away much of the hope in turning the other cheek—trusting that God is trustworthy when He declares, "Vengeance belongs to Me; I will repay" (Rom 12:19). Embracing some of McLaren's proposals could quite possibly lead to the kind of bloody violence and world wars that he believes Christians will be able to help end.

It is difficult to discern how McLaren's severing the ethics of the kingdom of God from eschatological judgment is much distinguishable from last century's Social Gospel movement. Even while typing out this sentence I received an e-mail alert from a well-known Christian political action group entitled, "Ready to end poverty now?" Perhaps the assumption behind such a question is that social ills such as poverty may be eradicated apart from the return of Christ. This is not to say that poverty is not something against which the church of Christ must fight—and continually so. But Evangelicals and Emergents alike may do well to remember that the kingdoms of this world can never overcome sin and death, and their subsequent ills. Only the Lord Jesus can do this—at the resurrection from the dead (1 Cor 15:54–57). Some within the emerging church movement are right to critique the fact that Evangelicals, as a whole, have too often been seen as just another voting bloc within the Republican Party. But replacing one's preference for a certain political party with another does not the kingdom of God usher in.[80]

It may be true that some evangelical Christians overemphasize the future cosmic reign of Christ, with little to no emphasis on the kingdom now. One potential problem with the view of the kingdom of God that is held by many emerging church leaders, though, is that there seems to be too much "now"—and not enough "not yet." In the person and work of King Jesus, the eschatological kingdom has reached back and broken into the present age, and is present wherever the rule and reign of God exists. Though the kingdom is now (i.e., Mark 1:15), it is also not yet, as it awaits

[80] One needs only examine the growing number of emerging church leaders aligned with the leftist Christian political organization Sojourners to see that this is precisely what many within the movement seem to be doing.

future consummation in which the reign of God in Christ will extend over all the cosmos (Rev 11:15). Though Jesus is currently reigning at the right hand of the Father, we do not yet see all things under His feet (Heb 2:8). But the goal of the kingdom of God is to do exactly that, "to subordinate all things to him as creator, judge, and redeemer. Of no other kingdom can this be said."[81] Embracing a proper balance between God's kingdom as both now and not yet may help Christians to avoid a sense of beatific utopianism on the one hand and utter despair on the other.

Perhaps such a view of the tension existing between the now and not yet of God's reconciling work in Christ could also help to provide a better framework for cultural engagement than it seems is currently present among many within the emerging church. In worship, the church that Karen Ward pastors "incorporate(s) mainstream music as well—everything from Rachel's to U2, Bjork to Moby, Dave Matthews to Coldplay. We have no need to 'Christianize' music. God is sovereign, and the whole world is God's so any music that is good already belongs to God."[82] Tony Campolo criticizes Brian McLaren's lack of a discerning framework through which he is able to enjoy cultural products of the secular culture. "[M]ost of what society offers up for our cultural digestion these days is just plain worthless," Campolo argues. "To act as though there is some profound truth waiting to be uncovered in cheap and tawdry stuff is hardly Christian."[83] One observer of an emerging church writes that the church's pastor "promises that his followers don't have to reprogram their iTunes catalog along with their beliefs—culture from outside the Christian fold isn't just tolerated here, it's cherished."[84]

Theologian Richard Mouw has pointed out the benefit of Christian cultural engagement, taking part in the work that even

---

[81] Carl F. H. Henry, "Reflections on the Kingdom of God," in *Journal of the Evangelical Theological Society* 35 (1992): 40.

[82] Karen Ward, "The New Church: Artistic, Monastic, and Commute-Free," in *The Relevant Church: A New Vision for Communities of Faith*, ed. Jennifer Ashley (Orlando: Relevant Books, 2005), 85.

[83] Campolo and McLaren, *Adventures in Missing the Point*, 125.

[84] Sandler, *Righteous*, 45.

God will do at the end of the age (Isa 60).[85] But Evangelicals may do well to remember that while we live in this time between the times, biblically honed wisdom and discernment must be used in such engagement and redemption. In Athens, the apostle Paul *did* quote pagan poets in preaching the gospel to his hearers—but the reason he even gained a hearing was "because he was telling the good news about Jesus and the Resurrection" (Acts 17:18). Such a message wasn't very culturally savvy two millennia ago; neither is it today. But it's the message that saves.[86]

Many emerging church leaders put great emphasis on caring now for the "whole" person—not just one's soul, but also the body—which is quite admirable, and biblical.[87] But perhaps this lack of focus on the eschaton is precisely the reason why McLaren seems to advocate a deemphasis on the future resurrection of the body, reminiscent of the kind of Gnosticism the apostles and the early church fathers anathematized. Holding in his hands the cremated ashes of a deceased friend, one of the characters in McLaren's novels realizes that such ashes are merely "borrowed" remnants of creation that his friend had embodied during her life. Later the character reflects, "The ashes fell between my fingers, but Kerry herself was somehow retained and preserved, saved and cherished, in the mind of God, the heart of God. *She doesn't need these ashes anymore.* She had become all she could in the matrix of matter, energy, and time on earth."[88]

McLaren is not alone in appearing to purport a lack of emphasis on the future resurrection of the body. If a person attends enough funerals—even those that operate under the name "evangelical"— he may hear a preacher speak of the deceased person's body as a discarded casing. After all, the preacher may reason aloud, the departed person's soul—what's *really* important—is in heaven

---

[85] Richard Mouw, *When the Kings Come Marching In: Isaiah and the New Jerusalem*, 2nd ed. (Grand Rapids: Eerdmans, 2000).

[86] Russell D. Moore, "Retaking Mars Hill: Paul Didn't Build Bridges to Popular Culture," *Touchstone: A Journal of Mere Christianity*, September 2007, 20–25.

[87] Though aspects of his biblical exegesis and the implications of such ministry are somewhat deficient, see, for example, Doug Pagitt's emphasis on holistic ministry—and the dangers of dualism—in Pagitt, *A Christianity Worth Believing*, 81–93.

[88] McLaren, *The Story We Find Ourselves In*, 194.

with Jesus. Such an outlook on the body hardly can be considered Christian. The Christian's hope lies not in a disembodied heaven in the presence of Christ, but rather in what New Testament scholar N. T. Wright has deemed the "life *after* 'life after death'"—that is, the resurrection of the body.[89]

The resurrection of Jesus after three days in the tomb is much more than an afterthought to the work done on the cross. Instead, as the Spirit of holiness raises from the dead this One whom sin and death could not keep in the grave, God is declaring to the principalities and powers that the new creation is here. Jesus, in His death *and* in His resurrection, serves as a forerunner on our behalf. The Christian hope, then, is that our Messiah-substitute has destroyed the penalty for sin—death—and that all who believe in Him, though they may die, will someday be raised from the dead as well—to rule and reign with Him in His consummated kingdom forever. And no one will be arguing over what has been "borrowed" then.

This resurrected Messiah has overcome judgment, sin, and death; in fact, at Calvary the Son of God even goes through hell in becoming a curse on our behalf.[90] Mark Driscoll believes unequivocally in hell as an eternal punishment for those who do not receive Christ as Lord and Savior in this life.[91] It seems that others—such as McLaren—are not so sure.[92] Spencer Burke and Barry Taylor assert that a "hell-obsessed theology of salvation makes for self-centered humans who actually negate the role and

[89] N. T. Wright, *Christian Origins and the Question of God,* vol. 3, *The Resurrection of the Son of God* (Minneapolis: Fortress, 2003), 31.

[90] Many books and articles on the doctrine of hell have been written in recent years. For a succinct survey of arguments for the traditional doctrine of hell from biblical, theological, historical, and pastoral perspectives, see the essays in *Hell under Fire,* ed. Christopher W. Morgan and Robert A. Peterson (Grand Rapids: Zondervan, 2007).

[91] "God is literally holy, we are literally sinful, Jesus literally died to forgive our sin, and if we fail to receive his forgiveness, we will literally stand before him for judgment and be sentenced to a literal hell as an act of literal justice." Driscoll and Breshears, *Vintage Jesus,* 222.

[92] For an overview of Brian McLaren's view of the doctrine of hell, with particular emphasis on McLaren's fictional works, see the essay by Greg D. Gilbert, "Saved from the Wrath of God: An Examination of Brian McLaren's Approach to the Doctrine of Hell," in *Reforming or Conforming? Post-Conservative Evangelicals and the Emerging Church,* ed. Ronald N. Gleason and Gary L. W. Johnson (Wheaton, Ill.: Crossway, 2008). Gilbert roots McLaren's deficient approach to the doctrine of hell in his deficient view of the gospel itself.

function of grace by striving to corral people into heaven."[93] While it may be true that some Evangelicals can be guilty of preaching a gospel that looks more like "eternal fire insurance" than the Christ-centered nature of salvation revealed to us through His Scriptures, it is also true that no one speaks of hell in the Bible more than our Lord Jesus Himself—and the biblical writers constantly warn of a judgment to come for all who do not trust in Christ for salvation.

An overemphasis on the doctrine of hell by some does not mean that such a doctrine is not true—it is—or even that it should not be emphasized in presenting the gospel—it should. "It is a terrifying thing to fall into the hands of the living God!" (Heb 10:31), the writer of the book of Hebrews says. And the apostle Paul writes to his young protégé, Timothy, that his preaching ought to be done with the knowledge of God's coming judgment, and His coming kingdom (2 Tim 4:1–2). Not falling prey to false teaching and condemnation of the devil, Paul knows that it is Christ Himself who "will rescue me from every evil work and will bring me safely into His heavenly kingdom" (2 Tim 4:18). Hell is the right punishment for all who have sinned against a holy God. But hell has no claim over those who are in Christ—this One who has already been through judgment and has been vindicated. And such a warning—such good news—must be preached in its fullness.

CONCLUSION

Some of the aspects of the emerging church most disturbing to some Evangelicals are the least enduring aspects of the movement. Evangelical church fads and consumer products will always be with us. There are other aspects—both positive and negative— of the emerging church conversation that can be obscured in all the buzz over the "branding" of the emerging church.

There are within the emerging church those the Scripture would categorize as false teachers. Where that is the case, Evangelicals must put priority on the gospel over other considerations. The exclusivity of Christ, penal substitutionary atonement, and

---

[93] Burke and Taylor, *A Heretic's Guide to Eternity*, 181.

biblical eschatology must not be traded away for anyone's mess of pottage. On the other hand, there are also some voices within the emerging church movement who are pointing out real deficiencies with the way Evangelicals have understood the doctrine of salvation. Where these voices are consonant with that of the Spirit of Christ as revealed in the Scriptures, we should listen humbly.

May evangelical Christians be faithful to discern the one from the other, even as we pray to God, "Your kingdom come." And that's something *all* believers in the Lord Jesus should long to see emerge.

THE CHURCH ACCORDING TO EMERGENT/EMERGING CHURCH

JOHN HAMMETT

THIS CHAPTER CONSIDERS THE ECCLESIOLOGY of the emerging church movement—that is, their vision of what the church is to be and do. Here we are dealing with what many in the emerging church movement see as their central concern. Speaking at the Fall Contemporary Issues Conference at Westminster Theological Seminary in 2006, Scot McKnight said, "At its core, the emerging movement is an attempt to fashion a new ecclesiology (doctrine of the church)."[1]

Dan Kimball says "I believe true emerging churches must go deep within, and from the inside out, rethink, reshape, and revalue how we go about everything as culture changes. We must rethink leadership, church structure, the role of a pastor, spiritual formation, how community is lived out, how evangelism is done, how we express our worship, etc." This process of rethinking he describes as "deep ecclesiological thinking."[2]

Gary Nelson, speaking at a Baptist World Alliance Symposium in March 2007, says the question being asked by the emerging

---

[1] The full text of the address by McKnight, "What Is the Emerging Church?" is available at http://www.foolishsage.com/wp-content/uploads/McKnight%20-%20What%20 is%20the%20Emerging%20Church.pdf. The quote in the text is from an adaptation of that address in Scot McKnight, "Five Streams of the Emerging Church," *Christianity Today* 51, no. 2 (February 2007): 37.

[2] Dan Kimball, "The Emerging Church and Missional Theology," in *Listening to the Beliefs of Emerging Churches: Five Perspectives*, ed. Robert Webber (Grand Rapids: Zondervan, 2007), 83–84, 86.

church—what does it mean to be church today?—is the same question that was asked centuries ago, by those who became the first Baptists. He adds that Baptists, above all other denominations, "should be the encouragers of this question," since it is "the natural expression of our historical ecclesiology."[3] Examples could be multiplied from observers both within and without the emerging church movement testifying to their pervasive interest in the question of ecclesiology. They are asking, what does it mean to be and to do church in the emerging, postmodern culture?

DEFINITIONAL DIFFICULTIES

Attempting to limit the scope of the discussion in this chapter requires defining two difficult terms. The first is the well-known problem of defining the diverse and somewhat diffuse movement called emerging or emergent. The second will be defining the ecclesiological issues within the broad field of ecclesiology of most importance to these churches.

DEFINING EMERGENT/EMERGING CHURCHES

Since other chapters in this book address the question of defining emerging churches in detail, this section will simply sketch the issues and state the assumptions governing this chapter. The first important distinction to make is between *Emergent* and *emerging*, a distinction which is becoming increasingly clear in discussions surrounding this movement. Scot McKnight distinguishes the two in these words: "Emerging is the wider, informal, global, ecclesial (church-centered) focus of the movement, while Emergent is an official organization in the U.S. and the U.K."[4] Thus, *emerging* is the broader, umbrella term for all those seeking to engage postmodern culture and *Emergent* is a subset of *emerging*.

But there have also been some who have given a more narrow definition for emerging churches. For example, Eddie Gibbs and

---

[3] Gary Nelson, "Everything Old Is New Again: Emerging Church Ecclesiology," 2. This was an address delivered at the Baptist World Alliance Symposium in Elstal, Germany, in March 2007. It is available at http://www.bwanet.org/media/documents/elstal%20paper -Nelson.pdf, accessed July 20, 2007.

[4] McKnight, "Five Streams," 36.

Ryan Bolger of Fuller Seminary have written the most thoroughly researched book to date on the emerging church, called by Andrew Jones, "[q]uite simply the best book yet on the emerging church."[5] It is in many ways an insightful and important work, with a fascinating appendix in which fifty emerging church leaders from the U.S. and U.K. give their stories in their own words. On the basis of five years of extensive research, they define emerging churches as those possessing three core practices: "(1) identifying with the life of Jesus, (2) transforming secular space, and (3) living as community." From these three core practices they derive six additional practices. Emerging churches: "(4) welcome the stranger, (5) serve with generosity, (6) participate as producers, (7) create as created beings, (8) lead as a body, and (9) take part in spiritual activities."[6] They see these nine patterns as "most prevalent in churches that take culture, specifically postmodern culture, seriously."[7]

They place Gen-X megachurches, seeker churches, purpose-driven churches, and Vineyard churches as outside the emerging church because they do not fit their criteria. They seem to see Chris Seay, Mark Driscoll, and Erwin McManus and their churches as churches in which the "bulk of church practice remained the same as their conservative Baptist, seeker, new paradigm, purpose-driven predecessors; only the surface techniques changed," whereas they believe "[t]aking postmodernity seriously requires that all church practices come into question."[8] But this seems to prejudge the question of what type of response postmodernity requires and unnecessarily excludes people like Driscoll and Seay, who are both widely identified with the emerging movement. For example, Driscoll was chosen to provide one of the five perspectives in *Listening to the Beliefs of Emerging Churches: Five Perspectives*, and Seay has served on the board of directors of Emergent Village.

Another unfortunate but understandable limitation of Gibbs and Bolger is that their study relates only to emerging churches

---

[5] The citation from Jones is on the back cover of Eddie Gibbs and Ryan K. Bolger, *Emerging Churches: Creating Christian Community in Postmodern Cultures* (Grand Rapids: Baker Academic, 2005), which also gives Jones's Web site, tallskinnykiwi.com.

[6] Gibbs and Bolger, 43–45.

[7] Ibid., 43.

[8] Ibid., 30, 34.

in the United States and United Kingdom, because that was as far as they could extend their research, which involved extensive personal interviews. Thus some important contributions from Australia, New Zealand, and continental Europe are omitted.[9]

In this author's opinion, the defining and unifying feature of the diverse groups and individuals associated with the emerging church movement seems to be an intentional effort to seriously engage the emerging, postmodern culture. Views of what type of response that engagement requires differ from group to group and individual to individual. In fact, Ed Stetzer has identified three types of responses to postmodern culture among those in the emerging church and has categorized them on that basis: "some are taking the same Gospel in the historic form of church but are seeking to make it understandable to emerging culture; some are taking the same Gospel but questioning and reconstructing much of the form of church; some are questioning and revising the Gospel and the church." He calls these groups the Relevants, the Reconstructionists, and the Revisionists.[10] Driscoll comments, "What ties each of these types of Emerging Christians together is a missiological conversation about what a faithful church should believe and do to reach Western culture."[11] Stetzer's formulation has been widely affirmed by emerging church leaders[12] and avoids limiting the emerging church to only some of the Reconstructionists and Revisionists, as the definition of Gibbs and Bolger seems to do.

[9] From Australia, there is an important book by Michael Frost and Alan Hirsch, *The Shaping of Things to Come: Innovation and Mission for the 21st-Century Church* (Erina, New South Wales: Strand, and Peabody, Mass.: Hendrickson, 2003); from New Zealand, Steve Taylor, *The Out of Bounds Church* (El Cajon, Calif.: emergent YS/Grand Rapids: Zondervan, 2005); a European perspective is found in Wolfgang Simson, *Houses that Changed the World: The Return of the House Church* (Waynesboro, Ga.: OM, 2003). I know of no contributions from Africa or Asia, perhaps due to the limited effect of postmodernism on cultures in those areas.

[10] Ed Stetzer, "First-Person: Understanding the Emerging Church," January 6, 2006, *Baptist Press*, available at http://www.bpnews.net/bpnews.aso?Id=22406, accessed January 23, 2006. See also Stetzer's comments in his contribution to this book.

[11] Driscoll, "A Pastoral Perspective on the Emerging Church," *Criswell Theological Review* n.s.3, no. 2 (Spring 2006), 90.

[12] See Andrew Jones, "Ed Stetzer gets it," available at http://tallskinnykiwi.typepad.com/tallskinnykiwi/2006/01/ed_stetzer_gets.html, accessed July 19, 2007, who says, "According to Ed, some are: –Relevants, and Ed thinks they rock. –Reconstructionists and Ed will put up with them. –Revisionists and Ed does not have to agree with them." Driscoll uses Stetzer's categories in Driscoll, "A Pastoral Perspective," 89–91.

A second overly narrow definition of emerging church may be drawn by some from D. A. Carson's book, *Becoming Conversant with the Emerging Church*.[13] Though he acknowledges the diversity of the movement, Carson chose to focus his critique on two books, *A Generous Orthodoxy* by Brian McLaren and *The Lost Message of Jesus* by Steve Chalke, with help from Alan Mann. This may lead some to identify all the emerging church with those two exemplars. Carson's book has itself been widely critiqued in emerging church circles as focused on too narrow a representation of the emerging church as a whole and for largely missing the point of what emerging church leaders are saying. Scot McKnight says, "I have probed and prodded emerging church leaders and ordinaries for about two years now, and I have almost never heard anything that resembles what Carson thinks is so typical of the emerging 'church.'"[14] He sees this overly narrow definition of the emerging church as of crucial importance:

> Here's my point: if you narrow the emerging movement to Emergent Village, and especially to the postmodernist impulse therein, you can probably dismiss this movement as a small fissure in the evangelical movement. But, *if you are serious enough to contemplate major trends in the Church today, at an international level, and if you define emerging as many of us do—in missional, or ecclesiological terms, rather than epistemological ones—then you will learn quickly enough that there is a giant elephant in the middle of the Church's living room. It is the emerging church movement and it is a definite threat to traditional evangelical ecclesiology.*[15]

Perhaps *challenge* would be a better word to use than "threat" to describe what the emerging church is bringing to traditional evangelical ecclesiology, but in any case an adequate understanding of the movement requires a due consideration of its breadth. From this author's perspective, limiting the emerging church to only those

---

[13] Grand Rapids: Zondervan, 2005.
[14] McKnight, "What Is the Emerging Church?", 2.
[15] Ibid., 9 (emphasis in original).

aligned with Emergent or only those considered emerging by Gibbs and Bolger or only those like Brian McLaren misinterprets the movement and omits some of its key figures, who have much in common with and much to offer to traditional Evangelicals. This chapter will adopt a broader definition of the emerging church, as including all those who intentionally focus on engaging postmodern culture. Furthermore, while interacting with all emerging churches exhaustively is impossible, this chapter will attempt to interact with representatives from all three of the categories developed by Stetzer.

DEFINING KEY ISSUES IN EMERGING ECCLESIOLOGY

Traditional treatments of ecclesiology typically discuss issues such as the nature of the church, the marks of the church, different forms of church government, different views of the ordinances (or sacraments), and the various ministries of the church.[16] While some aspects of these issues are important for some in the emerging church, most are not interested in fighting the battles that split Catholics, Presbyterians, Methodists, Baptists, and others. This author's research has not discovered any significant interest in emerging church material in discussions of congregational versus presbyterian polity or infant baptism versus believers' baptism or the nature of Christ's presence in the Supper or the proper marks of a true church. The emerging church movement spans many denominations, and denominational differences do not seem to be an important point of division or discussion among those in the movement.

What ecclesiological issues do matter to those in the emerging church movement? Though not all in the emerging church are equally interested in each of these issues, nor do all respond in the same way, four issues seem to be important ecclesiological concerns for the great majority of those in the emerging church: the church's nature as community, the church's missional ori-

---

[16] See, for example, the topics treated under ecclesiology in evangelical systematic theology textbooks like Millard Erickson, *Christian Theology*, 2nd ed. (Grand Rapids: Baker, 1998), chs. 50–55; Wayne Grudem, *Systematic Theology* (Leicester, England: InterVarsity Press and Grand Rapids: Zondervan, 1994), chs. 44–51; *A Theology for the Church*, ed. Daniel L. Akin (Nashville: B&H Academic, 2007), 766–856; or the topics in an ecclesiology textbook such as John S. Hammett, *Biblical Foundations for Baptist Churches: A Contemporary Ecclesiology* (Grand Rapids: Kregel, 2005) or Edmund Clowney, *The Church* (Downers Grove: IVP, 1995).

entation to the culture, the church's worship, and the church's leadership.[17]

THE CHURCH AS COMMUNITY IN EMERGING ECCLESIOLOGY

It would be hard to overstate the emphasis on the nature of the church as community and the importance of experiencing community in the church for those in the emerging church. This is one area where the differing wings of the emerging church movement seem to agree. One of the three core practices Gibbs and Bolger identify as present in all emerging churches is "living as community." They define emerging churches as "communities that practice the way of Jesus within postmodern cultures" and include the note of community in the subtitle of their book.[18] Emerging churches as different as Mars Hill (Seattle), Mars Hill Bible Church (Grandville, Mich.), and Solomon's Porch (Minneapolis) all emphasize the centrality of community in the life of the church.[19] In fact, it is difficult to find any emerging church that does not refer to itself as a community, and most include some statement about community in their key values.

One common factor undergirding the importance of community in postmodern culture is their desire to reach those whose politics, interests, and background are not typical of members of most traditional, evangelical churches. A common motivation for planting emerging churches was the perception by many that existing churches were stifling, inauthentic, and completely out of touch with many segments of society.[20] On the basis of extensive

[17] Other topics, such as preaching and evangelism, are crucially important elements in ecclesiology but will be the subject of other chapters in this book and thus will be considered only secondarily in this chapter.

[18] Gibbs and Bolger, *Emerging Churches,* 44–45. The subtitle of their book is *Creating Christian Community in Postmodern Cultures.*

[19] The Web sites of all three of these churches highlight the importance of community. See the Mars Hill Church Membership Covenant, which affirms the importance of forming "an authentic church community," and includes community as one of the four "core values" of Mars Hill. Mars Hill Bible Church, pastored by Rob Bell, lists community as one of their six shared values and begins their mission statement with the phrase, "living out the way of Jesus in missional communities." Solomon's Porch describes itself as "a holistic, missional, Christian community," where people "intentionally share life together," including the expectation of vulnerability and accountability to the community.

[20] Many of the stories in appendix A of Gibbs and Bolger, called "Leaders in Their Own Words," reflect their dissatisfaction with churches that they did not think would accept

226 PART 2 THEOLOGICAL SECTION

research, Ed Stetzer states that there has been a widespread failure among traditional churches to provide meaningful community,
especially for those different from traditional church members. He
says, "Most Christians don't like lost people. . . . We wish it were
not so, but it is. Lost people don't think like us; they often don't
vote like us; they influence our kids . . . they are not our people."[21]
Despite his critique of emerging churches, D. A. Carson acknowledges their strength in connecting with many often overlooked or
untouched by traditional churches.[22]

Specific examples abound. Dan Kimball highlights the story
of Sky, a creative, artistic, non-Christian who had experienced
Christians as close-minded, judgmental, arrogant people, but who
came to Christ because in Kimball's church he met Christians who
became his friend and lived their lives for Christ before him.[23]
In his book *The Radical Reformission*, Mark Driscoll includes
interviews with those involved in the film industry, a radio disc
jockey, tattoo artist, rock band manager, and a brewer and pub
owner, showing the openness to cultural diversity characteristic of
postmodern culture and a necessary prerequisite to building community with postmodern people.[24] Rob Bell describes the motivation for founding his church as the desire to speak the language
of postmodern people: "A hundred people a day were calling and
saying, 'Dude! Give us the real thing.' I was like, If someone could
speak to them in their mother tongue, they'd be here in droves."
The church Bell founded, Mars Hill Bible Church, did in fact grow
to number ten thousand attenders within two years.[25]

Another common but not universal expression of the importance of community is a commitment to smallness, either keeping

the non-Christian friends they were seeking to win to Jesus.

   [21] Ed Stetzer, cited in Shawn Hendricks, "Secret to becoming a 'comeback church'
explored in new B&H book," *Facts & Trends* (July/August 2007): 45. Stetzer's research is
detailed in Ed Stetzer and Mike Dodson, *Comeback Churches: How 300 Churches Turned
Around and Yours Can Too* (Nashville: B&H, 2007).

   [22] Carson, *Becoming Conversant,* 52–53.

   [23] Dan Kimball, *The Emerging Church: Vintage Christianity for New Generations*
(Grand Rapids: Zondervan/Youth Specialties, 2003), 21–23.

   [24] See the interviews preceding each chapter of Mark Driscoll, *The Radical Reformission: Reaching Out Without Selling Out* (Grand Rapids: Zondervan, 2004).

   [25] David van Biema, "The Hipper-Than-Thou Pastor," found at http://www.time.com/
time/magazine/article/0,9171,1692051,00.html, accessed January 14, 2008.

the church intentionally small, or seeing the church as a network of small groups. Gibbs and Bolger state frankly, "Emerging churches have no desire to grow big."[26] They quote Dwight Friesen of Quest Church in Seattle: "We committed to never growing beyond forty, and so we never built the infrastructure to enable us to go beyond that. We believed that our community would self-regulate. We have a radical commitment to being small."[27]

Other churches have grown but have come to view the church, not so much as the large group that gathers on Sunday as a network of small groups, or home communities. Even when the large group does gather, some churches make a conscious attempt to structure the very room to be more conducive to community. Dan Kimball describes emerging church worship services as occurring in a room "arranged to focus on community, striving to feel more like a living room or coffeehouse while worshiping."[28] Doug Pagitt describes the reaction to entering the worship area of Solomon's Porch: "People expecting to find rows of folding chairs find instead groupings of couches, chairs, end tables, recliners, and the like arranged in the round with an open center area."[29]

However, at least a handful of emerging churches have experienced significant growth and meet in more traditional settings. Two examples are the two churches that have both chosen Mars Hill as their name (Mars Hill Church in Seattle and Mars Hill Bible Church in Grandville, Mich.). Both have grown to megachurch size, with Mars Hill Seattle numbering more than five thousand members, and Mars Hill Bible Church having eleven thousand attenders each Sunday. However, both of these churches also emphasize small groups. Membership at Mars Hill Seattle includes not just regular attendance at corporate worship but also "involvement in a small group or class,"[30] and Mars Hill Bible Church sees involvement in smaller house churches as their "way

---

[26] Gibbs and Bolger, *Emerging Churches,* 110.

[27] Ibid.

[28] Kimball, *Emerging Church,* 185.

[29] Doug Pagitt, *Church Re-Imagined: The Spiritual Formation of People in Communities of Faith* (Grand Rapids: Zondervan, 2003/2005), 59.

[30] See "Mars Hill Membership Covenant," available at http://lite.marshillchurch.org/site/?id=BAAE0F06-5159-47A4-BBAE-649BD70D1725, accessed April 18, 2006.

of living out church" and becoming "more like Jesus together in community."[31] The use of small groups seems to be a common approach for maintaining fellowship in emerging churches that have grown.

No doubt this emphasis on community in the emerging church is part of their response to postmodern culture. One of the most common contrasts often drawn between modern and postmodern culture is that of the individualism of modernity, especially modernity in North America, and the preference for the communal in postmodern culture.[32] But the importance of community is also clearly found in Scripture. The early church was notable for their devotion to fellowship and the quality of their common life (Acts 2:42–47), and the dozens of "one-another" commands in the New Testament require community. And so it is not surprising to find that a commitment to community is found in a wide variety of churches beyond the emerging church movement, who may draw their emphasis on community not from engagement with the emerging culture but from a careful reading of Scripture.

There is evidence that many in megachurches find fellowship and community in those churches, particularly in small groups.[33] Leading seeker churches like Saddleback Community Church and Willow Creek have a strong emphasis on community.[34] A recent book profiling what the authors called "simple churches" found that these growing churches include a strong emphasis on community, or connecting with others, as an important part of the process of making disciples.[35]

[31] See http://www.marshill.org/groups/hc/, accessed January 15, 2008.

[32] See, for example, the contrasts drawn by Kimball, *Emerging Church*, 60–61, or Brian McLaren, *A New Kind of Christian* (San Francisco: Jossey-Bass, 2001), 16–18, 99.

[33] Scott Thumma, "Megachurches Today: Summary of Data from the Faith Communities Today Project," available at http://www.hirr.hartsem.edu/org/faith_megachurches_FACTsummary.html, accessed October 15, 2004.

[34] Fellowship is one of the purposes of the church, according to Rick Warren, *The Purpose Driven Church* (Grand Rapids: Zondervan, 1995), and an article by Verla Gillmor on Willow Creek claimed "Community Is Their Middle Name," *Christianity Today* 44, no. 13 (November 13, 2000), 50.

[35] Thom Rainer and Eric Geiger, *Simple Church: Returning to God's Process for Making Disciples* (Nashville: B&H, 2006). Chapters 2 and 4 profile the process of four churches, each of whom placed a high emphasis on community, usually using various types of small groups.

These examples show that while the emphasis on community in emerging churches is strong, it is not distinctive to them alone. Their emphasis on community is to be applauded, and it may be that they have been much more successful than traditional churches in creating community for those in emerging culture, but the desire for community is part of the created nature of humans and the provision of community to all types of people should be a key ministry of all healthy, biblical churches. On this point, the emerging church may be credited with challenging traditional churches and recalling them to an important New Testament emphasis.[36]

THE CHURCH'S MISSIONAL ORIENTATION

Rivaling community for importance in the emerging church is its orientation to the emerging culture. Where traditional churches may be unaware of the growth of postmodern culture around them or entrenched in modernity or confrontational toward new developments in the culture, the orientation of emerging churches toward their culture is missional. For many in the emerging church, a missional orientation to culture is the most important and distinctive difference in their churches. Scot McKnight urges us to "define emerging as many of us do—in missional, or ecclesiological terms, rather than epistemological ones."[37] Many use the terms *missional* and *emerging* as virtually interchangeable. Andrew Jones says, "you will often hear the word 'missional' added to 'emerging' to form the description 'emerging-missional church.'"[38]

The most thorough exploration of the background of the term *missional* comes from Ed Stetzer, who notes that while "missional" appeared in dictionaries more than a hundred years ago, it became popular in the latter part of the twentieth century through the work of missiologists Lesslie Newbigin, David Bosch, and the Gospel

[36] For example, Scott Smith, in *Truth & the New Kind of Christian: The Emerging Effects of Postmodernism in the Church* (Wheaton: Crossway, 2005), 108, says of emerging churches, "they rightly call our attention to the need to live out our faith in community."

[37] McKnight, "What Is the Emerging Church?", 9.

[38] Andrew Jones, "What I Mean When I Say 'Emerging-Missional' Church," available at http://www.the-next-wave-ezine.info/issue86/index.cfm?id=9&ref=ARTICLES%5FEME, accessed February 23, 2006. Jones adds that the hyphenated phrase is particularly "favored by Aussies and Kiwis" (Australians and New Zealanders).

and Our Culture network, who emphasized the need for churches to impact their culture and be contextually relevant.[39] While originally, discussions of missional churches were largely limited to ecumenical circles, more recently a growing number of Evangelicals have recognized that being missional is essential for churches in the changing cultural context in which they find themselves. In fact, Stetzer documents usage of the term *missional* recently by leaders from Southern Baptists, Methodists, the United Church of Christ, the Presbyterian Church in America, the Evangelical Free Church, the Nazarene Church, Wesleyans, and even the Unitarian Universalists.[40]

What do those in the emerging church movement mean by missional? While most acknowledge a common starting point, and perhaps a common core of meaning, there seem to be two basic directions different members of the movement have taken in developing the meaning of missional. One camp sees a missional orientation as requiring churches to contextualize their methods, structures, and mind-set but doing so precisely to communicate the unchanging gospel. They retain a strong concern for sound doctrine alongside the concern for cultural relevance. The second camp sees a missional orientation as requiring a radical reconsideration, not only of methods, but also of the gospel itself.[41]

Within the first camp, the most detailed description of what it means for the church to be missional comes from Australians Michael Frost and Alan Hirsch, whose book *The Shaping of Things to Come* is seen by Andrew Jones as second only to Gibbs and Bolger as "essential reading on the emerging church."[42] They introduce their work as an attempt "to reframe our ecclesiology *entirely* on missional grounds" and speak much more of the church as missional than emerging.[43] They describe the older or tradi-

[39] See Ed Stetzer, "Toward a Missional Convention," a paper delivered at the Baptist Identity Conference, February 17, 2006, at Union University in Jackson, Tennessee, available at http://www.uu.edu/events/baptistidentity/schedule/htm, accessed August 1, 2007.

[40] Ibid., 4–7.

[41] In terms of the classification of Relevants, Reconstructionists, and Revisionists, the first two fall within the first approach, while the third follows the second approach.

[42] Andrew Jones, "The 50 Books on My Emerging Church Bookshelf," available at http://tallskinnykiwi.typepad.com/tallskinnykiwi/2006/06/the_50_books_on.html, accessed on July 9, 2007.

[43] Frost and Hirsch, xi.

tional church as *attractional* (planting a church and asking people to come), *dualistic* (sharply separating sacred and profane), and *hierarchical* (bureaucratic, authoritarian, top-down management). By contrast, the missional church must be *incarnational* ("seeping into the host culture like salt and light"), *messianic* (engaging the culture in the same mode as the Messiah), and *apostolic* (in terms of its leadership style).[44] Their book gives a number of specific suggestions for developing an incarnational ecclesiology, messianic spirituality, and apostolic leadership, with multiple chapters of their book devoted to each of these three topics. Of most interest to this chapter is the first element. Their description of the pattern they suggest bears quoting at length:

> The missional-incarnational church should be living, eating, and working closely with its surrounding community, developing strong links between Christians and not-yet-Christians. It would be best to do this in the homes of not-yet-Christians and in their preferred public spaces . . . but also in the homes of Christians. By creating a net of deep, loving friendships, more and more people will be swept into the community.[45]

This approach does seem to involve a more radical change than merely tinkering with the worship service. Rather than approach a church plant with the idea, "if we build it, they will come," this approach seeks ways to become indigenous to the host culture. It is rooted in missiological principles often used by traditional missionaries, but the need is now to apply it in settings not always recognized as mission fields, places that were formerly part of Christendom but are now post-Christian.

Thus, the missional church envisioned by Frost and Hirsch seeks to thoroughly contextualize the church, making it indigenous to its culture, but it retains a strong commitment to a traditional understanding of the gospel. They say, "the emerging missional church must see itself as being able to interact meaningfully with

---

[44] Ibid., 18–21, 30. The apostolic form of leadership will be discussed in a later section of this chapter.

[45] Ibid., 57.

culture without ever being beguiled by it. This is the classic task of the cross-cultural missionary: to engage the culture without compromising the gospel. We cannot emphasize this enough."[46]

A similar approach to being missional is found in the works of Dan Kimball. In addition to engaging the culture and making friendships with nonbelievers, he offers numerous specific suggestions for worship, preaching, leadership, and congregational life that are culturally relevant to postmodern people, many of which will be considered in later sections of this chapter. But he clearly recognizes the need for changes in practice to be rooted in sound theology. He says, "Absolutely everything we do in church is a reflection of what we believe theologically, whether we are consciously aware of it or not."[47] Among Kimball's theological beliefs are his commitment to Scripture as inspired, a compass, an anchor, and authority.[48] Like Frost and Hirsch, he is seeking both cultural and contextual relevance and biblical faithfulness.

Mark Driscoll is seen by some as "not typically emerging"[49] and as mentioned above, he falls outside the criteria used by Gibbs and Bolger to define emerging churches. Yet he seems to fall within the same overall approach to being missional as Frost, Hirsch, and Kimball. He passionately argues that America is a mission field filled with people who "need a gospel and a church that are faithful both to the biblical text and to the cultural contexts of America," and insists that churches must understand and engage the culture.[50] He does have an element of what Frost and Hirsch call "attractional ecclesiology," because he does call people "to come and see the transformed lives of God's people," believing that "the transformed lives of people in the church are both the greatest argument for, and the greatest explanation of, the gospel."[51] At the same time, he calls on all the members of his church to be missionaries to the culture, building friendships with lost people and

---

[46] Ibid., 16.
[47] Kimball, "The Emerging Church and Missional Theology," in *Listening*, 103.
[48] Ibid., 94–97.
[49] Robert Webber, "Introduction: The Interaction of Culture and Theology," in *Listening*, 16.
[50] Driscoll, *Radical Reformission*, 18–19.
[51] Ibid., 68.

bringing them to experience life in the church, through which they will come to see the gospel lived and preached. They seem to be readily connecting, with Mars Hill Church having grown at a rate of 60 percent per year since its inception.[52]

Frost and Hirsch, Kimball, and Driscoll would all affirm that a missional church should be "biblically faithful and culturally appropriate,"[53] and would understand biblical faithfulness as limiting how far cultural contextualization can go and requiring a stable meaning for the gospel. In the same vein, Ed Stetzer calls for missional churches to be "biblically-faithful, culturally-relevant, counter-culture communities," and sees being missional as crucial to evangelistic effectiveness in the North American context.[54] Thus, while there seems to be agreement on what it means to be missional among these representatives from the "Relevant" and "Reconstructionist" camps within the emerging church, some of those from the "Revisionist" point of view develop missional in a different direction. This includes many (but not all) of those classified as emerging by Gibbs and Bolger.

At first glance, being missional may not seem important for these churches. The term *missional* does not appear in any of the criteria found by Gibbs and Bolger to characterize these churches and is almost absent from *An Emergent Manifesto of Hope*, a recent book edited by Doug Pagitt and Tony Jones and representative of the views of those in Emergent Village. Rather, the idea of being missional comes in via the idea of "identifying with Jesus" (the first of the criteria of Gibbs and Bolger) and his proclamation of the gospel of the kingdom. Jesus came proclaiming the kingdom, and in that way he participated in the ongoing mission of God. The church is missional as it follows Jesus into the world, proclaiming the gospel of the kingdom.

---

[52] Ibid., 66.

[53] This phrase is taken from the description of a missional church found on The Missional Network Web site. See http://missionalnetworkweb.com/about.aspx, accessed August 1, 2007.

[54] Stetzer, "Toward a Missional Convention," 25; in 12–13 he documents the present ineffectiveness of Southern Baptist churches in penetrating the culture and reaching lost people in North America.

This gospel of the kingdom has a bit different focus or emphasis than that described above, in that it is not entirely or even primarily focused on personal salvation in terms of forgiveness of sins received through faith in what Christ did on the cross. For example, Brian McLaren says that whereas earlier he had understood the kingdom in terms of heaven, now he says, "I see the kingdom as primarily being about God's will being done on earth, in history, with a forward light cast beyond this life."[55] Gibbs and Bolger say, "The gospel of emerging churches is not confined to personal salvation. It is social transformation arising from the presence and permeation of the reign of Christ."[56] Sherry and Geoff Maddock describe their involvement in a missional community as including actions like joining neighborhood associations and working on issues of poverty, protection of the environment, and ministry to AIDS sufferers and the homeless. They see such action as coming from "the assumption that God's kingdom is in the present tense."[57]

The emphasis on social transformation, issues of social justice, and God's will being done on earth now signals a significant difference in the missional nature of the church in this branch of the emerging church. While all branches of the emerging church movement would affirm the importance of both social justice and evangelistic outreach, it seems that the emphasis on the former is markedly greater among the churches that fit under the criteria of Gibbs and Bolger, whereas evangelistic ministries seem to have a higher emphasis in missional churches following the thinking of Frost and Hirsch or emulating Mark Driscoll and Dan Kimball.

The difference here should not be seen in terms of black and white but differing emphases. For example, when Gibbs and Bolger say, "Emerging churches have no desire to grow big,"[58] that does not seem to fit what is happening in numerous churches

---

[55] Brian McLaren, "An Interview with Brian McLaren," *Criswell Theological Review*, n.s. 3, no. 2 (Spring 2006); 7.

[56] Gibbs and Bolger, *Emerging Churches*, 63.

[57] Sherry and Geoff Maddock, "An Ever-Renewed Adventure of Faith: Notes from a Community," in *An Emergent Manifesto of Hope*, eds. Doug Pagitt and Tony Jones (Grand Rapids: Baker, 2007), 88.

[58] Gibbs and Bolger, *Emerging Churches*, 110.

in the Acts 29 Network, a network which has been developed by Mark Driscoll and reflects his passion for evangelism. It is not that bigness is their goal; it is that winning people to faith in Christ is the priority. Likewise, what prompted Dan Kimball's movement toward the emerging church movement was the lack of response of non-Christian youth to outreach methods of the past.[59]

Again, this is not to deny the evangelistic concern of many in Emergent Village or those regarded as emerging by Gibbs and Bolger or those in what Stetzer calls the Revisionist camp, but there is a discernible difference in emphasis. Gibbs and Bolger say that in welcoming the stranger, those in the emerging church believe that "Christians cannot truly evangelize unless they are prepared to be evangelized in the process," and that "God might be involved in other faiths," and that it is important to be "accepting of other faith communities," without feeling compelled to try to convert them.[60] Samir Selmanovic, a pastor serving on the Coordinating Group for Emergent Village, in an article entitled "The Sweet Problem of Inclusiveness," writes concerning the relationship of Christianity to other world religions, "The gospel is not *our* gospel, but the gospel of the kingdom of God, and what belongs to the kingdom of God cannot be hijacked by Christianity," and "If the Christian God is not larger than Christianity, then Christianity is simply not to be trusted."[61]

While respect and listening to others would be affirmed by all, this understanding of the gospel of the kingdom seems to further deemphasize evangelism in this branch of the emerging church. One of the common criticisms of emerging churches has been a weakness in the area of evangelism. As Scot McKnight said, "The emerging movement is not known for [evangelism], but I wish it were."[62] Rick Warren and Mark Driscoll echo this criticism, though Driscoll's own church is one of a number of exceptions.[63] Part of the reason for

[59] Kimball, *Emerging Church*, 34.

[60] Gibbs and Bolger, *Emerging Churches,* 131.

[61] Samir Selmanovic, "The Sweet Problem of Inclusiveness: Finding Our God in the Other," in *An Emergent Manifesto of Hope*, 194, (emphasis in original).

[62] McKnight, "Five Streams," 38.

[63] Warren reported in an e-mail correspondence with this author, dated December 7, 2005, that his researchers had found few emerging churches that were winning significant

this weakness may be that the definition of missional among some emerging churches deemphasizes the evangelistic aspect of that mission in favor of social transformation, and that change of emphasis seems to be linked to their vision of the kingdom.

The emphasis on the present aspect of the kingdom is especially seen in the works of Brian McLaren. In an insightful review, Greg Gilbert sees two problems with McLaren's view of the kingdom: (1) in emphasizing the present, here and now aspect of the kingdom, he never really integrates the eschatological aspect, and (2) in emphasizing the kingdom as political and social, he overlooks the spiritual. The second is the more serious in that it leads to a weakness in McLaren's view of the cross:

> McLaren's gospel is so socially and politically oriented, so focused on the present, and so unwilling to address the reality of eternity, that it has no obvious place for concepts like substitution, justification, atonement, sacrifice, or propitiation. Yet those are the concepts and themes that come together in the Bible's narrative to give meaning to the cross. The fact is that the kind of kingdom McLaren wants Jesus to have preached . . . doesn't have any real use for a cross. . . . [for it is only] a superfluous illustration of the kind of life the kingdom would call us to live.[64]

McLaren doesn't deny justification by faith or that Christ's death is atoning in some sense. But in reaction to a gospel he saw as too focused on just getting people into heaven, he seems to have moved to a position that does in fact make the cross problematic, and may contribute to the weakness or hesitancy in evangelism, mentioned above, that some even within the emerging church see as a problem.

Evaluation of the missional aspect of emerging church ecclesiology depends largely on which wing of the emerging church

numbers of nonbelievers to faith in Christ. Driscoll states that the "common critique" of all three types of emerging churches is that they are not seeing "significant conversion growth." See Driscoll, "A Pastoral Perspective," 90.

[64] Greg Gilbert, "Brian McLaren and the Gospel of Here & Now," *9News* 4, no. 5 (July/August 2007): 14, available at http://www.9marks.org/CC/CDA/Content_Blocks/ CC_Printer_Friendly_Version_Utility?1, accessed on July 19, 2007.

one is discussing. The approach of Frost and Hirsch seems well grounded and sound evangelistically and missiologically. The similar approach advocated by Kimball and Driscoll seems to have produced thriving churches, especially that of Driscoll in Seattle and in many of the churches sponsored by his Acts 29 Network. The approach of McLaren and others in his camp can be helpful in reminding us that God's redemptive work does include social justice and transformation of life here and now, but needs to take care not to forget that Jesus said in the end, "My kingdom is not of this world" (John 18:36). A mission that stops short of ultimately bringing people to the cross to receive forgiveness and eternal life is not the mission to which Christ calls His church. But on the whole, the call for churches to be missional in terms of being both biblically faithful and culturally relevant is a very positive contribution of the emerging church movement, and the increasingly widespread use of the term *missional* among Evangelicals is a hopeful sign that perhaps the call is beginning to be heard and heeded by churches well beyond the bounds of the emerging church movement.

THE CHURCH'S WORSHIP AND EMERGING ECCLESIOLOGY

As with almost every aspect of the emerging church, views on the church's worship vary. On one extreme, there are a small number who are "meetingless," in that they "have moved away from a central gathering. They are relational, organic, and flowing."[65] On the other extreme, there are some, mostly those in the Acts 29 Network, that accentuate the traditional preaching of Scripture in worship, with Mark Driscoll's sermons usually lasting longer than an hour. But most emerging churches have continued to have a large weekly gathering, even if small groups are seen as the heart of the church's life.

Their chief concern in worship has been to develop gatherings that allow people from the emerging culture to experience God. The familiar debates between traditional, contemporary, and blended music are not the point for these churches, for they see

[65] Gibbs and Bolger, *Emerging Churches,* 102.

both traditional and contemporary churches as "marginal to the culture at large."[66] Many in the emerging church believe that post-modern culture is so radically different from modern culture that worship must undergo similarly radical changes if churches are to genuinely engage worshipers that come from that culture.

One of the most common emphases to appear in discussions of worship among emerging church leaders is the need for worship to be experiential. Sally Morgenthaler and Dan Kimball both see the emphasis on experience linked with how people in the emerging culture come to know. Morgenthaler says, "Having shifted from 'knowing-by-notion' to 'knowing-by-narrative,' realignment [her term for worship] in emerging congregations is experiential more than mental, sensory more than read," involving worshipers on every level: "visual, aural, tactile, kinetic, emotional, and cerebral."[67] Dan Kimball explains that while modern people begin with learning facts, which then influence beliefs which then guide behavior, for postmodern people everything begins with experience, which influences behavior, which only then leads to beliefs.[68]

For worship to be experiential, it must also be participatory, rather than passive. Emerging church leaders see both traditional and contemporary worship as encouraging a consumer approach, where the worshiper comes and is offered a "worship service."[69] The emerging church sees worship as involving "participating as producers."[70] These two ideas of experience and participation set the background for much of what is distinctive about emerging worship.

One of the most noticeable differences is the use of art, both in places of worship and as part of worship. Even Mark Driscoll, who is more traditional than most in the emerging church, says, "We display paintings, photos, and works in other media for the sake

[66] Ibid., 77.

[67] Sally Morgenthaler, "Emerging Worship," in *Exploring the Worship Spectrum: 6 Views*, ed. Paul A. Basden (Grand Rapids: Zondervan, 2004), 224, 229.

[68] Kimball, *Emerging Church*, 187.

[69] For this reason, Kimball prefers the phrase "worship gatherings." Ibid., 116–17.

[70] This is the title of chapter 8 of Gibbs and Bolger and a major theme in their discussion of emerging worship.

of beauty and the encouragement of artists. . . . We take aesthetics very seriously in everything from our building to our website."[71] In some places, emerging churches meet in art galleries and have been more successful than traditional churches in reaching the artistic community, in part because they have valued their contributions. In addition to art, visual symbols contribute to the worship experience. Dan Kimball comments on the widespread use of candles in emerging worship: "they symbolize sobriety, spirituality, simplicity, quietude, and contemplation."[72]

Beyond participation in a visual way, emerging worship seeks to be multisensory. The sense of hearing is obviously involved in music, which is sung, played, and often composed by members in the community.[73] The sense of smell is brought into play by the use of incense, and the senses of sight, smell, taste, hearing, and touch are all involved in communion, which Kimball calls "the ultimate experiential act of worship."[74] Some have experimented with participation in labyrinths, praying through the stations of the cross, drawing sketches during the service to illustrate responses to Scripture,[75] as well as more traditional activities such as reading Scripture, praying, giving, sharing testimonies, and the hearing of the preached word, though the last is not central generally in emerging worship.[76]

The postmodern preference for diversity seems also reflected in emerging worship. Ancient liturgies and practices are combined with and even presented via modern technology; diverse geographies and ethnicities can be highlighted; extreme participation can

[71] Driscoll, *Radical Reformission*, 186–87.

[72] Kimball, *Emerging Church*, 139.

[73] Driscoll, *Radical Reformission*, 186, and Pagitt, *Church Re-Imagined*, 35, both comment that much of the music they sing in worship is written by members of their respective congregations.

[74] Kimball, *Emerging Church*, 162.

[75] See Pagitt, *Church Re-Imagined*, 59–82, for discussion of some of these methods used in worship at Solomon's Porch.

[76] Since there is a chapter in this book on preaching in emerging churches, I will limit comments here to the observation, that, with a few exceptions like Mark Driscoll, preaching is retained but not central in most emerging church worship. However, interestingly, Dan Kimball encourages emerging church pastors to preach on topics like the exclusivity of Jesus, hell, the Trinity, and the truthfulness of Scripture. See Kimball, *Emerging Church*, 181–82.

be coupled with times of absolute silence; paradox and eclecticism are acceptable in worship. Sally Morgenthaler calls this "radical recontexting" and identifies it as "the most noticeable difference between emerging worship and other forms." She further notes that in radical recontexting, *the order of service may be more concurrent (several things happening at once) than homogeneous (everyone doing the same thing at a time)*."[77]

Thus, emerging churches seek to involve people in an experiential time of worship, utilizing their creativity, participating with all their senses, recombining diverse elements in an almost endless variety of ways, for the purpose of glorifying God. Kimball notes that the goal is not experience for the sake of experience, or novelty for its own sake; the goal is a "community oriented participatory gathering which points us toward experiencing God in a transcending way."[78] Leonard Sweet has described the distinctive emphases of emerging churches under the acronym EPIC (experiential, participatory, image-driven, connected);[79] the same acronym forms a good summary of the distinctive emphases of their worship as well.

What may be said in evaluation of emerging church worship? The reclamation of beauty and the arts in service to God in worship is a matter than many, even in traditional churches, would argue is long overdue, and emerging churches should be applauded for providing the initiative on this point. Likewise, many traditional churches would agree that worship should be experiential and participatory. They would say they remind their people often that God is the audience and we are not passive spectators but active worshipers. They desire for their people to engage, encounter, and experience God in worship. Many are incorporating various media in worship, but perhaps most have not made "*holistic* fundamental shifts to truly engage the emerging culture."[80] In their defense, Kimball acknowledges that not all areas or even all young people

---

[77] Morgenthaler, 226 (emphasis in original).
[78] Kimball, *Emerging Church*, 123.
[79] See Leonard Sweet, *Postmodern Pilgrims: First Century Passion for the Twenty-first Century World* (Nashville: B&H, 2004).
[80] Ibid., 105 (emphasis in original).

have transitioned to postmodern. Those churches still in modern contexts should engage modern culture.[81]

Most traditional and seeker churches could profit from a greater emphasis on the Lord's Supper, the reading of Scripture, and times of prayer, and it would not be out of order for churches to reconsider what liturgy may have to offer and what symbols could be helpfully used. Moreover, the fact that God made us multisensory creatures should have some impact on our worship. There is much for churches to ponder and gain from the worship of emerging churches. Of course, there are also questions to ask and points open to criticism.

For some, a commitment to the regulative principle (the idea that nothing should be used in church that does not have an explicit or implicit biblical warrant) will limit what may be properly utilized in public worship. Even for those without such an explicit commitment, Evangelicals have always wanted to test everything by Scripture. If we guide our practice of worship solely by the principle of engaging culture, could we not be in danger of creating another set of consumers, with the only difference being that they are postmodern consumers rather than modern? For this reason, it is important that changes in worship be carefully considered in the light of the church's nature and calling and in light of the nature of the God to whom worship is offered, as Scripture informs our understanding. For example, the idea of concurrence (different members of the congregation doing different things at the same time) seems particularly out of place in the church's celebration of the Lord's Supper, for that is the place where the members of the body not only remember Christ but renew their unity with one another. Taking it together seems an integral aspect of its meaning.[82]

Another common question is the practicality of many of their suggestions. Even Robert Webber, who is very friendly to much in the emerging church, responds to Sally Morgenthaler's description of a service: "I would very much love to be at this service.

---

[81] Ibid., 61–65.

[82] Kimball, *Emerging Church*, 163, specifically mentions that individual members need not take the Supper together. Gibbs and Bolger, 229, cite a similar example, and this author witnessed the same practice in an emerging church I attended in Raleigh, North Carolina.

Once, maybe twice a year. But every Sunday? The burnout rate of the worship creators . . . would be excessively high, as would the burnout for the worshipers."[83] Paul Zahl and Harold Best express similar reservations. Zahl says, "the practical burden laid on us by her ideas . . . is considerable," and that in the long run, "planners and leaders always fall back on routine. It is part of human nature."[84] Best raises the question: "How would an average, well-trained worship leader be able to come up with the kind of variety from week to week without succumbing to a set of habits that could only be called 'liturgically repetitive'?"[85] Gibbs and Bolger acknowledge, "Sustainability is a struggle for a number of groups," and so some churches limit their very creative events to once a month or quarter. Other churches have recognized the helpfulness of liturgy to insure structure and content over the long haul. Otherwise, "a Christian community is at the mercy of the spiritual ebb and flow and creative output of the current leadership."[86]

On the whole, the emerging church's worship offers some helpful reminders and challenges to churches to recapture beauty and the arts, to intentionally involve worshipers in multisensory worship experiences, and, as missional churches, to engage the culture in which they are planted. While there have been some common elements of Christian worship through the centuries, this author believes Scripture prescribes little in terms of the specifics of worship and thus allows ample room for worship to adapt to different cultures. At the same time, care should be taken not to devalue elements that have a clear biblical basis, such as the preaching of Scripture, or to practice an ordinance like the Lord's Supper in a novel way that distorts its meaning. Finally, while creativity may be part of being made in God's image and should be encouraged, we need not seek endless novelty. Tradition can help

[83] Robert Webber, "A Blended Worship Response," in *Exploring the Worship Spectrum*, 248.

[84] Paul Zahl, "A Liturgical Worship Response," in *Exploring the Worship Spectrum*, 231–32.

[85] Harold Best, "A Traditional Worship Response," in *Exploring the Worship Spectrum*, 236.

[86] Gibbs and Bolger, *Emerging Churches*, 173, 224.

us root our experience of God in words and practices that have proven useful to generations of Christians.

LEADERSHIP IN THE EMERGING CHURCH

Polity or church government has traditionally been a significant topic in most ecclesiological discussions and has received renewed attention in recent years, especially among Baptists.[87] The emerging church movement, however, spans many denominations and has not engaged in traditional congregational versus episcopalian versus presbyterian polity debates. What has been a subject of considerable discussion in the emerging church movement has been what form leadership should take, especially in the context of emerging, postmodern culture. Dan Kimball notes, "most growing up in our emerging culture are fairly critical of anything that looks like 'organized religion,'" and thus are somewhat suspicious of leadership.[88] In fact, a number of early emerging churches "experimented with the idea of leaderless groups" as a response to "the postmodern critique of modern forms of control."[89] But nearly all emerging churches have seen some form of leadership as inevitable and necessary.

---

[87] In Baptist life, the discussion has been sparked by a number of churches adopting the terminology of *elders* for their church leaders and a consideration of the relationship of elders and the congregation in church government. Among the works discussing this question, see Mark Dever, *Nine Marks of a Healthy Church* (Wheaton: Crossway, 2000) and *A Display of God's Glory* (Washington, D.C.: Center for Church Reform/9 Marks Ministries, 2001); John Piper, "Biblical Eldership," available at http://www.desiringgod.org/library/tbi/bib_eldershi.html, accessed September 24, 2004; *Perspectives of Church Government: Five Views of Church Polity,* ed. Chad Brand and Stan Norman (Nashville: B&H, 2004); *Who Runs the Church: 4 Views on Church Government,* ed. Steven B. Cowan (Grand Rapids: Zondervan, 2004); Phil Newton, *Elders in Congregational Life: Rediscovering the Biblical Model for Church Leadership* (Grand Rapids: Kregel, 2005); Gerald Cowen, *Who Rules the Church? Examining Congregational Leadership and Church Government* (Nashville: B&H, 2003); Alexander Strauch, *Biblical Eldership: An Urgent Call to Restore Biblical Church Leadership*, 2nd ed. (Littleton: Colo.: Lewis & Roth, 1988; and Hammett, *Biblical Foundations for Baptist Churches*, 135–215. For a collection of earlier Baptist works on polity, see *Polity: Biblical Arguments on How to Conduct Church Life,* ed. Mark Dever (Washington, D.C.: Center for Church Reform/9 Marks Ministries, 2001).

[88] Dan Kimball, "The Paradox of Emerging Leadership," found at http://blog.christianitytoday.com/outofur/archives/2006/03/the_paradox_of.html, accessed on April 11, 2006.

[89] Gibbs and Bolger, *Emerging Churches,* 196.

In this section, we will look at three approaches to leadership in emerging churches. Two are very much minority opinions but serve to illustrate the breadth of the movement on this issue. The third approach, which is most prominent within emerging churches, has to do more with attitudes than particular structures and allows for still further diversity on the particular form leadership takes in a given church.

TRADITIONAL LEADERSHIP

The first approach to leadership to be examined comes from an unusual but important emerging church, one whose approach to leadership is much like that of traditional Evangelical churches, that of Mark Driscoll and the Mars Hill Church in Seattle, Washington. As noted earlier, Driscoll is not included among the emerging church leaders interviewed by Gibbs and Bolger in their study of emerging churches, and Driscoll himself has been somewhat hesitant to be identified as part of the emerging church, due to some theological differences he has with other well-known leaders of the emerging church.[90] Still, he seems to fit within our discussion here for two reasons.

First and most obviously, as Mark DeVine notes, Driscoll has been "spectacularly effective at reaching precisely that demographic the heroes of the Gibbs/Bolger type churches insist will only respond to sufficiently postmodern-immersed and shaped ministries."[91] In fact, his is one of the few churches that has won large numbers of those in the emerging culture, with more than six thousand gathering each weekend. The success of his church suggests that he is effectively engaging the emerging or postmodern culture, despite the fact that he is confronting and opposing the culture on some points. It also suggests that part of the problem many postmodern people have with the leadership in traditional churches may be not that it is traditional, but that it is poor; that is, it is leadership by those whose character falls far short of that

---

[90] Collin Hansen, "Pastor Provacateur," *Christianity Today* 51, no. 9 (September 2007), 46.

[91] Mark DeVine, "Fast Friends or Future Foes: The Emerging Church and Southern Baptists," 15–16, available at http://www.theologyprof.com/free-theological-resources, accessed August 1, 2007.

called for in Scripture. Driscoll's experience suggests that the problem may not be a traditional approach to leadership, *per se*, but the manner in which leadership is exercised.

A second reason why the approach of Driscoll is important to examine is that it is being replicated through the numerous churches being planted by the Acts 29 Network, whose stated goal is to plant one thousand new churches in the next twenty years, churches characterized by faithfulness both to "the content of unchanging Biblical doctrine" and "the continually changing context of the culture."[92] In a word, Acts 29 is planting emerging churches, according to the broad definition adopted at the beginning of this chapter. Though Acts 29 is deliberately nondenominational, in that their statement of faith "omits some finer points of doctrine and secondary issues as we allow the elders in our local churches to operate according to their convictions on these matters," they do advocate a particular approach to leadership, one that matches that of their founder.[93]

What is Driscoll's approach? In a word, it is traditional, surprisingly so. In this area, Driscoll believes the church must oppose trends in contemporary culture in order to be biblically faithful. He concedes that the demons of modernity did need to be cast out of the church, but he also sees new demons of postmodernism that need to be avoided. Two of these postmodern demons relate directly to the topic of leadership.

The first Driscoll calls "the photocopy heresy," which involves "the silly notion that everyone is equal" and leads to "confusion over gender issues" and "a peculiar commitment to making sure that everyone's voice is equally heard and everyone's input is equally considered, whether or not it is foolish."[94] He specifically critiques churches who "replace a preaching monologue from a

[92] "Acts 29 Doctrine," available at http://www.acts29network.org/about/doctrine/, accessed July 24, 2007. An article on Mark Driscoll (Hansen, "Pastor Provacateur," 44) gives the number of Acts 29 churches as 170, as of September 2007.

[93] Ibid. Interestingly, Mars Hill itself, on a number of these secondary points (such as local church autonomy and believer's baptism) takes a Baptist position, and, according to Acts 29 vice president Darrin Patrick, around half of Acts 29 Network churches are Southern Baptist. See DeVine, *Fast Friends*, 12.

[94] Driscoll, *Radical Reformission*, 172–73.

recognized leader to a spiritual dialogue among a group of peers who refuse to acknowledge any leader in authority over them,"[95] comparing them to patients who shoot their doctor and then diagnose and prescribe remedies for each other, all in the name of equality. He recognizes that the church is called to "work among cultures that despise hierarchy" but affirms nonetheless differing roles and responsibilities for wives and husbands as well as church leaders and church members "because the governments of home and church belong to God and not the culture."[96]

Driscoll sees Scripture as teaching male only leadership and holds to that commitment in the face of a culture that is increasingly egalitarian. Speaking to a reporter with *The Seattle Times* about Paul's teaching on gender roles, "If I could change one part of the Bible, that would be the part, just so I could be left alone."[97] The Acts 29 Network Web site says clearly, "We are not egalitarians and do believe that men should lead their homes and male elders should lead their churches with masculine love like Jesus Christ."[98]

Gibbs and Bolger, by contrast, affirm the egalitarian position they see as characteristic of the emerging church, voicing their approval of the fact that virtually all those they identified as emerging churches "support women at all levels of ministry."[99] Sally Morgenthaler objects to the fact that while 60 percent of the members of what she calls the "average entrepreneurial congregation" are female, they account for less than 1 percent of the leadership, outside of the realms of children's and women's programs. She sees changes in the culture calling for a new style of leadership that females are especially equipped to offer. "Female Christ-followers who possess true leadership skills . . . need to lead because, more often than not, they get this new world and they get it really well."[100]

---

[95] Ibid., 173. He seems to be referring to the approach of Doug Pagitt and others, discussed later in this same section.

[96] Ibid., 174.

[97] This comment is reported in Collin Hansen, "Pastor Provocateur," 48, but the date of the story in *The Seattle Times* is not given.

[98] "Acts 29 Doctrine."

[99] Gibbs and Bolger, *Emerging Churches*, 11.

[100] Sally Morgenthaler, "Leadership in a Flattened World: Grassroots Culture and the Demise of the CEO Model," in *An Emergent Manifesto of Hope*, 183, 187.

Dan Kimball seems to recognize that women serving in some roles may be an issue for some. Nonetheless, he says:

> In the emerging culture, the role of women in the church is a huge issue. People in the emerging generations think of churches as male-dominated and oppressive of females. So whatever your theology may be about the role of women in the church, I would still highly encourage you to have females in up-front roles as much as possible, whether it is teaching, giving announcements, leading worship, sharing testimonies, or reading Scripture. This is critical for the emerging church.[101]

Women do serve as deacons (but not elders) at Mars Hill, but that church's example and success question the idea that women must be involved in leadership for an emerging church to attract those in the emerging generations. At any rate, the approach to leadership at Mars Hill frankly conflicts with the strong egalitarian impulse in postmodern culture.

The second postmodern demon related to leadership Driscoll terms "the hyphenated Christian," specifically, the postmodern-Christian. Driscoll's concern here is that a commitment to being fully postmodern is incompatible with a commitment to being Christian, because certain aspects of postmodernism are antithetical to Christianity. He sees this as especially so in terms of power and authority. Postmodern thought is suspicious of truth claims because such claims involve matters of authority and power; postmodern thought devalues authoritative truth claims to merely personal perspectives and opinions to remove or reduce their claims to be authoritative. Driscoll believes the postmodern attitude toward power leads to a rejection of "any form of officially responsible leadership," and to the demand "that ministry be facilitated rather than led."[102]

Driscoll challenges this second postmodern demon with an approach to leadership that does not hesitate to see leaders as those who do far more than merely facilitate; they actively lead.

---

[101] Kimball, *Emerging Church*, 150.
[102] Driscoll, *Radical Reformation*, 176.

The Mars Hill Church Web site offers this statement on church leaders:

> The elders ("pastors") of Mars Hill are appointed by God to shepherd and lead the flock of Mars Hill. It is our desire to lead this Church through this culture in a way pleasing to the Lord. Leading is not always easy or pleasurable, but as God continues to work through the elders by washing his children with His word the Lord is presenting [to] himself a radiant Church.[103]

Clearly, this church's leaders *lead*. The church's membership covenant specifies eleven commitments the church's leadership makes to members, including covenanting to provide pastoral care, teaching, prayer, and seeking God's will for the church community. For their part, among the ten responsibilities members accept is that of "submission to church leadership."[104]

At the same time, the approach to leadership depicted in the membership covenant seems to reflect many of the values Kimball recommends for emerging church leaders. Whereas he sees modern church leaders as CEOs, with a hunger to maintain all power for themselves, driven by goals, and leading by virtue of their role, Kimball says emerging church leaders need to be spiritual guides and fellow journeyers, with diffuse power, relationally driven, and earning the right to lead by deserving trust.[105] Many of those latter elements seem to be implied in the Mars Hill covenant. Leaders pledge an extensive commitment of personal ministry to the member that would be inescapably more relational than hierarchical. There are a plurality of elders and a larger number of deacons to diffuse power, and the leaders covenant to meet the criteria required for leaders in Scripture and to join members in fulfilling the duties of church members as fellow journeyers.[106] It would seem that Driscoll includes such elements not because he

---

[103] "Who We Are > Elders," available at http://lite.marshillchurch.org/site/who_we_are/elders/, accessed on April 18, 2006.

[104] "Mars Hill Church Membership Covenant," available at http:// lite.marshillchurch.org/site/?id= BAAE0F06–5159–47A4-BBAE-649BD70D1725, accessed April 18, 2006.

[105] Kimball, *Emerging Church*, 229.

[106] "Mars Hill Membership Covenant."

is seeking to adapt to postmodern culture, but because he is trying to incorporate what Scripture teaches about church leaders. Again, the problem may not be modern conceptions of leadership but simply nonbiblical conceptions.

At any rate, nothing in this approach seems particularly innovative. It may be called traditional not because it is the norm in most churches, but because it represents what many Evangelicals would see as a traditional interpretation of biblical teaching on church leadership. The difference may be that at Mars Hill the leaders actually lead in a way that reflects that teaching. Their approach is knowingly contrary to postmodern culture at a number of points. Based on his interpretation of biblical teaching, Driscoll chooses to challenge rather than adapt to postmodern culture on such issues. While this approach is not at all characteristic of emerging churches as a whole, it is one that has had significant success, and one that will be seen more often if the Acts 29 Network accomplishes their church-planting goals.

THE APEPT FIVEFOLD MINISTRY

A distinctively different approach to leadership has been developed, primarily by Australians Michael Frost and Alan Hirsch. It, too, is a distinctively minority approach in emerging churches. While Peter Wagner and some in the charismatic and Pentecostal community have shared some of their perspective, Frost and Hirsch have been the most influential advocates in emerging church circles of what is called "the fivefold ministry," which goes by the acrostic APEPT, standing for apostles, prophets, evangelists, pastors, and teachers, taken from Ephesians 4:11. They contrast this apostolic leadership model with the hierarchical model they see as characteristic of Christendom, and see a change in leadership as essential to the long-range health of missional churches. They say, "without this [shift to apostolic leadership] the missional church is unlikely to rise at all, and if it does manage to survive birth, it will not last long because it will lack the leadership structure to sustain it over the long distance."[107]

---

[107] Frost and Hirsch, *The Shaping of Things to Come,* 165.

The acronym APEPT does not designate five offices but five
roles or functions that must be "operating within the leadership
of a local congregation" and embraced by the congregation as a
whole within its corporate life.[108] They apply the APEPT model to
both the nature and structure of the whole church's ministry and
to the nature and structure of the church's leadership. That is, the
community as a whole is called to be apostolic, prophetic, evangelistic, pastoral, and didactic, and those five functions should be
especially seen in the church's leadership. They believe all five
functions are essential to the growth of the body in maturity and
mission, and that all members of the body are gifted and called
to minister in some way in one of those five areas. But, in addition, some are gifted and called "to be an APEPT leader to the
rest of the APEPT body."[109] These five functions are described as
follows:

> *Apostolic function*, usually conducted translocally, pio-
> neers new missional works and oversees their develop-
> ment. *Prophetic function* discerns the spiritual realities in
> a given situation and communicates them in a timely and
> appropriate way to further the mission of God's people.
> *Evangelistic function* communicates the gospel in such a
> way that people respond in faith and discipleship. *Pas-
> toral function* shepherds the people of God by leading,
> nurturing, protecting, and caring for them. *Teaching func-
> tion* communicates the revealed wisdom of God so that
> the people of God learn how to obey all that Christ has
> commanded them.[110]

Hirsch and Frost anticipate some of the objections to their proposal and make some good points in defense. While they accept
some unique aspects in the ministry of the twelve apostles of
Christ, they argue that nothing in the text of Ephesians 4 indicates
that the roles of apostle, prophet, and evangelist are temporary
or that only the roles of pastor and teacher are normative. They

---

[108] Ibid., 225.
[109] Ibid., 172.
[110] Ibid., 169 (italics in original).

point out that many scholars believe that Ephesians was written as a general epistle, not addressed to one specific congregation, but giving teaching for churches in general.[111]

The idea of widespread participation in the five functions finds support in the biblical idea of the priesthood of all believers, is reflected in the dozens of "one another" commands in the New Testament, and resonates well with postmodern culture. In fact, Baptists, as congregationalists and champions of the doctrine of the priesthood of all believers, could possibly adopt elements of the fivefold ministry as a model for the ministry of the church as a whole.

However, its viability as a pattern for leadership is weakened by the fact that Frost and Hirsch do not connect this single verse with other texts, especially in Acts and the Pastoral Epistles, that give more comprehensive and explicit directions on church leadership that qualify the application of Ephesians 4:11. To put it simply, Ephesians 4:11 alone is not sufficient to give us all we need to construct a biblical pattern of church leadership. Moreover, much of the criticism of the hierarchical model they oppose is provided in the New Testament teaching on leadership and supremely in the example of Jesus. Yet the APEPT model proposed by Frost and Hirsch is being promulgated through the Forge Mission Training Network in Australia and is championed as well by house church advocate Wolfgang Simson, who has been influential in the European house church movement.[112] It seems likely to be a pattern of leadership in at least some segments of the emerging church movement for the foreseeable future.

LEADERSHIP BY THE BODY

The third pattern of leadership to be examined is probably the one practiced by most emerging churches. In fact, Eddie Gibbs and Ryan Bolger, from their extensive research of emerging churches, list this type of leadership as one of the nine identifying characteristics of emerging churches: "Emerging churches . . . lead as a

---

[111] Ibid., 166–68.
[112] Simson, *Houses That Change the World*, 102–29.

body."[113] Dan Kimball expresses a similar idea, saying that emerging church leaders need to see themselves as spiritual guides or fellow journeyers, who approach their role with the thought, "I'll lead as we solve this together."[114] Kimball draws here on the comparison originally made by Stanley Grenz between Captain Kirk of the original *Star Trek*, representing the modern leader, and Captain Picard of *Star Trek: The Next Generation*, representing the postmodern leader.[115] The latter, says Kimball, "is very much a leader, but his approach is quite different and fits much better with the emerging culture."[116]

This pattern of leadership could be described in a number of ways: *open*, *consensual*, *facilitative*, *relational*, and *servant* are some of the terms often used. There is a strong opposition to any form of authoritarian or hierarchical leadership, which is seen as stifling creativity and freedom, and destructive of community. One example of how that idea is fleshed out is found in Solomon's Porch, an emerging church in Minneapolis, and the leadership pattern of its pastor, Doug Pagitt.

One of the clearest places where the intentionally communal nature of Pagitt's leadership is seen is in his sermon preparation, which occurs through a Tuesday evening Bible discussion. Pagitt says of this group:

> The Bible discussion group differs from a traditional Bible study. We aren't just getting together to read and extract from the Bible and deepen our own understanding. Rather, this group is like a microcosm of our community, standing in for others as we enter into the passage. In many ways this group sets the form and feel and content for what will happen on Sunday night during our worship gathering. Together we explore the questions and issues so that when the same passage is presented to our larger group, it will be clear that it has been wrestled with not

---

[113] Gibbs and Bolger, *Emerging Churches,* 45.

[114] Kimball, *Emerging Church*, 229.

[115] Grenz's lengthy comparison can be found in *A Primer on Postmodernism* (Grand Rapids: Eerdmans, 1996).

[116] Kimball, *Emerging Church*, 229.

just by the theologian who gives the sermon (me) but by "regular" people as well.[117]

He calls this discussion group his "primary time of preparation for the following Sunday's sermon" and likes the idea that the sermon is "more than just my thoughts and research on a passage."[118]

The communal nature of leadership carries over into what happens at the Sunday evening worship gatherings, which Pagitt sees as "a time when people contribute to the creation of a setting in which we are transformed, not a setting in which we come to be serviced by professionals or qualified volunteers."[119] Members participate by reading Scripture, singing and playing music, sharing stories, partaking of communion, and responding to the sermon, which has already been shaped by the previous Tuesday evening discussion. Pagitt says, "On most occasions the sermon is followed by a time of open discussion where I ask for comments, interpretations, and thoughts of significance from our community. During these few minutes not only are brilliant observations made, but people are also reminded that we are called to listen to one another and be taught by each other and not only by the pastor."[120]

This pattern of leadership displays a number of strengths and weaknesses. On the positive side, as a Baptist believing in congregational government, this author supports the idea that the ultimate human authority in the church is that exercised by the members of the community. Moreover, the idea of mutual ministry is supported by the doctrine of the priesthood of all believers, which in turn is supported by the many "one another" commands of the New Testament, such as to teach and admonish one another (Col 3:16). Moreover, Pagitt's behavior evidences a winsome humility that is commanded of all who follow Christ and is especially welcome in leaders (1 Pet 5:1–5).

Negatively, however, there are a number of biblical and theological weaknesses as well as practical difficulties in this pattern.

[117] Doug Pagitt, *Church Re-Imagined*, 115.
[118] Ibid., 119.
[119] Ibid., 63.
[120] Ibid., 77.

To follow the pattern of leadership by the body, one must ignore or at least minimize biblical teaching on leadership that assigns a certain measure of authority to recognized leaders in the body. Certainly, leaders are commanded to exercise their authority with humility, to serve those they lead, to listen to the counsel of others, and, for Baptists, to serve ultimately under the governance of the congregation. At the same time, there are commands given to members of churches to obey their leaders and submit to their authority (Heb 13:17; 1 Cor 16:16; 1 Thess 5:12–13), while leaders are to manage, take care of, direct the affairs of, and shepherd the church (1 Tim 3:5; 5:17; 1 Pet 5:2).

One of the major ways they exercise their authority is in teaching, for the leader is responsible "both to encourage with sound teaching and to refute those who contradict it" (Titus 1:9). One of the requisite gifts for a leader is the ability to teach (1 Tim 3:2), for the pastor is to be a teacher. He may not be the only teacher, and there are many contexts where discussion and mutual teaching is appropriate (such as small groups or Sunday school classes). But the responsibility of pastors to teach their congregations is not a relic of modernity that may be safely discarded in postmodernity, but a staple of Christian practice for two thousand years, firmly rooted in biblical example and precept.

Moreover, the New Testament makes a distinction between leaders and members, for leaders must meet certain criteria or qualifications. It is not that leaders are called to a higher standard; all believers are called to Christlikeness, and that is essentially what the qualifications reflect. But leaders must have made enough progress toward Christlikeness so that they can serve as examples to the church (1 Pet 5:3). Whereas Mars Hill documents on leadership specifically cite texts like 1 Tim 3:1–7 and Titus 1:6–9 in giving their definition of an elder, neither these texts nor the issue of qualifications for leaders is discussed by Pagitt; the only qualification mentioned in the discussion of leaders by Gibbs and Bolger is "the primary qualification" of being one who is "actively learning how to live in the kingdom of God as an apprentice of Jesus."[121]

---

[121]   Gibbs and Bolger, *Emerging Churches,* 215.

This oversight of qualifications for leaders is perhaps the most surprising omission in the discussion of leadership by the body. In view of the multiple and explicit discussions of qualifications in Scripture, it suggests that this leadership pattern may be more culture-driven than Scripture-driven.

In addition to biblical/theological problems, there are also practical difficulties encountered in practicing leadership by the body. One is the simple inevitability of leadership. As Gibbs and Bolger acknowledge, "Whenever a group of people meets together for any length of time, someone will emerge as a leader."[122] Despite attempts in emerging churches to keep leadership open, people tend to spot and identify leaders and look to them for leadership. An interesting feature of Pagitt's book is the inclusion of excerpts from journals kept by a number of members of Solomon's Porch. Some of their comments reflect their perception that Pagitt is indeed *the* leader of Solomon's Porch. One member commented on a Sunday when Pagitt was absent, "The worship gathering on Sunday was very unusual because Doug was gone. . . . It was great to hear so many different people's expressions, but I definitely missed having a message."[123] From this member's perspective, without the pastor's presence, there was no message. It would seem that the people of Solomon's Porch do regard the pastor as *the leader*, perhaps more than he would like them to.

Also, leadership by the body increases in difficulty as churches grow. Most of the emerging churches examined by Gibbs and Bolger are quite small, with a surprising number existing as house churches or cell churches. Some choose to stay small intentionally to preserve community; others remain small due to a lack of evangelistic effectiveness. Emerging churches that do grow will find it increasingly difficult to maintain open leadership or to involve everyone in decision making and will tend to move toward some sort of representative leadership.

[122] Ibid., 199.
[123] Pagitt, *Church Re-Imagined,* 62, 60.

EVALUATION

At least two positive lessons and two warnings may be drawn from these approaches to leadership in emerging churches. The first positive lesson is in the fact that all three of the approaches to leadership considered here agree that leadership is not to be arrogant, authoritarian, high-handed, or modeled after a business CEO.[124] Rather, the example is to be Christ, who served as a leader, and was highly relational. In the approaches of Driscoll and Frost and Hirsch, this concern is reflected in the responsibilities of leaders in the Mars Hill membership covenant and in the rejection of hierarchical leadership by Frost and Hirsch. The third approach, in rejecting hierarchical, authoritarian leadership, may overreact with a minimizing of the importance of recognized leaders, but all three approaches identify important attitudes which church leaders must exemplify.

Another positive contribution, particularly from the third approach, is the emphasis on congregational involvement in church government. While leadership by the body may not be a fully adequate approach to church leadership, calling members to see themselves as having a significant role in the leadership of the body is refreshing, particularly to this convinced congregationalist, and especially in a day when many church members see themselves as nothing more than consumers and are content to leave real concern for the church to the so-called "professionals."

One warning, seen particularly in the second and third approaches, is the danger of not incorporating all of biblical teaching on leadership. The APEPT model takes its starting point and acronym from Scripture, and relates helpfully to culture, but elevates a single verse to undue proportions. Frost and Hirsch manifest a careful attention to theology throughout most of their discussion of the emerging church, but in the area of leadership they seem to

---

[124] It is this author's belief that some in the emerging church who seem to espouse relativistic ideas of truth do not fully accept postmodern skeptical epistemology but are simply appalled at what they see as the lack of humility in many who defend absolute truth. They are right to value humility but wrong to think humility means we can never say that anyone is wrong, or that any idea is heretical. The goal must be "speaking the truth in love" (Eph 4:15).

become surprisingly focused on one verse. Their approach fails to take into account all of the biblical teaching on leadership.

The third view runs the danger of being culture-driven. Cultural relevance demands carefulness in avoiding sinful arrogance and worldly styles of leadership; biblical faithfulness demands equal carefulness in recognizing the rightful authority and importance of scripturally qualified and properly functioning leaders. Kimball seems to take his cue from what postmodern culture desires in a leader, without carefully critiquing those desires in the light of what Scripture says about leadership. Likewise, Pagitt's approach seems to be very culture-friendly in the area of leadership, but raises questions about how fully Scripture is being utilized to evaluate culture. Postmodern culture is mentioned more often than Scripture as the key shaper of their approach to leadership. Ben Witherington's caution, though given to Rob Bell concerning different issues, is apt on this point as well: "above all he must not fall into the trap of so identifying with the culture he is trying to reach, that instead of actually critiquing that culture from a Biblical point of view, he baptizes certain prevailing cultural values and calls them good, and even mistakes them for Biblical values."[125]

A second warning is seen in the simple existence of three approaches. The warning is to resist the temptation to reduce the emerging church to only one model of leadership, or anything else. It is a diverse movement, unified by its desire to engage emerging culture but differing widely in the specifics of what that engagement requires of churches.

CONCLUSION

The emerging church movement has sparked extensive discussions, to which this book and many others bear witness, not to mention the almost endless ongoing conversations conducted on Web sites and blogs. Some of the discussions have been sharply critical of the emerging church, in ways that many of its leaders

---

[125] Ben Witherington, "Rob Bell Hits Lexington and a Packed-Out House," found at http://benwitherington.blogspot.com/2007/02/rob-bell-hits-lexington-and-packed-out. html, accessed January 14, 2008.

have thought were unfair. In particular, many have found D. A. Carson's book, *Becoming Conversant with the Emerging Church*, an inaccurate portrayal of the movement. Scot McKnight faults Carson for not recognizing that "the center of the movement is about *ecclesiology not epistemology*."[126] While there does seem to be reason for concern about the corrosive effect postmodern thought may be having on the epistemology of some in the emerging church movement, this chapter has sought to focus on what seem to be central ecclesiological issues for the emerging church. On the issues that were the concern of this chapter, the verdict, while mixed due to the diverse nature of the movement, is more positive than negative.

The call for churches to cultivate community and adopt a missional orientation toward culture is altogether fitting and helpful. While many emerging churches seem to have adopted these emphases due to the cultural context, there is even stronger support for them in Scripture. Though the evidence seems to indicate that the majority of emerging churches have not translated their missional orientation into evangelistic fruitfulness, still they have highlighted the missional nature of the church in a way that has been very helpful. Ed Stetzer says, "Within the wider world of evangelicalism, the issue is settled—most evangelical denominations have decided they need change and they want to be 'missional.'"[127]

Likewise, in the area of worship, the emphases on art and beauty and the desire to experience God's transcendence are commendable. This author believes Scripture allows a good deal of liberty within broad guidelines in terms of specific ways we seek to implement those emphases in worship, and some ways may be more effective in some cultural settings than others. If so, then by all means let creative people use their creativity to find new ways to give God glory in worship that connect with people in the emerging culture. However, there are some staples of Christian worship that should not be left behind. In particular, the tendency in some emerging circles to minimize preaching seems contrary to Scripture, contrary to evangelical worship since the Reforma-

---

[126] McKnight, "What Is the Emerging Church?", 7 (emphasis in original).
[127] Stetzer, "Toward a Missional Convention," 32.

tion, and contrary to the fact that it is churches with strong biblical preaching that seem to be experiencing the most success in reaching the emerging generation.

Finally, in the area of leadership, the emerging church's objection to arrogant, authoritarian, heavy-handed leadership and the CEO mentality of many pastors is eminently justified, but not so much because it is contrary to postmodern sensibilities as because it is contrary to the leadership modeled by Christ and taught in Scripture. Here, the failure of some in the emerging church to ponder carefully all that Scripture has to say about leaders has led some to patterns of leadership that are overreactions to failures in other churches (the idea of leadership by the body) or simply patterns that have only a very slender foundation in Scripture (the APEPT model). Mark Driscoll's approach to leadership prioritizes biblical fidelity over cultural accommodation, while at the same time incorporating biblical emphases in leadership that are especially appreciated by those in the emerging culture (such as strong emphasis on relationships, leaders as shepherds and fellow journeyers, authenticity in terms of character).

In all these ecclesiological issues, the emerging church has thus far served effectively, as Mark DeVine suspects it will continue to serve, "as a conduit for certain ideas, values and emphases back into established churches."[128] At the same time, there are some areas of concern.

The lack of evangelistic impact by most emerging churches raises questions, especially since one of the rationales for the development of emerging churches was the lack of effectiveness of existing churches in reaching the postmodern generation. The fact that most emerging churches are not doing very well evangelistically, coupled with the fact that those who are doing well are regarded as on the fringe of the movement (Mars Hill, Mosaic, and a number of churches in the Acts 29 Network, for example), or are not associated with the emerging movement at all (Redeemer Presbyterian in Manhattan is one notable example) suggests that the missional focus of many emerging churches needs adjustment.

---

[128] DeVine, *Fast Friends,* 20.

A second area of concern for the emerging church and all churches is the relationship of cultural sensitivity and biblical fidelity. For Evangelicals, the latter should clearly have priority. Most if not all of the positive emphases that emerging churches have derived from their concern to relate sensitively to postmodern culture could have been as easily derived from a careful reading of Scripture; most of the weaknesses noted in postmodern ecclesiology can be traced to allowing postmodern culture to override biblical teaching. The problem with elevating culture over Scripture is of course that postmodern culture, like all cultures, is fallen, and thus cannot be followed uncritically.

Much that has been written has been critical of the emerging church, especially in conservative evangelical circles, and there are certainly causes for concern over the ideas and directions being taken by some (not all) in this movement. But the passion among many in the emerging church to develop churches that are both biblically faithful and culturally relevant is something to applaud, learn from, and join. May this book contribute both to the understanding of areas of concern and appreciation for the positive contributions of many in the emerging church, in winning postmodern people and in stimulating reexamination of biblical teaching on ecclesiology.

PART THREE
PRACTICAL SECTION

THE EMERGING CHURCH AND ETHICAL CHOICES: THE CORINTHIAN MATRIX

DANIEL L. AKIN

ETHICAL DECISION MAKING in the twenty-first century is confronted with new and diverse challenges, not only from the culture itself but also within the church. The rise of the so-called Emergent Church movement has sparked a great deal of conversation, if not consternation, with respect to traditional Christian ethics. Consider the following examples:

- Emerging pastor Mark Driscoll, once labeled "the cussing pastor" for his frequent use of expletives in delivering his messages,[1] described himself as having been a teetotaler until shortly after his conversion and entrance into the ministry. Soon thereafter, however, Driscoll recalled that one day he was "studying the Scriptures for a sermon about Jesus' first miracle of turning water into wine, as reported in John's gospel, a miracle that Jesus performed when he was about my age. My Bible study convicted me of my sin of abstinence from alcohol. So in repentance I drank a hard cider over lunch with our worship pastor." Driscoll goes on to note his personal longing for the return "to the glory days of Christian pubs, where God's men gather to drink beer and talk theology." He later adds, perhaps humorously, that

[1] Driscoll has since repented of his use of profanity. He also distances himself from the Revisionist stream of Emergent, preferring to be thought of as Relevant and Reformed.

while drinking itself is not sinful, "drinking light beer" is indeed a "sin."[2] Driscoll is hardly alone—a casual Internet search reveals numerous Emergent churches and leaders that not only espouse positive views concerning the "moderate" consumption of alcohol but even advertise their meeting locations as pubs, bars, or breweries.[3]

- Tony Jones, former national coordinator of Emergent Village, recently admitted that after years of having not made up his mind regarding the issue of homosexuality, he *"now believe[s] that G[ay]L[esbian]B[isexual]T[ransgendered] Q[ueer] can live lives in accord with biblical Christianity (at least as much as any of us can!) and that their monogamy can and should be sanctioned and blessed by church and state."* Jones does acknowledge that this newfound position will likely be tested as to "whether I have good theological and philosophical reasons for supporting the rights of GLBTQ persons to marry, or whether I've simply caved to the mushy inclusivity of pluralized nothingness."[4]

- Brian McLaren, Tony Jones, and Doug Pagitt (among others) have called for a recasting of ethical priorities, urging the elevation of environmentalism and social justice to a status equal to (if not greater than) traditional evangelical ethical concerns like abortion and homosexuality.[5]

---

[2] Mark Driscoll, *The Radical Reformission* (Grand Rapids: Zondervan, 2004), 146–47, note also the title of chapter 6, "The Sin of Light Beer."

[3] See for example http://churchinabrewery.com/, a Web site of Sojourn Church, Huntsville, Alabama.

[4] Tony Jones, "How I Went from There to Here: Same Sex Marriage Blogalogue" [on-line]; accessed January 12, 2009; available from http://blog.beliefnet.com/tony jones/2008/11/same-sex-marriage-blogalogue-h.html; Internet, emphasis original.

[5] McLaren, for example, recalled that his involvement in environmental issues raised eyebrows amongst some in his own community because ". . . they're surprised that a Christian pastor would be out here doing this sort of thing. . . . I know what they're thinking, *Christians are part of the problem, not part of the solution. They read James Dobson, Chuck Colson, and Jerry Falwell, not Wendell Berry, Herman Daly, or Al Gore; they focus on the family and the military, not the environment,"* in *A Generous Orthodoxy: Why I Am a Missional, Evangelical, Post/Protestant, Liberal/Conservative, Mystical/Poetic, Biblical, Charismatic/Contemplative, Fundamentalist/Calvinist, Anabaptist/Anglican, Methodist, Catholic, Green, Incarnational, Depressed-yet-Hopeful, Emergent, Unfinished Christian* (Grand Rapids: Zondervan, 2004), 233 (emphasis original). He adds in a footnote, "All the names in the latter group, by the way, see their environmentalism as an expression of their Christian faith."

How should evangelicals respond to such scenarios? A radically biblical perspective is demanded. A genuinely Christian mind-set is required. What is needed is what Don Carson calls a "world Christian." What does he mean by that? Four things will stand out and be true of such men and women:

1. Their allegiance to Jesus Christ and His kingdom is self-consciously set above all national, cultural, linguistic, and racial allegiances.
2. Their commitment to the church, Jesus' messianic community, is to the church everywhere, wherever the church is truly manifest, and not only to its manifestation on home turf.
3. They see themselves first and foremost as citizens of the heavenly kingdom and therefore consider all other citizenship a secondary matter.
4. As a result, they are single-minded and sacrificial when it comes to the paramount mandate to evangelize and make disciples.[6]

World Christians recognize that they are citizens of a different kind of nation, a different kind of kingdom, a different kind of community. And yet, they also recognize that they live in this world as well, a world that is not their home but one in which they serve as royal ambassadors fulfilling the ministry of reconciliation (2 Cor 5:18–21). They are here as divine representatives to call men and women from this world kingdom into God's glorious kingdom. This assignment calls for *wisdom* and *winsomeness*. It calls for *conviction* as well as *compassion*. It requires that we plant our feet in the *Scriptures* while keeping a watchful and discerning eye on the *culture*.

How can we live out this calling to be God's people in God's world? I want to provide for us a biblically based strategy for faithfully accomplishing this assignment, one that is transferable to any cultural context, whether in North America or around the world. There are biblical principles that are true anywhere, anytime, and under any circumstances that will help us communicate

---

[6] D. A. Carson, *The Cross and Christian Ministry* (Grand Rapids: Baker, 2003), 117.

and "live out" the gospel more clearly. A great place to discover this strategy is Paul's first letter to the Corinthians. Here was a church gone wild, a church in a titanic battle in terms of its moral and ethical decision-making. They were struggling, and struggling mightily, both inside and outside their community, and they had the awesome task of being the Church in a radically secular, immoral, non-Christian context. Maintaining a clear gospel witness was difficult and problematic. Therefore, Paul wrote this letter in order to instruct the Corinthians in how to live out a gospel-centered ethic.

TEN PAULINE PRINCIPLES

Within 1 Cor 6:12–13:13, Paul sets forth a number of universal, nonnegotiable principles that would enable them to engage the culture with integrity while staying true to the gospel of Jesus Christ, both in what they said and in how they lived. I have identified ten that speak not only to those who lived in the first century but also to those of us who are living in the twenty-first century. These principles, as Ed Stetzer says, will enable us to be biblically missional, which means "*doing mission* right where you are."[7]

(1) WILL THIS ACTION BE HELPFUL TO ME?

> *"Everything is permissible for me," but not everything is helpful. "Everything is permissible for me," but I will not be brought under the control of anything.—1 Cor 6:12*

> *"Everything is permissible," but not everything is helpful. "Everything is permissible," but not everything builds up.—1 Cor 10:23*

Certain actions are simply not helpful for believers. They accomplish little to nothing. To understand this principle, examine the following four statements. "Everything is permissible for me" (6:12; 10:23). "'Foods for the stomach and the stomach for foods,' but God will do away with both of them" (6:13). "Every sin a person can commit is outside the body" (6:18). "It is good

---

[7] Ed Stetzer, *Planting Missional Churches* (Nashville: B&H, 2005), 19.

for a man not to have relations with a woman" (7:1). I believe these were all Corinth slogans. In other words, these statements were not things Paul was affirming. On the contrary, these were popular sayings that Paul was correcting because they were rooted in a misunderstanding of the implications of the gospel. The first three erred on the side of antinomianism; the last one erred on the side of legalism and asceticism. All were infected with a view of reality that was grounded in a Platonic type of philosophy that saw matter as evil or, at best, inferior. Thus, some went to one extreme and said, "The body does not matter, so indulge." Others said, "The body is bad, so I will punish it."

Paul said there is a third and better way. The Lord is for the body (6:13) and He is going to raise it (6:14). In other words, the body is a wonderful gift from God, and it is a great thing when handled properly. So ask: Is a particular activity helpful, profitable, beneficial? Will a particular activity make me better in Christ and build me up? In other words, the question should not be, "Am I free to do it?" The question is, "Is it good for me to do this as a man or woman in Christ?"

(2) WILL THIS ACTION POTENTIALLY ENSLAVE ME?

> *"Everything is permissible for me," but not everything is helpful. "Everything is permissible for me," but I will not be brought under the control of anything.—1 Cor 6:12*

Paul is confident that he is a slave to only one master. His name is Jesus. No one or no thing is to "be master" (*NIV*) over us other than Him. I will choose to live a radically Christ-centered life because I belong to Him. There is a danger in living "too close to the edge." It can be the edge of antinomianism and libertarianism or legalism and asceticism. Either extreme is going to draw you away from Christ, and you will run the risk of being enslaved. Later, in 1 Cor 10:14–22, Paul will point out that living near the edge of sin can even make one vulnerable to demonic attack and influence. There is little, if any, wisdom in hanging around out there.

The boasts: "I have liberty in Christ" and "I am free under grace" becomes something of a moral rationalization that is more likely a personal idol erected for satisfying sensual pleasure. In the long run, when you convince yourself that something will not hurt anyone, it will in fact lead you yourself into a world of slavery and bondage to the cruelest taskmaster of all: yourself and your own carnal desires. True spiritual freedom is not the right to do what you want; it is the supernatural enablement of Christ to do what you ought and enjoy doing so! Gordon Fee says, "There is a kind of self-deception that inflated spirituality promotes, which suggests to oneself that he/she is acting with freedom and authority, but which in fact is an enslavement of the worst kind—to the very freedom one thinks one has."[8] Christians must consistently guard themselves against any action that will potentially enslave them.

(3) WILL THIS ACTION ENCOURAGE MY BROTHER OR SISTER IN CHRIST?

Therefore, if food causes my brother to fall, I will never again eat meat, so that I won't cause my brother to fall.—1 Cor 8:13

No one should seek his own good, but the good of the other person.—1 Cor 10:24

Give no offense to the Jews or the Greeks or the church of God.—1 Cor 10:32

Paul, for the sake of others, was willing to adjust his life that they might not be hurt or harmed. His brother or sister in Christ mattered more to him than his rights or liberties. This principle is grounded in the "mind of Christ" text of Phil 2:3–5. For the sake of the body of Christ, your community of faith, "consider others as more important than yourselves." Paul drives ethics to the gospel and to the cross. The gospel demands that the needs of others outweigh selfish desires. When it comes to wise decision-making, a believer in Christ should always have an eye toward a potentially weaker brother. As John MacArthur says, "Right or wrong is not the issue, but offending someone is."[9]

---

[8] Gordon Fee, *The First Epistle to the Corinthians*, NICNT (Grand Rapids: Eerdmans, 1987), 253.

[9] John MacArthur, *Giving Up to Gain* (Panorama City, Calif.: Word of Grace, 1982), 5.

(4) WILL THIS ACTION HELP OR HINDER
MY GOSPEL WITNESS?

*If others share this authority over you, don't we even
more? However, we have not used this authority; instead
we endure everything so that we will not hinder the gospel
of Christ.—1 Cor 9:12*

*For although I am free from all people, I have made myself
a slave to all, in order to win more people. To the Jews I
became like a Jew, to win Jews; to those under the law,
like one under the law—though I myself am not under the
law—to win those under the law. To those who are outside
the law, like one outside the law—not being outside God's
law, but under the law of Christ—to win those outside the
law. To the weak I became weak, in order to win the weak.
I have become all things to all people, so that I may by all
means save some. Now I do all this because of the gospel, that I may become a partner in its benefits.—1 Cor
9:19–23*

*Give no offense to the Jews or the Greeks or the church
of God, just as I also try to please all people in all things,
not seeking my own profit, but the profit of many, that they
may be saved.—1 Cor 10:32–33*

This principle is so crucial Paul states it at least three times. He
makes it very clear that his ethics are missiologically and evangelistically motivated. He did not allow anything to hinder the gospel from going forth in the most effective way possible.

Some misunderstand Paul to mean that he is infinitely flexible.
However, antinomianism has no place in Paul's theology, missional strategy, ethics, or personal life. He would never say, "I am
free to do anything that I want." He is "under the law of Christ"!
To say, "to the thief I became a thief to win the thief; to the drunkard, I became a drunkard to win the drunkard" is utter nonsense
and a total misinterpretation of what Paul is saying. Paul is not
infinitely flexible; he is not free from the law of Christ that places

the souls of men and women at a premium. Again, the insights of
D. A. Carson are helpful:

> All of God's demand upon him [Paul] is mediated
> through Christ. Whatever God demands of him as a new-
> covenant believer, a Christian, binds him; he cannot step
> outside those constraints. There is a rigid limit to his
> flexibility as he seeks to win the lost from different cul-
> tural and religious groups: he must not do anything that
> is forbidden to the Christian, and he must do everything
> mandated of the Christian. . . . Today that expression,
> "all things to all men," is often used as a form of deri-
> sion. He (or she) has no backbone, we say; he is two-
> faced; he is "all things to all men." But Paul wears the
> label as a witness to his evangelistic commitment. Even
> so, he could not do this if he did not know who he was
> as a Christian. The person who lives by endless rules
> and who forms his or her self-identity by conforming to
> them simply cannot flex at all. By contrast, the person
> without roots, heritage, self-identity, and nonnegotiable
> values is not really flexing, but is simply being driven
> hither and yon by the vagaries of every whimsical opin-
> ion that passes by. Such people may "fit in," but they
> cannot win anyone. They hold to nothing stable or solid
> enough to win others to it![10]

The bottom-line: nothing must hinder or obscure the gospel!

(5) IS THIS ACTION CONSISTENT WITH MY NEW LIFE IN CHRIST?

> *Do you not know that the unjust will not inherit God's*
> *kingdom? Do not be deceived: no sexually immoral peo-*
> *ple, idolaters, adulterers, male prostitutes, homosexuals,*
> *thieves, greedy people, drunkards, revilers, or swindlers*
> *will inherit God's kingdom. Some of you were like this;*
> *but you were washed, you were sanctified, you were justi-*

---

[10] Carson, *The Cross and Christian Ministry,* 120–21.

*fied in the name of the Lord Jesus Christ and by the Spirit
of our God.—1 Cor 6:9–11*

*Do you not know that your body is a sanctuary of the Holy
Spirit who is in you, whom you have from God? You are
not your own.—1 Cor 6:19*

Sometimes in our desire to communicate the gospel clearly
and without unnecessary baggage, we go too far and actually
miscommunicate the message and send an uncertain sound. To
gain a hearing from our "cultural despisers" we adjust our vocabulary, compromise purity and holiness, and thereby hide the glorious gospel that transforms and changes life. The gifted German
theologian Wolfhart Pannenberg in a *First Things* article entitled,
"How to Think About Secularism" provides needed words of wisdom in this context:

> The absolutely worst way to respond to the challenge of
> secularism is to adapt to secular standards in language,
> thought, and way of life. If members of a secularist soci-
> ety turn to religion at all, they do so because they are look-
> ing for something other than what that culture already
> provides. It is counter productive to offer them religion
> in a secular mode that is carefully trimmed in order not to
> offend their secular sensibilities.
>
> Christians should not shy away from the fact that our
> lives are centered on the divine things. We offer a differ-
> ent way of making sense of reality and a different way of
> living, which go against the grain of what modern society
> offers as the norm. We also should not shy away from
> referring to the wrath of God against human sin even
> though most moderns ignore, disbelieve, or sweeten the
> pill with deceptions about God's complaisance over sin.[11]

Tim Keller wisely informs us,

[11] Wolfhart Pannenberg, "How to Think About Secularism," *First Things* 64 (June/July
1996), 31.

All of our personal problems and church problems come
because we don't come continually back to the gospel to
work it out and live it out. . . . Christians are enormously bold
to tell the truth, but without a shred of superiority [remem-
ber 6:9–11!], because you are sinners saved by grace. The
balance of boldness and utter humility, truth and love, is not
somewhere in the middle between legalistic fundamentalism and relativistic liberalism. It is actually off the charts.[12]

When considering how to live for Christ in the twenty-first century, our new life demands that we proclaim and live the message
with great holiness, boldness, and humility.

(6) WILL THIS ACTION VIOLATE MY CONSCIENCE?

*Eat everything that is sold in the meat market, asking no
questions for conscience' sake, for the earth is the Lord's,
and all that is in it. If one of the unbelievers invites you
over and you want to go, eat everything that is set before
you, without raising questions of conscience. But if someone says to you, "This is food offered to an idol," do not
eat it, out of consideration for the one who told you, and
for conscience' sake. I do not mean your own conscience,
but the other person's. For why is my freedom judged by
another person's conscience?—1 Cor 10:25–29*

It is risky, even dangerous, to ignore the inner voice of conscience. It is God-given and under redemptive reconstruction
through the Spirit and the Word. A well-informed, Scripture-
saturated, Spirit-sensitive conscience will be an asset in warning
us of things that are sinful, evil, and unwise.

Now, I do not think Paul would say, "Let your conscience be
your guide," as if conscience by itself is a sufficient umpire or arbi-
trator when it comes to good decision-making. Rather he would
say, "Let your conscience *guided by Scripture* and *controlled by
love* be your guide." This will involve some tension in your lifestyle
preferences, but it will also result in God conforming you more to

---

[12] Tim Keller, "Being the Church in Our Culture," at http://www.journeyon.net/media/
being-the-church-in-our-culture.pdf, accessed January 18, 2008.

the mind of Christ. We must get used to living with this tension. While most would love for every decision to be crystal clear, that is naïve and simplistic. Thus, Christians must know what is going on in their own cultural context. The internal voice of a believer's conscience can be a great aid when guided by Scripture and controlled by the ethic of love.

(7) WILL THIS ACTION FOLLOW THE PATTERN OF THE LIFE OF JESUS?

Be imitators of me, as I also am of Christ.—1 Cor 11:1

Recently I was listening to N. T. Wright lecture. As he raised the issue of Christian ethics he noted that a number of his British friends had poked fun at and dismissed the silly, shallow American phenomena of the WWJD (What Would Jesus Do?) bracelet. However, he then went on to note that several of his children were now making their pilgrimage through the teenage years. Suddenly, he did not find WWJD to be a silly and shallow consideration at all. In fact, he rather hoped his children might adopt such an ethic in this postmodern, anything and everything goes culture of the West. Of course, it is essential to KWJD (Know What Jesus Did) if asking WWJD is going to be of any benefit. In other words, this gospel-centered, Christ-centered ethic requires an immersion into the Scriptures, and in particular the Gospels. To live like Jesus you must know Jesus!

(8) WILL THIS ACTION SHOW LOVE TO OTHERS?

If I speak the languages of men and of angels, but do not have love, I am a sounding gong or a clanging cymbal. If I have the gift of prophecy, and understand all mysteries and all knowledge, and if I have all faith, so that I can move mountains, but do not have love, I am nothing. And if I donate all my goods to feed the poor, and if I give my body to be burned, but do not have love, I gain nothing.—1 Cor 13:1–3

"Love is the magnet that attracts others to Christ."[13] It is also the fulcrum that balances freedom and responsibility, theology and moral behavior. The emerging church has an admirable emphasis on love and community. If our actions are not grounded in love, it does not matter how much we know. D. A. Carson is again helpful on this balancing act:

> Strong Christians may be right on a theological issue, but unless they voluntarily abandon what is in fact their right they will do damage to the church and thus "sin against Christ" (8:12). To stand on your rights may thus involve you in sin after all—not the sin connected with your rights (there, after all, you are right!), but the sin of loveless-ness, the sin of being unwilling to forgo your rights for the spiritual and eternal good of others.[14]

I like the insight of John MacArthur on this crucial point:

> Now a Christian who is truly well-rounded, positive, and effective, thinks and acts in two ways: conceptually and relationally. He has the ability to understand concepts and communicate to people. He has knowledge plus love and this is the way it should be in the church. Our knowledge needs to be balanced with love. The great fear is that with all our knowledge we would not have love and would therefore wind up being nothing. We have to be concep-tual and relational. I think that in the name of liberty some of modern-day Christianity has violated the conscience of weaker brothers and created division in the body. Variations in behavior are the major cause of division in the body, not variations in doctrine. These variations in behavior are not even necessary since we could restrict our liberty for the sake of the weaker brother and create unity. We must make sure that love is the response to knowledge.[15]

---

[13] Chuck Swindoll, *1 Corinthians Bible Study Guide* (Fullerton, Calif.: Insight for Liv-ing, 1977), 16.

[14] Carson, *The Cross and Christian Ministry,* 125.

[15] MacArthur, *Giving Up to Gain,* 13.

(9) WILL THIS ACTION HONOR MY BODY, WHICH BELONGS TO GOD?

> *Do you not know that your body is a sanctuary of the Holy*
> *Spirit who is in you, whom you have from God? You are*
> *not your own, for you were bought at a price; therefore*
> *glorify God in your body.—1 Cor 6:19–20*

In these verses Paul declares that we are not our own and have
been bought with a price. Therefore, we should honor God in all
we do with our bodies. Chuck Swindoll reminds us that our bodies are: (1) a physical extension of Christ, (2) a moral illustration
of the Lord, and (3) a spiritual habitation of God.[16] John Piper
says six things are true because Jesus bought your body: (1) God
is for the body not against it. (2) The body is the dwelling place of
the Holy Spirit. (3) The body will be resurrected from the dead.
(4) The body is not to be mastered by anything but Christ. (5)
The body is not to be used for any immorality. (6) The body is to
be used for the glory of God. What is the result? "Use your body
in ways that will show that God is more satisfying, more precious, more to be desired, more glorious than anything the body
craves"[17]

(10) WILL THIS ACTION GLORIFY GOD?

> *Therefore, whether you eat or drink, or whatever you do,*
> *do everything for God's glory.—1 Cor 10:31*

This climactic and overarching principle has been called "the
joyful duty of man." It is right in its God-focus, for He is the most
beautiful and valuable person in the entire universe. It is right in
its human perspective, for it makes clear why we are here: to live
for God's glory. John Piper gets it right: "God is most glorified in
us when we are most satisfied in him!"[18] No part of life is exempt
from this principle. It is comprehensive and it is satisfying!

---

[16] Swindoll, *1 Corinthians*, 12.

[17] John Piper, "You Were Bought with a Price," at http://www.desiringgod.org/Re-
sourceLibrary/Sermons/ByScripture/19/817_You_Were_Bought_with_a_Price/, accessed
January 18, 2008.

[18] John Piper, *Desiring God* (Sisters, Ore.: Multnomah, 1996), 9.

PUTTING ALL OF THIS INTO PRACTICE

When making ethical choices, world Christians will not wed their cultural and personal preferences to the gospel of Jesus Christ. They will vigorously keep them separate and distinct. They will not insist on their rights or their special interests that could cloud the beauty and purity of the gospel. How can a devoted Christ-follower stand beneath the cross of their Savior and insist on their rights? To give up our rights for the spiritual and eternal blessing of others will be a joy and not a burden.

How will this influence the way we live as Christians? I believe the following theological matrix derived from the Corinthian correspondence can give us some guidelines to consider. Several years ago, when I served at the Southern Baptist Theological Seminary, my good friend Al Mohler and I often discussed how the church should worship. He helped me create the following paradigm that holds ramifications for how the church continues to live out the gospel in today's cultural context.

A THEOLOGICAL PARADIGM
FOR BEING THE BODY OF CHRIST

− Bad Church (Christian) + Good Way	+ Good Church (Christian) + Good Way
− Bad Church (Christian) − Bad Way	+ Good Church (Christian) − Bad Way

Obviously, we want to be a good Christian in a good way. It is not difficult to discern a good Christian because we have a perfect manual called the Bible. We can go to the counsel of the Old and New Testaments and discover God's idea for gospel ethics. Some things are nonnegotiables. However, being a good Christian in a good way is not always as easy to discover. There are many gray areas. How can we discover the good way? I believe the ten principles found in the Corinthian correspondence, along with the following six guiding axioms, can help us find the "good way."

SIX GUIDING AXIOMS FOR FINDING THE "GOOD WAY"

(1) Love will *regulate* liberty.

(2) Love will *rein in* legalism.

(3) That which *detracts* from the gospel will be avoided.

(4) That which *distracts* from the gospel will be avoided.

(5) Follow the *witness* principle.

(6) Follow the *wisdom* principle.

ALCOHOL ABSTINENCE: A TEST CASE

One cannot examine the ethics of Emergent without dealing substantively with the issues of alcohol. I readily confess to a personal bias when it comes to the issue of alcohol. My wife Charlotte grew up in the Georgia Baptist Children's Home because her parents were alcoholics. Her father died a lost alcoholic. Her mother, by God's grace, was saved on her deathbed. Her body had been ravaged by the twin killers of alcohol and tobacco. Today her brother is a lost alcoholic, as is most of the rest of her family. My sister Joy and her husband Kevin King adopted a daughter born with fetal alcohol syndrome. She began life with two strikes against her through no fault of her own. Today there are more than 40 million problem drinkers in America. Alcohol is the number one drug problem among teenagers. One in three American families suspects that one or more family members have a drinking problem. Misuse of alcohol costs our nation $100 billion a year in quantifiable cost. Because of these experiences and many more, I have often said that even if I were not a Christian I would still have nothing to do with alcohol. There is simply too much sorrow and heartache connected to it. Avoiding this devastating drug is simply the wise thing to do.

In my own denomination, several years back Southern Baptists again passed a resolution calling for abstinence from alcohol. The resolution passed overwhelmingly, but it did generate significant debate both during and after the Convention meeting. Some have accused those supporting the resolution of being pharisaical and legalistic, traditionalists and antibiblical. It is said that we fail to understand Christian liberty and freedom, and that we even stand against Jesus. These are strong accusations from fellow brothers and sisters in Christ. However, are they correct? Are those like myself who believe abstinence to be the best lifestyle choice really guilty of these charges? Let me respond as graciously and kindly as I possibly can, explaining why I hold the position I do. I share my heart with no malice or ill will toward anyone but from a desire to honor the Lord Jesus and to protect others from the evils alcohol has visited on so many.

We should remember from a Baptist perspective that there are *historical* precedents for affirming abstinence. In 1886 Southern Baptists issued their first resolution on alcohol. Since then there have been almost sixty resolutions that in a united voice have addressed the risk of alcohol and the wisdom of abstinence. For 120 years Southern Baptists have made clear their stand on this issue. Individual Baptists no doubt continue to take a drink as they had before 1886, but the Southern Baptist Convention as a whole has been consistent in its stands as it pertains to beverage alcohol. I am confident that our forefathers understood the issue of Christian liberty as they passed these resolutions. I am grateful for this tradition. I believe we should continue it.

There are *moral* reasons for affirming abstinence. John Piper teaches the wisdom of abstinence because alcohol can be a mind-altering drug, and it can be addictive. It does not help one in doing the will of God and can genuinely be a hindrance. Further, he notes "the carnage of alcohol abuse," and therefore he personally chooses to boycott such a product. He then adds, "Is it really so prudish, or narrow to renounce a highway killer, a home destroyer, and a business wrecker?"[19] Some questions are in order and deserve an answer. Does alcohol make me a better person? Does

[19] John Piper, "Total Abstinence and Church Membership," at http://www.desiringgod. org/ResourceLibrary/Sermons/ByDate/1981/313_Total_Abstinence_and_Church_Membership/, accessed January 21, 2008.

alcohol draw me closer to God? Does alcohol help me run the race faithfully to the end (Heb 12:1–2)?

Some respond by saying the issue is not abstinence but moderation. They draw an analogy to both eating and sex. There is however a significant difference. We must eat to live. We must engage in sex to procreate. Alcohol is not a necessity for life or good living.

I am in total agreement with my spiritual hero Adrian Rogers who said, "Moderation is not the cure for the liquor problem. Moderation is the cause of the liquor problem. Becoming an alcoholic does not begin with the last drink, it always begins with the first. Just leave it alone." My friend James Merritt wisely says, "It is impossible to be bitten by a snake that you never play with." Alcoholism cannot strike unless it is given the opportunity. That potential becomes real with the first drink one takes.

There are *biblical* reasons for practicing abstinence. Let me quickly note several that draw on our study in this chapter. (1) It is consistent with the principle of *edification* (1 Cor 6:12). Alcohol does not build you up or make you better for Jesus. Avoiding it ensures you will not harm yourself with it. (2) It is consistent with the principle of refusing that which *enslaves* (1 Cor 6:12). Alcohol is a drug that can impair the senses and has a potential addictive element. Like addictive pornography, it should be avoided at all cost. (3) It is consistent with the *ethic of love* for believers and unbelievers alike (1 Cor 8:13; 9:19–22; 10:32–33). Because I am an *example* to others, I will make certain no one ever walks the road of sorrow called alcoholism because they saw me take a drink and assumed, "if it is alright for Danny Akin, it is alright for me." No, I will choose to set an uncompromising example of abstinence because I love them. (4) I will seek my joy and filling in the Spirit, not in alcohol. I love the J. B. Phillips translation of Ephesians 5:18, which reads, "Don't get your stimulus from wine (for there is always the danger of excessive drinking), but let the Spirit stimulate your souls." Psalm 4:7–8 adds, "You [O LORD] have put more joy in my heart than they have when their grain and wine abound. In peace I will both lie down and sleep; for you alone, O LORD, make me dwell in safety" (ESV). (5) It is true Jesus drank wine, and I am sure I would have had I lived in the first century. However, there is no evidence that He ever partook of "strong drink." As Bob Stein has carefully documented, "The term 'wine' or *oinos* in the ancient world, then, did not mean wine as we understand it today but wine mixed with water. . . . To consume the amount of alcohol that is in two martinis by drinking wine containing three parts water to one part wine [a fairly common ancient ratio], one would have to drink over twenty-two glasses. In other words, it is possible to become intoxicated from wine mixed with three parts water, but one's drinking would probably affect the bladder long before it affected the mind."[20] It should also be noted that children would have drunk this diluted mixture of water and wine. It seems clear that there is no one-to-one correspondence with first-century wine and twenty-first century distilled liquor. Concerning the latter I believe the Lord Jesus would have no part.

Let me conclude with some practical considerations. Should those who practice abstinence look down on those who do not? The answer is an unqualified no. That is pride and therefore is sin. It is true that alcohol has contributed to many going to hell, but pride, no doubt, has done so in even greater numbers. A smug, prideful abstainer without Jesus is just as lost as the poor drunkard who is always in search of another drink. Those who believe in abstinence should be gracious and humble, kind and caring, loving and patient.

As a pastor or church leader, would I demand abstinence for church membership? No, I would not. Would I demand it for leadership? Absolutely! The principle of Prov 31:4–5 is appropriately applied here, "It is not for kings, Lemuel, it is not for kings to drink wine or for rulers to desire beer. Otherwise, they will drink, forget what is decreed, and pervert justice for all the oppressed."

I agree with John MacArthur. Can I say it is always a sin to take a drink? No. Can I say it is almost always unwise? Yes, because it violates the biblical principles of wisdom and witness. One of

[20] Bob Stein, "Wine Drinking in New Testament Times," *Christianity Today* 19 (June 20, 1975), 10–11.

America's leading pastors, Andy Stanley, wrote a book entitled *The Best Question Ever*. That question is this, "What is the wise thing for me to do?" I challenge anyone to show me the superior wisdom of drinking "in moderation," as opposed to not drinking at all. This is not legalism but love. This is not being antibiblical but pro-brother and sister. This is not working for evil but for good. Given the world in which we live, I believe such a lifestyle honors the Lord Jesus. I believe it pleases Him. It is the wise thing to do.

TO PREACH OR NOT TO PREACH

AN EVANGELICAL RESPONSE
TO THE EMERGENT HOMILETIC

JIM SHADDIX

> *To be, or not to be: that is the question:*
> *Whether 'tis nobler in the mind to suffer*
> *The slings and arrows of outrageous fortune,*
> *Or to take arms against a sea of troubles,*
> *And by opposing end them? To die: to sleep;*
>
> *. . .*
>
> *To sleep: perchance to dream: ay, there's the rub;*
> *For in that sleep of death what dreams may come.*

IT MAY VERY WELL BE the most familiar line from all drama or literature—*To be, or not to be: that is the question.* It is, of course, from Shakespeare's play *Hamlet* written in 1603.[1] What Hamlet is deliberating is the comparison between the pain of life—which he sees as inevitable—and the fear of the uncertainty of death and possible damnation due to suicide. His dilemma is that although he is dissatisfied with life and identifies its many torments, he is uncertain of what death may bring. Will it be mere sleep or perhaps an experience worse than life?

Many leaders in the emerging church movement—especially the revisionists—find themselves in a similar dilemma as Hamlet when it comes to preaching. While identifying what they might consider the "torments" of traditional homiletics, they fail to be able to identify an acceptable alternative with any authority, clarity,

---

[1] Shakespeare's actual title was *The tragedie of Hamlet, prince of Denmarke.*

or consistency with either biblical or historical preaching. Of this "emerging" homiletic, Richard Holland rightly observes that

> [the emerging church] phenomenon is distinguished by its iconoclastic dismantling of accepted worship forms. Every nuance of ecclesiology is being questioned and reconsidered under the twin-lens microscope of postmodernism (culturally) and postconservatism (theologically). That preaching too is receiving a theological, philosophical, and methodological facelift from leaders in the EC movement should surprise no one.[2]

I think we must be clear in recognizing that there are many solid preachers within the broader emerging church movement who are theologically conservative and truly evangelical. They're faithfully seeking to remain true to God's Word and the right proclamation of it. At the same time, the *Emergent* strand of the movement often is represented by individuals whose theology and homiletic is characteristic of the description above. It is this strand that causes the greatest concern.

Even a cursory consideration of preaching philosophy and practice surfacing in the Emergent movement indicates that what's happening is not a mere facelift but a blatant redefinition. Anyone giving serious credence to many of the Emergent homiletical tenants will find himself in a Hamlet-like quandary: *To preach, or not to preach—that is the question.* Following are some responses to several major characteristics of Emergent homiletics that indicate— while we may be using some of the same terms (e.g., *preaching*, *sermon*)—we're probably not talking about the same ministry.

THE CONVERSATION IS OVER

I can remember as a child periodically being in an argument with one of my parents that ended with their emphatic declaration, "This conversation is over!" What they were always saying was that there was nothing more to discuss. Their assertion or decision

---

[2] Richard L. Holland, "Progressional Dialogue & Preaching: Are They the Same?" in *The Master's Seminary Journal*, vol. 17, no. 2 (Fall 2006): 207–8.

was final, and I needed to accept it and move on. As with Emergent theology that sees truth as an ongoing "conversation," much Emergent homiletics refuses to accept the concept of absolute truth and, therefore, has a difficult time moving on to authoritative propositional preaching.

If Brian McLaren is the Emergent church's "most influential thinker"[3] and the movement's "de facto spiritual leader,"[4] Doug Pagitt is its premier homiletician. As a member of the "Organizing Group" in the Emergent Village, he serves as founding pastor of Solomon's Porch, a self-described "Holistic, Missional, Christian Community"[5] in Minneapolis, Minnesota. In his book *Preaching Re-Imagined: The Role of the Sermon in Communities of Faith*, he calls for traditional preaching to be replaced by "progressional dialogue" that "involves the intentional interplay of multiple viewpoints that leads to unexpected and unforeseen ideas. The message will change depending on who is present and who says what. This kind of preaching is dynamic in the sense that the outcome is determined on the spot by the participants."[6] McLaren acquiesces, saying, "I've found that the more my preaching mirrors the flow of a conversation, the more people connect with it."[7]

As an additional component to this idea of preaching as an ongoing conversation, many Emergent revisionists view Scripture as simply one of the participants. Rejecting the idea that the Bible is the sole authority on spiritual truth, they believe that the Christian community has an equal role to play in the preaching event. Pagitt asserts,

> The Bible ought to live as an authoritative member of our community, one we listen to on all topics of which she speaks. Understanding the Bible as a community member

---

[3] Albert Mohler, "What Should We Think of the Emerging Church? Part One" *Al Mohler's Weblog* (June 29, 2005), online at: http://www.albertmohler.com/commentary_read.php?cdate=2005-06-29, accessed January 10, 2008.

[4] Andy Crouch, "The Emergent Mystique," *Christianity Today* (November 2004):38.

[5] See their Web site at http://www.solomonsporch.com/, accessed January 10, 2008.

[6] Doug Pagitt, *Preaching Re-Imagined: The Role of the Sermon in Communities of Faith* (Grand Rapids: Zondervan, 2005), 52.

[7] Brain McLaren, "Preaching to Postmoderns," in *Preaching with Power: Dynamic Insights from Twenty Top Pastors*, ed. Michael Diduit (Grand Rapids: Baker, 2006), 119.

means giving the Bible the freedom to speak for herself. Sometimes that will mean getting out of the way and putting less effort into interpreting Scripture for others, instead letting them carry out their own relationship with what the Bible says.[8]

So, as opposed to being the sole authority for faith and practice, the Bible is merely one contributor sitting around the table— alongside experience and collective wisdom—as "an authoritative member of the community."[9]

If you think this idea is strange, consider a recent study conducted by my own denomination based on interviews with eighteen to thirty-four-year-olds from all over the United States. Some were unchurched, some were regular church attendees, and some were even church leaders. The research indicated that one of the things that characterizes this generation is the search for "authentic answers." But the study went on to report that both the churched and the unchurched said "they desired to participate in Bible study that minimizes finding pat answers in the exploration of Scripture." One of the researchers concluded, "The lost and the saved in this age group are looking for just what the church can provide in Biblical community. They want absolute truth but they embrace the struggle of finding it themselves. They don't want it to be spoon-fed to them." Respondents cited "the combined knowledge and experiences of the group" as well as "a climate of honesty" as appealing characteristics of small group meetings in the church.[10]

Obviously, these opinions are couched in lingo that is characteristic of Emergent homiletics. But I would call for great caution before we build our preaching and teaching ministries around that research. Any time you listen to the combined voice of both the regenerate and the unregenerate, you're going to come away with a skewed opinion at best. The very suggestion that the regenerate and unregenerate are saying the same thing ought to tell us that

[8] Pagitt, *Preaching Re-Imagined*, 195.

[9] Ibid., 31, 195.

[10] Libby Lovelace, "LifeWay Research Examines the New View of Young Adults," http://www.lifeway.com/lwc/article_main_page/0%2C1703%2CA%25253D164570%252 526M%25253D200725%2C00.html, accessed January 10, 2008.

we've got a problem. But according to Pagitt, "Every person has experience, understanding, and perspective; there is no one who is totally devoid of truth."[11] So, progressional dialogue allows even unbelievers not only to come to the gathering of believers, but to enter into the preaching event by speaking with the same authority as that of the regenerate persons and their Bibles. I would submit, however, that you don't provide authentic answers to a starving generation by minimizing objectivity in Bible study, democratically polling the group to determine truth, and leaving the conclusions in the hands of those championing for self-discovery. Our all-too-frequent approach to Bible teaching of going around the room and asking, "What does this verse mean to you?" will be the death of evangelical orthodoxy, especially when we're asking and listening to unregenerate minds.

To be completely fair, let me say at this point that the Bible certainly entertains the idea of corporate dialogue in the preaching event. New Testament preachers often sought to lead their listeners to examine with them the truths of Scripture and to seek an understanding of them. The word *suzēteō*, for example, means to seek or to examine together. That's what Paul did in Jerusalem when he "conversed and *debated* with the Hellenistic Jews" (Acts 9:29; emphasis mine). At Thessalonica, he "reasoned with them from the Scriptures" (Acts 17:2). The word "reasoned" is *dialegomai*, which means to speak through, ponder, or revolve in the mind. It came to mean to converse with or to discuss. A similar thought is found in the verb *homileō*, which means to converse or talk with (e.g., Acts 20:11). It also carries the idea of engaging in conversation. Certainly, New Testament preaching often had a conversational nature about it, engaging the listeners in a journey of discovery. Biblical preachers preached and the people listened, but the listeners sometimes responded with feedback.[12]

But there is a major difference between this dialogue in New Testament preaching and that being proposed by some Emergent preachers. Dialogical preaching in the New Testament was always

[11] Pagitt, *Preaching Re-Imagined*, 139.

[12] For further treatment of the biblical words that inform the preaching event, see Jerry Vines and Jim Shaddix, *Power in the Pulpit* (Chicago: Moody, 1999), 17–23.

directed by the preacher toward a particular end. In other words, he
was trying to get the listeners to arrive at a particular conclusion.
Acts 17:3, for example, clarifies the purpose and approach to Paul's
dialogical reasoning mentioned above (Acts 17:2) by saying that
he was "explaining and showing that the Messiah had to suffer and
rise from the dead." Dialogue and conversation in biblical preaching
always involved the intent of guiding listeners to a preestablished
conclusion, not to "unexpected and unforeseen ideas." Let's consider for a moment some biblical roots that I believe provide clear
indication that "progressional dialogue" is a long way from historical preaching as it's revealed on the pages of Scripture.

First and foremost, biblical terminology indicates that preaching is rooted in the divine, not in the collective "wisdom" of a
group. God has chosen to reveal Himself to mankind, and He
has chosen human vessels to be mediums of that revelation. The
Hebrew word *nābî*, one of the most common terms for prophet,
conveys the idea of one who pours forth or announces. It includes
the implication of being moved by divine impulse to prophesy (see
Deut 13:1; 18:20; Jer 23:21; Num 11:25–29). Two other Hebrew
words are translated "seer" in the Old Testament. *Hōzeh* suggests
to glow or to grow warm (e.g., Amos 7:12). *Rōéh* simply means
one who sees (e.g., 1 Chr 29:29; Isa 30:10). These terms indicate
that the prophet was one whose heart had been warmed by something the Lord allowed him to see.

Some New Testament terms also imply the divine origin of
preaching as opposed to the discovery of a group. The word *logos*
is used to refer to a word or saying. Sometimes the communication
of God's message to man is referred to as preaching the Word, or
logos, to people (e.g., 2 Tim 4:2). Another word, *rhēma*, emphasizes that which has been uttered by the living voice (see Rom
10:17). When the Word was spoken in the New Testament, God
actually was communicating Himself through the act of proclamation. New Testament preaching was in actuality divine instruction
by those who communicated the gospel (see Eph 3:17). It wasn't
a group of gospel communicators fleshing out divine instruction
through corporate discovery.

Furthermore, the frequently used word *kērussō* means to pro-claim after the manner of a herald. In ancient times heralds com-municated only the edict of royalty, not their own messages or the messages of fellow heralds. This word also implies a message of authority that calls upon the listeners to read and to obey (see Rom 10:14–15; 1 Cor 1:21,23; 2 Tim 4:2). Jesus used this word to commission His followers prior to His ascension, ordaining preaching as the primary method of dispensing the gospel (see Mark 16:15; Luke 24:47). The New Testament preacher was one who proclaimed the message of the King of kings to men. The preaching event, then, was accompanied by an atmosphere of seri-ousness, authority, and divine mandate. This is a far cry from the "progressive dialogue" of the Emergent homiletic.

Another element of New Testament preaching included the idea of teaching. The word used to describe this element is *didaskō*. The apostles "continued teaching and proclaiming the good news that Jesus is the Messiah" (Acts 5:42). In listing the requirements of the bishop-pastor, Paul said the man had to be "an able teacher" (1 Tim 3:2). He also charged the young pastor, "Hold on to the pattern of sound teaching that you have heard from me, in the faith and love that are in Christ Jesus. Guard, through the Holy Spirit who lives in us, that good thing entrusted to you. . . . And what you have heard from me in the presence of many witnesses, commit to faithful men who will be able to teach others also" (2 Tim 1:13–14; 2:2). New Testament preachers prioritized the systematic, intentional teaching of basic doctrine, not the coordination of people sitting in a group with equal opportunity to share their personal story with God or their perspective on a given passage of Scripture.

To take it a step further, most preaching and teaching in the Bible is informed by the idea of public discourse before a corporate assem-bly. The Hebrew word *qōhelet* means a caller, preacher, or lecturer (e.g., Eccl 1:1). The root word is *qāhal,* which means to assemble together. The implication is of one who spoke before an assembly of people. And the word *qārā'* means to call out to a group of peo-ple (e.g., Isa 61:1), addressing the message of God to them. This runs quite contrary to Pagitt's criticism of traditional preaching. He pejoratively refers to it as "speaching . . . the style of preaching that is hardly distinguishable from a one-way speech."[13] Furthermore, he says that it doesn't work and is "a tragically broken endeavor."[14] The testimony of Scripture clearly differs with this position.

One final component of biblical preaching that runs against the grain of Emergent homiletics is the important element of persuasion. Describing his own preaching, Pagitt says:

> In many ways the sermon is less a lecture or motivational speech than it is an act of poetry—of putting words around people's experiences to allow them to find deeper connection to their lives. As we read through sections of the Bible and see how God has interacted with people in other times and places, we better sense God interacting with us. So our sermons are not lessons that precisely define belief so much as they are stories that welcome our hopes and ideas and participation.[15]

So instead of shaping belief through instruction and persuasion, this dialogical approach to preaching depends upon the multiple viewpoints of the participants to change the perspectives of others.[16]

The New Testament gives a different impression, however. For example, the word *peithō* means to use words to persuade others to believe. In Acts 13:43 we are told that Paul and Barnabas spoke to Christian converts, "persuading them to continue in the grace of God." In Corinth, Paul "reasoned in the synagogue every Sabbath and tried to persuade both Jews and Greeks" (Acts 18:4). Paul brought the whole matter of persuasion as a part of preaching into focus when he said, "Knowing, then, the fear of the Lord, we persuade people" (2 Cor 5:11). The particular word used in this passage means to persuade or to induce one by words to believe. The Bible preachers were persuaders. By use of Bible preaching

---

[13] Pagitt, *Preaching Re-Imagined*, 10–11.

[14] Ibid., 19. For further discussion of Pagitt's belief in the serious consequences of "speaching" for the community of faith, see Holland, *Progressional Dialogue & Preaching*, 210–11.

[15] Doug Pagitt, *Church Re-Imagined: The Spiritual Formation of People in Communities of Faith* (Grand Rapids: Zondervan, 2005), 166.

[16] Holland, *Progressional Dialogue & Preaching*, 212.

they brought men to the point of believing Jesus was the Christ and then deciding to commit themselves to Him.

Complementing that idea is the fact that New Testament preaching was apologetic in nature. The word *apologia* suggests a verbal defense or a speech in defense of something. Addressing the Jerusalem mob, Paul said, "Brothers and fathers, listen now to my defense before you" (Acts 22:1). Other passages use the same terminology (see Phil 1:7,17; 2 Tim 4:16). Bible preachers, in the best sense of the term, gave a defense for the gospel. They were not hesitant to present the message of the Lord Jesus in the most convincing, appealing, and persuasive way possible.

So when it comes to the issue of discovering and communicating spiritual truth, preachers in the Bible saw their responsibility simply to teach propositionally what God had revealed and persuade their listeners to act on it. They weren't asking a lot of questions; they were giving a lot of answers. I agree with Holland's assessment of the Emergent view of preaching: "The Bible raises its hand in a conversation, politely waiting until it is called upon to speak. However, in history the Bible has been the thunder of God for reformation, revival, and regeneration."[17] If we take biblical revelation as our guide to preaching, the conversation is *over!*

UNDERSTANDING IS ESSENTIAL

Like all sincere preachers, Emergents desire for their preaching to result in the supernatural life-change of their listeners. Pagitt says that our preaching practices "ought to be judged by their effects on our communities and the ways in which they help us move toward life with God."[18] But his answer to how we go about this involves the abandoning of traditional preaching because of its employment of *knowledge* as the agent of transformation. He writes, "I have become convinced that our misguided belief that life change can come through proper knowledge acquired through education has failed to produce the kind of radical commitment to life in harmony with God and the way of Jesus that we are

[17] Ibid., 216.
[18] Pagitt, *Preaching Re-Imagined*, 28.

called to."[19] He further states, "I truly believe progressional dialogue is necessary to move people into fuller, richer lives of faith. People's lives are not changed by the information they get. Lives are changed by new situations, new practices, and new ways of experiencing the world."[20]

The roots of discovering truth through experience as opposed to gaining understanding through teaching can be traced back to some of the precursors of the Emergent movement. In 1992, Leith Anderson (Doug Pagitt's former pastor and current president of the National Association of Evangelicals) spoke of the new emerging twenty-first-century church:

> The old paradigm taught that if you had the right teaching, you will experience God. The new paradigm says that if you experience God, you will have the right teaching. This may be disturbing for many who assume propositional truth must always precede and dictate religious experience. That mindset is the product of systematic theology and has much to contribute. . . . However, biblical theology looks to the Bible for a pattern of experience followed by proposition.[21]

Anderson's perspective essentially became canonized as part of the Emergent church's creed of choosing experience over doctrine.[22]

Once again, Scripture takes issue with such an assertion. God rebuked the preachers of Hosea's day because they failed to help the people know and understand His Word. He said, "My people are destroyed for lack of knowledge. Because you have rejected knowledge, I will reject you from serving as My priest. Since you have forgotten the law of your God, I will also forget your sons" (Hos 4:6). People's understanding and knowledge of truth is absolutely critical for life change. Bill Hull said that "transformation comes through the commitment of the mind. Without the proper

[19] Pagitt, *Church Re-Imagined*, 21.
[20] Pagitt, *Preaching Re-Imagined*, 163.
[21] Leith Anderson, *A Church for the 21st Century* (Minneapolis: Bethany House, 1992), 21.
[22] Roger Oakland, *Faith Undone* (Silverton, Ore.: Lighthouse Trails, 2007), 55.

knowledge and thinking we have no basis for personal change or growth. The mind is the pivotal starting place for change."[23]

You can trace this emphasis all the way through the Bible. Ezra and his fellow teachers banked on the people's understanding of God's Word during the great revival of Israel's worship recorded in Nehemiah 8. The passage indicates twice that all who could "understand" were gathered together (Neh 8:2–3). Understanding was considered to be so important that the capability of doing it was at least part of the price of admission! Later in the service the scribes attempted to foster understanding via the following process: "They read from the book, from the Law of God, clearly, and they gave the sense, so that the people understood the reading" (v. 8 ESV). The word "clearly" is the Hebrew word *pārash*, which means to distinguish or to specify clearly. "Gave the sense" is likely a reference to translating the Scriptures from Hebrew to Aramaic. The word is *śēkel,* which technically means to give the meaning, indicating perception or insight. Its root means to break up section by section. Essentially, what they were doing was exposing the meaning of Scripture that had been covered up by language, time, culture, social setting, and other factors so the people could understand what God was saying. And all this was done "so that the people understood the reading." The word for "understood" is *bîn,* which means to separate mentally or to assist in understanding. The idea of clarity in making understanding possible was paramount.

These Hebrew scribes served as conservators of God's truth as they interpreted Scripture, copied Scripture, and preserved the oral law. The later development of synagogue services included Scripture reading and exposition as a part of worship. Regular meetings in the synagogue included a time when rabbis would read a portion of Scripture and then explain it to the people in attendance. This activity constituted the focal point of the meetings and gave the synagogue an educational quality.[24]

---

[23] Bill Hull, *Right Thinking* (Colorado Springs: Navpress, 1985), 8.

[24] I. Sonne, "Synagogue," in *The Interpreter's Dictionary of the Bible,"* vol. 4, ed. George Arthur Buttrick (Nashville: Abingdon, 1962), 487.

Jesus Himself was set upon providing clear explanation to His hearers, both in the synagogue worship and in other contexts. He often read and explained the Scriptures as a visiting rabbi (see Luke 4:16–21). He explained Scripture in personal conversations, as with the disciples on the Emmaus road: "Then beginning with Moses and all the Prophets, He interpreted for them the things concerning Himself in all the Scriptures" (Luke 24:27). The word translated "interpreted" is the Greek word *diermēneuō*, which means to unfold the meaning of what is said or to explain through. Reflecting upon the teaching of Jesus, those disciples used a similar word when they asked, "Weren't our hearts ablaze within us while He was talking with us on the road and explaining the Scriptures to us?" (Luke 24:32). The word "explaining" is *dianoigō*, which means to open thoroughly. It means to open the sense of the Scriptures or to explain them. Another word used to describe preaching is *epiluō*, which literally means to unloose or to untie. It was used to describe the preaching ministry of Jesus and His use of parables (see Mark 4:34). The word conveys the idea of explaining what is obscure and hard to understand, in other words, to interpret.

The apostle Paul followed the same practice in Thessalonica, "explaining and showing that the Messiah had to suffer and rise from the dead" (Acts 17:3). To the Romans he said that life transformation comes about by "the renewing of your mind" (Rom 12:2). To the Colossians he wrote that believers "have put on the new man, who is being renewed in knowledge according to the image of his Creator" (Col 3:10) and that they should consequently "Let the message about the Messiah dwell richly among you, teaching and admonishing one another in all wisdom" (Col 3:16). The apostle Peter acquiesced, saying, "May grace and peace be multiplied to you through the knowledge of God and of Jesus our Lord. For His divine power has given us everything required for life and godliness, through the knowledge of Him who called us by His own glory and goodness" (2 Pet 1:2–3).[25]

---

[25] For further discussion on the biblical emphasis on knowledge and understanding, see Holland, *Progressional Dialogue & Preaching,* 216–18.

The Emergents' oversight of this obvious emphasis in Scripture has a direct correlation to the doctrine of the perspicuity—or *clarity*—of Scripture. Furthermore, one's view of the clarity of the Bible directly reflects one's view of God's character. John MacArthur keenly observes,

> In Scripture, the person of God and the Word of God are everywhere interrelated, so much so that whatever is true about the character of God is true about the nature of God's Word. Thus, to deny the clarity of Scripture is to call into question God's ability to communicate clearly. But by affirming the fact that the Bible's message is inherently understandable, the doctrine of perspicuity rightly acknowledges that the Spirit of God has revealed divine truth in a comprehendible form.[26]

When knowledge and understanding are dismissed as non-essentials in sanctification, the implication is that the Bible is vague, mysterious, difficult, or impossible to understand. And not only does that assertion reflect on the character of God, it defaults to a place where no objective truth is possible, or at least possible to know with any significant degree of certainty. And that's precisely why so many Emergents dismiss propositional truth statements as a way of understanding and preaching the Bible.

Scripture's emphasis on the essential nature of knowledge and understanding for spiritual development, along with the belief in objective truth, are just some of the reasons I believe propositional Bible exposition is the contemporary preacher's assignment. Our primary task is not to give opinions, indirect implications, extrabiblical principles, or even inspiration for mutual dialogue, but instead to reveal the Holy Spirit's intended meaning in Scripture so that people's minds are exposed to supernatural truth. That's why explanation is foundational to expository preaching and is its primary distinguishing factor. Explanation is the process of making something clear or plain, and therefore more understandable.[27]

---

[26] John MacArthur, "Perspicuity in Scripture: The Emergent Approach" in *The Master's Seminary Journal*, vol. 17, no. 2 (Fall 2006): 154.

[27] Al Fasol, *Essentials for Biblical Preaching* (Grand Rapids: Baker, 1979), 73.

Robert Thomas said, "The unique contribution of Bible exposition is its substantial enhancement of the listeners' comprehension of Scripture's intent."[28] Explanation is the element that vaults the supernatural truth of God's Word into the mind of the listener, thus enabling transformation. It's the means to the end of understanding, and understanding is the highway to life change.

THE BIBLE IS ENOUGH

James Bond fans will remember *The World Is Not Enough* as the title of the nineteenth spy film of the famed British spy series. The title traces its origins to the English translation of the Latin sentence *Orbis non sufficit*. In the film, Bond utters the words in response to the temptation of Elektra King when she offers him the world. The words are taken from Bond's family motto that adorned his coat of arms in *On Her Majesty's Secret Service*. That's quite a statement that suggests that one possesses some value greater than all the world has to offer!

It appears that the revisionists in the Emergent church movement claim to possess a greater value than God has to offer when it comes to preaching. Many are saying the same thing about the Bible regarding preaching to contemporary culture: *The Bible is not enough*. Will Sampson, who serves on the Coordinating Group of Emergent Village, writes:

> A rallying cry of the Protestant Reformation was *sola scriptura*, or Scripture alone. And while this doctrine may have arisen as a necessary corrective to abuses of church leadership in the Reformation period, it is in full effect today. Preachers speak of the Bible as an instruction book or as the only data necessary for spiritual living. But this diminishes some critical elements of theological knowledge. . . . Sola scriptura also tends to downplay the role of God's Spirit in shaping the direction of the church.[29]

---

[28] Robert L. Thomas, "Exegesis and Expository Preaching," in John MacArthur, Jr., *Rediscovering Expository Preaching*, ed. Richard L. Mayhue (Dallas: Word, 1992), 138.

[29] Will Sampson, "The End of Reinvention," in Doug Pagitt and Tony Jones, *An Emergent Manifesto of Hope* (Grand Rapids: Baker, 2007), 155–56.

Whether by claim or practice, they suggest that our radically different culture needs more than the Bible can give. And the disappearance of the centrality of Scripture and the primacy of propositional preaching within the movement rival the performances in the world's best magic shows. True preaching in many Emergent venues has all but vanished, and authoritative proclamation has been replaced by a progressive conversation about the perceived "mystery" of God's revelation.

The Bible, however, tells a radically different story. Scripture's testimony regarding itself is that the Bible, in fact, *is* enough to redeem mankind, restore righteousness, and provide all that mankind needs for life and godliness. Psalm 19:7–9, for example, refers to God's Word with six different titles—*instruction* (law), *testimony*, *precepts*, *command*, *fear*, and *ordinances*. A careful word study of these designations reveals that all six terms are references to the written record of God's revelation. Furthermore, the undeniable connections between the Old Testament and Jesus (see Matt 5:17; Luke 24:27; John 5:39; Rom 10:4), between Jesus and the apostolic teaching in the Gospels (see Acts 2:42; Eph 2:20), and between the apostolic teaching and the Pauline writings (see 2 Pet 3:14–16) would indicate that we are on safe ground applying these six synonyms to both the Old and New Testaments.

In this passage the psalmist describes the Bible as being in perfect internal harmony with the nature of God. It is *perfect* (v. 7), reflecting God's blameless character, integrity, uprightness, and fidelity. It is *sure* (v. 7) and trustworthy in the sense that God's statutes are true in principle and verifiable in the situations of life. It is *right* (v. 8), not perverse or crooked. The Bible is an open book devoid of any hypocrisy. It is *pure* (v. 8), reflecting the radiance and brightness of God's glory. It is *clean* (v. 9), pure and flawless like refined silver. It is *true* (v. 9), reflecting God's fidelity and loyalty.

But the most needful word for Emergent leaders from Psalm 19:7–9 is that each of these six qualities of God's Word affect a particular practical outcome. To begin with, Scripture *renews one* (v. 7). God's Word revives by restoring the whole person, by assuring forgiveness and cleansing, and by giving life to the godly. To the Romans Paul said, "Faith comes by hearing, and hearing by the word of God" (Rom 10:17 NKJV), thus claiming God's Word as the originator of saving faith. Paul told Timothy that the Scriptures "are able to instruct you for salvation" (2 Tim 3:15). James spoke of the Word's ability to foster sanctifying wholeness when he told his readers to "lay aside all filthiness and overflow of wickedness, and receive with meekness the implanted word, which is able to save your souls" (Jas 1:21 NKJV). The apostle Peter spoke somewhat at length about the work of the Word. He said,

> By obedience to the truth, having purified yourselves for sincere love of the brothers, love one another earnestly from a pure heart, since you have been born again—not of perishable seed but of imperishable—through the living and enduring word of God. For
>
> *All flesh is like grass,*
> *and all its glory like a flower of the grass.*
> *The grass withers, and the flower drops off,*
> *but the word of the Lord endures forever.*
>
> And this is the word that was preached as the gospel to you.
>
> So rid yourselves of all wickedness, all deceit, hypocrisy, envy, and all slander. Like newborn infants, desire the unadulterated spiritual milk, so that you may grow by it for your salvation, since you have tasted that the Lord is good. (1 Pet 1:22–2:3)

No doubt contemporary culture is populated with people whose souls need purity, whose lives need to be born again, and whose infant Christianity could stand some simple spiritual nourishment. The Bible claims to do all of that in reviving the soul.

The Scriptures also are said to *make the inexperienced wise* (Ps 19:7). The Bible is the source of wisdom to all who are ready to receive it (see 119:130; Prov 21:11), the already wise as well as the simple-minded and foolish (see Ps 14:1–3). It also *makes the heart glad* (19:8). Scripture produces heartfelt joy, inner peace, and tranquility. Jeremiah offered some encouragement for times when preachers are staring into the solemn faces of parishioners who reflect a desperate need for a good dose of joy. He excitedly announced,

> Your words were found, and I ate them,
> And Your word was to me the joy and rejoicing of my heart;
> For I am called by Your name,
> O Lord God of hosts. (Jer 15:16 NKJV)

The Bible also *makes the eyes light up* (v. 8). Scripture's radiance gives light to the eyes to see and receive God's blessings. Surely people in contemporary culture need direction for navigating life's journey. The psalmist later proclaims, "Your word is a lamp for my feet and a light on my path" (Ps 119:105). And imagine that—all without calling a 900 number to confide in a fortune-teller, tarot card reader, or other self-professed psychic! There was some holy heartburn—or heart change—that took place in the disciples on the road to Emmaus after Jesus explained the Scriptures to them. They rhetorically asked, "Did not our heart burn within us while He talked with us on the road, and while He opened the Scriptures to us?" (Luke 24:32 NKJV). God's Word opens the eyes and lights the path! Furthermore, it also *endures forever* (v. 9). Scripture does not change with the times and the incessant variations in fashion and culture, even the post-Christian ones of our day. It's always "in"! It's always relevant (see Matt 5:18; 1 Pet 1:23–25).

The pinnacle of all these claims, however, is that Scripture is *altogether righteous* (v. 9). This phrase actually is a verbal form that means that Scripture is not merely righteous in its nature, but it reflects God's righteousness in an effectual way. Our Lord has given us every truth, principle, standard, and warning that we will ever need for restoration into His image! The New Testament is filled with claims about the sanctifying power of Scripture. Jesus Himself acknowledged the Word's role in sanctification when He prayed to the Father for His disciples: "Sanctify them by Your truth. Your word is truth" (John 17:17 NKJV). The apostle Paul

got in on the action, too, recognizing the Scripture's power to foster spiritual growth and advancement toward glorification in the
believer. He told the Ephesian elders that God's Word "is able to
build you up and give you an inheritance among all those who are
sanctified" (Acts 20:32 NKJV). He told Timothy that the Spirit-
inspired Scriptures were not only "able to instruct you for salvation," but also to train him "in righteousness" (2 Tim 3:15–17).
The Scriptures are the primary agent that God uses for fostering
righteousness.

If these and other claims that the Bible makes about its own
sufficiency as God's primary purveyor of life and godliness are
true, why would contemporary preachers feel the need to give
their people anything else? Surely the Bible *is* enough!

IRRELEVANCE IS RELEVANT

"From the Issacharites, who understood the times and knew
what Israel should do: 200 chiefs with all their relatives under
their command" (1 Chr 12:32). Several years ago I heard and read
this verse quoted by four different people in three different venues
within a span of about two weeks. I first heard it from one of the
most popular pastors of our day who used it in his conference on
preaching to contemporary listeners. A few days later I read it in
a book on preaching to postmoderns. And finally I heard two different students use it in succession on the same day in a seminary
classroom to introduce their paper presentations on preaching
to postmoderns. And all four individuals used the verse to make
essentially the same assertion: *If preachers are going to be beneficial and relevant to contemporary listeners, they must understand
their times by being students of this postmodern culture.*

After hearing the proposed mantra for the fourth time, my curiosity got the best of me. My mind began to wander during the eloquent presentation by the second seminary student, and I started
asking a couple of questions: *What were the times, and what was
Israel supposed to do?* So I quietly opened my Bible to the passage and began to read the context (multitasking, of course, as
I listened to the second student's presentation!). My search was

quite revealing. The immediate passage in 1 Chronicles 12 is a roll call of David's mighty men. And within that chapter and the one preceding it, both questions are clearly answered numerous times! What were the times? Well, it was time to turn the kingdom over to David because of Saul's sin (see 1 Chr 11:3,10; 12:23,38). How did the men of Issachar know what Israel was to do? Simple. They knew that Israel was supposed to take this action because it was "according to the Word of the Lord" (1 Chr 11:3,10; 12:23). I almost gasped out loud while the student was waxing eloquent on preaching to postmoderns. Not only did this passage *not* say what I heard asserted four times; it said basically the opposite! To be sure, being a student of one's culture certainly is important. But the preacher will know how to prophetically tell his listeners what to do only by knowing the Word of the Lord, not by studying his culture! Scripture is what defines, determines, and dictates relevance for every culture.

For whatever reason, many Emergent preachers have been led to believe that the Bible is irrelevant—or at least not relevant enough—for contemporary culture. But this is nothing new. Emergent preachers are really not emerging at all when it comes to calling for more relevance in preaching. They're just *re-emerging*. Harry Emerson Fosdick was calling for more relevance in preaching early in the twentieth century. He, too, wanted to involve more of the experiences of the congregation. Criticizing expository preaching, he wrote,

> [Expository preachers] take a passage from Scripture and, proceeding on the assumption that the people attending church that morning are deeply concerned about what the passage means, they spend their half hour or more on historical exposition of the verse or chapter, ending with some appended practical application to the auditors. Could any procedure be more surely predestined to dullness and futility? Who seriously supposes that, as a matter of fact, one in a hundred of the congregation cares, to start with, what Moses, Isaiah, Paul, or John meant in those special verses, or came to church deeply concerned about

it? Nobody else who talks to the public so assumes that
the vital interests of the people are located in the meaning
of words spoken two thousand years ago.[30]

There are so many things wrong with that denigration, not the least
of which is the suggestion that preaching is only relevant when the
audience is "concerned" with, "cares" about, or has an interest in
what the preacher has to say. Try telling that to Isaiah, Jeremiah,
Paul, or Stephen! On the contrary, much preaching in the Bible
and throughout history was prompted because people were just
the opposite—unconcerned, uncaring, and disinterested.

Furthermore, what Fosdick and his reemerging children fail to
realize is that overcontextualization quickly begins to de-throne
Scripture as the authority in people's lives, thus removing any
chance at true life change. The truth of the matter is that real
relevance is found in *exposing* the timeless application of "what
Moses, Isaiah, Paul, or John meant in those special verses." Few
would argue that Jesus spoke relevantly to the two travelers on the
road to Emmaus when, "beginning with Moses and all the Prophets, He interpreted for them the things concerning Himself in all
the Scriptures" (Luke 24:27). And their response seemed to indicate that what they heard was relevant for their lives as they rhetorically asked, "Weren't our hearts ablaze within us while He was
talking with us on the road and explaining the Scriptures to us?"
(Luke 24:32). While many leaders simply start out trying to make
their music, outreach, and preaching more contextual to emerging
culture, they don't realize when they begin to measure relevance
by their contemporary context instead of the historical Scriptures.
When that happens, contextualization begins to drive the train and
true relevance ceases to happen.

More importantly, contextualization that no longer lets Scripture define and dictate relevance misses one of the most profound
theological truths and supernatural components of gospel ministry. In a very real sense the apostle Paul suggested that the perceived "irrelevance" of the message and the medium (proclaiming

---

[30] Harry Emerson Fosdick, "What Is the Matter with Preaching?," in *What's the Matter with Preaching Today?*, ed. Mike Graves (Louisville, Ky.: Westminster John Knox,
2004), 9.

the cross) actually was the key to an effective preaching ministry! The secular culture of his day emphatically thought that Christianity was foolish. Just like contemporary culture, Paul's culture considered the idea of salvation coming through a guy's death on a cross and the subsequent proclamation of it as an absolutely absurd thought (see 1 Cor 1:18–25).

But therein rests the genius of the plan of God. He intentionally designed it this way so that nobody could get the glory that belongs only to Him! Paul said it twice in 1 Corinthians 1:27–31:

> Instead, God has chosen what is foolish in the world to shame the wise, and God has chosen what is weak in the world to shame the strong. God has chosen what is insignificant and despised in the world—what is viewed as nothing—to bring to nothing what is viewed as something, *so that no one can boast in His presence.* But it is from Him that you are in Christ Jesus, who became God given wisdom for us—our righteousness, sanctification, and redemption, in order that, as it is written: *The one who boasts must boast in the Lord.* (emphasis mine)

That's just one of the reasons why messing with the gospel message—the cross—and God's ordained means of propagating it—preaching—are such incredibly tragic acts. Any perversion of either one renders Christianity impotent.

The Emergent homiletic appears to mess with both the gospel and the preaching of it. For example, Pagitt asserts that the gospel is entering into the broader story of God in the world. Championing that the gospel itself needs to be "re-imagined," he ponders:

> It seems to me that this call to communal spiritual formation challenges us to re-imagine the gospel itself. Perhaps the challenges of living the dreams of God in the post-industrial world go beyond methodology problems. Perhaps we have been propagating a limited message, reducing biblical authors to sound bytes that cut the gospel message into so many pieces that we are left with little more than statements of what we believe rather than

the broader story of how we are to enter into God's story
through a life lived in faith.[31]

Not only does Pagitt reject the concept that the gospel is propositional truth to be believed; he suggests that subjective experience
is the doorway for entering into God's story. It's no wonder that D.
A. Carson concluded of several noted Emergent writers: "I have to
say, as kindly but as forcefully as I can, that to my mind, if words
mean anything, [they] have largely abandoned the gospel."[32]

Furthermore, if God's supernatural power is lashed to the foolishness of preaching as much as it is the cross, what sense does it
make to redefine preaching or even model it after the prowess of
contemporary public speakers in an effort to make it more effective? None at all. God purposefully chose a message and a medium
that the world would always consider foolish and irrelevant so that
when His supernatural power is manifested through them, only He
will get the credit. That makes the message and preaching of the
cross the most relevant things in the universe! In the preaching
ministry, the irrelevant actually becomes the relevant. And when a
contemporary preacher either changes the message or models his
preaching after the expertise of a public entertainer, politician, or
therapist in an attempt to make it less foolish and more relevant to
his culture, he may just be pulling the rug of supernatural power
right out from under his ministry.

THE MEDIUM IS THE MESSAGE

Several years ago I read a review of a music video in *Time*
magazine that described the piece this way: "Provocative images
fill the TV screen. Over a driving, syncopated rock beat, a woman's voice—urgent, seductive—tells a story of possession and
salvation."[33] It wasn't the description that caught me off guard as
much as what the video was about—a contemporary rendition of
the Luke 8 passage when Jesus cast out the host of demons from

---

[31] Pagitt, *Church Re-Imagined*, 31.

[32] D. A. Carson, *Becoming Conversant with the Emerging Church* (Grand Rapids:
Zondervan, 2005), 186.

[33] "Short Takes," *Time* (December 7, 1992): 83.

the man of Gadara! Chuck Colson was shocked by the same video presentation and offered a warning to Christians:

> The almost surrealistic style was so vivid that for all practical purposes it drowned out any biblical teaching. . . . The producers' goal was admirable—reaching out to young people raised on MTV—but if even a secular reviewer can sense a discrepancy between the biblical message and the style in which it is communicated, then surely we, too, must become more aware.[34]

The *Time* magazine reviewer summarized: The "message is overwhelmed by the medium." Make no mistake about it: the *form* of Christian communication also can cancel out the *message!*

Herein lies a word of caution not only for the revisionists among the Emergents, but also for the relevants within the larger movement. One of the contentions that keeps surfacing in the emerging church movement is the need to "contextualize" the gospel and its preaching. Consequently, there's a whole lot of emphasis on preaching in ways that relate to the emerging generations. We often hear calls for things like *changing the methods without changing the message*. The feeling is that we can change the medium so as to identify with the culture without changing the nature of the gospel. Certainly, there is both sincerity and validity in many of those claims.

However, educator Marshall McLuhan actually may have been right when in 1967 he proposed that "the medium is the message" in his work by the same name. Contemporary preachers must understand that *what* we say often times can affect people as much as *how* we say it. At least Paul seemed to think so when he wrote, "When I came to you, brothers, announcing the testimony of God to you, I did not come with brilliance of speech or wisdom" (1 Cor 2:1). The word translated "brilliance" doesn't indicate something that's aloof, erudite, or intellectual. Instead, it means "rising out above" and carries the idea of having preeminence or superiority.[35]

---

[34] Charles Colson and Nancy Pearcey, *How Now Shall We Live?* (Wheaton, Ill.: Tyndale House, 1999), 471.

[35] F. W. Grosheide, *Commentary on the First Epistle to the Corinthians*, in The New International Commentary on the New Testament (Grand Rapids: Eerdmans, 1953), 58.

Paul didn't say he refused to utilize good speech, nor did he say that he never gave attention to his thought processes or those of his listeners. He simply claimed to never allow those realities to overshadow—or *rise out above*—the message in the presentation of the sermon.[36]

Personally, I believe this is why God did not choose music to be the primary means of propagating the gospel. It's such an emotional medium. There's nothing wrong with it. In fact, music is an incredible gift from God and one that we can use to worship Him in profound ways. But music is so emotionally charged that we often are moved by the medium even when the content is lacking. Video can be the same way. It is possible for certain mediums of communication to *rise above* the message that they are carrying.

This reality is incredibly important in light of the emerging emphasis on the need to shape preaching style to reach certain audiences. As we've already observed, some Emergent preachers suggest that preaching today will only connect if it's characterized by things like progressional dialogue, conversational speech, relational presentations, visual imagery, contemplative atmospheres, and other components that appeal to the postmodern mind. But some methods of presentation can actually overshadow the message because of their emotional nature or other qualities that bypass understanding and appeal to another aspect of people's flesh. So to prevent anything from usurping his message, Paul intentionally avoided any dependence on fine dialectical oration, striking speculative thought, and certain other qualities of secular communication. Sincere efforts to make the Bible message more palatable to contemporary audiences can easily result in obscuring the message when the means of presentation or the nature of a given audience are stressed to the point of *rising out above* the message itself.

Some emerging preachers suggest that preachers today need to learn from stand-up comedians, Hollywood actors, journalists, and other secular communicators. The implication often is made that a failure to do so will result in an inability to communicate the

---

[36] Jim Shaddix, *The Passion Driven Sermon* (Nashville: B&H, 2003), 30.

gospel effectively to contemporary culture. Consequently, many preachers spend more time attending conferences and reading books on secular communications skills than they do immersing themselves in their message. But Paul refused to take his cue on speaking to the culture from secular public orators. He refused to embrace a preaching philosophy that gave primary attention to exceptional oratorical prowess or a keen analysis of how the human mind worked. Something else dominated his presentation that contrasted him from the secular public speakers of the day— the supernatural message of Jesus Christ.

Before leaving this discussion it's important to understand that it's not just the way the message is presented that the Emergents desire to change. The revisionist theology previously noted in this and other chapters actually is a driving force behind the move for new mediums in preaching. McLaren himself admitted,

> It has been fashionable among the innovative [emerging] pastors I know to say, "We're not changing the message, we're only changing the medium." This claim is probably less than honest. . . . In the new church we must realize how medium and message are intertwined. When we change the medium, the message that's received is changed, however subtly, as well. We might as well get beyond our naïveté or denial about this.[37]

Certain mediums purposefully can be chosen in corporate communication in order to send a certain message. To be sure, some Emergents are choosing particular methods and means of communication in order to send a revised message.

For preachers today, it's not as easy as simply changing the medium and method but keeping the message the same. Sometimes the medium or method can speak so loudly that the message is never heard. Sometimes the medium is intentionally chosen in order to communicate a different message. This can happen with the way the preacher presents himself, the things he uses to augment his presentation, or the atmosphere in which he speaks. Every preaching approach, sermon illustration, and prop must be

---

[37] Brian McLaren, *Church on the Other Side* (Grand Rapids: Zondervan, 2000), 68.

carefully analyzed and selected on its own merit with regard to its potential to overshadow the message that is being preached. If it's not, the sincere effort to make the age-old message of the gospel more understandable and relevant to a contemporary audience can backfire. The audience may like the medium but still miss the message.

SOME FINAL THOUGHTS . . .

We live in an age where every new wave fizzles faster. In our explosive media environment we run everything to its limit and exhaust it at a more rapid pace through television, radio, cell phones, PDAs, iPods, the Internet, and blogs. And the more recent the movement or mind-set, the shorter its existence will be. Each one will have a shorter shelf life than the one preceding it. This world experienced thousands of years of premodernism, but only hundreds of years of modernism. I propose that we'll have a few years of postmodernism and Emergent philosophy, and then something else will come along if it hasn't already. The Emergent church and its homiletic will be short-lived, and its constituents will move on to something else in hopes that it will satisfy the longing in their souls.

But Emergents have something else working against them. Like every nontraditional preaching philosophy built on unbiblical premises, I believe the Emergent homiletic will expire due to its void of lasting substance. Go back to the Christian psychological preaching of Harry Emerson Fosdick, which gave birth to the power of positive thinking championed by Norman Vincent Peale. Follow it through to the new neo-orthodox motivational speeches of Robert Schuller, and then to the seeker-targeted talks of Bill Hybels. Ultimately you'll find yourself at the self-help prescriptions of the postmodern communicators. It doesn't take long to identify each one's day in the sun and each one's setting on the horizon of evangelicalism. The progressional dialogue of the Emergents likely will be no different. It will run its course and fizzle out.

God has chosen the faithful preaching of the Bible and its cross to be that which redeems the souls of men and women and gives them hope for better things. Holland is right to remind us that the sermon rightly understood interprets the Scriptures for the community of faith, and such is the biblical and historical legacy of preaching. The ones Pagitt refers to as "speachers"—the preachers, orators, expositors, evangelists, reformers, teachers, missionaries, and apologists—actually are the ones who have made a difference in Christian history. Holland reflects,

> To read church history is to understand that the pulpit has come to us on a river of blood. Men were martyred because they refused to dialogue about the truth. Many could have saved their own lives had progressional dialogue been their conviction. But the truthfulness of Scripture anchored their souls and shook continents. The church does not need to be convinced that everyone is a preacher. The church needs more men who are faithful to the sacred desk, the public speaching of Holy Scripture.[38]

In the aforementioned familiar Shakespearean drama, Hamlet goes on to call death the "undiscover'd country from whose bourn no traveller returns." I pray that our well-meaning friends among the Emergents will turn from their vain search in this deathly territory before it's too late. The better place to give one's life is on the altar of that which is lasting.

---

[38] Holland, *Progressional Dialogue & Preaching*, 222.

THE EMERGING CHURCH AND EVANGELISM

CHUCK LAWLESS

MORE THAN ONE CHURCH GROWTH RESEARCHER has noted the evangelistic failure of the North American church. Thom Rainer, president and CEO of LifeWay Christian Resources, observes that it now takes eighty-six church members per year to reach one person for Christ.[1] George Barna has shown that fewer than one-third of churchgoers believe they are responsible for sharing their faith with someone who believes differently.[2] Moreover, Christians who do evangelize face an unchurched world that sees little lifestyle difference between believers and nonbelievers.[3]

The American church is without a doubt in crisis. Few churches are growing by reaching nonbelievers. Most churches that are growing are doing so by "swapping sheep" with other congregations or by reaching those who were formerly churched. The unchurched world sees the church as outdated, irrelevant, and unconcerned. As shown throughout this book, the emerging church movement is one attempt to address some of these issues.

The goal of this chapter is to examine the emerging church's beliefs and approaches concerning evangelism. This task is complicated, of course, by the various and debated understandings

[1] Thom S. Rainer, "The Dying American Church," accessed at http://www.mmiblog.com/monday_morning_insight_we/2006/04/the_dying_ameri.html.

[2] "Religious Beliefs Vary Widely by Denomination," accessed at http://www.barna.org/FlexPage.aspx?Page=BarnaUpdate&BarnaUpdateID=92.

[3] See "Christianity in Crisis," accessed at http://www.willowcreek.com/wcanews/story.asp?id=WN04I12008.

of both terms. This entire book has worked to define *emerging church*, recognizing that the movement includes relevants, reconstructionists, and revisionists.[4] So diverse is this movement that anyone who wants to disprove the movement's character described in this chapter is sure to find at least one exception to any conclusion herein. Proving diversity is not, however, the equivalent of disproving general characteristics.

Defining *evangelism* is equally difficult, especially as understood by leaders of the emerging church. Indeed, it is easier to *describe* evangelism in the emerging church than it is to *define* it (which, as we will see, is also problematic). For now, suffice it to say that while many in the emerging church have a heart to see lives transformed, their approaches to get there are not always connected to a biblical understanding or practice of evangelism.

EMERGENT EVANGELISM: REACTIONARY AND REFORMING

It is difficult to read writings of this movement and not get a sense that emerging church leaders are passionate about seeing lives changed through their ministries. For example, Rob Bell tells the story of Yvette, a student of witchcraft who had been attending Bell's church. Yvette had been listening to Bell's teachings, hated everything he was saying, disagreed with his conclusions, and in fact, "wanted to stand up on her chair and yell at me."[5] Through conversations with Bell, however, Yvette became a follower of Christ and began to share her story with other witches.

The story of Brooke, a participant in John Burke's Gateway Church, is no less captivating:

> I first opened my heart to even trying church and seeking God after relocating to Austin. Once I made the first step to go to Gateway, God went to work. . . . God began the process of healing my broken spirit and revealed many things about my life (current and past) that needed

---

[4] See pp. 70–73 of Ed Stetzer's chapter.

[5] Rob Bell, *Velvet Elvis: Repainting the Christian Faith* (Grand Rapids: Zondervan, 2005), 89. Yvette's entire story is found on pages 89–90 of this work.

healing. . . . Through this healing process, I became a
Christian and committed myself to Jesus. I see God's
work every day in my life now. I look for him in every
situation, and I can see how clearly he knows just what I
need personally. Nothing compares![6]

Even emerging church critic D. A. Carson admits that this
movement is driven "in part, by a concern for evangelism, in
particular the evangelism of a new generation of people who are
shaped by postmodern assumptions."[7] These are churches that do
indeed strive to "welcome the stranger" and "serve with generosity," as Gibbs and Bolger have noted.[8]

This commitment to reaching a new generation is, though,
more than simply a passion for changed lives; it is also a reaction
to what are perceived to be faulty approaches to evangelism in the
traditional church. In some cases, the issues raised are significant,
and the call for reformation is justified—but the solution offered
is troublesome.

EC EVANGELISM IS A REACTION AGAINST REDUCTIONISTIC EVANGELISM

Most of us have encountered what one emerging church writer
first experienced as evangelism in the church: "At the end of the
service, the pastor asked if anybody wanted to become a Christian.
He said that people could repeat a prayer after him and become a
Christian, right there at that moment in their seats. He said that if
people repeated this prayer after him, they could be sure that when
they died, they would go to heaven and not hell."[9] A call to pray a
simple prayer, sometimes ignoring repentance and genuine faith,
and followed by eternal assurances apart from lifestyle—that is

[6] John Burke, *No Perfect People Allowed: Creating a Come-as-You-Are Culture in the Church* (Grand Rapids: Zondervan, 2005), 176.

[7] D. A. Carson, *Becoming Conversant with the Emerging Church: Understanding a Movement and Its Implications* (Grand Rapids: Zondervan, 2005), 52.

[8] Eddie Gibbs and Ryan K. Bolger, *Emerging Churches: Creating Christian Community in Postmodern Cultures* (Grand Rapids: Baker, 2005), 45.

[9] Bell, *Velvet Elvis*, 176.

the type of evangelism that alarms not only emerging church leaders but others as well.[10]

Others have done door-to-door evangelism, often prefacing sharing the gospel with a spiritual interest survey. Tony Jones goes so far as to call this evangelism a "scam, a classic bait-and-switch" where the survey is only a premise to get in the door. The goal was to share the gospel quickly and move on to the next prospect.[11] Evangelism of this sort reduces the prospect to a project, and the person to be reached becomes only a target to be hit.

Conversion is also reduced to a single moment, "an event or point at which a person 'gets it.'"[12] Too often, those who testify of such an experience give scant evidence of a change of lifestyle after their perceived conversion. The unbelieving world that sees little difference between the "saved" and the unsaved thus no longer accepts "Jesus is the answer" as a response to their spiritual questions.

George Barna's research shows that these concerns are not unjustified. In fact, a 2006 study showed that lifestyle differences between believers and nonbelievers were statistically indistinguishable. The similarities were so strong that researcher David Kinnaman concluded, "the lifestyles and relationships of born again believers are not much different than others."[13] What the world then sees is a gospel message that apparently is not life transforming.

Now, according to Emergent leader Dan Kimball, unbelievers must cross a chasm of their negative perceptions of Christianity and the church before bridging the gap between themselves and God.[14] At least one cause of this chasm is faulty evangelism

---

[10] See, for example, Mark Dever and Paul Alexander, *The Deliberate Church* (Wheaton, Ill.: Crossway, 2005); Will Metzger, *Tell the Truth* (Downers Grove, Ill.: InterVarsity, 1984).

[11] Tony Jones, *The New Christians* (Hoboken, N.J.: Jossey-Bass, 2008), 100–101.

[12] Brian D. McLaren, *More Ready than You Realize* (Grand Rapids: Zondervan, 2002), 106.

[13] "American Lifestyles Mix Compassion and Self-Oriented Behavior," accessed at http://www.barna.org/FlexPage.aspx?Page=BarnaUpdate&BarnaUpdateID=264.

[14] Dan Kimball, *They Like Jesus but Not the Church* (Grand Rapids: Zondervan, 2007), 233–36.

that has resulted in professions of faith without an accompanying change of lifestyle.

EC EVANGELISM IS A REACTION AGAINST EVANGELISM DIVORCED FROM RELATIONSHIPS

In some ways, evangelism has become more about inviting others to church than about leading them to Jesus. If we can get them to church, there they will hear the gospel. Consequently, "outreach" is more likely what Michael Frost and Alan Hirsch have called "in-drag."[15] Relationships with nonbelievers are shallow at best and nonexistent at worst. The church has become more an insulation from the world than a training ground for evangelism. In fact, it is Brian McLaren who perhaps best summarizes this trend in the established church:

> One of the greatest enemies of evangelism is the church as fortress or social club; it sucks Christians out of their neighborhoods, clubs, workplaces, schools, and other social networks and isolates them in a religious ghetto. . . . Thus, Christians are warehoused as merchandise for heaven, kept safe in a protected space to prevent spillage, leakage, damage, or loss until their delivery.[16]

As noted earlier, evangelism in such a context (when it happens) reduces nonbelievers to trophies to be won rather than people to be loved. The emerging church seeks to counter this growing tendency by emphasizing the relational nature of the gospel. We are to love others not because they need to be converted, but simply because Jesus commanded us to love our neighbors (Matt 22:39). Love tied to an agenda—even an evangelistic agenda—is not truly love.

In turn, Kimball has shown that the emerging generation desires a church that loves all people unconditionally.[17] They are open to the church community, but they are unlikely to enter that community without first developing a relationship with another

---

[15] Michael Frost and Alan Hirsch, *The Shaping of Things to Come* (Peabody, Mass.: Hendrickson, 2003), 41.

[16] "The Place of Absolute Truth in a Postmodern World—Two Views," accessed at http://www.christianitytoday.com/ct/article_print.html?id=11412.

[17] Kimball, *They Like Jesus*, 226–28.

member of the community. In Kimball's words, "They don't want a stranger walking up to them on the street and handing them a tract. Nor do they want a casual acquaintance putting pressure on them in a weird way to come to their church."[18] Heather Kirk-Davidoff puts it this way: "We can spot a sales pitch a mile away."[19]

The proper response, according to emerging church leaders, is to pursue Christ in the context of community—and to show our faith as much by our actions as by our words. In the eyes of a generation that is generally skeptical of the church, the consistent, loving example of a true believer strengthens the credibility of the gospel. The gospel is the message, but relationships are the context in which that message is best shared. In fact, even lost people sometimes become evangelists as they tell others what they are learning about Jesus.[20]

EC EVANGELISM IS A REACTION AGAINST EVANGELISM FOCUSED MORE ON ETERNITY THAN ON THE IMMEDIATE

I confess that a fear of hell and a desire for heaven strongly influenced me toward following Christ. Hell scared me as a thirteen-year-old nonbeliever, even though I doubted I would face eternity anytime soon. Honesty demands that I also confess delayed growth as a young believer, as I focused more on getting ready for the next world than on living faithfully in this world. Had the emerging church leaders been writing then (in the early 1970s), I would have been a poster child for misdirected evangelism and Christian living. My error was that I focused on the kingdom to come more than the kingdom that is now.

In this scenario, life here becomes only a means to an end: heaven. Little else matters as long as we miss the judgment of hell and experience eternity in heaven. At least according to Spencer Burke, "everything becomes about evangelizing and gathering

---

[18] Ibid., 231.

[19] Heather Kirk-Davidoff, "Meeting Jesus at the Bar," in *An Emergent Manifesto of Hope*, ed. Doug Pagitt and Tony Jones (Grand Rapids: Baker, 2007), 37.

[20] Mark Driscoll, *Radical Reformission* (Grand Rapids: Zondervan, 2004), 70.

souls . . . [and] striving to corral people into heaven."[21] Other issues
such as social justice are neglected at best.

Missed in this approach to evangelism is the kingdom of God
in its present tense. The gospel "is concerned as much with life
before death as with life after death,"[22] and eternal life begins in
the here and now as we experience God's grace daily. Properly
understood, the invitation to follow Christ is also an invitation to
join a kingdom community where relationships are central and
grace is lived out.

Indeed, emerging church leaders contend that nonbelievers
today are likely to join a community before they are willing to follow Christ. Following the work of George Hunter, Kimball offers
this approach to evangelism today:

1. You first establish community with people or bring them into
   the fellowship of your community.
2. Within fellowship, you engage in conversation, ministry,
   prayer, and worship.
3. In time, as they discover what you believe, you invite them to
   commit.[23]

Within the context of community, nonbelievers learn the value
of following Christ in the present as the church seeks to transform
culture through social action and holistic ministry. Complete persons leading to whole societies *today* are thus a primary goal of
Emergent evangelism. In John Burke's words, the aim is

> not to get people to "convert" by repeating one prayer.
> The goal is to love God and people, living out of the full-
> ness of life in God's kingdom, inviting all to come and
> enjoy the fruits of life in us, because the door has been
> flung wide open through Christ. A prayer for salvation is
> the beginning of relational confidence with God, but the

---

[21] Spencer Burke and Barry Taylor, *A Heretic's Guide to Eternity* (Hoboken, N.J.:
Jossey-Bass, 2006), 181.

[22] Gibbs and Bolger, *Emerging Churches*, 54.

[23] Kimball, *The Emerging Church: Vintage Christianity for New Generations* (Grand
Rapids: Zondervan, 2003), 284–85; Kimball refers to Hunter's *The Celtic Way of Evangelism* (Nashville: Abingdon, 2000).

goal must be to help people trust God in very mundane, practical ways more and more every day.[24]

EC EVANGELISM IS A REACTION AGAINST EVANGELISM FOCUSED ONLY ON PROPOSITIONAL TRUTH

This reaction is as much a response to changing culture as it is a reply to the church's perceived failures in evangelism. Others in this book have more fully described postmodernism; thus, I will focus specifically on the emerging church's reaction to postmodernism and its denial of propositional truth.

Emerging church leaders understand that many in the unbelieving world reject any sense of absolute truth. They have seen competing truth claims, and they respond simply, "there must not be any truth, if everybody is saying, 'this is true, and that's true, and something else is true.' They all contradict, and it's just people arguing among themselves."[25] Nobody has a corner on truth, and anyone who speaks of only one truth is perceived as arrogant. Evangelism based on propositions is thus rendered powerless.

Consequently, emerging church leaders emphasize telling our stories more than telling propositional truths. Evangelism is not about convincing others of a truth; rather, it is about telling them our stories—"case studies in God's power to change."[26] Effective evangelism is then more dialogue than monologue, more question-and-answer than proclamation. Christians are to be more "travel guides" than traveling salesmen.[27] Indeed, community becomes that much more important if shared lives become the context in which the gospel is illustrated.

Here, McLaren's understanding of evangelism as "dance" is best understood. When the song of the gospel enters our lives, we cannot help but believe that "the entire world was meant to share in this song with its message, its joy, its dance."[28] All who

[24] John Burke, *No Perfect People*, 175–76.

[25] Harry Lee Poe, *Christian Witness in a Postmodern World* (Nashville: Abingdon, 2001), 146.

[26] McLaren, *More Ready*, 13.

[27] Rick Richardson, *Reimagining Evangelism* (Downers Grove, Ill.: InterVarsity, 2006), 19–27.

[28] McLaren, *More Ready*, 16.

really hear the song naturally dance, and they want to invite others to dance with them. This kind of dancing is difficult when one partner strives only to trump the other with his perception of truth:

> Evangelism in the postmodern world has to be less like an argument. This is not to say that it will not be logical, but rather that it will not be about winning and losing, which is why I think the image of dance works so well. Dance is not about winning and losing. When the music ends, you don't sneer at your partner and say, "Gotcha! I won that dance, 7 to 3!" And if you try to pull someone into a dance against her will, the term we use to describe that behavior is not "bold dancing," but rather "assault."[29]

EC EVANGELISM IS A REACTION AGAINST EVANGELISM SEPARATED FROM THE EVANGELIST'S LIFESTYLE

I have the privilege of working with several churches a year in my role as a church consultant. In most of these churches, evangelism is a task that only a few believers do—and then only once in a while. Many evangelism strategies in these churches stress inviting unbelievers to large events rather than personally modeling and sharing Christ in relationship. In these settings, the believer's lifestyle as a disciple of Jesus matters far too little.

Emerging church leaders attempt to counter this tendency by emphasizing evangelism as the natural result of a growing relationship with Christ. Conversion is not the ending point; instead, it is the beginning of a never-ending pilgrimage. That journey requires believers to be light in a world that is increasingly dark. Missions and evangelism thus become "not something they [believers] do but something they are."[30]

This analogy of a "journey" or "adventure" to describe the Christian life implies that believers are to be always growing in their understanding of Christ and the Christian life. Followers of Jesus are characterized by humility, knowing that they are ever learning and changing. Indeed, some emerging church leaders are

---

[29] Ibid., 27.
[30] Driscoll, *Radical Reformission*, 66.

quick to emphasize that evangelism is an opportunity for learning: "The followers of God are not called to be master teachers of God, but to be master learners. . . . That's why evangelism is to be a two-way street. If we expect others to learn from us and be changed, we must first allow for a real possibility that we have something to learn from them and be changed by what we learn."[31]

Peter Rollins calls this process "a type of reverse evangelism,"[32] and Gibbs and Bolger echo that thought: "Christians cannot truly evangelize unless they are prepared to be evangelized in the process."[33] Hence, in a rather strange twist, evangelism *and* evangelizing both occur in this spiritual journey. More on this concept will come later in this chapter.

SUMMARY AND AFFIRMATIONS

What, then, is evangelism according to the emerging church? McLaren (who admits his discomfort using the word *evangelism* because it has been so "bastardized") offers this definition that summarizes much of Emergent teaching: "Good evangelism is the process of being friendly without discrimination and influencing all of one's friends toward better living, through good deeds and good conversations. For a Christian like myself, evangelism means engaging in these conversations in the spirit and example of Jesus Christ."[34] This definition is not to suggest that speaking about Christ is avoided—in fact, McLaren encourages telling our story and God's story as well[35]—but the relational aspect is clearly prioritized. Needless to say, this definition demands critique that will occur later in this chapter.

Borrowing from the works of McLaren, Kimball, and Driscoll, the chart on the next page also describes evangelism according to the emerging church.[36]

[31] Samir Selmanovic, "The Sweet Problem of Inclusiveness," in *An Emergent Manifesto of Hope*, 197.

[32] Peter Rollins, *How (Not) to Speak of God* (Brewster, Mass.: Paraclete, 2006), 54.

[33] Gibbs and Bolger, *Emerging Churches*, 131.

[34] McLaren, *More Ready*, 15.

[35] Ibid., 172–73.

[36] See Driscoll, *Radical Reformission*, 68; Kimball, *Emerging Church*, 201; McLaren, *More Ready*, 135–43.

MODERN CHURCH	EMERGING CHURCH
Evangelism is an event that you invite people to so that they will hear a gospel presentation.	Evangelism is a process that occurs through relationship, trust, and example. Conversations matter as much as conversions.
Evangelism is primarily concerned with getting people into heaven.	Evangelism is concerned with people's experiencing the reality of living under the reign of his kingdom now. The Christian community is often the context of conversion.
Evangelism calls hearers to make a decision about Jesus.	Evangelism occurs when the nonbeliever sees authentic faith and ministry lived openly and participates in it.
Evangelism is done by evangelists.	Evangelism is done by disciples. Disciples are always learning and growing, and evangelism is part of discipleship.
Evangelism is a message dominated by propositions.	Evangelism is a conversation. Stories of transformed lives matter.
Evangelism uses reason and proofs for apologetics.	Evangelism uses the church being the church as the primary apologetic.
Evangelism calls for conversion to Christ first, followed by acceptance into the church.	Evangelism begins with acceptance and fellowship in the church, followed by conversion.

To be fair, the emerging church has identified legitimate issues with the established church's approach to evangelism. Thus, a brief summary of positives is in order prior to raising concerns about the emerging church and evangelism.

First, Emergent leaders are unafraid to speak of the failures of the North American church—and are thus quite willing to propose change. We may not agree with all of their proposals, but their willingness to face the brutal truth about the church is welcomed. Population growth is exceeding the rate of church growth, and evidence of the church's influence on culture is difficult to find. In some ways, the emerging church has filled a void because too few others have called the church to recognize its apparent inability to make a difference in society.

Second, McLaren and other leaders are correct to recognize that the church has become a "fortress or social club." I often ask church leaders and laity to give me the names of ten nonbelievers with whom they are relationally close enough that they could easily share the gospel with them—and *very few* believers can name ten. The church has become a cocoon, a place of retreat and refuge rather than a place to be equipped for evangelism. We should not be surprised that we do not reach nonbelievers if we have no relationships with them in the first place.

Third, many contemporary evangelistic strategies are indeed suspect, as emerging church leaders have indicated. Too many of us can point to someone who walked an aisle, prayed a prayer, raised a hand, entered baptismal waters, or signed a paper, but whose life hardly changed. Repentance is often omitted as mandate for following Christ (and is seldom called for by emerging church leaders, either), and one result is a church that looks remarkably like the rest of the world. The church cannot much threaten the devil when our members continue to live like the devil.

Fourth, while I do not accept that confrontational evangelism is no longer effective, it does seem clear that relationships are key to sharing Christ today. The gospel message is hardly dependent on relationships for its power (1 Cor 1:18), but it is in relationships that we model Christ and gain a hearing. In that sense, the emerging church has much to teach a church that has separated itself from the people we are called to reach. A single holy life lived obediently before others can sometimes overcome the influence of a multitude of hypocrites.

Fifth, emerging church leaders recognize that a highly individualized approach to evangelism has been one cause of an equally individualized approach to church.[37] *I* get saved, and *I* am now going to heaven—and as long as I am going to heaven, why worry much about how I live today? Church is thus a place to go rather than a congregation of believers who help me to mature in my faith. Accountability is not expected, and Christian growth seldom

[37] See, e.g., Robert Webber, quoted in Jimmy Long, *Emerging Hope* (Downers Grove, Ill.: InterVarsity, 2004), 207.

occurs. The result is a church for whom the "body of Christ" imagery of 1 Corinthians 12 means little.

Sixth, emerging church leaders properly raise concerns about attractional evangelism. Many of these same leaders never themselves call for personal, verbal evangelism, but they do recognize that invitations to attractive events are not enough. In Kimball's words, "If you build it, they will come" has not proven true for postmoderns.[38] Events simply cannot be the relationships for which many nonbelievers seek.

Seventh, emerging church leaders at least talk in terms of tying together the tasks of outreach and social ministry. Evangelicals fear that evangelism tied to social ministry will ultimately devolve into the social gospel, but such is not always the case. Churches such as the First Baptist Church of Leesburg, Florida, have clearly proven otherwise.[39] In some ways, though, the emerging church has been more attentive to these issues than the traditional church.

Eighth, the appeal for evangelism that is lifestyle rather than program is a needed one. I am not generally opposed to programs for doing evangelism, but programmed outreach will never be sufficient to reach the unchurched in North America. Too few believers enroll in evangelism training programs, and even fewer actually complete the programs. The church will begin to make a significant difference only when we can cry out as Peter and John did in describing their walk with Christ: "we are unable to stop speaking about what we have seen and heard" (Acts 4:20).

Ninth, emerging church leaders properly emphasize that missions is not limited to overseas. North America is now a mission field not only because the world has come to us but also because many North Americans no longer have any connections to Christianity. The church that fails to recognize this change may quickly find itself irrelevant in North American culture.

Thus, evangelism in the emerging church is both reactionary and reforming—reactionary against poor evangelism in the established church and reforming in its offering a way to do evangelism

[38] Kimball, *Emerging Church*, 197–200.
[39] See "Doing Well, Doing Good," accessed at http://www.worldmag.com/articles/10941.

that is perceived to be more effective today. Their diagnosis of the problem is not without merit, but their prescription for a cure is problematic. To that topic this chapter now turns.

EMERGENT EVANGELISM: TROUBLESOME AND UNCLEAR

Scot McKnight, who is generally a friend of the emerging church, is also a critic of the Emergent commitment to evangelism. Referring to Emergent skepticism about the "in vs. out" mentality of Evangelicals, McKnight concludes,

> This emerging ambivalence about who is in and who is out creates a serious problem for evangelism. The emerging movement is not known for it, but I wish it were. Unless you proclaim the Good News of Jesus Christ, there is no good news at all—and if there is no Good News, then there is no Christianity, emerging or evangelical.
>
> Personally, I'm an evangelist. Not so much the tract-toting, door-knocking kind, but the Jesus-talking and Jesus-teaching kind. I spend time praying in my office before class and pondering about how to teach in order to bring home the message of the gospel. So I offer here a warning to the emerging movement: Any movement that is not evangelistic is failing the Lord.[40]

So, notwithstanding D. A. Carson's earlier cited affirmation about evangelism and the emerging church, at least one scholar recognizes that emerging church leaders are simply not known for evangelism. That critique in itself demands the emerging church's ear, particularly because the challenge comes from a friend. At the same time, more substantial critique is still in order.

EC EVANGELISM RISKS NEGLECTING TRUTH ESSENTIAL TO NEW TESTAMENT EVANGELISM

Noted earlier is the emerging church's reaction to evangelism that is simply the stating of propositional truths. For nonbelievers

---

[40] See Scot McKnight, "Five Streams of the Emerging Church," accessed at http://www.christianitytoday.com/ct/2007/february/11.35.html?start=1.

in a postmodern culture that questions absolute truth, propositions are ignored at best and rejected entirely at worst. Listen to further emerging church comments addressing these issues:

> Evangelism is a way of life. By this we mean we are a community and introduce people into our community all the time. We don't really feel as though the gospel can be packaged into a proposition that is dispensed in slick programs or presentations.[41]

> Theology propositions and truth claims are more important than ever but not as litmus tests of correct belief or practice; rather, truth claims become launching pads for differentiated conversational relationship, marked by mutual exploration, humble submission, deference, and wonder. . . . The problem with orthodoxy or authoritative truth claims is that they are conversation stoppers.[42]

> I no longer believe that evangelism means the arguing of propositional ideas about God but rather that is the telling of one's story. There's a big difference between sitting down with someone and talking about one's life experiences and sitting down with someone and offering them a set of concepts about God on which their eternal destiny is said to depend.[43]

A fair assessment demands that we recognize some of the concern behind this "propositionless evangelism." For some emerging church leaders, the point is simply that propositions unsupported by lifestyle lose their credibility. John Burke, for example, argues that we must "test the effectiveness of our beliefs through the grid of relationship"; that is, "we must not fall into the trap of the educational model, thinking that teaching and testing assent to correct doctrine yields fruit—it alone does not."[44] Where our preached

---

[41] Brad Cecil, quoted in Gibbs and Bolger, *Emerging Churches*, 108–9.
[42] Dwight J. Friesen, "Orthoparadoxy," in *An Emergent Manifesto*, 209, 211.
[43] Burke and Taylor, *A Heretic's Guide*, 207.
[44] John Burke, "Response to Mark Driscoll," in *Listening to the Beliefs of Emerging Churches: Five Perspectives*, ed. Robert Webber (Grand Rapids: Zondervan, 2007), 37, 38.

truths show no change in our lifestyle, nonbelievers certainly must question the strength of our "truths."

For other emerging church leaders, the concern is that postmoderns simply do not relate to propositions. When a postmodern responds "so what?" to the most logically reasoned, clearly developed argument, the evangelist who uses only propositions seemingly has little left to give. Community-based relationships and dialogue-centered discussions are thus central to evangelism. Indeed, the Socratic method of evangelism is promoted as a means to reach postmoderns.[45]

For some emerging church leaders, a skepticism about once-for-all settled theology leads to questioning proposition-based evangelism. Theology is, according to Doug Pagitt, always changing, making it impossible to find "complex understandings meant for all people, in all places, for all times."[46] Tony Jones argues even more forcefully, "We must carry our theologies with an open hand, as it were. To assume that our convictions about God are somehow timeless is the deepest arrogance."[47] The church might hold their beliefs with conviction, but those convictions must be held humbly because they are ever subject to change.

Noted theologian Wayne Grudem affirms that systematic theology "focuses on summarizing each doctrine as it should be understood by present-day Christians."[48] In that sense, contemporary application does matter—but that reality in no way diminishes the truth that the gospel is expressed in propositional statements. As Justin Taylor has reminded us, "While Scripture is *more* than a set of propositions, it is not *less*."[49] The danger with a propositionless evangelism, of course, is that the church will fail to teach propositional truths that are essential to the gospel.

The apostle Paul was quite clear about the gospel: "For I passed on to you as most important what I also received: that Christ died for our sins according to the Scriptures, that He was buried, that

---

[45] Long, *Emerging Hope*, 202; Kimball, *Emerging Church*, 206–7.
[46] Doug Pagitt, "The Emerging Church and Embodied Theology," in *Listening*, 137.
[47] Jones, *New Christians*, 114.
[48] Wayne Grudem, *Systematic Theology* (Grand Rapids: Zondervan, 1994), 23.
[49] Justin Taylor, "An Emerging Church Primer," accessed at http://9marks.org/CC/artic le/0,,PTID314526%7CCHID598014%7CCIID2249226,00.html.

He was raised on the third day according to the Scriptures" (1 Cor 15:3–4). It is through proclaiming this message that God has chosen to save those who believe (1 Cor 1:21). The message of the gospel is undeniably a set of truth claims, and apart from these truths there can be no true evangelism. Indeed, these truths direct us to the One who saves.

While not all emerging church leaders would deny the necessity of these truths, their leaning away from propositional truth risks doing "evangelism" without ever getting to the message essential to New Testament evangelism. The frightening result is that some might assume their salvation apart from knowing essential truths; for example, McLaren relates the story of a man who becomes a follower of Jesus while not knowing why Jesus died (in fact, while accepting McLaren's assertion that even *Jesus* did not know why He had to die).[50]

New Testament evangelism is much more than McLaren's understanding of evangelism as friendliness in the spirit of Jesus; instead, it is the announcement of clear biblical truths that point the way to salvation. Mark Driscoll serves here as a foil to his own emerging church counterparts, as he strongly emphasizes the authority of God's Word, the nature of God as Trinitarian, and the substitutionary death of Jesus.[51]

EC EVANGELISM RISKS BEING LESS THAN GENUINE EVANGELISM

Understanding this concern requires defining "presence evangelism" and "proclamation evangelism." Presence evangelism is "getting next to people and helping them; doing good in the world"—with the hope of, but not necessarily leading to sharing about Christ.[52] Proclamation evangelism is simply speaking the gospel so that persons might respond to its truth. In the emerging church, presence evangelism is much more common than proclamation.[53]

---

[50] McLaren, *More Ready*, 79–82.

[51] Mark Driscoll, "The Emerging Church and Biblicist Theology," in *Listening*, 21–35.

[52] C. Peter Wagner, Win Arn, and Elmer Towns, eds., *Church Growth: State of the Art* (Wheaton, Ill.: Tyndale, 1988), 297.

[53] Gibbs and Bolger, *Emerging Churches*, 129.

This evangelism is relational and nonconfrontational, thus avoiding any sense that the nonbeliever is to be "won" to the Lord. Some emerging church leaders reject even the concept of "friendship evangelism" because it assumes that friendship is only the means to an end. Hear the presence evangelism so evident in this leader's thoughts: "The concept of friendship evangelism has always been something we have struggled with, as this is hardly unconditional love! We feel the call to serve the community and to be a presence for good, and our prayer is that along the way we will see people find faith."[54]

Much of this understanding is connected to the emerging church's call to live out the kingdom of God in the immediate context. Social ministry, political-social actions, and community development are often more emphasized than proclaiming the message of Christ. To illustrate, McLaren could declare that the "greatest outreach opportunities of our day" might include:[55]

1. recruiting one million believers to sacrifice for AIDS sufferers in Africa, and so show the love of Christ
2. recruiting one million Christians to befriend Muslims especially, but also all neighbors of other races and religions and political parties, invite them to their home for dinner, accept reciprocal invitations, and so show the love of Christ
3. recruiting one million Christians to protest the wasteful Industrial Consumerist system which destroys the planet, human communities, and human culture, and to proclaim in its place a vision of the kingdom of God, and so show the love of Christ.

In these cases, the Great Commandment (Matt 22:37–39) appears to take priority over the Great Commission (Matt 28:18–20). In fact, McLaren argues that "it is fruitless to engage in the Great Commission" if disciples are not first following the Great Commandment.[56] Any evangelistic strategy should be "a gentle,

---

[54] Chris Matthews, quoted in Gibbs and Bolger, *Emerging Churches*, 127.
[55] Brian McLaren, "The Strategy We Pursue," accessed at http://bgc.gospelcom.net/ise/RTpapers/Papers04/mclaren.pdf.
[56] Ibid.

humble strategy which relies primarily on the vulnerable rhetoric of good fruit, good deeds, good lives rather than coercive
argument."[57]

This understanding raises at least three critical issues. First,
this approach fails to see that New Testament evangelism is never
less than proclamation of the gospel. The New Testament does
not use the word *evangelize*; however, the word transliterated as
"evangelize" (*euangelizō*) is understood as "preach the gospel"
more than fifty times in the New Testament (e.g., Luke 4:43; Acts
8:4, 14:7; Rom 1:15; 1 Cor 15:1–2). The word was used in the
ancient world to describe announcing good news, such as the birth
of a baby or the victory of an army. Central to its meaning were (1)
the content of the message—the message itself was good news,
and (2) the proclamation of the message—someone intentionally
announced the good news.[58]

Given this understanding, it is difficult to see anything less
than verbalizing the gospel as New Testament evangelism. Our
good works point to God (Matt 5:16), but our lives only affirm the
gospel rather than proclaim it. In McLaren's example above, we
undeniably must minister to AIDS sufferers in Africa—but if we
do so without telling the good news of Jesus, we have done valid
ministry that is not yet evangelism.

Second, claiming to show Christ's love without ever speaking
of Christ's love is hardly fully loving. Granted, emerging church
leaders assume that showing Christ's love may lead to an opportunity to speak about Christ, but that opportunity is not guaranteed. If
the opportunity never arises, is my responsibility complete simply
because the non-believer never dialogued with me about Jesus? The
multi-fold expressions of the Great Commission in the New Testament (Matt 28:18–20; Luke 24:46–47; John 20:21; Acts 1:8) suggest
not. New Testament evangelism is proactive rather than reactive.

That is not to deny the church's responsibility to minister
among the poor, the hurting, and the disadvantaged. Love of God
is linked to love for our neighbor (Matt 22:37–40). Jesus left little

[57] Ibid.
[58] See "*euangelizomai, euangelion*" in *Theological Dictionary of the New Testament*,
ed. Gerhard Kittel (Grand Rapids: Eerdmans, 1964), 707–37.

room to deny that our faith is evidenced in our actions toward strangers and those who are hungry, thirsty, naked, sick, and imprisoned (Matt 25:31–46). Social ministry and Christian justice do matter—but apart from the proclamation of the gospel, they are not evangelism.

Finally, evangelism that is more presence than proclamation raises questions about the power of the gospel. If the gospel will not be heard apart from our obedience to minister to others, is the power of the gospel then dependent upon us? Our faithfulness is still mandatory, but the power of the gospel is surely independent of the messenger. So Duane Litfin responds negatively to McLaren's assertion that it is fruitless to engage in the Great Commission if the Great Commandment is not being fulfilled: "Apparently, the gospel is utterly without its own potency. It is powerless, it seems, without us. The power lies, not in the Spirit's convicting application of the message of the cross to human hearts, but in the messenger, so much so that if we fail, all gospel efforts will prove 'fruitless.'"[59] Genuine New Testament evangelism is based on a gospel that is powerful apart from us.

EC EVANGELISM LACKS A SENSE OF URGENCY

I am struck by the passion of the apostles as they preached the gospel in the book of Acts. In a pluralistic society that followed multiple spiritualities, they nevertheless stood up for the one true God regardless of the cost. Ordered by the authorities not to preach, they preached anyway (Acts 4:13–31; 5:17–42). Church historian Michael Green concludes that their obedience was motivated by three factors: personal gratitude to God for their own salvation, a sense of responsibility to live faithfully in response to God's love, and a genuine concern about the eternal destinies of nonbelievers.[60] Urgency drove these early believers to do evangelism.

In many churches today, however, evangelistic urgency is typically brief, connected most often to deathbed opportunities to share Christ or early enthusiasm for a new evangelism program.

---

[59] Duane Litfin, "Response to Brian McLaren's 'The Strategy We Pursue,'" accessed at http://bgc.gospelcom.net/ise/RTpapers/Papers04/litfin3pdf.pdf.

[60] Michael Green, *Evangelism in the Early Church* (Grand Rapids: Eerdmans, 2003), 273–99.

Teaching on the doctrine of hell is so infrequent that hell's reality is not a strong motivator to evangelize. Even the church that believes that evangelism is necessary often fails to do evangelism with urgency.

Some of the definitions of evangelism proposed by emerging church writers reflect this same lack of urgency:

> So "evangelism" is not something we do to attract seekers; instead we simply invite others to join us and be part of what God is doing in the world around us, and to help us put God's eschatology into practice by doing justice, loving kindness, and walking humbly with God.[61]

> If Christians would be quiet for a year and only do good works, that would be evangelism.[62]

> Evangelization is not a hit-and-run activity but one that entails a long-term commitment.[63]

One cause of this lack of urgency may be the emerging church's concern for living out the kingdom of God today. Focusing on the immediate, while also attempting to counter evangelism strategies that emphasize only the afterlife, has counter-productively weakened attention to the eternal state of nonbelievers. If Jesus were concerned more about bringing in the kingdom on earth—and *we* are the ones who worry about "who's in and who's out," as McLaren suggests—urgency about the afterlife surely wanes.[64]

The emerging church stands against any such tendency to differentiate between "who's in and who's out." Terms such as *lost*, *unChristian*, *nonbeliever*, and *unsaved* are considered hindrances to spiritual conversations. One proposed answer is to "stop thinking of everybody primarily in categories of in or out, saved or not, believer or nonbeliever."[65] Evangelistic apathy, however, is sure

---

[61] Karen Ward, "The Emerging Church and Communal Theology," in *Listening*, 171.
[62] Dieter Zander, quoted in Gibbs and Bolger, *Emerging Churches*, 147.
[63] Gibbs and Bolger, *Emerging Churches*, 153.
[64] Brian McLaren, "Brian McLaren's Inferno 2: Are We Asking the Wrong Questions about Hell?," accessed at http://blog.christianitytoday.com/outofur/archives/2006/05/brian_mclarens_1.html.
[65] Bell, *Velvet Elvis*, 167.

to follow when we stop thinking about persons as believers or nonbelievers.

Moreover, striving to live out the kingdom through social ministry will often weaken a commitment to evangelism. The needs are so great, and church resources are often so limited, that meeting those needs requires full attention. The temporary work of ministering to others—as mandatory as meeting needs is—unintentionally consumes the eternal unless the church intentionally strategizes to do both. Few emerging churches appear to be doing so.

In addition, a general question about the reality of hell is apparent in the writings of the emerging church movement. Spencer Burke admits the possibility of hell while also denying "a place filled with fire, brimstone, and flames that burn bodies forever in eternal torment."[66] McLaren encourages readers to "consider the possibility that many, and perhaps even all of Jesus' hell-fire or end-of-the-universe statements refer not to postmortem judgment but to the very historic consequences of rejecting His kingdom message of reconciliation and peacemaking. The destruction of Jerusalem in AD 67–70 seems to many people to fulfill much of what we have traditionally understood as hell."[67]

In an interview that is both confusing and frustrating, Doug Pagitt seems to deny the reality of hell.[68] If hell is not real in the first place, and evangelism is most about a conversation, urgency is simply no longer an issue.

Mark Driscoll, again in a manner contrary to other writers, strongly affirms the reality of hell, including providing twenty footnotes of biblical proofs for hell.[69] "What is at stake," according to Driscoll, "is nothing less than the gospel of Jesus Christ and people's eternal destinies."[70] We can only wish that other emerg-

[66] Spencer Burke, *A Heretic's Guide*, 198.

[67] Brian McLaren, "Brian McLaren's Inferno 3: Five Proposals for Reexamining Our Doctrine of Hell," accessed at http://blog.christianitytoday.com/outofur/archives/2006/05/brian_mclarens_2.html.

[68] Hear the Pagitt interview at http://www.vcyamerica.tv/view_video.php?viewkey=b633e50cdf1b20de6f46.

[69] Driscoll, "The Emerging Church and Biblicist Theology," *Listening*, 34–35.

[70] Ibid., 35.

ing church leaders would recognize the stakes here and respond
with equal urgency.

EC "EVANGELISM" SOMETIMES LACKS
A BIBLICAL FOUNDATION

Note the addition of quotation marks to "evangelism" in this
section's heading.

The marks are intentional, as the focus of this section is the
faulty view of some in the emerging church regarding followers of
other faiths. For some, "evangelizing" believers in other religions
is more about learning from them than teaching them the truths
of the gospel. Central to this discussion is the emerging church's
insistence on holding one's theology lightly and humbly, always
being willing to revise it as needed.

A first group affected by this discussion are those who know
about Jesus but have chosen not to follow Him. Chuck Smith and
Matt Whitlock wonder aloud if God might redeem those who
rejected a Jesus misrepresented by their spiritual leaders.[71] They
further tell the story of a good, moral woman and then question
the logic that "an all-good, all-wise, all-loving God . . . would
take pleasure in allowing this person to suffer for all eternity."[72]
McLaren simply declares as unknown "how things will be after
this life for people who don't believe but who lived better lives
than many who do."[73]

Apparently, the Bible's teaching that salvation is by grace through
faith—and *not* as a result of works (Eph 2:8–9)—is not clear.

A second group included in this discussion are those who have
never heard the name of Jesus. At least for some emerging church
leaders, the fact that these have not heard of Jesus is not a hindrance to their salvation. John Burke, who bases his conclusion on
the salvation of Old Testament saints, is especially certain about
his position: "I do know that there will be people in heaven, made
right with God, who never heard the name of Jesus! . . . I'm con-

---

[71] Chuck Smith Jr., and Matt Whitlock, *Frequently Avoided Questions* (Grand Rapids:
Baker, 2005), 166–67.

[72] Ibid., 167–68.

[73] Brian D. McLaren, *A Search for What Makes Sense: Finding Faith* (Grand Rapids:
Zondervan, 2007), 175.

fident God won't send anybody to hell for lack of knowledge or place of birth or ethnicity."[74] Spencer Burke goes further to say, "If you think about it, there is a certain madness to the idea that members of only one religious group can make it into heaven because they happen to know Jesus or some other religious figure."[75]

Other leaders may not be as forceful, but their conclusions are equally worrisome. McLaren agrees with David Bosch that we do not know of any way of salvation other than Jesus, but we cannot limit God's saving power.[76] Likewise, Karen Ward writes, "I affirm no other Savior than Jesus Christ, yet at the same time, I feel no need to know with certainty the final destination of those of other faiths who either have no knowledge of Christ or who do not accept the Christian claims of the atonement."[77]

Here the aforementioned "reverse evangelism" becomes more relevant. For some in the emerging church, evangelism includes an intentional willingness to learn from followers of other faiths, to grow personally through their insights and devotion, and to admit the possibility that "the Spirit has been with these people all along."[78] Evangelism is thus no longer "going," but it is rather seeking to determine where God is already at work. Pip Piper perhaps best describes this approach:

> Evangelism or mission for me is no longer persuading people to believe what I believe, no matter how edgy or creative I get. It is more about shared experiences and encounters. It is about walking the journey of life and faith together, each distinct to his or her own tradition and culture but with the possibility of encountering God and truth from one another.[79]

Undoubtedly, much is at risk here. If the goal of this mutual "journey" is to show respect to another person while seeking to proclaim Christ as the only way to God, this approach may be jus-

---

[74] John Burke, *No Perfect People*, 142.
[75] Spencer Burke, *Heretic's Guide*, 197.
[76] Brian McLaren, *A Generous Orthodoxy* (Grand Rapids: Zondervan, 2004), 262.
[77] Karen Ward, "Response to Mark Driscoll," in *Listening*, 46.
[78] Gibbs and Bolger, *Emerging Churches*, 132.
[79] Pip Piper, quoted in Gibbs and Bolger, *Emerging Churches*, 131.

tified. The risk is that the relationship never leads to a clear proclamation that Christ is not just *a* way to encounter God; rather, He
is the *only* way to encounter God, and that only through a personal
response to Him (Acts 4:12; Rom 10:9–13). This risk is exponen-
tially increased if one's theology views the necessity of belief in
Jesus as Burke's "certain madness."

Brian McLaren is again at the front of these conversations. In
response to a question about exclusivism, inclusivism, condition-
alism, and universalism, McLaren is quoted as saying, "I think
that people can be good Christians with any of these views, and
I also think they can be bad Christians."[80] Noted herein first is
the emerging church's tendency to evaluate Christian living by
actions, often with too little regard for beliefs and doctrine. More
specifically, McLaren apparently believes that good Christians
can hold fundamentally different beliefs about salvation—which
would then influence their commitment to evangelism.

The universalist sees little need for evangelism, for all will be
saved in the end anyway. The inclusivist is not inclined to evangelize, as a personal relationship with Christ is not necessary
for salvation. The conditionalist may still evangelize, though his
understanding of the noneternal nature of damnation may weaken
his urgency. The exclusivist is the most likely evangelist, for he
believes that Jesus is the only way to God, a personal relationship
with Christ is necessary for salvation, and hell awaits those who
do not follow Christ.

Once again, Driscoll (along with Gerry Breshears) counters
other emerging teaching and brings biblical truth to this discussion:
"The exclusivity, superiority, and singularity of Jesus are precisely
the teaching of Scripture. . . . Indeed, when we are speaking of
salvation we must speak only of Jesus, always of Jesus, and assur-
edly of Jesus."[81] On these truths true evangelism must be built.

[80] Brian McLaren, "The Last Word, and the Word after That: An Interview with Brian
McLaren," accessed at http://www.the-next-wave.org/stories/storyReader$700.

[81] Mark Driscoll and Gerry Breshears, *Vintage Jesus* (Wheaton, Ill.: Crossway, 2007),
188–89.

CONCLUSION

The emerging church rightly recognizes serious issues with the established church's approach to evangelism, especially in attempting to reach a postmodern society. The problem, however, is that their proposed response is too weakly tied to the proclamation of propositional truth. Combine that reticence to proclaim propositions with a theology that sometimes questions the lostness of human beings and the reality of hell, and there is no New Testament evangelism.

In moving toward the end of his book, *They Like Jesus but Not the Church*, Dan Kimball raises questions that all churches should hear:

> Isn't something going terribly wrong when so many outside the church are getting so many negative impressions of the church and Christianity? Isn't something going wrong when so many people don't even know a Christian? If the gospel really is good news and repentance is about being refreshed, shouldn't we be doing anything possible to help bring this good news and refreshment to others outside the church?[82]

We may not agree with all of Kimball's teachings, but his questions are probing. In fact, he further challenges pastors: "Evangelism needs to bleed from your church's entire being and should motivate Christians to be more hardcore disciples."[83] To that statement we add a resounding "Amen"—*if* evangelism is urgently proclaiming the clear propositional truths of Scripture to all men and women around the world.

[82] Kimball, *They Like Jesus*, 241–42.
[83] Kimball, *Emerging Church*, 209.

CONCLUSION

ADAM W. GREENWAY

THE PURPOSE BEHIND the preceding pages of this work was for leading voices from Evangelical life's broad spectrum to constructively analyze and critique the movement (or "conversation," if you prefer) known as Emergent.[1] Concerns ranging from the biblical and theological to the pastoral and practical have been raised throughout. A few brief concluding thoughts are now in order, culminating with some speculative musings about the movement/conversation's future.

Perhaps the most consistent criticism leveled against Emergent in this volume (and elsewhere) has been the overarching lack of concern for doctrinal content and precision. While "generous orthodoxy"[2] seems to be the Emergent desire, many of its leaders have clearly moved beyond the pale of orthodoxy in order to uphold some overarching sense of generosity. Whether it be the redefining of hell and eternal punishment, the embracing of forms of soteriological inclusivism or pluralism, the discounting of Jesus' deity and

---

[1] "Evangelical life's broad spectrum" as envisioned by this book's editors does not include Emergent itself, despite its leaders' attempts to appropriate the term as a befitting descriptor. See "Response to Recent Criticisms" [article on-line]; available from http://tallskinnykiwi.typepad.com/tallskinnykiwi/files/response2critics.pdf.

[2] While this slogan has clearly been best popularized by Brian McLaren's *A Generous Orthodoxy* (Grand Rapids: Zondervan, 2004), he credits Stanley J. Grenz, *Renewing the Center: Evangelical Theology in a Post-Theological Era* (Grand Rapids: Baker, 2000), for his first acquaintance with the term *generous orthodoxy*. The phrase is mentioned in a quotation by Hans Frei, "My own vision of what might be propitious for our day, split as we are, not so much into denominations as into schools of thought, is that we need a kind of generous orthodoxy which would have in it an element of liberalism . . . and an element of evangelicalism" (325). Grenz later comments, "The postmodern condition calls Christians to move beyond the fixation with a conflictual polarity that knows only the categories of 'liberal' and 'conservative,' and thus pits so-called conservatives against loosely defined liberals. Instead, the situation in which the church is increasingly ministering requires a 'generous orthodoxy' characteristic of a renewed 'center' that lies beyond the polarizations of the past, produced as they were by modernist assumptions—a *generous orthodoxy*, that is, that takes seriously the postmodern problematic" (331, emphasis mine).

penal substitutionary atonement, or the minimizing of the need for evangelism and missions because of nonconversionist theological worldviews (to simply highlight again a few issues treated within this book), the serious evangelical observer notices tragically little within Emergent that resonates with "the faith that was delivered to the saints once for all" (Jude 3) and much that resembles "another Jesus" (2 Cor 11:4) and "a different gospel" (Gal 1:6).

Ironically, there is much within Emergent theology that resonates with twentieth-century neo-orthodoxy: dynamic views on Scripture's inspiration and avoidance of descriptors like "inerrant" and "infallible," emphasis on Jesus' human nature and moral example rather than divine essence and redeeming sacrifice, strong commitment to social justice and ministry, discomfort with Reformational theology, ecumenism, center-left political values—the list could go on. Since having noticed these striking parallels as a researcher probing into the Emergent world, I have often described the movement to my students and others (quasihumorously, of course) as "neo-orthodoxy with a soul patch." All joking aside, the similarities between the two movements should be a cause for caution and concern.

Yet it would be unfair to simply state that nothing good has come from anything Emergent/emerging church. To its credit, the genesis behind the "conversation" was a willingness to honestly recognize and confront the fact that all is not well within the visible Church. No serious reader can deny that for all of the boasting about the "buildings, budgets, and bodies," too little genuine and lasting spiritual transformation is occurring in both individual lives and communities. At this historic moment when the Church, particularly in North America, has more resources than ever to fulfill the Great Commission mandate (Matt 28:18–20), the evidence indicates that the situation is getting worse, not improving. Population increases continue to outpace baptisms and church growth. The moral and cultural influence of Christians and local churches continues to wane. Even sincere efforts at stemming the tide are falling short.[3]

---

[3] A recent example is the year-long campaign to "witness, win, and baptize one million" undertaken by the Southern Baptist Convention, the largest evangelical denomination in the United States, in 2006. Entitled "The 'Everyone Can' Kingdom Challenge!", the

There is indeed a problem, Houston, and many engaged within
Emergent are at least acknowledging this reality and are asking the
hard questions that need to be put on the table, particularly with
respect to the continuing impact of traditional church methodologies. Regrettably, too many voices from the ranks of Emergent are
advocating that *methods* alone are not simply the problem, but that
the *message* itself must also "evolve" or "change"—into something
that hardly resembles the evangelical gospel of grace. In the quest
to be "relevant" to the so-called postmodern culture, far too much
biblical and theological ground has been conceded. The alarm bells
are rightly being sounded, but it's not Emergent to the rescue.

So what does the future hold for Emergent? At the time of this
writing (fall 2008), some leaders are now choosing to jettison the
term "emerging church" itself.[4] Talk continues about new networks
and collaborative relationships forming to move beyond the current Emergent/emerging church options.[5] New publications will
undoubtedly continue to come forth from both supporters and critics, pushing the envelope further and keeping the "conversation"
stimulated. The passing of time will sort out whether Emergent
will be remembered as a passing theological fad (what many of its
critics think) or rather as something more transformative and long-
lasting in the body of Christ (what most of its sympathizers hope).

In conclusion, it remains the editors' prayer that the addition
of our Evangelical voices to the "conversation" will both provide
counsel to those outside Emergent and provoke contemplation on
the part of insiders. Readers seeking either hagiography or hatchet-
job will likely have emerged from these pages disappointed; those
desiring honesty and helpfulness will hopefully have found both
within. May God be glorified.

cause was heavily promoted by Convention leadership, most notably by then-SBC president Bobby Welch, now SBC Strategist for Global Evangelical Relations and pastor emeri-
tus of First Baptist Church, Daytona Beach, Florida. Total baptisms actually *dropped*, however, from 371,850 in 2005 to 364,826 in 2006. See Russ Rankin, "SBC Baptisms Down
Amid Other Growth," *Baptist Press*, April 17, 2007 [article on-line]; accessed August 17,
2007; available from http://www.bpnews.net/bpnews.asp?id=25408; Internet. Additional
information on "Everyone Can" remains available online at http://www.everyonecan.net.

    [4] *Dan Kimball and Andy Jones are the leaders cited in Url Scaramanga,* "R.I.P. Emerg-
ing Church" [article on-line]; available from http://blog.christianitytoday.com/outofur/ar-
chives/2008/09/rip_emerging_ch.html.

    [5] See http://www.dankimball.com/vintage_faith/2008/09/emerging-and-em.html.

NAME INDEX

337

SUBJECT INDEX

SCRIPTURE INDEX